THE JOHNS HOPKINS UNIVERSITY STUDIES IN HISTORICAL AND POLITICAL SCIENCE

Under the Direction of the Departments of History, Political Economy, and Political Science

SERIES LXIII   NUMBER 3

THE SLAVE STATES IN THE PRESIDENTIAL ELECTION OF 1860

BY

OLLINGER CRENSHAW

0772338

GLOUCESTER, MASS.

PETER SMITH

1969

COPYRIGHT 1945, THE JOHNS HOPKINS PRESS
Reprinted, 1969 by Permission of
The Johns Hopkins Press
Baltimore, Maryland

PRINTED IN THE UNITED STATES OF AMERICA

TO

J. MONTGOMERY GAMBRILL

PREFACE

Within recent years several scholarly studies have appeared which directly or indirectly focus upon the presidential election of 1860 and the eve of the Civil War. Reinhard H. Luthin's *The First Lincoln Campaign* (Cambridge, 1944) is the first comprehensive re-study of this important election to appear since the publication of Emerson D. Fite's pioneer monograph in 1911. Several other books, all largely concerned with Lincoln or the North, by James G. Randall, David M. Potter, William E. Baringer, and Dwight L. Dumond, have presented a fairly complete picture of the Northern, or free state, aspects of the fateful election. In none of these, however, is a thoroughgoing study made of the shades of political opinion in the Southern, or slave state, areas, interaction of Southern ideas, and the reaction in the South to Northern events.

The present volume attempts to set forth these shades of political opinion held by individuals and groups in the then far from solid South—area by area, and, at the risk of repetition, state by state. Perhaps a better understanding of this complex and critical presidential contest may be gained by a consideration of the ideas, plans, and actions of Southern leaders and, as far as possible, of the Southern rank and file. At least it is hoped that these pages may fill such gaps as exist and supplement the aforementioned studies.

It will be seen that, while I have found segments of material to support each of the several " theses " with respect to the coming of the Civil War, I have been unable to accept entirely any one. The following pages may suggest, however, that in recent years the pendulum of historical interpretation has swung too far towards " revisionism " in overlooking the existence of desperate extremists in the South.

This study was begun a number of years ago under the direction of Dr. W. Stull Holt of the Johns Hopkins University, now of the University of Washington, and was brought to completion under the supervision of Professor J. Montgomery Gambrill of the Johns Hopkins University. Several chapters

7

were criticized by members of the advanced seminar in the Department of History at Johns Hopkins. Dr. Reinhard H. Luthin of Columbia University gave me the advantage of his unmatched bibliographical knowledge, and Dr. W. G. Bean of Washington and Lee University kindly read several chapters of the manuscript.

My obligations to the librarians throughout the United States are deep, especially to the curators of manuscripts, newspapers, and rare book collections. I wish to thank the following: the librarians at the Manuscript Division of the Library of Congress, the Southern Historical Collection of the University of North Carolina, Duke University Library, the Tennessee State Library, the Alabama Department of History and Archives, the Maryland Historical Society, the Mississippi Department of History and Archives, the University of Chicago Library, the Texas State Library, the Library of the University of Texas, the Louisiana State Department of Archives, the University of Virginia, the Virginia State Library, Emory University Library, the Johns Hopkins University Library, and the Charleston Library Society. Mr. Foster E. Mohrhardt, Mr. Richard H. Shoemaker, Miss Ellinor P. Gadsden, and Miss Evelyn M. Nelson of the Cyrus H. McCormick Library of Washington and Lee University have helped me almost daily. Mrs. Marjorie Burford Crenshaw, my wife, has aided me at every stage of the book's preparation. I am deeply grateful to all these for their invaluable help. Finally, I wish to thank Miss Lilly E. Lavarello, Secretary of the Department of History at the Johns Hopkins University, for her editorial assistance in preparing the book for publication. *The North Carolina Historical Review* has kindly given me permission to reprint in somewhat different form materials comprising Chapter V, which originally appeared in that magazine.

OLLINGER CRENSHAW

Lexington, Va.
1945

CONTENTS

0772338

66032

CHAPTER I

THE CONVENTIONS AND THE CANDIDATES

American politicians had concentrated upon the coming presidential election of 1860 long before that year arrived, and individuals were planning—usually under cover—to win the party nominations. Of course such Titans of the political scene as Senator William H. Seward and Senator Stephen A. Douglas were primarily concerned with securing the Republican and Democratic party nominations, respectively, in 1860, but there were numerous lesser hopefuls, who, mindful of the success in the past of such obscure " dark horses " as Polk, Harrison, Taylor, and Pierce, eagerly schemed to bring the coveted prize to themselves. Thus there were a half-dozen contestants for the Republican nomination, including the " rail-splitter," Abraham Lincoln of Illinois; the dubious Simon Cameron of Pennsylvania; Edward Bates of Missouri, who had taken his own chances seriously; that perennial seeker of the Presidency, Judge John McLean of Ohio; Salmon P. Chase of Ohio; and such favorite sons as Jacob Collamer of Vermont and William L. Dayton of New Jersey.[1]

In the Democratic ranks, where sectional fissure was only too apparent, it was the field against the Little Giant, Senator Douglas. Passed by in 1852 and in 1856, he gracefully yielded on those occasions but insisted that 1860 should be " his " year. The determined hostility of the Buchanan adminstration and of the Southern Democrats, however, made it unlikely that he could win the prize without a fearful struggle. President Bu-

[1] James Ford Rhodes, *History of the United States from the Compromise of 1850* (8 vols., New York, 1893-1919), II, 440-502, is an older account. The standard monograph is Emerson D. Fite, *The Presidential Campaign of 1860* (New York, 1911). For a recent scholarly treatment, with emphasis on the campaign in the free states, see Reinhard H. Luthin, *The First Lincoln Campaign* (Cambridge, 1944). See also Dwight L. Dumond, *The Secession Movement 1860-1861* (New York, 1931), Chaps. III-VI. Useful source books are Howard C. Perkins, *Northern Editorials on Secession* (2 vols., New York, 1942), esp. I, 3-27, and Chap. I, and Dwight L. Dumond, *Southern Editorials on Secession* (New York, 1931). For a recent study of the background, see Avery O. Craven, *The Coming of the Civil War* (New York, 1942).

chanan himself was not a candidate for renomination, and thus there were many persons who were mentioned, or who had some local support for the 1860 nomination. Among these were such possibilities as Daniel S. Dickinson of New York, James Guthrie of Kentucky, R. M. T. Hunter of Virginia, Andrew Johnson of Tennessee, Joseph Lane of Oregon, and John C. Breckinridge of Kentucky. There were those who thought that Jefferson Davis of Missisippi would make a satisfactory nominee. There were some like Henry A. Wise of Virginia and Howell Cobb of Georgia whose booms were punctured by their home states, and also there was the picturesque figure of Alexander H. Stephens who was urged to accept the nomination should it be proffered to him. The lively hopes of all these men rested upon the defeat of Douglas, and with the traditional two-thirds rule in effect, that might be achieved.

Among the old-line Whigs, some of whom hoped to engineer a fusion of Opposition-American elements with the Republicans, were such border-state leaders as John J. Crittenden of Kentucky and John Minor Botts of Virginia. Defying classification in any of the existing categories was Sam Houston, Governor of Texas, who had demonstrated some strength as a nationalist candidate, but who, if he were to succeed, had to obtain at least one of the regular group nominations. The abolitionists, of course, opposed the compromising politicians of all parties, the Republican included, and although some eschewed all political activity, Gerrit Smith ran for President on an abolitionist ticket. His candidacy was not taken seriously, however, even by himself.[2]

The story of the national nominating conventions in 1860 has often been told, but the outlines of the proceedings of each convention may be sketched here, together with an account of the nominees and the platforms of each party. The national Democratic convention convened at Charleston, South Carolina, the nucleus of sectional discontent and the home of the Rhetts and their Charleston *Mercury* newspaper. To this forum, therefore, was transferred the long drawn-out battle between the Douglas and Buchanan-Southern Democratic factions, and once

[2] Ralph V. Harlow, *Gerrit Smith* (New York, 1939), pp. 427-428; New York *Times*, Aug. 30, Sept. 17, 1860.

again was demonstrated the irreconcilable nature of the differences between them. Douglas and the Northern Democrats were determined that his principles should prevail in the platform, and his adversaries that they should not; indeed, the latter were determined to erect a platform altogether unacceptable to Douglas.

The convention met on April 23, at Institute Hall, with Caleb Cushing of Massachusetts as president. After some preliminary maneuverings the issue came to a crisis when the " majority " platform, brought in by a committee on which each state was equally represented, was rejected by the convention after eloquent speeches by Yancey of Alabama and Pugh of Ohio, and amidst scenes of confusion. When the Douglas platform was adopted by the convention, the lower Southern delegations, led by Alabama, seceded, and Charleston went mad with joy. At last Yancey and Rhett had come into their own, and on the night after disruption, May 1, while Yancey spoke, the proposal of an " Independent Southern Republic " was enthusiastically cheered. A Northern newspaper man, who described the scene, found a " fourth of July " atmosphere prevalent in Charleston. The Douglas men, who at first were afraid that, after all, the lower South might not secede from the convention,[3] and who desired the secession of perhaps a few Gulf states to strengthen Douglas in the North, took a serious view of the situation. It began to look, as Congressman Keitt had said of the Union, as if the party were rent from " turret to foundation-stone."

The Charleston convention then adopted the resolution which required for nomination two-thirds of the official total, which of course meant that Douglas' chances were diminished. On the first ballot Douglas received 145½, Hunter 42, Guthrie 35½, Andrew Johnson 12, with scattering votes cast for Dickinson, Lane, Davis, Toucey, and Pierce. As this was not sufficient to nominate Douglas, the convention balloted through the next several days, amidst increasing bitterness of the Northwestern Democrats, and some openly expressed the view that the Chicago convention would nominate the next President. For fifty-

---

[3] Austin L. Venable, " The Conflict Between the Douglas and Yancey Forces in the Charleston Convention," *Journal of Southern History*, VIII (Nov., 1942), 226-241, makes this point.

seven ballots the essential picture was unchanged, Douglas' vote being stabilized at approximately 152½, while Guthrie was runner-up with 65½ on many ballots. On the tenth day, May 3, the convention adjourned to reassemble at Baltimore, June 18.[4]

Meanwhile the seceding delegates held a three-day convention elsewhere in the city and adopted the rejected platform of the regular convention, heard a number of speeches, and adjourned to meet in Richmond the second Monday in June. This faction extended an invitation to the Democratic party to endorse their principles and to elect delegates to attend the Richmond meeting.[5]

The adjourned Democratic national convention met at Baltimore at the scheduled time, but at once the fierce contest was resumed.[6] This time the questions concerned the readmission of delegates who had seceded at Charleston, the deciding between contesting sets of delegations from the Southern states, and the requiring of a pledge that delegates be bound to support the nominee of the convention. The issue of credentials was referred on the second day to a committee, which deliberated for two days on the troublesome disputes, while the convention marked time. On Thursday, June 21, after a temporary delay caused by a collapse of the floor in the center of the Front Street theatre, perhaps symbolical of the party's condition, the Credentials Committee reported in favor of seating the contesting Douglas delegates from Alabama—thus excluding the Yancey delegation, and those from Louisiana. The Committee recom-

---

[4] Murat Halstead, *Caucuses of 1860. A History of the National Political Conventions* . . . (Columbus, 1860), pp. 1-97. This is an eye-witness account, marred by the author's obvious Republican sympathy and flippancy. The hostile John P. Kennedy wrote: "Talking of the politicians—those glass-eyed, scurvy fellows—what a witch cauldron have they been cooking at Charleston!" Kennedy to Mrs. Henry Duncan, May 27, 1860, MS, Letter Book, John P. Kennedy Papers, Peabody Institute Library, Baltimore.

[5] Halstead, pp. 155, 231-232.

[6] In the interim, both factions were at work. An agent of the seceders tried to line up votes for their admission at Baltimore, W. A. Richardson noted, but he had already "attended to that." He informed this agent that he wished the balloting to take precedence; nor did he desire the readmission of the seceders without their re-election. "I will see them in Hell before I change anything." It was a showdown between Union and disunion, he wrote, and he was uncompromisingly for the former. Richardson was Douglas' principal manager. W. A. Richardson to S. A. Douglas, May 13, 1860, MS, Stephen A. Douglas Papers, Library of the University of Chicago. Hereafter referred to as Douglas Papers.

mended compromise in the cases of Georgia, where each delegation was seated to cast a half vote, and of Arkansas where an
adjustment was reached. As no contestants appeared from
Texas and Mississippi, the seceders from those states were
admitted, while Florida and South Carolina presented no
credentials. In scattered contests from Massachusetts and
Missouri, Douglas delegates were seated.

A minority report, presented by Isaac I. Stevens of Oregon,
recommended the seating of the seceders and other anti-Douglas
men, stating at some length reasons for such conclusions. The
convention voted to seat the contestants from Alabama and
Louisiana, but rejected the majority report's compromise in the
case of Georgia, and by its action seated that state's seceding
delegation. The result of the action of the Douglas-controlled
convention in excluding the Alabama and Louisiana seceders
brought matters to a climax on the evening of June 22. The
chairman of the Virginia delegation, Charles W. Russell, rose
to announce that his group was quitting the convention, and
numerous others followed suit to proclaim their individual or
collective decision to withdraw, while still others retired for
consultation.

The sixth and final day was the occasion for further with-
drawals, including the resignation of Caleb Cushing, the president of the convention. He was succeeded by David Tod of
Ohio, and the convention, having disposed of all business but
that of the nominations, resumed the voting which had been
interrupted by the Charleston adjournment. The first roll-call
disclosed an all but unanimous vote for Douglas, but, under the
rule adopted at Charleston, he must have a two-thirds majority
of the original membership. A second ballot was taken in
which Douglas had 181½ to 7½ for Breckinridge and 5½ for
Guthrie, and a resolution was passed declaring Douglas the
unanimous nominee of the party. Senator Benjamin Fitzpatrick
of Alabama was nominated by a unanimous vote for Vice President, and the Baltimore convention adjourned *sine die* just
before ten o'clock on the evening of June 23. Thus closed the
stormy chapter which began at Charleston, and ended with the
party irreconcilably split.[7]

[7] Halstead, pp. 160-216. Fitzpatrick declined the nomination, and Herschel V.

The dissident Southern delegations and their sympathizers from the free states met in the Maryland Institute Hall and organized a convention which they styled the regular Democratic national convention. This harmonious body speedily adopted the Southern platform on slavery in the territories and nominated John C. Breckinridge of Kentucky for President and Joseph Lane of Oregon for Vice President. The skeleton convention at Richmond, constituted principally of the South Carolina delegates, ratified the platform and nominated Breckinridge and Lane.[8]

At Baltimore on May 9 the national Constitutional Union party convened with twenty-one states represented. This body was presided over by Washington Hunt of New York, and contained many old Whig leaders from North and South. It adopted a platform notable for its brevity and evasiveness, which condemned the platforms of other parties, and endorsed " the Union, the Constitution, and the Laws." The leading candidates for the presidential nomination were John J. Crittenden of Kentucky, John Minor Botts of Virgina, Sam Houston of Texas, John McLean of Ohio, and John Bell of Tennessee. Edward Everett of Massachusetts was often mentioned for Vice President. The first ballot gave Bell 68½, Houston 57, Crittenden 28, and Everett 25, with scattering votes for Rives, Goggin, and Botts, all of Virginia; Sharkey of Mississippi, and Graham of North Carolina. Bell was nominated on the second ballot, and Edward Everett was named for Vice President by acclamation.[9]

The Republicans assembled at the Wigwam, Chicago, May 15, in the interim between the Charleston and Baltimore conventions, with every prospect of selecting the successful candidate for President. The most eminent member of the party and eager contender for the nomination was Senator William H. Seward of New York, a man, however, too long in politics, who had accumulated too many enemies, including the powerful Horace Greeley of his own state. Other aspirants were Abra-

Johnson of Georgia was substituted for him as the vice-presidential candidate. Fitzpatrick's declination amazed J. J. Seibels of Alabama, who had Fitzpatrick's " assurances." Seibels to S. A. Douglas, June 25, 1860, MS, Douglas Papers.

[8] Halstead, pp. 217-230.

[9] *Ibid.*, pp. 105-120.

ham Lincoln of Illinois, John McLean of Ohio, Edward Bates of Missouri, Simon Cameron of Pennsylvania, N. P. Banks of Massachusetts, Salmon P. Chase of Ohio, and a few favorite sons.

The story of the nomination of Lincoln, after the success of the stop-Seward forces, has often been recounted. Lincoln's advantages included his own recently growing reputation, his residence in a doubtful state, the presence of a favorable gallery, and the possession of such clever managers as David Davis and Norman Judd, who did not scruple to engage in necessary vote-trading. An example of the trading was the " deal " with Simon Cameron, as a result of which the slippery Pennsylvanian became a member of Lincoln's cabinet. For Vice President, the Republicans cast two ballots before deciding on Hannibal Hamlin of Maine. The celebrated Kentucky abolitionist, Cassius M. Clay, received 101½ votes on the first ballot, but a heavy trend developed for Hamlin and he was chosen as Lincoln's running mate.[10]

The platform retreated from the radicalism of 1856, much to the chagrin of such an abolitionist-Republican as Joshua Giddings, but it was sufficiently inclusive to promise a protective tariff designed to satisfy Pennsylvania,[11] Congressional restriction of slavery in the territories, a homestead law, and a Pacific railroad, with which to win various blocs of voters. One issue could be emphasized in one region, and another stressed elsewhere.

It may be in order at this point to describe briefly the careers of the candidates of the four political parties. It should be said at the outset that there were at least several versions of the public and even the private lives of these men. First there was the version of the campaign biography and of the party headquarters and of the partisan orators and presses. At the other extreme was the version of political adversaries. Indeed, so divergent were these accounts that it is scarcely believable that

[10] *Ibid.*, pp. 120-154. On the Chicago convention, see W. E. Baringer, *Lincoln's Rise to Power* (Boston, 1937), pp. 188-329.

[11] For intra-party conflict on this subject, see Thomas M. Pitkin, " Western Republicans and the Tariff in 1860," *Mississippi Valley Historical Review*, XXVII (1940), 401-420. See also Reinhard H. Luthin, " Abraham Lincoln and the Tariff," *Am. Hist. Rev.*, XLIX (July, 1944), 609-629.

they could be descriptive of the same person. Thus the " record " of each candidate was searched far back into his history, and remarkable consistency was " proved " or, by a different selection of facts and their distortion and the use of " roorbacks," " proved " to be a mass of contradictions. The bitterness of the sectional warfare caused much talk about the soundness and the loyalty or the unsoundness and disloyalty of such men as Breckinridge, Bell, and Douglas towards the South. And Lincoln was often violently attacked as an abolitionist whose election would surely produce disruption and national ruin.

For Lincoln's career to 1860, which was hardly more distinguished than that of his competitors, one may turn to several adequate biographies and studies.[12] It should be remembered that in 1860 Lincoln was but one of many American politicians, and that his apotheosis was some years in the distance. The future American hero was born in Hardin county, Kentucky, in 1809, and spent a hard youth—so much popularized by later writers—in the back-country of Kentucky, moving with his peripatetic family to Indiana, and thence in the 1830's to New Salem, Illinois. The young Lincoln entered politics as a Henry Clay Whig, and served for seven years in the Illinois legislature. His attitude towards slavery was characteristic of his life-long admixture of the conservative and radical: he was antislavery, but not an abolitionist. During this period, he moved to Springfield, where he became a lawyer, and on the prairies earned a high reputation in that profession. Lincoln served one term as an unimportant Whig Congressman, 1847-1849, during which time he criticized Polk's Mexican war policies and formed a friendship with a fellow-Whig Southern Congressman, Alexander H. Stephens of Georgia.

After his retirement from Congress in 1849, Lincoln quit politics for a time, devoting his energies to the law, until the furor created by the Kansas-Nebraska bill caused him to return

[12] There is no completely satisfactory biography of this eminent American. For his early career, see Albert J. Beveridge, *Abraham Lincoln, 1809-1858* (4 vols., Boston, 1928). The best brief treatment is James G. Randall's sketch in the *Dictionary of American Biography*, XI, 242-259. Professor Randall is writing a biography of Lincoln which should fill this long-existing need. For Lincoln's political rise, see W. E. Baringer, *Lincoln's Rise to Power*.

to political activity in the mid-fifties. A Republican by 1856, Lincoln received 110 votes for Vice President in the first Republican convention, and became the party's nominee in the senatorial contest against Douglas in 1858. The race against the famous Little Giant commended Lincoln to the free states, and his penetrating question at Freeport, which exposed vividly the weak point in Douglas' popular sovereignty argument, proved to be of great significance. Earlier in this same contest he had made the sensational Springfield "House-Divided" speech, which was often alluded to by his enemies in the campaign of 1860.

Shrewdly watching the beginnings of the preconvention campaign, Lincoln captured the Illinois delegation. He had agreed late in 1859 to furnish biographical material to a supporter,[13] and he observed developments among the Democrats whose antics played so much into Lincoln's hands. He especially followed the fortunes of his old adversary, "Judge" Douglas, but on one occasion he appeared to miscalculate the probable outcome of the Charleston convention.[14] After his nomination at Chicago, he did all he could to bring together the conflicting elements of the party.[15] During the canvass when Douglas spoke frequently and Breckinridge occasionally, Lincoln remained silent in Springfield. As he told one friend: ". . . in my present position, when by the lessons of the past, and the united voice of all discreet friends, I can neither write nor speak a word for the public . . . ."[16] Illustrative of his determination not to be embarrassed by requests for his views was the form letter prepared by J. G. Nicolay, his secretary, to inform inquirers that he would say nothing, as his record set forth everything.[17]

[13] Lincoln to J. W. Fell, Dec. 20, 1859, *Writings* (Federal Edition), V, 117-120. In this he noted that he had been defeated before the people but once during his political career—for the legislature in 1832.

[14] Lincoln actually thought that the cotton states' secession at Charleston would help Douglas, especially in the North, and that Douglas would be nominated: "This puts the case in the hardest shape for us. But fight we must; and conquer we shall in the end." Lincoln to C. M. Allen, May 1, 1860, Emanuel Hertz, *Abraham Lincoln A New Portrait* (2 vols., New York, 1931), II, 772. Earlier, he thought Douglas would fail at Charleston. Lincoln to H. Taylor, April 21, 1860, *Writings*, V, 180-181.

[15] For example, Lincoln to Carl Schurz, June 18, 1860, Hertz, II, 778-779.

[16] Lincoln to S. Galloway, June 19, 1860, *Writings*, V, 185-186.

[17] J. G. Nicolay to ————, (1860), *ibid.*, pp. 183-184.

On occasion, Lincoln did write brief letters concerning his prospects, which seemed " very flattering," and corrections as to his alleged past actions, or encouragement to party workers. He urged people to write to him; now and then he replied with a short " private " or " confidential " letter.[18] Such a letter he wrote to A. Jonas, in which he denied that he had ever been in a Know Nothing lodge at Quincy, Illinois, in 1854. He added: " And now a word of caution. Our adversaries think they can gain a point if they could force me to openly deny the charge by which some degree of offense would be given to the Americans." [19]

During the summer and fall of 1860, pressure was brought to bear upon Lincoln to make a statement of reassurance to the South, from which section were emanating disquieting sounds of secession threats.[20] He made no public utterance on this matter, but in private he opposed secession, and asserted that it was the duty of the President to operate the governmental machine as it existed. No doubt Lincoln welcomed a letter sent him through an intermediary, John B. Fry, from the Virginia leader, John Minor Botts. This contained, said Lincoln, " one of the many assurances I received from the South that in no probable event will there be any very formidable effort to break up the Union. The people of the South have too much of good sense and good temper, to attempt the ruin of the government, rather than see it administered as it was administered by the men who made it. At least, so I hope and believe." And a month before election, he told another correspondent: " . . . I certainly am in no temper and no purpose to embitter the feelings of the South, but whether I am inclined to such a course as would in fact embitter their feelings you can better judge by my published speeches than by anything I would say in a short

[18] Lincoln to S. Colfax, May 31, 1860, Paul M. Angle (comp.), *New Letters and Papers of Lincoln* (Boston, 1930), p. 244. Charles Sumner had sent him his speech, " Barbarism of Slavery," and Lincoln acknowledged its receipt by saying that he had not yet read it, " but I anticipate much both of pleasure, and instruction from it." Lincoln to Sumner, June 14, 1860, *ibid.*, p. 249. On his prospects, see Lincoln to Hannibal Hamlin, July 18, 1860, *Writings*, V, 186; and Lincoln to N. D. Sperry, Sept. 26, 1860, Angle, p. 258.

[19] Lincoln to A. Jonas, July 21, 1860 (confidential), MS, Jeremiah S. Black Papers, Library of Congress.

[20] Angle, p. 259.

letter if I were inclined now, as I am not, to define my position anew." [21]

This oracular sentiment, vague and expressed in private as it was, could clear up nothing. Lincoln allowed those who would interpret his past as conservative to do so, and those who would stress the radicalism of the " House-Divided " speech, could likewise do so. Thus the debate continued through the campaign of 1860, and as late as 1930, two distinguished scholars, one a Northerner, and the other a Southerner, could still reach opposite conclusions as to Lincoln's intentions towards the " peculiar " institution.[22]

It has long been known that the choice of the frontier-type for President was not well received by certain cultured Eastern Republicans and others,[23] and the adverse comment of such a Southern radical as Rhett was to be expected.[24] Not all Southern opinion of Lincoln was so violent, and it may be of interest to note a sample of editorial comment in Southern papers at the time of Lincoln's nomination.

The New Orleans *Crescent* was restrained in its obervations. According to this conservative paper, Lincoln had conducted the debates with Douglas in an able manner, and his moral and personal character, so far as known, was " unexceptionable." His penchant for balancing radicalism and conservatism did not escape notice, and, everything considered, his nomination was the strongest that the party could have made. Nevertheless, it

[21] Lincoln to John B. Fry, Aug. 15, 1860 (Private), MS, Black Papers. It may be of significance that this letter of Lincoln's reposes in the Library of Congress. J. S. Black was the political manager for the Buchanan administration. Lincoln to L. Montgomery Bond, Oct. 15, 1860, *Writings*, V, 192.

[22] Arthur C. Cole, " Lincoln's Election an Immediate Menace to Slavery in the States?" *American Historical Review*, XXXVI (July, 1931), 740-767, contends that the South's fears for the immediate future of slavery because of Lincoln's election were groundless. J. G. deR. Hamilton, " Lincoln's Election an Immediate Menace to Slavery in the States?" finds the Republican party based upon (1) a desire to kill slavery, and (2) hatred of the South. He emphasizes Lincoln's radical utterances, 1856-1860, as well as those of Seward, Giddings, Henry Wilson, Sumner, and others. He believes that, if the South had not seceded, slavery in the states would have been attacked, *ibid.*, XXXVII (July, 1932), 700-711. A recent Northern scholar, Dwight L. Dumond, agrees with Hamilton as to Lincoln's radicalism, *Antislavery Origins of the Civil War in the United States* (Ann Arbor, 1939), pp. 106-114.

[23] New York *Herald*, May 19, 1860, thought Lincoln worse than Pierce.

[24] Charleston *Mercury*, June 7, Oct. 15, 1860.

CC032

was the duty of the South to exert itself to defeat this dangerous candidate.[25] A competitor newspaper in the same city, the *Bee*, described Lincoln as a man of agreeable manners, an effective speaker, self-instructed and self-made, who had a strong following in the West. This paper believed his nomination " a masterstroke." [26] The former Whig sheet, the Lynchburg *Virginian*, printed a favorable account of Lincoln, praising his Whig principles, but entirely rejecting his slavery views.[27] The Lexington, Kentucky, *Statesman*, a Democratic paper in Breckinridge's home town, praised Lincoln as " second to none in his party as a man of ability, prudence and sagacity." He was described as a radical, but a " delusive " one.[28] Other Southern papers either ignored the Chicago nominations, or agreed with the Fort Smith *Times* that " the South cannot abide in the Union with such a man as Lincoln for President." [29]

The Republican candidate for Vice President, Hannibal Hamlin of Maine, was born in 1809 in that state, became a successful lawyer, and entered politics as a Jacksonian Democrat. He was chosen to serve several terms in the legislature, and was elected Speaker of the Maine House of Representatives. From 1843 to 1847 he served in the national House of Representatives, and went to the United States Senate in 1848 as an antislavery Democrat. There he remained throughout the next decade, with a brief interregnum as Governor of Maine, and it was as a senator that he won the vice-presidential nomination on the Lincoln ticket in 1860.[30]

Recently there has been a revival of interest in the career of Stephen A. Douglas of Illinois, recipient of the Baltimore convention's nomination for President and principal foe of Lincoln in the free states. For many years, Douglas' reputation has been overshadowed by that of his now more famous rival, Lincoln. Indeed at times Douglas has seemed to have been no more than a foil for Lincoln's career. The " Little Giant " of the fifties was born at Brandon, Vermont, in 1813, but joined

[25] New Orleans *Daily Crescent*, May 19, 1860.
[26] New Orleans *Bee*, May 21, 1860.
[27] Lynchburg *Daily Virginian*, May 21, 1860.
[28] Lexington *Kentucky Statesman*, May 22, 1860.
[29] Fort Smith *Times*, May 31, 1860.
[30] D. A. B., VIII, 196-198.

the westward migration, which took him in the 1830's to Illinois. In that frontier state, Douglas became a lawyer and for a brief time a judge (hence the life-long appellation), and a Democratic politician. He followed the familiar pattern of service in the state legislature, was elected to the House of Representatives in the 1840's, and finally to the U. S. Senate in 1847.

In the Senate the youthful Douglas rose to the position of chairman of the Committee on Territories, a post he held until party factionalism removed him on the eve of the conventions of 1860. He had contracted a Southern marriage which some charged influenced his course in the fifties, but which probably did not. Senator Douglas attracted a following among the " Young Americans " who were so ebullient and confident of their country's progress, and was a serious contender for the Democratic presidential nominations in 1852 and 1856. Each time, however, when another received the prize, the contender gracefully stepped aside, but by 1860 he and his followers believed that the time had arrived for Douglas' nomination for President.

Meanwhile, his name had become unpopular, first in the North as the result of the furor created by the Kansas-Nebraska bill's passage in 1854 under his sponsorship, and afterwards, as a consequence of his rejection of the Lecompton constitution and his answer to Lincoln's Freeport question, he lost much support in the South. Thus after 1857 Douglas was faced with the Republicans on one flank and the Buchanan-Southern Democratic faction on the other, and in the Senate sessions just preceding the presidential election, the anti-Douglas Democrats filled hundreds of pages of the *Congressional Globe* with attacks upon him. His quest for the Presidency was closely related to the final sectional cleavage, and it was his fate, as a middle-of-the-road statesman, to fall between the fires of the extremists.[31]

At first the Baltimore convention had nominated Senator

[31] For a brief but well-balanced account, see Allen Johnson, *The Life of Stephen A. Douglas* (New York, 1908) ; a recent study, packed with details and based on hitherto unused materials, but vehemently pro-Douglas, is George Fort Milton, *The Eve of Conflict* (Boston, 1934) ; Allen Johnson's study in the *D. A. B.*, V, 397-403, is good.

0772338

Benjamin Fitzpatrick of Alabama for Vice President on the Douglas ticket, in an effort to appease the South by honoring a senator from Yancey's home state, and perhaps to open up a senatorship for the great orator. Senator Fitzpatrick declined the nomination, and the name of former Governor Herschel V. Johnson of Georgia, was substituted. Johnson was born in Burke county, Georgia, in 1812, and had earned distinction as a lawyer, as a member of the United States Senate in 1848-1849, as a state judge, and as Governor from 1853 to 1857. A strong state-rights man in the crisis of 1850, during the next decade his views had become moderate, and he was selected as a Southerner who not only was a Unionist, but one who had voted for the Kansas-Nebraska bill and at the same time was willing to go along with Douglas. No doubt Johnson's nomination caused him some embarrassment at home, where his course was denounced by the extremists, and where he was subjected to personal abuse.[32]

John C. Breckinridge was born near Lexington, Kentucky, in 1821, was educated at Centre College, studied law, and after a brief residence in Iowa, returned to Lexington in 1845, where he practiced law. Noted for his oratory, he made a stirring oration in July, 1847, in which he commemorated the Kentuckians who had fallen in the Mexican war, a war he entered belatedly as a Major of volunteers. He won no glory as a soldier, however, and entered politics first as a member of the legislature and then of Congress from Clay's old district in 1851. Although a Democrat, his dignity and serenity and his attractive personality caused many to regard him as the inheritor of Henry Clay's mantle. He served two terms in Congress before his nomination for Vice President on the Buchanan ticket in 1856. As Vice President he was personally respected even by his political opponents. A year and a half before his term expired he was chosen United States Senator from Kentucky by the legislature to succeed John J. Crittenden. Thus in 1860 this personable young man of thirty-nine was at the same time Vice President, Senator-elect from Kentucky, and a presidential nominee. Although he was the candidate of the element in the Democratic party associated with secession, he personally

[32] D. A. B., X, 102-103.

was a moderate, and vigorously defended himself against charges of inconsistency and disunion.[33]

Because Yancey, Rhett, and others in the lower South supported him, Breckinridge was widely charged with being a secessionist.[34] The charge of inconsistency as to his interpretation of the Kansas bill and his attitude towards slavery in the territories was often brought up against him. Certain speeches of his, especially in 1854 and 1856, were cited to show that earlier he had agreed with Douglas. Bell and Douglas newspapers quoted a speech he delivered in the House of Representatives in 1854, and one on June 9, 1856, at Lexington, Kentucky, and attention was emphatically directed to Breckinridge's address at the Tippecanoe battlefield, Indiana, during the campaign of 1856. Douglas himself at Petersburg, Virginia, alluded to this " Tippecanoe " speech, and Bell papers quoted alleged passages from it with horror: " 'I am connected with no party that has for its object the extension of slavery, nor with any to prevent the people of a State or *Territory* from deciding the question of its existence or non-existence with them for themselves.' " [35] Also there was some discussion as to whether

[33] *D. A. B.*, III, 7-10. There is no satisfactory biography of Breckinridge. For campaign sketch, see *Biographical Sketches of Hon. John C. Breckinridge . . . and General Joseph Lane . . .* (Washington, 1860), pamphlet, pp. 32, Library of Congress. New York *Herald*, June 25, 1860. The Breckinridge Family Papers, MSS, Library of Congress, are barren of material pertaining to John C. Breckinridge's 1860 campaign.

[34] Rev. Dr. Robert J. Breckinridge, a vigorous Unionist, former Clay Whig and Know Nothing, uncle of John C. Breckinridge, supported the latter in 1860 on the ground that he was completely devoted to the Union. Dr. Breckinridge resented the abuse of his nephew as a traitor. He also thought that the Bell and Douglas candidacies promoted Lincoln's chances. If the country could escape convulsions in 1860, he predicted that by 1864 there would be a consolidation in the South under John C. Breckinridge's leadership. Robert J. Breckinridge to W. F. Warner, Oct. 20, 1860 (copy), MS, Breckinridge Family Papers.

[35] For the inconsistency charges, see Carrollton (Ala.) *Pickens Republican*, July 12, 1860; Athens (Ga.) *Southern Watchman*, Sept. 13, 1860; Fayetteville (N. C.) *Observer*, July 5, 1860; and St. Louis *Daily Missouri Republican*, Sept. 7, 1860. It has not been possible to check the references to all Breckinridge's speeches, in which he was alleged to have been inconsistent. Especially elusive is the so-called Tippecanoe speech. In no instance did the Bell or Douglas paper quoting it cite a specific reference. According to the Charlottesville (Va.) *Review*, Oct. 5, 1860, Breckinridge said, Sept. 10, 1856, as reported by the Pittsburgh *Daily Union*, Sept. 12, 1856: "I would be the last to attempt to extend slavery to any new State or Territory. My desire is quite to the contrary." On March 23, 1854, Breckinridge said in the House: "Among the many

he was or was not a slaveholder.[36] He was accused even of being a sympathizer with John Brown,[37] and on the ground that some former Know Nothings supported him it was charged that he was a Know Nothing.[38]

The candidate for Vice President with Breckinridge was Joseph Lane of Oregon, who as Senator from that recently admitted state had closely cooperated with the Jefferson Davis faction in the Senate. Lane was born in Buncombe county, North Carolina, in 1801, and early in life migrated westward, settling in Vandenburg county, Indiana. In this state he entered politics and served in the Indiana legislature from 1822 to 1846, after which he won some fame in the Mexican war. For his services in that war he was brevetted Major General and won

misrepresentations sent to the country by some of the enemies of this Kansas-Nebraska bill, perhaps none is more flagrant than the charge that it proposes to legislate slavery into Nebraska and Kansas. Sir, if the bill contained such a feature, it could not receive my vote. The right to establish involves the correlative right to prohibit, and denying both, I could vote for neither. I go further, and express the opinion that a clause legislating slavery into those Territories could not command one southern vote in this House. . . . What, then, is the present condition of Nebraska and Kansas? Why, sir, . . . a law remains on the statute-book forever prohibiting slavery in these Territories. It is proposed simply to take off this prohibition, but not to make an enactment in affirmance of slavery there. . . . The effect of the repeal, therefore, is neither to establish nor to exclude, but to leave the future condition of the Territories dependent wholly on the action of the inhabitants, subject only to such limitations as the Federal Constitution may impose." He went on to say that the domestic institutions of the people could be regulated by them in their own way, except that whatever they did must be in accord with the Constitution. Thus property rights under the Constitution were left to the federal courts. Breckinridge then concluded with an explicit description of the two interpretations of the Kansas-Nebraska bill, saying that both parties left the matter to the Supreme Court of the United States for decision. (*Appendix to the Congressional Globe*, 33d Cong., 1st sess., p. 441.) In view of the later Dred Scott decision, it seems difficult to see wherein lay Mr. Breckinridge's inconsistency, unless it be in regard to his disclaimers as to legislating slavery into Kansas.

[36] Savannah *Daily Republican*, Sept. 3, 1860, compared Bell, a large slaveholder, to Breckinridge, who owned no slaves. A letter from I. R. Gross, Sheriff at Lexington, Ky., was introduced. Gross said that for the past three years, Breckinridge had listed no real or personal property for taxation. The Breckinridge press bestirred itself to prove their candidate a slaveholder. See correspondence of L. W. Powell of Henderson, Ky., in Waynesboro (Ga.) *Independent South*, Sept. 7, 1860, and also letter from the Postmaster of Lexington, Ky., to the effect that he was, and had been for years, a slaveholder. Fernandina *East Floridian*, Oct. 11, 1860.

[37] Richmond *Examiner*, Aug. 7, 1860.

[38] *Ibid.*, Aug. 10, 1860; Memphis *Daily Appeal*, Oct. 4, 1860.

the sobriquet, " The Marion of the Mexican War," which was repeated by his friends during the 1860 campaign. President Polk appointed him Governor of Oregon Territory in 1848 which post he held until 1850, and from then till 1859 he was Oregon's Territorial delegate. With the admission of Oregon in the latter year, Lane was chosen United States Senator for the term expiring in 1861. As a Westerner Lane was of particular value to the Southern Democrats in the controversy over slavery in the territories, because Lane agreed with the demand for Congressional protection to slavery there, and entirely rejected Douglas' doctrine.[39]

Lane's biographer has called attention to his availability as a presidential candidate in 1860. A frontier politician of humble birth, and a Mexican war hero, Lane possessed a Jacksonian appearance and a following among members of Congress. He was the leader of the administration Democrats in Oregon, which apparently constituted the overwhelmingly dominant Democratic faction. After some difficulty, Senator Lane received the endorsement of the Oregon delegation to the Charleston convention for either President or Vice-President, and when the seceders departed from that convention, Lane wired Lansing Stout of the Oregon delegation, to " go out and stand by them." In Baltimore, Lane was the unanimous first-ballot choice of the Southern Democrats for the Vice Presidency.[40] Between the Charleston and Baltimore meetings, Lane wrote an Oregon friend condemning what he termed Douglas' rule-or-ruin policy. " One thing, however, is certain, that is Douglas cannot nor will not be nominated, or if he should be the South will bring out a candidate and run him with the certainty of giving him the entire South. We are in a muss, and I can hardly see how we can get out with whole bones, but we will see." [41]

So experienced a politician as Lane realized that the situation in Oregon would be hopeless with two Democratic tickets in the field, and he wrote Judge Deady in a characteristic ungram-

[39] D. A. B., X, 579-580.
[40] M. Margaret Jean Kelly, *The Career of Joseph Lane, Frontier Politician* (Washington, 1942), pp. 164-185, covers Lane's part in the campaign of 1860.
[41] Joseph Lane to M. P. Deady, May 13, 1860, MS, Joseph Lane Papers, Oregon Historical Society. I am indebted to the Society for copies of pertinent letters in this collection.

matical letter to see to it that only one Democratic ticket remained in the race.[42] The political trend in Oregon was against Lane, however, and no fusion was arranged of the warring Democratic factions. Rather, the Douglas Democrats seemed to cooperate with the Republicans; together they gained control of the Oregon legislature in 1860, and elected two new Senators, one E. D. Baker, a Republican, and the other, J. W. Nesmith, a Douglas Democrat. The loss of Oregon during the campaign caused much rejoicing in the anti-Breckinridge press, and Lane's telegram to Charleston was paraphrased to read that the Oregon voters had told " Jo Lane to go out."

Lane traveled during the campaign and made a number of addresses in behalf of his ticket. He was hissed at Philadelphia, however, and after a brief visit to his native North Carolina, he campaigned in Indiana. Although one modern writer has called Lane an open and avowed secessionist,[43] he joined the head of his ticket during the campaign in denying that he was a disunionist.[44] There was talk that the ultimate goal of the secessionists was to take advantage of the complicated electoral machinery and the four presidential tickets, and by throwing the election into the House of Representatives and blocking an election there, eventually to make Lane President by electing him vice president in the Senate. Just how seriously Lane himself took this possibility, the evidence does not disclose, but it was a far-fetched scheme. There is some evidence to show that Lane had given up hope of defeating Lincoln before election, and that he favored action by South Carolina to " sustain " her honor, to stand firm, and by that means to win " an immense body of support North." [45]

Lane's state of mind can be described from letters he wrote not long after the election. On December 2, he informed Judge Deady that no adjustments could or would be made, and that the Union was broken up.[46] On January 27, 1861, he predicted

[42] Lane to Deady, July 13, 1860. For senatorial election in Oregon, see Providence *Daily Journal*, Oct. 23, 1860.

[43] *D. A. B.*, X, 579-580.

[44] Kelly, p. 174; Lane, in a speech at Indianapolis on Sept. 17, said that he would not rebel and that four years would pass quickly. Rome (Ga.) *Weekly Courier*, Oct. 12, 1860.

[45] J. F. Hammond to James H. Hammond, West Point, N. Y., Oct. 29, 1860, MS, James H. Hammond Papers, Library of Congress.

[46] Lane to M. P. Deady, Dec. 2, 1860, MS, Lane Papers.

the permanent establishment of a Southern Confederacy of fifteen slave states, which would receive immediate foreign recognition, as he had heard from foreign representatives in Washington. In the light of these facts, coercion would be most unwise. Lane then concluded:

The Republican party have brought all this calamity on the country. Their total disregard of the constitution, of the rights of the states and of the decision of the Supreme court has made it necessary for the slave states to act just as a portion of them have acted. Their preservation and self respect made it absolutely proper & necessary to do all they have done, they did their duty. Let the blame and responsibility rest upon that sectional fanatical party who have destroyed the best form of government ever created by the wisdom of man.[47]

But when secession and war came, Lane returned to Oregon, where he spent the remainder of his life in obscurity.

The nominees of the Constitutional Union party, John Bell of Tennessee, and Edward Everett of Massachusetts, were men of exceedingly high personal, political, social, and economic standing in their respective communities. Bell was born near Nashville in 1797 and graduated from the college in the city of Nashville, which later became his life-long place of residence. He soon became a lawyer of eminence and an active local politician. A Jacksonian at first, he broke with the great leader and became a foremost Whig in his state. Between 1827 and 1841, Bell was a member of the national House of Representatives, and in 1834 was elected Speaker of that body over the Jacksonian James K. Polk. Another honor fell to him when in 1841 he was appointed Secretary of War by President Harrison, but in common with his fellow Whigs, quit the cabinet when his party quarreled with President Tyler.

From 1847 to 1859, John Bell served in the United States Senate as a nationalist and a conservative. Although Bell was a large slaveholder who disliked abolitionists, he was not aggressively pro-slavery, and indeed, opposed extremists in both sections. During this long public career, Bell made that record upon which, like Lincoln, he stood in the canvass of 1860. His defense of the reception of abolition petitions had aligned him with John Quincy Adams in that memorable contest; though he

---

[47] Lane to Deady, Jan. 27, 1861, MS, *ibid.*

conceded the constitutionality of Congressional exclusion of slavery in the territories, he opposed its exercise. His opposition to the Kansas-Nebraska bill made him almost unique among Southern Senators, and his defiance of the Tennessee legislature's instructions to support the Lecompton constitution underscored his lack of Southern orthodoxy. With the disintegration of the Whig party, Bell naturally participated in the American movement, and like such Southern men as Botts, Crittenden, and Bates, toyed briefly with the idea of uniting moderate Republicans with old Whigs.[48] On the tariff, he was acceptable to the Republicans as a protectionist.

During the campaign this long record was combed by friend and foe with the usual partisan objectives in view. A Southern man for whom Greeley's *Tribune* had a good word was anathema to those desiring advanced Southern rights unity.[49] The Southern Bell papers exerted themselves to demonstrate that he was sound on all issues involving the South. The *Congressional Globe* was used by both sides in this appeal to the record. But like Lincoln, Bell maintained silence, with one or two exceptions, on the issues of the campaign.

Historians have scarcely scratched the surface in their analyses of the Constitutional Union movement.[50] They have often accepted the hostile estimates of partisans and have dealt with the Bell candidacy in terms of contempt. Bell's platform has been called evasive, and " the old gentlemen " who composed

---

[48] For the facts of Bell's career, see *D. A. B.*, II, 157-159, and these may be compared with the bitter partisan accounts of his " record." For a favorable campaign biography see *The Life, Speeches, and Public Services of John Bell* . . . (New York, 1860), pamphlet, Library of Congress pp. 31. For a sympathetic sketch, see Philadelphia *Press*, May 11, 1860, which suggested that Bell would not make a bad candidate for the Republicans as well. Forney's paper declared that " the hereditary antagonists " of the Democrats had made a good selection. For a pro-Bell article, see Little Rock *Arkansas State Gazette*, Sept. 22, 1860, and for a typical effort to prove Bell unsound and disloyal to the South, see Little Rock *Arkansas True Democrat*, Oct. 13, 1860. Tallahassee *Floridian and Journal*, Sept. 8, 1860, accused Bell of justifying murders of foreigners and Roman Catholics in Baltimore, New Orleans, and Louisville.

[49] New York *Tribune*, Jan. 12, 1860, which also said: " History at least will do Mr. Bell no reluctant justice."

[50] Cf. S. S. Nicholas to J. J. Crittenden, July 13, 1860. Nicholas concluded that if Pennsylvania could not be carried by fusion, the only " fun " would be in beating the Democrats in Tennessee and Kentucky. MS, John J. Crittenden Papers, Library of Congress.

his following described as timid men unwilling to face the great moral issues of the time. Fortunately, in the Boteler papers at Duke University there is a long letter from John Bell to Congressman Alexander Robinson Boteler of Virginia, who acted as director of the National Executive Committee of the Constitutional Union party. In this lengthy and confidential communication of July, 1860, the candidate unbosomed himself as to his expectations and offered strategic suggestions for the party to follow. Bell declared that his ticket had a good chance to carry most of the Southern states, if his friends exerted themselves, but that that would not mean electoral success, because, " In the present state of public sentiment in the *free* States, Lincoln, if the election were to come off now, would be elected by the people,—by the Colleges." All would be in vain, therefore, unless somehow Lincoln could be defeated.

Pennsylvania held the key to the situation, according to Bell.[51] That state must be made to see that if Lincoln triumphed, her particular interests, coal and iron, would be doomed to many years of neglect.

I had hoped that the enlightened friends of her particular interests (iron & coal) would see that the election of any sectional candidate would be fatal to them. But it seems they do not. They are *infatuated* from some cause. I presume it is the passion for novelty in part—for seeing a new power at Washington.—A new dynasty on the throne, & the gratification of seeing the hated Democracy—pretty nearly synonymous with *Southern Oligarchy* (in their vocabulary) overthrown.

Bell would stress to them that peace was a *sine qua non* for the development of such interests, and that peace would never come with a sectional candidate like Lincoln. The wheels of government would be stilled by the opposition of the entire South, within thirty days after Lincoln's election.

Yet he feared that Pennsylvania would vote Republican anyway. Therefore, the only way to defeat Lincoln was by fusion in the important free states, such as New York, Pennsylvania, New Jersey, and others. But on this matter Bell

[51] The Bell-Everett party established a weekly party newspaper, the *Union Guard*, published at Washington. It had a protectionist, Unionist tone. It assailed the alleged secessionist clique, and tried to prove Lincoln to be a Sumnerite. See *Union Guard*, complete file, Library of Congress. See especially issues July 12, 19, Aug. 16, Sept. 20, 27, 1860.

preferred not to advise his friends directly as to their course, remarking that, if the election should go to the House, he would probably not receive the support of Republican states.

Pressure of business interrupted Bell's letter, begun July 2, so that he could not resume it until July 30, because, as he said, he was swamped with a voluminous correspondence. Most of his letters came from Southern writers, demanding that he make explicit statements regarding slavery. But, again, like the wily Lincoln, Bell referred them to his past course during a quarter century of public life. Some of these requests came from real friends and others from concealed enemies.

After the lapse of nearly a month, Bell thought he could peer through the future more clearly. He still believed that he could carry all the South except two or three of the more radical states. This should be driven home to the North:

If our ticket can, by any means meet with success in either one of the large states of Pennsylvania, N. York—or Ohio,—I may be elected by the Colleges! which I am strongly impressed with the belief, is the only way in which I can be elected.—An election by the House, I could hardly hope to receive,—the way things go now a days.

Further reflection upon the question of a coalition with the Douglas men in the free states caused Bell to think that, after it was obvious that Douglas could not be elected, the fusion electors would vote for him, and that such votes could elect Bell and Everett. Breckinridge could not get a single vote North. Such were his optimistic calculations at the end of July.

Another matter Bell dwelt upon at some length, which appeared in the campaign arguments, was the " conspiracy " theory.

Since the first part of this letter was written, I have become satisfied from information received from the South, that a more wide-spread and determined purpose exists in the South, to attempt a separation of the states in the event of the election of Lincoln, than I had before thought existed. It is now almost certain, that in that event, a secession of three or four States, if not more, will take place, unless the leaders are foiled in their designs, or discouraged by the vote—the unexpected strength of the vote of the Union party cast in those states, in November: and I am now firmly persuaded that the *secession* from the Convention at Charleston & and again at Baltimore was *instigated*, & finally passed to consummation by those artful and able instigators, who said, or believed, that the movement would lead *to the election* of *Lincoln*. It was designed that it should. They could not have supposed, or believed, for a moment, that Breckinridge could get a single vote in any of the free states: and they must have known that, weakened as he was sure to be, Douglas could not carry any one state, except perhaps Ill. The conspirators did not dream that the Union party could rally strength enough to defeat their designs. Hence, I repeat, the Breckinridge movement must have been made designedly to elect Lincoln. This *design*, you will remark, I impute to the *few* arch leaders, not to the rank & file of the delegates from Va. N. C. Tenn. Ky. & Mo. These latter, are dupes, but not altogether innocent. The malignancy of some of them, led them to prefer the election of Lincoln, with all its *possible* evil consequences, to the election of Douglass.

This being true, Bell concluded that it was of the first importance that Lincoln be defeated, and he listed some seven free states " to be operated on."

Here the candidate suggested certain material for pamphlet distribution, such as a strongly written document, the text of which should be " peace," while " the success of either of the other three [candidates] is endless strife, it may be, civil war." He also suggested the preparation of a pamphlet which would set forth the imminent danger of secession of the Southern states, and the certainty, in any event, of the solid bloc of Congressional opposition to Lincoln's adminstration. Bell even suggested that a Mr. Welling of the *National Intelligencer* be approached to undertake the task. John Bell closed with a note of guile in his manner of transmitting this confidential letter to Boteler.[52]

Former Governor Washington Hunt of New York, an active Bell manager, described the formation and composition of the fusion ticket in his state. An understanding existed between the ten Bell and the twenty-five Douglas electors, that if the entire thirty-five votes were necessary to elect Bell in the college they would be cast for him. Hunt replied in confidence that they ought to do just that, " . . . and in that event that you will not fail to appreciate their patriotism and to exhibit your proverbial

[52] John Bell to Alexander R. Boteler, July 2-30, 1860, MS, Alexander Robinson Boteler Papers, Library of Duke University. Earlier, Bell had written W. Ridgeway, May 29, 1860, that either Lincoln would be elected in the college, or that the election would go to the House, where the Union candidate would be chosen. Here he referred Ridgeway, of the Richmond *Whig*, to his main speeches in regard to slavery. MS, John Bell Papers, Library of Congress.

sense of justice." Bell need not reply, Hunt told him, but " in the course of human events I may have to ask you to remember it." [53] But the " course of human events " made it unnecessary for Bell to recall this incident—he had no Federal offices to dispense.

In the summer of 1860, the New York *Herald* carried an article describing Bell's character and personality, and published an interview he granted to that paper's correspondent. Bell spoke with optimism as to his or Mr. Everett's chances of winning the Presidency, and declared the mission of his party to be to prevent dissolution. His comments on Lincoln may be quoted:

Mr. Lincoln he regarded as a fair, candid, open hearted, common sense man. He was in the House of Representatives when he (Mr. Bell) was in the Senate. If left to himself, Mr. Bell had no fears about Mr. Lincoln; but it would be the counsels of the leaders of his party, Seward and others, that he feared, and which would be fraught with injustice to the South and eventual danger to the Union.[54]

If John Bell had had a distinguished career prior to his nomination for President, that of the vice-presidential candidate, Edward Everett, was even more so. Born in Massachusetts in 1794, he became for a time a Unitarian clergyman, and was elected to the chair of Greek at Harvard, his Alma Mater, in 1815. Continuing his education, he was the first American to received the Ph. D. degree from Göttingen (1817). This scholar-clergyman-educator entered politics and was elected to Congress in 1825, where he served for ten years, after which he held the Governor's chair for four terms. Under Harrison and Tyler he was American minister to London, and upon his return, was chosen to be president of Harvard College. This briefly held and not altogether happy post he relinquished to become Secreetary of State at the close of Fillmore's term. From this office he stepped to the Uniter States Senate, of which he was a member when the sectional controversy reached new intensity.

[53] Hunt to Bell, Aug 19, 1860, MS, *ibid.* For the private reflections of a Constitutional Unionist leader and eminent literary figure, see the " Journal of John P. Kennedy," XII (Dec. 7, 1859 to Sept. 9, 1861), pp. 27-203, *passim*, MSS, John Pendleton Kennedy Papers, Peabody Institute Library, Baltimore.
[54] New York *Herald*, Aug. 8, 1860. It is remarkable that even Bell should misjudge Seward's essential conservatism.

Throughout his career he had deferred to the South in politics, and his absence on the Kansas-Nebraska roll-call, together with increasing fire from antislavery elements, led to his resignation. Meanwhile, he had become famous as an orator and for his work in the Washington Monument Association.[55] Thus he had achieved a career of distinction not matched by many contemporary public figures. A recent writer has characterized him as the " spokesman of the powerful New England industrialists." [56]

Everett's correspondence reveals that the nomination came to him as a painful surprise. Only the crisis of 1859-1860 had induced him to emerge from retirement.[57] He described his dilemma to a well-wisher:

The nomination was wholly unexpected to me and as unwelcome as unexpected. I took effectual measures to prevent a nomination to the Presidency, and if I had dreamed that a nomination to Vice-Presidency would be tendered to me, I should positively have declined it, in advance. I cannot now decline it, without exposing my motives to misconstruction, throwing cold water on the cause, and greatly disobliging the friends who have bestowed upon me this mark of their confidence. I have accordingly accepted it.

He regretted that for a time he must " creep " out of his "shell" of retirement.[58]

---

[55] D. A. B., VI, 223-226.

[56] Merle Curti, Growth of American Thought (New York, 1943), p. 351.

[57] Edward Everett to Anna Ella Carroll, Dec. 12, 1859, MS, Anna Ella Carroll Papers, Maryland Historical Society.

[58] Everett to Anna Ella Carroll, May 29, 1860, MS, ibid. Indeed, he meditated a declination. Everett to John J. Crittenden, May 28, 1860, MS, John J. Crittenden Papers, Library of Congress. He desired to be excused, he wrote Washington Hunt, and would delay his official answer. Everett to Hunt, May 14, 1860, MS, ibid. John P. Kennedy to Edward Everett, May 23, 1860, implored Everett to accept the Vice Presidency as he would be a tower of strength to the ticket. It was necessary to nominate a Southern man for President, because of the discord at Charleston; but for that the ticket would have been reversed. The chances were not favorable, but who knew what might happen. MS, Letter Book, Kennedy Papers, Peabody Institute Library, Baltimore.

Chapter II

THE DOCTRINE OF CONGRESSIONAL PROTECTION OF SLAVERY IN THE TERRITORIES

In the period after the Mexican war the acute territorial question, temporarily quieted after the passage of the Compromise of 1850, flared up with renewed intensity upon the adoption in 1854 of the Kansas-Nebraska bill. In these years four distinct proposals were offered which sought to solve this vexing problem, but despite the efforts of Congress, the Executive, and the Supreme Court to reach a final and generally accepted solution, none was agreed upon during the decade of the 1850's. The four proposals were: (1) the Wilmot proviso, the demand that slavery be forbidden forever in the territories by Congressional enactment, which became the basic creed of the Republican party; (2) the antithetical insistence of the aggressive pro-slavery Democrats that Congress should legislate to protect slavery in the territories; (3) the Popular Sovereignty idea of Stephen A. Douglas, which he made clearer in his Freeport doctrine of 1858, that the people of the territories, prior to the writing of a state constitution, could maintain or banish slavery by action of the territorial legislature; [1] and (4) the suggestion that a geographical line, 36'-30", be drawn through the West to divide free from slave soil. It is with the second of these propositions that the following treatment is concerned, as it became a central issue of the campaign of 1860. It was the dogma upon which the Southern Democrats generally decided to stand; and by so doing, split the party at Charleston and created a new party at Baltimore. The demand for the

---

[1] The Buchanan Democrats and the Southern Democrats insisted that by the term Popular Sovereignty was meant the act of people in a territory in writing a state constitution. It was at that point that they conceded that the people might establish or reject slavery; but before that point, slavery existed in the territories by force of the Constitution, and no power could disturb it there. No clarification was made apparently during the debates on Kansas-Nebraska, and the Cincinnati platform of 1856, upon which Buchanan was elected, continued the dual interpretation. But after Douglas' Freeport speech, 1858, the term Popular Sovereignty meant Douglas' interpretation of the doctrine.

Congressional protection of slavery in the territories was the immediate *raison d'être* of the Breckinridge party.[2]

As early as 1848, under the leadership of William L. Yancey of Alabama, an " Alabama platform " which demanded Congressional protection of slavery in the territories had been put forward as a party test. After the failure of the Southern extremists in 1850, and the experiment with the Kansas-Nebraska bill in the mid-fifties, Southerners returned to this doctrine, and in the Davis Senate resolutions of February 2, 1860, they formulated with finality their immovable position.[3]

It will be pertinent to examine the expositions and criticisms of this Congressional Protection dogma made by orators and party newspapers during the campaign. Whence came the demand for this, and what tangible result did the Southern Democrats expect to secure from this demand? If they should win their point on slavery protection, where could it be applied, and would it actually win for the South more slave territory and states? What was the attitude of the former Southern Whigs, in 1860 Bell followers and pro-slavery men? Likewise what attitude did the Southern Douglas men assume in the matter? What were the realities indeed of this " burning " question?

Even before the party conventions the main lines of attack were clear: the advocates of the doctrine were to be challenged to produce proof of its practical benefit to the South. At the beginning of the year the Kentucky clergyman, Robert J. Breckinridge, wrote his nephew, John C. Breckinridge, a strong Unionist letter in which he probed the territorial question. In his opinion, no problem ever needed more wisdom in handling, lest it bring yet more difficulties to the territories and perhaps destroy the Union. The Constitutional right the South supposed she had won was of no practical value: the South could not send masters and slaves to the territories fast enough to compete in those regions. Surely the experience of Kansas was decisive. The South could not spare the slaves, and only the reopening of the African slave trade could put her in the race for territories. " As an American citizen I deplore the fearfully undue impor-

---

[2] James G. Randall, *The Civil War and Reconstruction* (New York, 1937), p. 128.
[3] *Ibid.*, p. 174.

tance which the control by Congress over slavery in the Territories has been made to assume in our national politics." [4]

Others from the border slave states, generally Bell men, expressed similar views. Senator John J. Crittenden of Kentucky declared that there was no case calling for Congressional legislation on slavery in the territories: " To make it a practical question you have to suppose a future territory of a character to attract slavery; that there shall be an emigration of slaveholders to it; that the Territorial Legislature which assumes to deal with property has committed a flagrant outrage; and that the individual has called upon Congress." He surveyed the American territories but saw not a single one to which slavery would go if invited. Why dispute over something in the distant future? he inquired. [5] He returned to this topic in an illuminating discussion at Independence, Kentucky, in mid-September. He dismissed Douglas' Squatter Sovereignty as harmless nonsense, and protested against what he termed air-beating over " a mere abstraction." Crittenden declared that the Kansas matter was settled. As for Nebraska, that area was too cold for habitation or slavery. Nobody who could get a livelihood elsewhere would desire to go there. Who desired to take slaves across the Rocky Mountains? What persons desired to inhabit treeless plains? He answered: " There is not, in my judgment, one single spot of any considerable extent in any territory of the United States where any man would desire to carry his slaves, and yet the whole contest is as to what is to be done when the people carry their slaves where they don't want to carry them." The Kentuckian protested against making the nation the tail to the kite of petty territorial squabbles, and pointed to the fact that no case had yet arisen that required Congressional interposition. It was all remote and should not be agitated. [6]

Congressman Garret Davis of Kentucky wrote in the same vein to George D. Prentice:

In the territories north of the cotton region, climate, soil and immigration exclude it [slavery] so inexorably as to require no aid by Congressional or territorial legislation, and none which they could give would

[4] Robert J. Breckinridge to John C. Breckinridge, Jan. 9, 1860, Augusta (Ga.) *Chronicle and Sentinel*, Jan. 28, 1860.

[5] Alexandria *Gazette*, Aug. 9, 1860.

[6] New York *Times*, Sept. 18, 1860.

force it there. The country west of Arkansas, and inhabited by Indian tribes, is the only theatre where the slave question can ever have a real and practical interest, and not even there so long as the tribes exist, and their rights are respected.

He discerned among the Republicans a "hypercritical simulation" of hatred of slavery, and in his opinion there was no reason for fanaticism in connection with the subject of slavery. It was time to ignore the whole thing, he added.[7] Mayor Thomas Swann of Baltimore said in the course of a Bell speech, July 18: "As to the Territories, what new complications are likely to spring up—if the politicians will leave them to laws of climate, and the people who control them?"[8] And another Marylander, J. Dixon Roman of Washington county, asserted that there was no territory where slavery could exist.[9] In these arguments the "ordinance of nature" thesis of Webster's Seventh of March speech will be recognized.[10]

The influential Richmond *Whig* insisted that to constitute a legitimate issue, the request for protection "must be founded upon an *existing unprotected* condition of slave property in the territories." Otherwise the demand for it was based upon a prospective situation, and was but an "abstraction." If Kansas did not ask for protection, what case was there? Inasmuch as Nebraska and Washington territories had failed to pass laws protecting slavery, it was ironically suggested that they might be in need of protection by Congress. The vote of all Southern Senators except three against the proposal of Senate Albert G. Brown for "protection now" seemed conclusive evidence of the theoretical nature of the protection "humbug."[11] Indeed, the fate of the Brown resolutions was widely discussed and emphasized as proof either that the "seceders" considered none of the territories owned by the United States as suitable for settlement by slaveholders, or that they were insincere in offering the Davis Senate resolutions.[12] The Ashland address of

[7] Davis to Prentice, July 4, 1860, *ibid.*, July 23, 1860.
[8] Baltimore *American*, July 19, 1860.
[9] *Ibid.*
[10] Rhodes, I, 146-147.
[11] Quoted in Augusta *Daily Chronicle and Sentinel*, Sept. 30, 1860.
[12] Baltimore *Clipper*, Aug. 14, 1860. Only Senators Johnson of Arkansas, Brown, and Mallory voted for this resolution. Mobile *Daily Advertiser*, Oct. 6, 1860.

Breckinridge was quoted to the effect that he hoped the time would never come when territorial authority would be so reckless of its Constitutional obligations " *as to make it necessary for Congress . . . to interfere for the protection of personal rights and private property.*" It was clear to the Savannah *Republican* that the hub-bub about protection was of no significance.[13]

Historians have long criticized the Constitutional Union party's evasiveness in the campaign of 1860, and it is true that the Bell arguments were much more forceful in attack than in propounding positive policies. This is especially true in the discussion of Congressional protection, in which the Bell forces sought to condemn the dogmas of the Southern Democrats and at the same time to reassure Southern slaveholders as to their " soundness " on Southern rights. The Louisville *Journal* conceded that as late as 1859 the Opposition party in Kentucky subscribed to the doctrine of Congressional protection, and that this was still the party's position. John Bell was said to be in accord, but that he and his party denied that this dogma was of greater importance than the nation's existence. In the view of this partisan, the Southern Democrats were " using " the Breckinridge candidacy and the plank of Congressional protection for the " infernal " purpose of destroying the Union.[14] It was necessary to convince the electorate in the slave states that Bell was " right " on Southern principles, because his strength was largely in the South. Benjamin H. Hill of Georgia came out for Congressional protection in a speech at Macon on June 30.[15] Later however Hill condemned Breckinridge's platform as containing no advantage to the South. It was " madness," he wrote.[16]

As a modern historian has pointed out, the Constitutional Union state convention of Alabama adopted a strong platform insisting on full protection for slaveholders in the territories.[17] And Thomas H. Watts of Alabama interpreted a communication from John Bell to mean that Bell believed the territories

[13] Savannah *Daily Republican*, Sept. 25, 1860.
[14] Quoted in Augusta *Daily Chronicle and Sentinel*, Sept. 16, 1860.
[15] Savannah *Daily Republican*, July 9, 1860.
[16] Hill to Savannah *Daily Republican*, Oct. 13, 1860; *ibid.*, Oct. 19, 1860.
[17] Dumond, *The Secession Movement, 1860-1861*, pp. 94-95.

were common property of the states, that citizens of each state had the right to go there with property of every description, and while there to have protection to property and persons.[18] Yet a Bell man could say: "Congressional Protection, of its own force, never has secured a slave State, and never will." A writer to a Bell journal considered the territorial question a closed matter, and a Bell speaker declared that the protection the South already had was sufficient.[19] During the course of a staunch pro-union Bell speech, Jere Clemens ignored the subject of Congressional protection.[20] Still another Bell partisan assured an Alabama audience that the Supreme Court of the United States had decided the Protection question.[21] Indeed, it was a common contention with Bell supporters to leave the question of slavery protection to the arbitrament of judicial tribunals.[22] It seems safe to conclude that in the lower South there was sharp difference of opinion in the ranks of the Constitutional Unionists on the doctrine of Congressional protection.[23] In the upper South there was a preponderant opposition to it among the Bell people.

The Douglas Democrats in the South were in agreement with the objections made by Bell partisans to the Congressional protection dogma. Throughout the campaign there was, in general, cordiality between the Bell and Douglas forces. Both fired on the Breckinridge territorial doctrine, but handled each other with tenderness. Congressman Lawrence O'B. Branch of North Carolina flayed the Congressional protection doctrine in a letter to his constituents, May 15. It would give the South nothing and would lose everything his section had gained within the past twenty years.[24] Henry W. Miller said at Raleigh, North Carolina, shortly afterwards on the same subject: " I have looked in vain for reasons which justify the spirit of bitter

---

[18] Watts to Daniel Sayre, July 30, 1860, Mobile *Daily Advertiser*, Aug. 4, 1860.

[19] *Ibid.*, Oct. 21, 9, Nov. 4, 1860.

[20] *Ibid.*, Sept. 6, 7, 9, 1860.

[21] *Ibid.*, Oct. 5, 1860.

[22] Nashville *Republican Banner*, Jan 21, 1860.

[23] Dumond, *The Secession Movement 1860-1861*, pp. 94, 95, 95 n., gives the impression that there was general identity in such states as Georgia and Alabama on this issue between the Bell and Breckinridge men.

[24] Raleigh *Semi-Weekly Standard*, June 23, 1860.

persecution with which he [Douglas] has been pursued by some of the politicians of the South." The speaker found the doctrine of Congressional protection fraught with danger to the South. It was of no practical importance: instead Southern politicians should be concerning themselves with the great issue of defeating the Black Republicans.[25]

In Georgia, Alexander H. Stephens questioned whether or not the South should "reverse" her course and demand Congressional protection as a condition of remaining in the Union. Should Congress fail to meet the demand, secession must follow, he reasoned. Stephens warned the South that if the power to protect be granted to Congress, the power to prohibit accompanied such a concession. With calmness he urged that differences as to the legality of action by Territorial Legislatures to exclude slavery be referred to the courts. Since the Dred Scott decision, he saw no reason to quarrel with the Northern Democratic interpretation. The Cincinnati platform of 1856 was acceptable to him. He could see no objection, "unless we are determined to have a quarrel with the North." The future vice president of the Confederacy would not make war on "the supposed shortcomings of our friends." As he later argued after Lincoln's election, let Georgia wait for real aggression. Moreover, even if Squatter Sovereignty were not a Constitutional impossibility, under that doctrine the South had the right of expansion. Squatters, he contended, had carried slavery to Alabama, Arkansas, Tennessee, Kentucky, and Missouri without laws to protect it, and to Texas in spite of hostile law, and "they will carry it to all countries where natural laws will permit."[26]

Harvey M. Watterson of Tennessee could find no principle involved. Congressional protection would "never, never" be needed, because the question was one which would be solved by interest—the "everlasting" dollar. He recommended that the country be saved from the Black Republicans, to accomplish which all should acquiesce in the Kansas-Nebraska bill.[27] E. C.

[25] *Ibid.*, June 13, 1860.
[26] Letter of May 9, Augusta *Daily Chronicle and Sentinel*, May 18, 1860. It will be noted that Stephens was a possibility for the Democratic nomination at the time this letter was written.
[27] Speech delivered in New York. Memphis *Daily Appeal*, July 3, 1860.

Cabell of St. Louis, a former resident of Florida and owner of cotton plantations in Arkansas and Mississippi, wrote that he considered the Southern demands on the Democratic party to be " unreasonable." It was an impossibility to obtain what was asked; in any event, it was the Northern Democratic group which would give the South most. Cabell had lived under territorial government in Florida, and his experience there led him to support Popular Sovereignty. He would have none of " *a mere impracticable* abstraction." It was regrettable that he could not have done the impossible by removing his orange and pomegranate trees from Florida to Missouri. " If we are to have a ' revolution ' let it be on more tenable ground." [28] O. A. Lochrane of Georgia wrote the Macon *Telegraph* that he was supporting Douglas because his mind " seizes upon the practical "; he pronounced Congressional protection to be " unnecessary and unwise." [29] Numerous others among the Douglas people deprecated the Breckinridge demand. Former Governor Herschel V. Johnson belonged to the " climate-products " school. Congressional protection would benefit the South but little and he would not infuriate the North by demanding it. The common law and the Constitution would afford the South ample protection.[30]

It has been reiterated in the foregoing arguments of those opposed to Congressional protection that in their opinion the doctrine was inapplicable to any other territories then under the American flag. A traveller who had journeyed from Memphis to New Orleans observed plentiful uncultivated land, which he cited as an argument against the necessity or possibility of the expansion of slavery. Because the South had not the slaves to spare, he predicted no new slave territory in a hundred years— unless the African slave trade were reopened.[31] And inasmuch as there had been considerable discussion since 1850 regarding the possibilities for slavery in New Mexico, the published letter of an army officer who apparently wrote with first-hand know-

[28] Cabell to Jos. Clisby, May 18, Tallahassee *Floridian and Journal*, June 9, 1860.

[29] Augusta *Daily Constitutionalist*, Sept. 8, 1860.

[30] Rome *Weekly Courier*, May 25, 1860. Congressman J. S. Millson of Norfolk, Va., opposed protection. Washington *States and Union*, Sept. 1, 1860.

[31] Memphis *Daily Appeal*, Oct. 2, 1860.

ledge of climatic and topographical conditions there was brought to bear on the problem. Lieutenant Lazelle concluded that the great staples of Southern labor would be limited by soil and climate to relatively restricted and insignificant areas in New Mexico. He protested against hasty judgment and lack of information which he believed to be responsible for the view that New Mexico would be a likely addition to slavery. He prophesied that slavery was doomed, and that the South with increased population would reverse her historic attitude. He added that if the South should not await this result and should break away from the Union, the same forces would operate and nothing would be gained.[32]

In view of such clear-cut challenges by the Bell and Douglas campaigners, it became incumbent upon the Breckinridge press and orators to present a defense of a doctrine upon which they were staking all. Indeed, before the political conventions, the passage of the Davis Senate resolutions and the nomination of Breckinridge, there had existed some doubt as to the wisdom of making an opinion on the territories a test of political fidelity. Governor Joseph E. Brown of Georgia, surely an ardent proponent of Southern rights, questioned whether territorial protecttion was a wise issue. Like others, he doubted if a case would ever come up where this legislation would be needed.[33]

No less a personage than Senator Robert Toombs wrote his friend Alexander H. Stephens that Senators Brown, Davis, and Pugh had each introduced a set of resolutions dealing with slavery in the territories, and continued:

Davis's are those approved by the Pres[iden]t and are in the main good; but I think all of them are wrong. It is the very foolishness of folly to raise and make prominent such *issues now*. By the Kansas act of 1854 we repealed the Missouri restriction, declared our purpose as far as possible to remove the question of slavery from the halls of Congress, and therefore gave the territorial legislatures all the power over it which the Constitution allowed them to exercise, and to test that limit provided that all cases involving liberty might be appealed to the Supreme Court. The court has decided that Congress can not prohibit slavery in the territories, and altho' I think it involves the power of the

---

[32] St. Louis *Daily Missouri Republican*, May 20, 1860. This letter was cited as a Douglas argument.

[33] Jos. E. Brown to Messrs. Collins, Gresham, *et al.*, May 12, Augusta *Daily Constitutionalist*, May 19, 1860.

territorial legislatures also, yet it is true that that precise point has never come directly before the Court and never may. It has not arisen in seventy years; it may not arise in seventy years more. Why then press it now when we have just as much weight as we can possibly carry? Hostility to Douglas is the sole motive of movers of this mischief . . . . The Democratic caucus meets tomorrow to try to carry out this business. I shall resist it to the last extremity.[34]

But the caucus adopted the Davis resolutions, and Toombs became a few weeks later one of the most insistent Congressional protection men. The reason for his shift is not apparent, but it is significant that as late as February, 1860, after the Brown raid and the election of Pennington, and in the midst of the tense atmosphere of Washington that the forthright and tempestuous Toombs should take such an unequivocal stand against the slave-protection dogma. It suggests that his conversion was a matter of political expediency rather than deep-seated conviction.[35]

A strong Southern rights paper, the Columbus (Ga.) *Times,* debated the point. Of course, if a Congressional protection plank could be obtained well and good; but if that was rejected and the alternative was the formation of another party, it was thought better to abandon the issue for the time being. Anyway, there was no necessity for immediate protection, and Southerners could take solace in a friendly executive and judiciary. And territories in southerly regions would come in as slave states because of proximity to slaveholders, climate, courts, and laws. It was plain that this paper was a reluctant advocate of Congressional protection. Later the *Times* pointed out that with the Republicans in control of the House of Representatives, what the South asked for would never be granted. Would it not be better, then, to be content with a compromise and a " sound " nominee? Let the South wait till a distant day to demand Congressional protection.[36] R. H. Glass of Virginia

[34] Toombs to Stephens, Feb. 10, 1860, *The Correspondence of Robert Toombs, Alexander H. Stephens, and Howell Cobb,* ed. Ulrich B. Phillips, *Annual Report of the American Historical Association for the Year 1911* (2 vols., Washington, 1913), II, 461.

[35] For his later views, see *ibid.*, pp. 480-481. Toombs' biographers, Pleasant A. Stovall, *Robert Toombs* (New York, 1892) and Ulrich B. Phillips, *The Life of Robert Toombs* (New York, 1913) shed no light on this point.

[36] Columbus *Daily Times,* May 16, 26, 31, 1860.

believed that most of the Virginia newspapers, including his own, before the Charleston convention took the position that the Cincinnati platform of 1856 should be " reaffirmed . . . without change or modification, believing as we did that any attempt to give it either a Northern or Southern construction would be attended with results fatal to the harmony and success of the Democratic party." [37] Senator David L. Yulee of Florida conceded that Davis' doctrine was of value only in the future, because the destiny of all territories possessed by the Union was settled. He believed that " no inconsiderable " numbers in the South favored non-intervention.[38] The Richmond *Examiner* feared that the Yancey platform would " stimulate activity " of Congress by recognition of its authority over property of any kind in the territories.[39] And even after the campaign had been in progress for over two months, a fiery Southern journal complained that a large " class of our people are unwilling to make this territorial issue," and that only the future would determine if that class were strong enough to undo the " true " men of the South.[40]

But in spite of doubters the Breckinridge party took its stand squarely on the doctrine of Congressional protection, although embarrassed during the canvass by the activities of Davis' Mississippi colleague in the U. S. Senate, the extremist Albert Gallatin Brown. His position on the Davis resolutions and senatorial activity has been earlier alluded to, and suffice it to say here that he was not satisfied with the theoretical demands of Breckinridge and Lane. Of course Brown's attitude gave comfort to those who maintained that the doctrine was a sham. He publicly displayed his displeasure both with the Charleston-Baltimore plank and with the letters of acceptance of the Southern-Democratic nominees. With reference to the latter, it distressed Brown that he did not find an assurance that the entire power of government would be utilized to protect slave

[37] Richmond *Daily Examiner*, July 10, 1860. Glass published the Lynchburg *Republican*.

[38] Fernandina *East Floridian*, June 14, 1860.

[39] Richmond *Examiner*, June 7, 1860. This paper favored Congressional protection but would not make it a party test. *Ibid.*, July 10, 1860.

[40] New Orleans *Daily Delta*, Sept. 14, 1860. There was no distinction between rights in territories and in states, in the opinion of the *Delta*. *Ibid.*

property in the territories and on the high seas—as other property was protected. It was all much ado about nothing.[41] However, there were few who saw eye to eye with Brown's ultraism in the South, and Brown supported Breckinridge in spite of this difference of opinion.

It now remains to describe the main lines of the case as presented by the militant champions of the Davis doctrine of Congressional protection. Never did a group assume a more rigid position than did the Southern Democrats on this dogma, which became the test of Southern political orthodoxy. That bellwether of extremism, the Charleston *Mercury*, departed at times from its lofty contempt for parties and elections, and deigned to undertake a defense of the Southern position on the territorial question. Rhett's paper addressed itself to those who disposed of the issue as "abstract" or "fictitious." At the outset it denied (1) that there existed no territory into which Southern people could go with property in slaves, and (2) that the South had no population to spare for colonization.

In a manner suggestive of Calhoun's method of appealing to history, the *Mercury* reviewed recent events in America. If in 1849-50 the United States government had done its duty by protection of slavery in the territories, Southerners would have gone there with slaves, and California would probably have become a slave state. But the federal government was notoriously unwilling to do its duty, surrendered to the North, and denied the South a chance. Kansas likewise would have become a slave state had it not been for the United States government and the Territorial government, both of whom denied the South equality. Argument in the case of Kansas was buttressed by the contiguousness of the slave state of Missouri, which possessed similar soil and climate. In the opinion of the *Mercury,* it was the political crusade which prevented a natural—that is, Southern—emigration to Kansas. If only slave property had been protected, non-slaveholders would have remained away, but instead the latter were encouraged to migrate to Kansas to "uproot" Southern institutions.

To the assertions that Nebraska and Washington territories

[41] A. G. Brown to L. T. Galloway, Washington *States and Union*, Aug. 27, 1860. James B. Ranck, *Albert Gallatin Brown* (New York, 1937), pp. 192-193.

were too cold, that Utah and New Mexico were too barren and arid, that the Indian territory belonged to the Red man, that Central America was too distant, that Mexico was forbidden, that Cuba—if and when the United States should annex her—would be slave territory willy-nilly, and that therefore all talk of slave protection in the territories was nonsense, the *Mercury* answered with a categorical denial in general and in each particular.

The Indian territory, adjacent to Arkansas, was a practical case in point, where it was important to apply the principle of protection to slave property. Unless the South asserted her rights this territory would become a free state or states. William H. Seward was represented as having said that if the four states possible to be created from Texas sought admission to the Union as free states they would be admitted, but if any sought entrance as slave states, the question would arise, " Is it just and right, wise and expedient to establish Slave States? " With regard to the Arizona and New Mexico region, it was suggested that slaves could probably work the mines of that country. In the midst of this hopeful survey of the frontier, the *Mercury* paused abruptly for what appeared to be a concession: " At any rate, it is cowardly and suicidal to determine that because there is just now no territory we care to occupy, that therefore our rights, which may be vital and invaluable, should be yielded to a hostile sectional sentiment at the North." [42]

Even if the American territories in actual possession in 1860 seemed unpromising, it was always possible to contemplate our " Manifest Destiny," a subject extensively discussed in this era by the Southern press, with special application to our neighbor Mexico. The fantastic charlatan, " General " George W. L. Bickley, founder of the filibustering organization, the Knights of the Golden Circle, was at this very time busy recruiting volunteers with whom he planned to seize Mexico. The fertile imagination of Bickley conjured up the vision of twenty-five new slave states to be carved out of the territory south of the Rio Grande.[43] Although the *Mercury* gave but scant attention

[42] Charleston *Mercury*, Feb. 28, 1860.
[43] *Daily Louisville Democrat*, Sept. 2, 1860. O. Crenshaw, " The Knights of the Golden Circle: The Career of George Bickley," *American Historical Review*, XLVII (Oct., 1941), 23-50.

to the noisy " General " its ideology regarding our Latin neighbors was substantially the same as that which he proclaimed.
Southerners were reminded that two Mexican states, Texas and
California, had already been absorbed by the United States. " Is
it to be expected that our onward march is to stop here? "
Indeed not: the irrepressible Anglo-Saxon would occupy and
assimilate that entire " splendid but undeveloped country."
These Anglo-Saxon agents of civilization would gradually remove " the worthless mongrel races that now inhabit and curse
the land." What could be more natural than that the " terres-
trial paradise," which bordered on the South, should be popu-
lated by " enterprising Southerners?" With this exposition, it
was clear that the *Mercury* had " proved " the case: the territorial question *was* eminently practical.[44]

It then " answered " the second " fallacy " which had been
disseminated by enemies of the protective principle—that the
population of the South was too sparse for expansion. To its
own satisfaction, the *Mercury* demonstrated that on the contrary, the population was ample for such purposes, if only the
protective principle were in operation. The emigration of
people from Virginia, North Carolina, South Carolina, Georgia,
Alabama, Kentucky, and Tennessee to fresher and better lands
in Florida, Arkansas, and Texas, was cited to prove the contention that it was not lack of people which prevented the expansion of the South. Slavery was cautious and sensitive: it would
not spread without protection. After all, it only required 90,000
population to make a state, and with the South's total population estimated at approximately ten million, it was clear that
the population " gag " was without foundation. Thus the
Mercury disposed of the population argument.[45]

Other journals in the South which had espoused the Breckinridge cause felt the necessity of grappling with the " miserable
abstraction." The Richmond *Enquirer* conceded the postulate
that slavery would go only where it was profitable, and also
admitted the superior facility of antislavery emigrants in
reaching the territories. Differing from the Charleston *Mercury*,
the *Enquirer* denied that there was a Southern surplus of popu-

[44] Charleston *Mercury*, Feb. 28, 1860.
[45] *Ibid.*, Feb. 29, 1860.

lation, capital, or labor. The North had overwhelming advantages in the race for settlement. Moreover, in the organization of territorial governments, the North would win, because fifty laborers had fifty votes, whereas a Southerner with fifty slaves had but one vote. Even if the climate were favorable in territories, the result would be the same under squatter sovereignty. It was recognized that whatever the conditions, the difficulties were great in settling slaves in unorganized territories. Indian raids, change of climate, lawlessness, and travel dangers were serious factors—any one of which might reduce an opulent slaveholder to penury. The slim chance of success for a Southerner as he sallied forth to the territories was described. The slaveholder departed for the West, armed with pick and rifle, with slaves left behind, "upheld by the hope that better days will establish around him to share the fruit of his toil . . . the dependents to whom he owes protection and control." If the abolitionists deprived him of even this hope, what was left? To the modern student this seems indeed a nebulous argument, but apparently it was the best case which this important journal could make for Congressional protection.[46]

From another source came the contention that it was dangerous to allow slavery to be shut up within its 1860 limits, while the North continued to expand. "Slavery cannot endure without the right of expansion." If the South surrendered on this issue, slavery was lost, as it would be smothered.[47] Indeed, it was common among the advocates of Congressional protection to take high ground, to assume a lofty Constitutional position and to avoid a detailed discussion of the actual operation of this allegedly imperative doctrine. It was time to stand firm against the Black Republicans, a party which was said to believe in the social, political, and moral inferiority of the Southern white man and woman.[48] And in order to " prove " the charge that after all the battle over slavery in the territories

[46] *Daily Richmond Enquirer*, May 12, 1860.

[47] Montgomery *Mail* quoted in New Orleans *Daily Delta*, May 6, 1860.

[48] Nashville *Union and American*, July 26, 1860; Troy (Ala.) *Independent American*, March 21, 1860, said: ". . . the ensuing Presidential contest is proposed to be made a final test of the disposition of the North to do us justice without a political rupture." Also *ibid.*, May 16, 1860: " The prime cause of all our misfortunes may be discovered in the yielding disposition of our Southern people to the demands of Northern cupidity and fanaticism . . . ."

was but a preliminary to an attack on slavery in the states, it was always possible for Southern extremists to quote from the more radical Northern press. The Breckinridge party organ in St. Louis, for example, called attention to an editorial from the Chicago *Democrat,* a Lincoln paper, whose editor was " Long John " Wentworth:

It [slavery] cares for nothing but itself; and would sacrifice everything for the promotion of its end, and that end is universal domination. Nothing short of this will satisfy it. We might as well make up our minds to fight the battle now as at any other time. It will have to be fought, and the longer the evil day is put off, the more bloody will be the contest when it comes. If we do not place slavery in the process of extinction now by hemming it in where it is, and not suffering it to expand, it will extinguish us and our liberties.[49]

The intransigent position on Congressional protection was not only a challenge to the Republicans but was also a warning to the Northern Democrats, whose alleged lukewarmness towards Southern rights " encouraged " the Republicans and the abolitionists.[50] Unless protection be demanded, the destruction of Southern sugar and rice plantations was predicted.[51] Thus it may be that certain extremist elements in North and South, anxious to hasten the final day of reckoning, seized upon the issue of Congressional protection as a means by which to consummate the " irrepressible conflict."

It has been brought out that moderates in the South had proposed that the whole question of the territories be left to the courts, and in the last analysis to the Supreme Court of the United States. Of course it was expected that such a suggestion would meet with Southern favor because of the recent Dred Scott decision, and the political complexion of the Supreme Court. But comparatively little attention was paid to this aspect of the question by the Breckinridge campaigners. When notice was taken of this proposal, it was rejected as a possible snare. In the first place, no judicial settlement of the matter was

[49] St. Louis *Daily Bulletin*, Aug. 10, 1860, quoting the Chicago *Democrat*.
[50] St. Louis *Daily Bulletin*, July 2, 1860, which said further: " Do not give the slaveholder the right to *enter* the territory with his slaves and then, as Mr. *Douglas* would do, turn loose upon them men hired by emigrant aid societies to deprive him of his property. This is Mr. Douglas' position, and *it is infinitely more odious than the Republican doctrine of total exclusion.*"
[51] Louisville *Daily Courier*, Oct. 12, 1860.

possible until someone went into a territory with slaves and was deprived of them. After which he must seek remedy for his wrongs in a court of justice. It was objected that this was a long and tedious process, which would have the effect of excluding slavery from the territories, and leave the " peculiar " institution open to attack by " hordes " from the free states. And in the second place, with the future rather than the present or past in mind, the South was warned against acceptance of the Supreme Court as the final arbiter of political questions. It was pointed out that three members of the Court were tottering on the brink of the grave—just the number needed to give the Court to the Republicans. Said the same source: " Our great respect for the present able and spotless Court, should not lead us to put implicit confidence in a Body which may become as corrupt and sectional as the party which threatens to make it subservient to the base ends of Black Republicanism." Not the Supreme Court, but the people of the states should decide such questions.[52] Another suspected that the Republicans were biding their time until they had control of the Senate and the Supreme Court, when they purposed to proceed against slavery in the states.[53]

Such were the exhaustive arguments of the main Southern political groups in respect of the doctrine of Congressional protection. No topic was more tirelessly and repetitiously discussed than this one. Alexander H. Stephens testified plaintively on this point:

We have heard it [Congressional protection] in the social circle—in the forum—on the hustings—and in the halls of legislation. The newspapers have literally groaned with dissertations on it. Pamphlets have been published for and against the respective sides. Congress has spent months in its discussion, and may spend as many years as they have months, without arriving at any more definite or satisfactory conclusion in relation to it than Milton's perplexed spirits did on which they held such high and prolonged debate when they reasoned. . . .[54]

---

[52] St. Louis *Daily Bulletin*, May 24, 1860.

[53] Louisville *Daily Courier*, Oct. 12, 1860. These remarks regarding the Supreme Court may be compared with twentieth-century attacks upon that body.

[54] Augusta *Daily Chronicle and Sentinel*, May 18, 1860. Of the Congressional debate, a recent student has said: " A tiresome, legalistic discussion it was, each speaker trying to support his position by logic, history, the 'laws of nature,' legal citations, and *arguments ad hominem*." Randall, p. 176.

The long-suffering historian may agree with Stephens, and also with a contemporary paper which declared: " The appeals to the masses are as labored as a bookman's thesis." [55]

Lincoln's victory at the polls made certain that the doctrine of Congressional protection of slavery in the territories had no chance of success in the immediate future. But with the secession of South Carolina, and the subsequent Congressional efforts late in 1860 and early in 1861 to effect a compromise which would save the Union, there was a continuation of the discussion of the eternal question of slavery in the territories. Whether or not slavery was doomed in the territories as they existed in 1860, as contended by Bell and Douglas men in the campaign, and regardless of whether the issue was a meretricious one, in its aftermath it came to play a profoundly important role in the final disposition of the ill-fated Crittenden Compromise.

It has been demonstrated above that the Breckinridge Democrats made out a weak case for the actual application of their principle of Congressional protection; that they met with difficulty the challenge that the question had been disposed of, as regarded existing territories. Yet it has been maintained that the Republicans were compelled to stand firm on "principle," come what may, because Southerners would (1) make demands for more slave territory in the direction of Mexico and the Caribbean, and (2) demand the reopening of the African slave trade.[56]

It is true that there were Southerners who demanded portions —or all—of Mexico, Central America (the Charleston *Mercury* pointed out that it was less distant than California), and Cuba. It is also true that there was much " Manifest Destiny " talk in the Southern press in 1860, that William Walker was active, that Buchanan's Mexican policy was expansionistic, and that the abortive Knights of the Golden Circle for a time attracted attention. Senator Joseph Lane of Oregon in a Senate speech, September 19, 1859, cited the case of Arizona, which possessed a warm climate and a soil adapted to cotton production, especially in the Gila valley.[57] Obviously Lane considered this region

[55] St. Louis *Daily Evening News*, June 1, 1860.

[56] The African slave trade was infrequently discussed in the South during the campaign.

[57] *Congressional Globe*, 36th Cong., 1st sess., p. 185.

as potential slave territory. Early in the next year, a U. S. army officer, James Longstreet, stationed in New Mexico, wrote a prominent Southern Congressman of his activities and aspirations in the extension of slavery. He said that several of his friends and himself had " been working very hard, for several years past, to get Chihuahua into the U. S." This Mexican area was ready to join the United States, and had applied to the President for support or protection; it was his opinion that Chihuahua might readily come into the Union as a slave state. Longstreet sought Congressman Miles' help and offered to raise a regiment of volunteers, which he would march into Mexico within forty days after the American President authorized such a move. " Once we got a foot hold in Chihuahua, Sonora, which is much more important, will very soon follow." [58]

But also it should be observed that the United States Senate rejected the McLane treaty in the spring of 1860, that responsible Southerners were by no means agreed as to the wisdom of expansion at the expense of Mexico, and that the filibusters Walker and Bickley had ended in fiasco—scorned by many in the South. Thus as far as the actual filibustering menace was concerned, it was not serious in 1860-1861. At any rate, confidence was expressed in the North that filibusters were well in hand, or would be when a Republican administration took over. Horace Greeley's New York *Tribune* as early as November, 1859, said:

If the sham Democracy are beaten in 1860, the struggle for and against Slavery extension will be virtually concluded. We shall have Kansas, Nebraska, Dakota, New-Mexico and Arizona added to the number of Free States during the ensuing Presidential term. After that . . . let those who will clamor and plot for the acquisition of more territory on which to plant Slavery.[59]

And the same influential journal later expressed its doubts as to the possibility of extending slavery in northern Mexico. It pointed out that slavery needed fertile soil, staple crops, and facilities for transportation, but that northern Mexico had little soil suitable for cotton or sugar culture. There were no harbors and rivers. In the opinion of the *Tribune,* it was doubtful if

[58] James Longstreet to W. Porcher Miles, Albuquerque, N. M., Feb. 27, 1860, MS, Miles Papers, Southern Historical Collection, University of North Carolina.
[59] New York *Tribune*, Nov. 22, 1859.

even the revival of the African slave-trade would make possible the introduction of slave labor there. And when the same paper took note of the activities of that " new blue-eyed man of destiny," " General " Bickley and his Knights of the Golden Circle, it condemned them severely but doubted that much could be accomplished before November, 1860, when a new order would be ushered in at Washington, which would " restrain the ardor of these gentlemen of medieval propensities." [60]

And there were Southerners who agreed that Mexico was not favorable to the spread of slavery. The Texan, a member of Congress and later of Jefferson Davis' cabinet, John H. Reagan, expressed himself in a letter to one who evidently had been interested in filibustering schemes. Reagan condemned Walker and filibustering.

We dread the bringing into the Union of new free States which are formed out of our own territory, and the policy of those of you who seek Mexico and Central America, is to bring in ready-made free States, not composed of American citizens but of the mongrels of those countries.

He doubted that slavery could go there, even if those people were disfranchised, unless they were exterminated.

I know you will shrink back at the idea that slavery may thus be well nigh circumscribed. But we must look at destiny as it is, not as we would have it. You would make slave states there, so would I, and we would make a slave state of Kansas, of New Merico, of Utah, of Arizona, but we cannot, as we did not of California. I see the last State Gazette wants Sonora. For what, in God's name. To make another free State? For that is the inevitable.[61]

Senator Louis T. Wigfall of Texas, a fiery Southerner, was reported as being opposed to the taking of Mexico and her " mongrel " population.[62]

Eli Thayer of Massachusetts, a Republican and one who had been closely associated with colonization projects, was completely satisfied with the outcome of the workings of Popular Sovereignty. It was to him the most practicable way of exclud-

[60] Ibid., March 31, 1860.
[61] John H. Reagan to J. W. Latimore, Oct. 7, 1858, MS, Reagan Papers, Texas State Library, Austin, Texas.
[62] Cincinnati Daily Gazette, March 1, 1860.

ing slavery from the territories.[63] The New York *Herald* saw nothing in the territorial question. It was but the " ranting of Demagogues." Kansas was free, and there was never the slightest probability of its being otherwise. According to this source, in no territory of the United States, except perhaps New Mexico—" a miserable region "—would slave labor triumph over free. The *Herald* believed that the South was waking up to this " humbuggery," and thought the North should do so.[64] Indeed, the intense concern with New Mexico, a desolate region with almost no slaves in 1860, may be reflected upon by the modern student who knows that it was not until 1912 that New Mexico and Arizona became members of the Union.

The same issue which so sharply divided contemporaries recently has had scholarly attention, and one modern student of the period has concluded that slavery had indeed reached its natural limits by 1860.[65]

Yet when in 1861 the Crittenden Compromise came so near to adoption, when the members of the Congressional committee which included Davis, Toombs, Seward, and others at last agreed to a compromise which probably would have been overwhelmingly accepted by Northern popular vote, with cities reported to be ready to compromise, what was it that prevented the acceptance of the Crittenden Compromise by the Republican party? It was the inexorable adherence to " principle" which prevented Lincoln from agreeing to the Compromise. This fateful decision made by the President-elect dealt a mortal blow to the compromise effort which seemed most likely to succeed, a decision extolled by the historian of the period.[66]

On the other hand, what shall be said of the Southern leadership in this trying epoch? They had long stressed their " principle," and budged from it in the Crittenden discussions with reluctance. We have seen that even some " sound " Southern Democrats had questioned in 1860 the wisdom of the principle.

[63] Richmond *Daily Examiner*, June 4, 1860. See Thayer's Worcester speech, New York *Times*, Aug., 30, 1860.

[64] New York *Herald*, Aug. 21, 1860. The hollowness of the furor concerning Negro slavery in New Mexico has been demonstrated by a recent investigator, Loomis Morton Ganaway, *New Mexico and the Sectional Controvery, 1846-1861* (Historical Society of New Mexico, Publications in History, XII [March, 1944], Albuquerque, 1944), pp. 123-124.

[65] C. W. Ramsdell, " The Natural Limits of Slavery Expansion," *Mississippi Valley Historical Review*, XVI (September, 1929), 151-171.

[66] Rhodes, III, 153-170.

If the arguments of Bell and Douglas men in the campaign were substantially correct, if the sentiments of the Reagan letter were descriptive of an actual condition, then the Southern leaders had made a tragic blunder in insisting on a hollow principle. If slavery were doomed in the territories, as Reagan asserted, and could spread nowhere, the Southerners were indeed defeated by destiny—a "manifest destiny" of a truly different sort. And if it were slavery itself which the statesmen of the Old South were frantically attempting to save, what is to be said of their rejection of the Republican offer of a Constitutional amendment to guarantee slavery forever in the states—an amendment which was passed and ratified by two states? It has been said that a Confederate soldier, contemplating the fate of the South after Appomattox, declared that the ruined South was the monument of John C. Calhoun. In view of the ultimate outcome of their policies, their dogmatic insistence on the territorial "principle," it would possibly be more just to substitute the Southern leaders of 1860-1861 as the authors of disaster. It may be objected that this is taking advantage of the "hind-sight" of the historian. But there were Northern and Southern contemporaries who likewise assessed the situation.

> When, in the next century, the historian of the United States shall write the history of the Presidential canvass of 1860, he will be compelled to record that, on the part of a portion of the Southern people, there was an exhibition of mingled folly, insanity, and perfidy, which was possibly without a parallel.

So said a border-state Douglas paper, a paper friendly to slavery and the South.[67]

Let us summarize the situation as it seems to emerge. The Southern Democrats espoused a doctrine which they had no chance to obtain, and which if they did gain would net them nothing. They rejected Douglas, no foe to the South, and took the course certain to secure the election of the hated Black Republican. If "manifest destiny" barred slavery from the territories, they refused to admit it. On the other hand, Lincoln refused to concede anything on the "principle." As President after March 4, 1861, he might have attended to absurd filibusters south of the Crittenden line. But he chose to stand on "principle." If slavery was doomed in the territories, as seems to be true, and hemmed in, and the Republicans were willing to

[67] St. Louis *Daily Missouri Republican*, Oct. 4, 1860.

guarantee slavery forever in the states, what indeed was the real reason for the failure to make adjustments, a failure which may be attributed alike to Northern and Southern statesmen? It may be said that there was something deeper which may have made the Civil War inevitable; surely on its face the territorial issue is hardly convincing. Yet Lincoln was unmovable on this very issue. Concering the Crittenden Compromise, he wrote the month after election:

Prevent, as far as possible, any of our friends from demoralizing themselves and our cause by entertaining propositions for compromise of any sort on "slavery extension." There is no possible compromise upon it but which puts us under again and leaves us all our work to do over again. Whether it be a Missouri line or Eli Thayer's popular sovereignty, it is all the same. Let either be done, and immediately filibustering and extending slavery commences. On that point hold firm, as with a chain of steel.[68]

At the other extreme, Congressman Keitt of South Carolina could say: "The territorial question was so important that the Democratic party had to be broken up because of it & the government thrown to the Republicans. *It is enough to risk disunion upon.*" [69] But there were many in both sections who did not believe that there was "work to be done again," and a recent careful scholar has concluded: ". . . nor did the territorial aspect of slavery mean much politically beyond agitation. Southerners cared little about actually taking slaves into existing territories." [70]

[68] Lincoln to William Kellogg, M. C., Dec. 11, 1860, John G. Nicolay and John Hay, eds., *Abraham Lincoln Complete Works* (2 vols., New York, 1907), I, 657-658. One may compare Lincoln's allusion to Thayer with comment by the New York *Times* upon Thayer's Worcester speech. Said the *Times*, Aug. 30, 1860: "He [Thayer] has less faith than Mr. Sumner and some other conspicuous Massachusetts agitators in epithets and denunciation, and a good deal more in the laws of social economy and common sense. . . . So long, therefore, as slavery is not likely to go into the Territories, it is worse than folly to insist on its exclusion by act of Congress."

[69] L. M. Keitt to James H. Hammond, Oct. 23, 1860, MS, Hammond Papers, Library of Congress.

[70] J. G. Randall, "The Blundering Generation," *Mississippi Valley Historical Review*, XXVII (June, 1940), 14. For a contrary view, see S. E. Morison and Henry S. Commager, *Growth of the American Republic* (2 vols., New York, 1937), I, 526-528. See also the challenging article, J. G. Randall, "Has the Lincoln Theme Been Exhausted?" *American Historical Review*, XLI (1936), 270-294.

CHAPTER III

SOUTHERN POLITICAL STRATEGY IN THE ELECTION OF 1860

Both at the time and to subsequent observers, the split of the Democratic party at Charleston and Baltimore and the nomination of a Southern-Democratic ticket against the Lincoln, Douglas, and Bell forces seemed to augur but one result—the election of Lincoln. Yet South Carolinians were not alone in the solemn assurance that if the detested " black " Republicans should gain power in the presidential election, the Union was at an end. These warnings were heard long before the clans began to gather for the several national party conventions in the spring of 1860.[1] Yet apparently the destruction of the one great national party, which had barely scraped through to victory in 1856, was the event most welcome to the Republicans: it would remove any doubt that the nominee of the Chicago convention was to become President of the United States. It has been contended that the Southern-Democratic action was guided by their determination to uphold " principle " at whatever cost.[2] But that maintenance of " principle " would very likely lead to political defeat, and encompass the direst result of all— " black " Republican triumph.

Since only the most blatant partisanship could claim that Breckinridge had a chance before the people, there was some discussion during the campaign of the chances of the election being thrown into the House of Representatives, where if the Southern Democrat were not chosen himself, at least Lincoln would be defeated. This explanation makes more reasonable

[1] See *Congressional Globe*, 36th Cong., 1st sess., Pt. I, pp. 94-97, 168-170, for examples. In fact the entire eight weeks of the Speakership contest was filled with Southern threats of secession if Seward or one like him was elected president. Henry Wilson, *History of the Rise and Fall of the Slave Power in America* (3 vols., Boston, 1874), II, 643-654.

[2] Emerson D. Fite, *The Presidential Campaign of 1860*, says (p. 116): " Not the death of the Democratic party, then, nor yet the dissolution of the Union of the states was the compelling force back of the Charleston and Baltimore secessions: the true motive was a desire to vindicate Southern principles, by securing the abasement of Stephen A. Douglas and his principles."

the Breckinridge candidacy, assuming that a well-directed effort would be made to secure that result. Historians have usually regarded the statesmen of the old South as masters of political maneuvering, and have assumed that they had a well-laid plan once more to gain their ends. Hence historians have adopted the view that the clever Southern leaders planned an election in the House, and what is more, came extremely close to consummation of their scheme.

Of course, during the campaign, partisans of Stephen A. Douglas attempted to pin the disunion label on the entire Breckinridge party. According to their interpretation of events, the Yancey-Rhett secessionist forces deliberately broke up the Democratic conventions, deliberately insisted upon the slave-protection plank, deliberately set up a Southern ticket which would elect Lincoln and lead to immediate secession.[3] Republicans echoed the charges, and after 1860 they became a part of the " aggressive slavocracy " thesis.

Many questions occur to the historian as he considers these explanations of the course of parties in the critical election of 1860. First, what evidence exists that the events at Charleston and Baltimore were based upon a belief that the Southern candidate would make the race primarily to reach the House of Representatives? What evidence exists to show that the party disruption was the result of sabotage? What Southerners desired the overthrow of the party? What evidence exists to prove that Southern politicians, supporting Breckinridge, believed in the chance of his success, either in the House or before the people? What proof is there for the contention that the anti-Lincoln strategists cooperated with those allies necessary to execute their plans? What was the situation in the House of Representatives? Assuming that the election eventually went there, was it a certainty that the anti-Lincoln forces could or would act in unison? Did the Republicans have a chance of victory there instead? How efficiently did the " Buchanan machine " function to achieve the success of Breckinridge, the adminstration candidate? An eminent student of Southern history wrote a generation ago: " It seems, therefore, fair to

[3] St. Louis *Daily Missouri Republican*, Oct. 4, 1860. See also *Daily Louisville Democrat*, Sept. 2, 1860.

conclude that . . . the able and well-organized aristocracy of
the South came near to winning their point, an election in the
House. . . ." [4]

Aside from grandiose considerations of "principle," what
was the problem which faced those who wished above all to
defeat Lincoln, in terms of votes, first in the electoral college,
and second in the House? The electoral vote in 1860 totaled
303. The fifteen slave states had 120, and the eighteen free
states 183. Therefore 152 votes were needed for election. Thus
the Southern problem was first to win a unified block of 120
Southern votes, plus 32 Northern votes, if not for a single
candidate, then scattered among Breckinridge, Bell, and Douglas. There existed in 1860 a confidence that California and
Oregon, whose Congressmen and Senators had been pro-Southern, would vote with the South. Counting the seven Pacific
Coast votes, 25 more were needed, which might come from
New York 35, Pennsylvania 27, Indiana 13, Illinois 11, and
Ohio 23. The rest of the free states, including New England,
the Southern calculators wrote off as hopelessly lost. Indeed,
some of the rabid Southerners dismissed the old Northwest,
and based their chances upon Pennsylvania and New York.[5]

Yet with four candidates in the field in all free states, it was
clear that Lincoln's chances became certainties. The feud begun
long before Charleston, between the Buchanan administration
and the Douglas Democrats, made cooperation between all
groups difficult at best in some states, and impossible in others.
Of course, the Republicans benefited by this internecine warfare.
Yet political exigency should have dictated that Douglas have
a clear field in the free states, and Breckinridge a clear field in
the slave states. But the Buchanan-Douglas feud prevented the
former, and the persistence of Southern Whiggery prevented
the latter.[6] It is true that a complete fusion ticket was belatedly

[4] William E. Dodd, "The Fight for the Northwest, 1860," *American Historical
Review*, XVI (July, 1911), 788.

[5] For some Southern estimates, see *Daily Richmond Enquirer*, Feb. 1, 1860,
which declared: "Farming States must unite with planting States." Paulding
(Miss.) *Eastern Clarion*, Aug. 1, 1860. Henry M. Phillips of Pennsylvania
calculated that if Breckinridge received 120 Southern votes, then 7 from the
Pacific Coast and Pennsylvania's 27 would make him President. Phillips to
Jeremiah S. Black, Sept. 27, 1860, MS, Black Papers.

[6] Sam Houston observed: "The strife of the two sections of the Democratic

formed in New York and Rhode Island, and an incomplete fusion in New Jersey and Pennsylvania. In the old Northwest and Pacific Coast, four tickets remained in the field to the end.

Professor Dumond has correctly contended that if the votes received by Lincoln's three opponents had been concentrated on any one of them, the Republicans would still have had an ample margin in the electoral college.[7] But undoubtedly the intra-party strife, the ineptness of the Buchanan office-holders, and the weakness of fusion against a single candidate, were factors which contributed to that result. Some believed that the situation might have been much more favorable if there had been harmony from the outset with Douglas the candidate in the free states, backed by a friendly group of federal office-holders.[8] If the Democratic managers, under the aegis of the "able" Southern strategists, wished to salvage enough Northern votes to save them from Lincoln, they executed their plans most imperfectly.

After the Charleston convention, the Charleston *Mercury* suggested that each faction of the party, Northern and Southern, make a nomination, thus polling the maximum anti-Republican vote in each section. The chances of throwing the election into the House would be enhanced, where each state had one vote, and where the opportunity of blocking the Republicans would be good.[9] The equally fiery Memphis *Avalanche* recom-

party is such that they would not unite, nor would the Bell men go to either, or either of the sections go to Bell." Houston to A. Daly, Aug. 14, 1860, Amelia W. Williams and E. C. Barker, *The Writings of Sam Houston, 1813-1863* (8 vols., Austin, 1943), VIII, 120.

[7] Dumond, *The Secession Movement 1860-1861*, p. 112.

[8] See analysis of the situation, New Orleans *Daily Crescent*, Feb. 20, 1860. Horace Greeley had just toured the Northwest, and had noted Douglas' popularity there. The *Crescent* admitted that Popular Sovereignty was not what the South desired, but it appeared unwise not to take the next best policy which could be obtained. "Sooner than a rabid Republican, let us have Douglas, liberal in his ideas and feelings toward the South." If Douglas were wrong on one point, it would be better to have him than a Republican, "wrong in all things." Later the *Crescent*, March 16, 1860, declared that Douglas could win the requisite electoral votes in the North.

[9] Charleston *Mercury*, May 26, 1860. Yet the same paper earlier said: "The Charleston Convention may fill an important page in history. It may tell of the rebound of a great and free people in the maintenance of their rights, or of their final submission and downfall." (*Ibid.*, April 21, 1860.) "The events of yesterday," the *Mercury* commented, "will probably be the most important which have taken place since the Revolution of 1776." (*Ibid.*, May 2, 1860.) With

mended that the Richmond convention proceed to make nominations, "which may not triumph at the polls, but which will win in the House of Representatives." [10] Likewise, the New Orleans *Delta* calculated that it would be well if there were several candidates. If the Constitutional Democrats could not win in the House, there was no hope indeed. The *Delta* conceded that the "Rump candidate" Douglas must win some electoral votes in the North, but this he must do by his own efforts, aided by the friends of the South.[11] It is interesting to note that ultra journals of the complexion of the *Mercury*, the *Delta*, and the *Avalanche*, were foremost in urging this strategy.

So far as the Bell candidacy was concerned, the Louisville *Journal* believed that its only chance lay in an election in the House.[12] John Bell himself, however, though not sanguine, told his campaign manager that he would win in the electoral college, if at all.[13] The depth of partisan feeling between Democrats and Whigs-Americans-Constitutional Unionists in the South would probably have worked against harmony if the election had reached Congress. Bell was bitter against some of the Breckinridge leaders, and intimated that he might receive Republican votes in a contest in the House.[14] But it was the Breckinridge managers, "the Southern oligarchy," who were supposed to be waging the battle with a chance of victory in Congress.

Just how many Breckinridge politicians actually believed he would be successful? [15] Publicly many assumed a bold front, declaring that their candidate was the only one who stood a chance of election. Some even deprecated the strategy which would place Breckinridge in the Presidency by means of an

which was the *Mercury* more concerned, an election in Congress, or the "revolution"?

[10] Memphis *Daily Avalanche*, June 4, 1860.

[11] New Orleans *Daily Delta*, May 2, 1860.

[12] Quoted in the Memphis *Morning Enquirer*, June 30, 1860. The Richmond *Whig*, May 8, 1860, declared that if the election went to the House, the Opposition candidate would be elected on a compromise basis.

[13] John Bell to Alexander R. Boteler, July 2-30, 1860, MS, Boteler Papers, Duke University Library.

[14] *Ibid*.

[15] Breckinridge told Mrs. Jefferson Davis immediately after his nomination: "I trust I have the courage to lead a forlorn hope." Mrs. Jefferson Davis, *Jefferson Davis, A Memoir* (2 vols., New York, 1890), I, 685.

election in the House of Representatives. By the time the campaign was well in progress, the Richmond *Examiner* scarcely mentioned this method, and a number of newspapers looked askance at the House.[16] Some feared bribery, apostasy of Douglas Congressmen, difficulties among Opposition members and the Democrats—as illustrated in the Speakership contest, and danger that Lincoln would be elected outright in the House.[17] One Southern paper thought that to take the election to the House would merely renew the impasse which existed at Charleston, and that the wild scenes of December, 1859—January, 1860, might be renewed.[18] Another inquired: " Have we assurance that opposing elements can be brought to cooperate in the House of Representatives? " Should the issue there be narrowed to Lincoln versus a Southern slave-protectionist, it was feared that the " exasperated " North would vote against the latter.[19]

After the nominations, what were the private expectations of the Southern Democrats? William H. Trescot of South Carolina, Assistant Secretary of State, saw Senator Judah P. Benjamin of Louisiana, " a shrewd calculator," who thought " the chances bad, very bad." Trescot found many who agreed with Benjamin: " I meet here and there a sanguine man but I think the general expectation is defeat." [20] As the campaign progressed, several South Carolina Congressmen wrote privately that they expected Lincoln's election.[21] John D. Ashmore wrote that it

[16] Richmond *Daily Examiner*, May 22, 1860. The *Examiner* vigorously denied that the Breckinridge campaign was based upon the hope of an election in the House. *Ibid.*, July 28, 1860.

[17] Bribery was said to be " *very* potent *in that assembly*." *Ibid.*, May 22, 1860; Nashville *Union and American*, Oct. 23, 1860.

[18] Fayetteville *Observer*, Aug. 16, 1860.

[19] Tuscumbia *North Alabamian*, Aug. 10, 1860.

[20] Trescot to William Porcher Miles, July 12, 1860, MS, Miles Papers, Southern Historical Collection, University of North Carolina. He did admit that Senator James Chesnut, Jr., was more hopeful.

[21] Congressman W. Porcher Miles of Charleston wrote: " I think the prospect very gloomy. I do not think Breck[inridge] can possibly carry Penn[sylvania] . . . Lincoln will be elected President." Miles to Hammond, Aug. 5, 1860, MS, Hammond Papers, Library of Congress. Miles was an influential member in the Southern group. He was very close to such men as Senators Hunter and Mason, and Congressman Muscoe R. H. Garnett of Virginia. Yet there is hardly a trace of any plan to secure Breckinridge's election in the House in the extensive Miles Papers in the Southern Historical Collection. W. W. Boyce came out for secession in a public letter. Fernandina *East Floridian*, Aug. 16, 1860.

was his private opinion that the Charleston convention had been deliberately broken up, although he did not say so publicly.[22] Laurence Keitt put the matter baldly: the territorial question had been so important that the Democratic party had to be destroyed, and the government turned over to the Republicans. Surely then, he argued, it was important enough to hazard disunion for.[23]

There is evidence to show that many Southern politicians doubted the wisdom of wrecking the party on the slave-protection issue. Toombs, while he later ardently supported Breckinridge, had earlier characterized the entire difficulty as due to hatred of Douglas, and a determination to destroy him.[24] Martin J. Crawford, a sound Southern Democrat, wrote a few days after the Charleston adjournment: " In reference to the difficulties at Charleston they all grew out of the Senatorial race in Alabama, the Platform in that State was made for the purpose of electing its author to the Senate of the U. S. and it may do it, but it has well nigh cost us a Republic." Crawford had long endorsed the doctrine of slave-protection, but it was his opinion that Alabama was the only delegation that would have demanded it in the platform. The others would have passed over it until the party was strong enough to win the point. The only outcome which Crawford could see was discord and ruin. Within five years the party might carry through such a fight successfully, but it was impossible in 1860. " I do not believe that a good General would risk his whole army in a battle when he was confident that defeat and disaster awaited him & certainly not when he could maintain his ground with honor and with safety & repulse the enemy whenever he was attacked." Crawford saw no pressing emergency which required Congressional slave-protection; the preservation of the Democratic party was of far more importance. He also attributed the Southern dislike for Douglas to the fear that if he were the Democratic nominee, the Know Nothings would carry the South. Let the party be saved first, and the " abstraction " afterwards.[25]

[22] Ashmore to Hammond, Aug. 30, 1860, MS, Hammond Papers.
[23] I. M. Keitt to Hammond, Oct. 23, 1860, MS, *ibid*.
[24] Toombs to Alexander H. Stephens, Feb. 10, 1860, Phillips, *Correspondence*, p. 461.
[25] Crawford to Alexander H. Stephens, May 11, 1860, MS, Stephens Papers, Library of Congress.

Toombs became bitter against Douglas, but if an adjustment could not be made at Baltimore, he saw only disaster ahead. Nevertheless, he was determined to back those who "struggle for our equal rights in the territories." On June 9, Toombs said: "I am fully aware that personal hostilities and personal advantages are at the bottom of the strife; but there is a right and wrong to the controversy for all that." The eminent Georgian did not believe that any Democrat could be elected; nor did he think that it mattered much if the party did win.[26]

The gossiping friend of A. H. Stephens, J. Henly Smith, noted from Washington that the Republican ticket would be a strong one. "We are distracting our forces, pursuing an *ignis fatuus* of protection to Slavery in the territories, where we will never take Slaves even if we had protection, and have not negroes to make Slave States out of Texas where Slavery is protected by law!"[27] Immediately before the Baltimore convention, Jefferson Davis deplored the absence of agreement among Southern men as to the candidate. He predicted that unless Northern men took the "proper action" at Baltimore, and voted to exclude the "spurious" delegates, the Democratic party would become "historic." If Northern men insisted upon Douglas, "we must be beaten." Davis had never seen the country in such danger, and those who might aid were unconscious of the real state of things. "If our little grog drinking, electioneering Demagogue [Douglas] can destroy our hopes, it must be that we have been doomed to destruction."[28] Sam

[26] On May 5, 1860, Toombs wrote Stephens that he wanted to reunite the party at Baltimore on the basis of the Tennessee resolutions. But if that could not be done, ". . . I shall stand by the bolters and let things rock on." He continued: "The real difficulty at Charleston was that a large number of Democrats North and South had committed themselves so far against Douglas that they were lost if he was nominated, and they therefore preferred ruining the party with themselves than ruining themselves without the party." Toombs was disgusted with it all. (Phillips, *Correspondence*, pp. 468-469.) Toombs believed that Douglas proceeded on the theory that the South so much feared Republican rule, that they would submit to him. By May, Toombs had recanted his hostility to the slave-protection platform, and sharply criticized Douglas. (Toombs to Stephens, May, 12, 1860, *ibid.*, pp. 477-478.) Later he interpreted Douglas' attitude as forcing every man to agree with him or do battle against him. (Same to same, June 9, 1860, *ibid.*, p. 481.)

[27] J. Henly Smith to A. H. Stephens, May 19, 1860, MS, Stephens Papers.

[28] Jefferson Davis to Franklin Pierce, June 13, 1860, Dunbar Rowland, ed., *Jefferson Davis, Constitutionalist* (10 vols., Jackson, Miss., 1923), IV, 495-496. (Henceforth referred to as Rowland.)

Milligan of Tennessee considered the withdrawal at Charleston " an irreparable error" on the part of the South.[29] James H. Hammond thought that action " silly" and the Southern politicians " blunderers."[30] B. Y. Martin predicted a " black" Republican victory, and a disrupted country. " I wish to defeat the abolition party & I do not believe we can do it with *any candidate*, if we insert as a *test* & plank in the platform the doctrine of affirmative Congressional intervention for the protection of Slavery in the Territories." [31]

L. Q. C. Lamar of Mississippi felt misgivings as to what had happened at Charleston, and U. S. Supreme Court Justice John A. Campbell of Alabama privately and flippantly wrote him: " If I had the powers of a Turkish Cadi, I should condemn all the Southern actors in that scene to wear veils for four years." [32]

The practical difficulties of welding an effective opposition to Lincoln among the disparate elements became plain enough. Hammond noted the lack of cooperation between the Breckinridge and Douglas groups in apportioning the states, with the object of gaining an election in the House. Hammond condemned A. G. Brown, Yancey, John A. Winston, and Pierre Soulé. Rhett was as " *odious* as ever Burr was." [33] And an ardent Southern sympathizer living in New York, S. J. Anderson, touched upon the same point at the close of the campaign: " Our disruption at Charleston and Baltimore encouraged our enemies and disheartened our friends." The " madness" had alienated Southern support in New York City. The " shattered" Democrats and the Bell-Everett men did not cooperate.[34] J. Henly Smith criticized the lack of cooperation in New York, and reported that the administration was alarmed lest Breckin-

---

[29] Sam Milligan to R. Johnson, May 28, 1860, MS, Andrew Johnson Papers, Library of Congress.

[30] James H. Hammond to W. Gilmore Simms, July 10, 1860, MS, Hammond Papers.

[31] B. Y. Martin to A. H. Stephens, June 8, 1860, MS, Stephens Papers.

[32] Edward Mayes, *Lucius Q. C. Lamar, His Life, Times, and Speeches* (Nashville, 1896), pp. 83-84.

[33] James H. Hammond to M. C. M. Hammond, July 4, 1860, MS, Hammond Papers.

[34] S. J. Anderson to A. H. Stephens, Oct. 21, 1860. Anderson later said: " In the breaking up of the conventions, we lost the last chance. That chance was the election of Douglas." The country was on the eve of world-shaking revolution. Same to same, Nov. 4, 1860. MSS, Stephens Papers.

ridge fail to enter the House, because " old Joe [Lane] cannot be President by the Senate." [35]

Thus many Southern men, among them those who supported the Southern ticket, deprecated the split of the party and saw it could not succeed. Indeed, the historian may wonder just how many of them actually desired its success, or believed in it. Those most urgent for the split, Rhett, Yancey, Keitt, the Memphis *Avalanche,* and the New Orleans *Delta,* were also the open disunionists. While Jefferson Davis has not been classified with this group, his recent biographer has said: " His demand of slave-protection, therefore, sounded the death knell of Democratic unity in the pending election. A Republican President was inevitable . . . ." [36]

There was another disturbing aspect of the problem of an election in the House, and that was the uncertain chance of anti-Lincoln success once the election went there. J. Henly Smith declared that the split at Baltimore was intended to make Lincoln President. Smith then outlined the strategy of " our friends." They were determined that Douglas should carry New York, which would assure an election in the House, where they would deliberately delay an election till March 4, 1860, to enable the Senate to elect Lane President. " This is the programme of our friends. This will fail them." [37]

Smith then analyzed the situation in the House. Of 33 votes, the Republicans were assured of 15. [38] Smith asserted that Con-

[35] J. Henly Smith to A. H. Stephens, Oct. 25, 1860. S. J. Anderson thought the administration's " war " on Douglas in Illinois, " the vindictive rivalry " in the Senate, the activity of " the Rhetts and the Yanceys " would combine to elect Lincoln by the electoral college. Anderson to A. H. Stephens, July 21, 1860, MSS, *ibid.*

[36] Robert McN. McElroy, *Jefferson Davis; The Unreal and the Real* (2 vols., New York, 1937), I, 207. McElroy continues: " It would still, however, be unfair to conclude that Davis' aim was secession. His desire was rather to prevent secession by preventing Douglas and his followers from precipitating conditions which would cause the south to secede." (*Ibid.*) But it was by no means certain that if Douglas had been nominated by the full party that the South would have seceded. Rather it was the division in the party, which McElroy says Davis brought about, which made doubly sure the precipitation of " conditions which would cause the south to secede." J. Henly Smith thought the South's course " suicidal." (Smith to A. H. Stephens, June 12, 1860, MS, Stephens Papers.)

[37] Smith to Stephens, June 26, 1860, MS, *ibid.* Cf. Philadelphia *Press,* July 3, 1860.

[38] Republicans controlled the House delegations of Connecticut, Indiana, Iowa,

gressman Isaac N. Morris, a Douglas Democrat from Illinois, had avowed that he would vote for none but Douglas. Smith believed that Morris would eventually cast his lot with the Republicans.[39] Also Congressman Lansing Stout of Oregon occupied a precarious seat, which was being contested by the Republicans. Inasmuch as they had organized the House, if it became necessary they would press the contest against Stout, unseat him, and win the Oregon vote and the election. To prevent this, Smith reported, the Democrats were determined " . . . to sit in the House and call the ayes & nays on motions to adjourn till Congress expires. I should think this to be the height of folly . . . . The country will not, and in my opinion, ought not, to endure such a procedure." [40] In subsequent letters, Smith insisted that Lincoln's election was assured either by the people or by the House.[41]

The instability of Congressman Morris was a matter of public knowledge, and the Nashville *Union and American,* a Breckinridge organ, sharing Henly Smith's fears, wished to prevent the election from going to the House.[42] On October 29, John Townsend, an ardent South Carolina secessionist, declared in a speech: " I know that there is, with some, a feeble hope entertained that, if the election goes into Congress, Breckinridge, or Bell, or Lane, by some skillful management or good luck, might be slipped into the Presidency instead of Lincoln." Townsend characterized that as a contemptible and " feeble " delusion; it was lamentably timid, an avoidance of what Townsend and many others in his community desired, " manly resist-

---

Maine, Massachusetts, Michigan, Minnesota, New Hampshire, New Jersey, New York, Ohio, Pennsylvania, Rhode Island, Vermont, and Wisconsin.

[39] Of the nine Illinois Representatives, 4 were Republicans and 5 Democrats. If Morris shifted, the Republicans would win the Illinois vote.

[40] Smith to Stephens, June 26, 1860, MS, Stephens Papers. Cf. A. H. Stephens to Z. P. Landrum, July 1, 1860, reflecting these ideas. A. H. Stephens, *A Constitutional View of the Late War Between the States* . . . (2 vols., Philadelphia, 1870), II, 685-691.

[41] Smith, an ardent pro-slavery man and bitter foe of the Republicans, favored a separation if Lincoln won. Occasionally he indulged the luxury of the thought that Lincoln would be beaten before the people, and added: " The House is our greatest danger. The blacks lack only the change of two men there." (Smith to Stephens, Sept. 17, 1860, MS, Stephens Papers.) But in October, he gave up all hope. A Southern Confederacy was " freely discussed " in Washington. (Smith to Stephens, Oct. 11, 1860, MS, *ibid.*)

[42] Nashville *Union and American,* Oct. 23, 1860.

ance." After all, why should the South longer place her trust in any President? Even Buchanan had failed to govern along " just " lines.[43]

Although Southerners expressed skepticism as to the success of what was at best a tenuous scheme, what of the Republicans? Perhaps because of their confidence of success in the electoral college, they gave little attention to the possibility of an election in the House. They did, however, circulate a pamphlet speech of David Dudley Field warning against chaos in Congress, if that body should be called upon to choose the President. Field characterized the electoral machinery as the very weakest part of the American system: " You must choose between Mr. Lincoln and the dangers and chances of a struggle in Congress, with its uncertain issues." Field depicted, doubtless with the recent Congressional scenes in mind, the juggling of 33 votes in " . . . a wild, excited, body, where one man from Oregon has the same power as 33 from New York." [44]

A few Southerners professed to believe that they could throw the election into Congress and there stave off defeat.[45] But as the campaign matured, less and less of that belief was expressed. Little but pessimism was heard from the Southern politicians, and by September 1 most had conceded Lincoln's election, some publicly. Moreover, it appears that even if they had succeeded in taking the election into Congress, there was a very good chance of Lincoln's election in the House. There was also the

[43] John Townsend, *The Doom of Slavery in the Union, Its Safety Out of It* (2d ed., Charleston, 1860), pamphlet, Library of Congress, pp. 23.

[44] David Dudley Field, *The Dangers of Throwing the Election of President into Congress*, pamphlet, Library of Congress, pp. 7. Cf. the view of Gov. Houston of Texas: " The people have been taught to dread such consummation." (In Houston's " Withdrawal," Aug. 18, 1860, *Writings*, VIII, 122.) " Occasional " John W. Forney wrote from Washington that if the presidential election went into the House of Representatives, all the conflicting factions would be arrayed against each other with unrelenting ferocity. He thought that such an occasion would be a terrible test for American institutions, in which the issue might hinge on one vote. (Philadelphia *Press*, Sept. 1, 1860.)

[45] W. D. Pike to W. P. Miles, May 6, 1860, MS, Miles Papers. A. H. Stephens momentarily thought that the election would go to the House, where if Douglas, Lincoln, and Bell were the contestants, Douglas might be elected. (Stephens to J. Henly Smith, Sept. 12, 1860, Phillips, *Correspondence*, p. 496.) James H. Hammond, despite his denunciations of Southern politicians, strangely persisted in the belief in the success of Breckinridge. (L. M. Keitt to Hammond, Aug. 4, 1860, MS, Hammond Papers.)

possibility of much strife in the House and Senate, similar to that which had characterized the Speakership contest and the Lovejoy incident. For the sake of American governmental processes and reputation before the world, it was doubtless fortunate that the Congress of the United States, tense with sectional hatred, was not called upon to settle so explosive a matter as the election of a President in 1860-1861.

Evidence seems lacking that a concerted drive at any time was in operation to achieve this purpose. Toombs, Hunter, and Davis, the Southern " triumvirate," who were believed to have guided policy during this period, appear to have said little of an election in the House. The recent biographers of Davis and Hunter ignore the subject, and Toombs' correspondence reveals him despondent as to the future, nowhere confident of success by any expedient.[46] Toombs and Davis were greatly exasperated with developments,[47] and, finally establishing their " principle " with the nomination of Breckinridge, assumed a fatalistic attitude. They seemed to do little to implement their precious principle in practical action.[48] Moreover many Demo-

[46] McElroy, I, 192-224, ignores the House of Representatives as a part of Davis' plans in the presidential campaign; Henry H. Simms, *Life of R. M. T. Hunter* (Richmond, 1935), pp. 133-145, omits the subject. Cf. Rowland, IV, *passim* for scattering correspondence of Davis; C. H. Ambler, *The Correspondence of R. M. T. Hunter, 1826-1876, Annual Report of the American Historical Association for the Year 1916* (2 vols., Washington, 1918), II, 285-337; Phillips, *Correspondence*, pp. 448-481.

[47] As early as December, 1859, Toombs wrote of the coming election: " If they beat us I see no safety for us, our property and our firesides, except in breaking up the concern . . . I think it madness to wait for what people call ' an overt act!'" (*Ibid.*, pp. 449-450.) Davis saw only gloom. (Davis to Pierce, Jan. 30, 1860, Rowland, IV, 185.)

[48] Years afterward, in his *apologia*, Davis asserted that he foresaw defeat, and described his unsuccessful effort to unite all elements opposed to Lincoln. He related that he had secured the pledge of Bell and Breckinridge to withdraw, if Douglas would do so. (Jefferson Davis, *The Rise and Fall of the Confederate Government* [2 vols., New York, 1881], I, 52.) George Fort Milton, *The Eve of Conflict* (Boston, 1934), p. 487, says that Davis wished to substitute Horatio Seymour for all. Thus it appears that Davis had no thought of an election in the House. William E. Dodd, *Statesmen of the Old South* (New York, 1911), pp. 228-229, accepts Davis' version of his conference with Douglas. Contrast this with Dodd, *American Historical Review*, XVI, 788. It appears that the Davis account and the whole episode need more light. Did Bell authorize his withdrawal in writing? Dodd commented upon the cavalier manner by which Davis would dispose of candidates of great political organizations. (*Statesmen of the Old South*, p. 229.) The student may well question the reaction among

crats, Northern and Southern, "sound and unsound," questioned the wisdom of demanding the slave-protection principle in 1860.[49] It may be of significance that Rhett and the fire-eating press stressed the plausibility of an election in Congress at first, only to drop the idea as time passed.

The historian may, therefore, conclude that the Southern politicians were not "well-organized," but were by turns confused, indifferent, despondent, and defeatist; that many gave up the fight long before election day; that if they " came near winning their point," they did not know it.[50] If they had won·

the followers of Bell to such summary withdrawal of his candidacy. Douglas refused on the ground that his followers would go to Lincoln. (Milton, p. 487.)

[49] It may be recalled that Toombs was bitterly opposed to this plan as late as February (Phillips, *Correspondence*, p. 461), and that Davis a few days before had written: " I have not been able to show him [Gov. Dana of Maine] how the question could be adjusted by ' resolution' but have told him of the only way I have seen, and which is that of nominating the man who will be accepted by both sections without a platform." (Jefferson Davis to Franklin Pierce, Jan. 30, 1860, Rowland, IV, 185.) What caused Toombs and Davis to change their minds so abruptly in the following weeks? Evidently aware of what was in store, Martin J. Crawford of Georgia, told Stephens that he had no hand in bringing about the present condition in the party. (Crawford to A. H. Stephens, Oct. 18, 1860, MS, Stephens Papers.) The contest in which Davis and Douglas fought each other to mutual destruction over the issue of Popular Sovereignty has baffled writers. Henry Wilson placed Davis' action " among the inscrutable mysteries," and saw the hand of Providence (*History of the Rise and Fall of the Slave Power in America*, II, 686). N. W. Stephenson has written: " Behind this ostensible issue was something else that is not quite apparent." Stephenson would not link Yancey and Rhett with Davis. (*D. A. B.*, V, 127.) Milton mentions abstract principle, and the determination of Southern leaders to protect their civilization; he believes the situation complex, but he thinks that the breach was accomplished by " ideologues" like Rhett and Ruffin, plus the concurrent activity of a small, powerful clique, who, accustomed for years to run the government, refused to part with place and power. This group did not have much economic interest in a retention of the status quo. (*The Eve of Conflict*, pp. 478-479.)

[50] Senator Joseph Lane of Oregon, the candidate for Vice President on the Breckinridge ticket, had no hope of victory. He conceded Lincoln's election, and believed that difficulties would follow. Dr. J. F. Hammond of West Point, New York, wrote that Lane had visited there " night before last," and that he had predicted a " Minister Plenipotentiary" from South Carolina within a month. Lane sent word to Senator Hammond to advise South Carolina to " sustain her honor" and take a firm hand. (J. F. Hammond to James H. Hammond, Oct. 29, 1860, MS, Hammond Papers.) Lane was surely close to the Southern group in Washington, and shared their innermost plans. R. B. Rhett, Jr. had written Jefferson Davis anticipating Lincoln's election. Davis replied cautiously suggesting that all the " planting States" be brought together before charting a new course. (David to R. B. Rhett, Jr., Nov. 10, 1860, Rowland, IV, 541-543.)

their point by securing an election by Congress, the evidence is that they would probably have been defeated in the House of Representatives. It is true that there was a Southern clique which welcomed the election of Lincoln, consisting of men like Rhett, Yancey, and Keitt, but their relationship to the most powerful Southern leaders was not close. The entire picture is one of confusion and drift. There certainly was no " united aggressive slavocracy " in the crucial battle of 1860, but the confusion and drift led to certain defeat—a defeat which created a situation for years desired by the Southern extremists and which brought at last the long-anticipated explosion.

CHAPTER IV

DOUGLAS APPEALS TO THE SLAVE STATES

That Senator Stephen A. Douglas began his campaign for the Presidency after receiving the nomination at the Baltimore convention, severely handicapped in most of the Southern states, has long been recognized by historians. The disappointments flowing from the operation of the Kansas-Nebraska bill, the enunciation of Freeport Doctrine, his opposition to the Lecompton constitution, his break with President Buchanan, and finally his determination to run for President, in spite of unyielding Southern opposition, as the champion of Popular Sovereignty, all these factors had transformed the leader of the Northern Democrats into a figure scarcely more popular in the South than Lincoln himself.

The regular Democratic party organizations and a large proportion of the Southern press were aligned against Douglas. The scattering politicians and newspaper editors who supported him did so with considerable force and ability, but they were woefully outnumbered. Among the Democratic supporters were ex-Governor John A. Winston, J. J. Seibels and his Montgomery *Confederation,* John Forsyth, former Minister to Mexico, and his Mobile *Register,* all of Alabama; James Gardner and his Augusta *Constitutionalist,* the Atlanta *Southern Confederacy,* Alexander H. Stephens—one of the most important Douglas men in the South, his half-brother Linton Stephens, and Herschel V. Johnson, the Douglas candidate for Vice President, of Georgia; Congressman A. J. Hamilton of Texas; the New Orleans *True Delta,* and Pierre Soulé, Louisiana; the Memphis *Appeal,* Tennessee; the St. Louis *Missouri Republican,* Missouri; the Louisville *Democrat,* Kentucky; and Governor John Letcher of Virginia. There were others and of course there were Douglas campaign papers, journals established for the duration of the campaign only. And the cordial tone of the Bell press towards Douglas should be noted. In spite of these allies, Douglas never had a chance to carry any lower Southern

state, although in certain areas he made a good popular showing. Missouri was the only slave state to cast her electoral vote
for Douglas.

Alert national figure that he was, Douglas was kept informed
as to local conditions and developments throughout the country
by faithful correspondents, and the Senator's private papers
contain a large number of letters from the South. Among these
writers were more or less well-known politicians as well as
obscure persons. Generally they were Douglas partisans who
assumed an optimistic attitude towards their favorite's candidacy in their localities. Occasionally a note of pessimism was
sounded, and few Southern friends of Douglas agreed with him
in the matter of Popular Sovereignty, although some sought to
soften or interpret that dogma so as to make it more palatable
to Southerners. Now and then a note of unintentional humor
crept into these letters. Requests for patronage after 1861 came
from not a few; others asked for speeches and documents; some
wanted money to keep alive feeble campaign newspapers; a
Georgian wanted one hundred dollars with which to " convert "
a hundred doubtful voters to Douglas.[1]

In the pre-convention weeks of 1860, Douglas was sounded
out by friends of lesser hopefuls and conciliatory gestures were
made in his direction. Friends of Andrew Johnson, R. M. T.
Hunter, Henry A. Wise, and Alexander H. Stephens were in
contact with Douglas. Scores of Southerners wrote advice as to
strategy which would win the nomination for Douglas. He was
told repeatedly that he should stand firm and make no compromise; that while the politicians were against him, the people
were for him; that the South was faced with a choice between
Douglas and a " black " Republican; that the Union was in dire
peril and that only he could save it; that if he should receive the
Charleston or Baltimore nomination, he would sweep the fifteen
slave states, including South Carolina. Perhaps in view of this
advice from the South, and the deep bitterness which existed
between the majority Democratic faction and the Douglas men,
subsequent actions of the Douglas managers at Charleston and
Baltimore may be understood. A few Southern Douglas men,
like Robert H. Glass of Virginia, finally advised Douglas to

---

[1] Summarized from mass of correspondence, 1859-1861, in the Stephen A.
Douglas Papers, Library of the University of Chicago.

withdraw in the interest of harmony and the Union, but the keynote of the majority of his Southern supporters was to fight to the bitter end. Douglas was left in no doubt that Lincoln's election would be the signal for serious trouble, and that Southerners would permit no interference with their slaves.[2]

As the summer passed and the situation became worse rather than better, Douglas received invitations from the South to come in person to appeal directly in behalf of the Union, and secondarily to advance his presidential candidacy. In 1860 and earlier there were many who professed to be horrified at the prospect of a presidential candidate on the hustings pleading his own cause. "The office should seek the man" was the accepted theory, and when Douglas announced his speaking dates he was assailed unmercifully. Especially indignant was the Breckinridge press when it learned that Douglas planned to invade the South. With regard to the Southern trip, much speculation arose as to his motives and "objects," and some Southern editors gave vent to threats against the Senator.

Nor did Douglas' rivals for the presidential chair engage in a personal canvass for the office. The New York *Herald* chided Lincoln for lack of moral courage because he declined an invitation to speak in Kentucky, his native state. He was represented as believing that Kentuckians misunderstood his position on slavery. This anti-Lincoln paper pointed out the advantages which would accrue from such a trip: should Lincoln suffer violence it would react favorably in the North, if not it would vindicate his courage. But if Lincoln would not move, let Douglas lead the way Southward, urged the *Herald*.[3] Before the summer ended, Douglas was speaking in Virginia, North Carolina, and Maryland. Lincoln remained in Springfield and allowed the Kentuckians to continue to misunderstand. For the most part John Bell was silent in the campaign, and John C. Breckinridge made but one public address.

In a remarkable analysis entitled, "What Douglas May Accomplish at the South," a metropolitan daily declared that Douglas' real field of effort was in the South, where disunion was the issue. "This is precisely the crisis in which Judge

[2] *Ibid.*
[3] New York *Herald*, Aug. 13, 1860.

Douglas may render a signal service to the country. Let him beard the Disunion Lion in his den."[4] And two days earlier the same paper asserted that Douglas was preparing for the election of 1864 by destroying the disunionists in 1860. A regeneration of his party was to be achieved between 1861 and 1864 under the leadership of the Little Giant.[5] Another journal agreed substantially with this interpretation. Douglas was depicted as having abandoned hope for his own success, and as preferring Lincoln's election to the possibility of an election in the House or Senate, where the chances of Breckinridge and Lane were alleged to be good. "*But he intends to crush out utterly and forever the disunion party,* if it is in his power to do so."[6] It was significant that the staunch unionist Richmond *Whig* requested Southerners to accord courteous treatment to Douglas.[7] After the completion of the trip to Virginia and North Carolina, a Washington correspondent of the New York *Times* pronounced Douglas' tour "a bold stroke of policy with reference to the North, where his strength is."[8]

Whatever his motives, Douglas made two extensive speaking tours into the South, the first taking him into Virginia, North Carolina, and Maryland, and the second, which came at the close of the campaign, into Missouri, Tennessee, Georgia, and Alabama. An examination of the first may now be made.

Perhaps the best known and certainly the boldest speech made by Douglas in the South was that delivered at Norfolk, Virginia, on August 25. During the course of a two-hour address there the speaker answered two questions propounded by Breckinridge men and printed in the Norfolk *Southern Argus*. The famous "Norfolk Questions" and Douglas' answers were as follows: 1. "On Lincoln's election will the South be justified in seceding?" 2. "If the South secede before an overt act of Lincoln, will you advise or vindicate resistance by force?" To both questions Douglas replied with unmistakable clarity: there was none of that tergiversation of which he had so often been

[4] New York *Times*, Aug. 16, 1860.
[5] *Ibid.*, Aug. 14, 1860.
[6] Richmond *Examiner*, Sept. 1, 1860. This information was attributed to an informant on the New York *Herald*.
[7] Richmond *Whig*, Aug. 21, 1860.
[8] New York *Times*, Sept. 26, 1860.

accused in the past. He answered the first in the negative, contending that a constitutional election could afford no justification for such action. It was his reply to the second question that caused a sensation: The duty of the President was to enforce the laws, to whom, if necessary, he pledged his aid. That none should misunderstand his meaning, Douglas asserted that what the country needed was " Old Hickory" measures. He conceded the right of revolution when the grievance became too great, but only as a last resort. The mere inauguration of a President "whose political opinions were in my judgment hostile to the Constitution and safety of the Union . . ." was not in itself sufficient cause for revolution or secession. He would uphold the President, but if the latter should exceed his Constitutional powers, he told his Virginia audience, he would hang such a President "as you hanged John Brown." Douglas pledged his love for the Union, insisted upon equality of all the people of all the states, and demanded obedience to law. Having thus disposed of the " Norfolk Questions," the adroit Senator turned to insist that John C. Breckinridge answer these poignant questions.

The desperate political situation of the country had been brought about by the nomination of Breckinridge upon the theory that Lincoln's election was preferable to the election of himself, Douglas continued. He would have defeated Lincoln had Breckinridge's friends not seceded at Baltimore, and with a show of logic he summarized: The secessionists, having brought about the situation, come forward to ask him if he will help them to dissolve the Union: " I tell them no—never on earth." [9]

Although Douglas' immediate hearers applauded his vigorous espousal of a coercive policy, the reaction elsewhere—especially among Breckinridge supporters in the far South—was one of bitter condemnation. " An infamous speech" was one characterization of the Norfolk address. It was plain, said the same observer, that Judge Douglas was the ally of Lincoln to stand against an outraged and insulted people.[10]   It was

---

[9] New York *Herald*, Aug. 27, 1860; for text of Douglas' speech see Norfolk *Southern Argus*, Aug. 27, 1860. This paper, which opposed Douglas, reported that the answers to the " questions " were followed by " great applause."

[10] Jackson *Semi-Weekly Mississippian*, Sept. 4, 1860. New York *Tribune*

remarkable that Douglas could utter such sentiment on the very soil of the "immortal" founders of the states-rights doctrine: he reached the lowest depths of federalism, thought a Georgia editor, who added: "His Norfolk speech must strip him, finally and hopelessly, of all Southern sympathy." [11] Jefferson Davis, reported the Oxford (Miss.) *Mercury,* displayed a grim type of humor when he commented upon Douglas' Norfolk answer. When Lincoln led his army to coerce Mississippi with Douglas in the role of Lieutenant General, said Davis, inasmuch as one was six-feet-four and the other five-feet-four, "the yard-arms of the gallows which our people would erect for them would have to be elevated accordingly." [12] Another fiery retort to Douglas exclaimed: "Let the desperate adventurer and traitor Douglas declare what he pleases about coercion, the chivalric South will bristle with armed men to repel such aggressions." [13] Another ardent critic of Douglas declared that it was a mistake that the questions should have been put to or answered by Douglas. The subject was too grave: Southern men should not disclose their policy to the Northern people. Breckinridge was commended for his silence.[14] And the Richmond Democratic press sneered at Lincoln's future aide-de-camp, one of which omitted to print the Norfolk speech. Even Douglas' remarks on Southern acquiescence in the United States Supreme Court were rejected by the Richmond *Examiner*: Lincoln would "pack" the Court.[15] And characteristically, Congressman Roger A. Pryor of Virginia, assuming the role of Brutus, promised that if the coercion policy were employed and no other effort to resist it were evident, he alone and single-handed would plant a dagger in the President's heart.[16] The secessionist William D. Porter of South Carolina denounced Douglas' Norfolk speech,

(semi-weekly), Sept. 4, 1860, reported that large crowds heard Douglas, attracted by novelty, and noted the hatred and contempt of Southern journals for him.

[11] Columbus *Daily Times*, Sept. 7, 1860. Several prominent men in Columbus were represented as quitting Douglas because of the Norfolk speech. *Ibid.*, Oct. 9, 1860.

[12] Oxford *Mercury* in Natchez *Daily Free Trader*, Oct. 3, 1860.

[13] Natchez *Daily Free Trader*, Oct. 3, 1860.

[14] Memphis *Daily Avalanche*, Sept. 14, 1860.

[15] *Daily Richmond Enquirer*, Aug. 30, 1860; *Daily Richmond Examiner*, Aug. 30, 1860.

[16] Norfolk *Herald* in Alexandria *Gazette*, Sept. 14, 1860.

in which he threatened the Southern States with military coercion in the event of secession, [and which] ought to startle and arouse the people of those States, like the blast of a hostile trumpet at midnight! The time, the place, and the circumstances under which the threat was uttered, give the last finish to its audacity and sanguinary significance! [17]

Inasmuch as the Illinois Senator spoke incessantly on his tours, sometimes making several speeches a day, it would be undesirable to attempt an analysis of his every utterance. Like Bryan a generation later, he was necessarily guilty of reiteration, and his address at Petersburg, Virginia, may suffice to illustrate further Douglas arguments. There he developed the theme of Popular Sovereignty. He inquired of Virginians if they thought that those who emigrated to the territories were less sensible when they reached there than when they were at home. There could be only praise for those who built their homes, who blazed the frontier, and "who split their own rails." With much apparent earnestness, Douglas, a Vermonter gone West, pleaded against narrow sectionalism, and extolled the liberalism of those who went West. As men went from valley to valley they lost their prejudices, and became "more liberal and more general and universal in . . . confidence in the patriotism of their fellow-citizens." The connection between Virginia and the Old Northwest was stressed, and the passionate regard of the latter for the Union was emphasized. To prove his point, Douglas used as an example a son of Virginia who moved to the Northwest, where he found his neighbors to be former residents of Connecticut, South Carolina, Maine, and Pennsylvania. Intermarriages, too, militated against sectionalism. So it was, he concluded, that the Northwest loved the Union by ties of blood, marriage, and commerce, and was bound to North and South. The Northwest would not endure an Ohio river boundary, nor pay duties at New Orleans for goods, nor be forced to secure passports to visit ancestors' graves in Virginia. To the charge that he had devised and put through the Kansas-Nebraska bill in order to cheat the South, Douglas replied by merely inquiring if the South's Representatives and Senators were that stupid. Congress would never be permitted

[17] W. D. Porter, *State Sovereignty and the Doctrine of Coercion* . . . 1860 Association Tract No. 2 (Charleston, 1860), p. 3.

to prohibit slavery anywhere if it were in his power to prevent it, the Senator told the Petersburg audience.[18]

After an address at Raleigh, North Carolina, which was given before the state Douglas convention, he was back in Virginia for a speech at Richmond.[19] If the New York *Herald* may be trusted, the champion of the Northern Democracy was cordially received in the Virginia capital, and on August 31 spoke to a large audience. Evidently the tour had exacted its toll, as the distinguished statesman looked more like a " weary, way-worn backwoods traveler " than one of of the nation's most eminent leaders, according to one observer.[20] In Richmond his exposition of Popular Sovereignty was interrupted by heckling, and it was in this city that the press illustrated vividly the bitter partisan methods then prevalent in American journalism. The Richmond *Daily Enquirer* declared that the Douglas procession resembled a funeral which included only " an old donkey, a few Douglas men, more Bell men, fifty four boys, and nearly 200 niggers." The hired band played, the " niggers " shouted, and Douglas bowed. As for the speech, it was largely " a mixture of squeaks and groans," and of course the crowd departed rapidly before the speech was half through. According to this jaundiced observer, the whole affair was " a miserable blunder." [21] On the other hand, another source pronounced the Richmond speech " able and ingenious," and described the audience as " attentive." [22] Indeed, there was no agreement as to the merits or the effects of Douglas' presentation of his cause in Richmond.[23]

The Douglas itinerary took him through the heart of Virginia on his way to the North. It included Charlottesville, Staunton, Winchester, and other towns in the Valley of Virginia, and as

[18] Augusta (Ga.) *Daily Constitutionalist*, Sept. 6, 1860.

[19] Raleigh *Semi-Weekly Standard*, Sept. 5, 1860; Baltimore *American*, Sept. 5, 1860.

[20] New York *Herald*, Sept. 1, 1860; New York *Times*, Sept. 5, 1860.

[21] Richmond *Daily Enquirer*, Sept. 3, 1860.

[22] New York *Times*, Sept. 5, 1860.

[23] A correspondent declared that Douglas lost votes in a " flat and uninspiring " speech. Yet the same writer reported that the Virginia Democrats were determined to crush Douglas, and were considering an invitation to Breckinridge to speak in those cities which Douglas had visited. New York *Herald*, Sept. 6, 1860. For text of the speech see Washington *States and Union*, Sept. 6, 1860.

Douglas crossed the Maryland boundary at Harpers Ferry, a partisan critic charged him with "running away" from the South.[24]

The next important slave-state appearance for the "somewhat prostrated" orator was at Baltimore. After he reached his hotel, he was handed a copy of the much-awaited Ashland address of Vice-President Breckinridge. A human picture was drawn of Douglas stripped and wrapped in a blanket, smoking a cigar, as he settled back to read his rival's only campaign utterance.[25] In the moderate political atmosphere of Baltimore, Douglas reiterated that "slavery is a question of political economy," and proceeded to echo Webster's argument of the Seventh of March speech. As for slavery in the territories, he would as soon attempt to grow cotton on the crest of the Rocky Mountains, as to attempt to force slavery where climate and topography were hostile.[26] With this address, Douglas concluded his first invasion of the slave states, and for the succeeding five or six weeks campaigned in the North. As he turned his face to the North, the Montgomery *Advertiser* taunted him: "Douglas did well to turn his course Northward—there are some portions of the South where the utterance of such sentiments might have led to the hoisting of that coat tail of his that hangs so near the ground to the limb of a tree, preceded by a short neck with grapevine attachment."[27]

At the close of September Douglas briefly visited slave-state soil by an appearance for a speech at Louisville, Kentucky. In that city, just across the Ohio river from Indiana, he consigned such issues as the bank, the tariff, distribution, and the subtreasury, to the past, and asserted that the only living issue was that of secession. The operation of the Buchanan "machine" was attacked on the score that office-holders who dared to support Douglas were "beheaded." In a city that was soon to cast a heavy vote for the moderate candidates, the Senator

[24] For a favorable account see New York *Herald*, Sept. 6, 1860; for hostile account see Richmond *Examiner*, Sept. 11, 1860. For a Bell paper's praise of Douglas' national sentiments, see Staunton *Spectator*, Sept. 4, 1860. See also Washington *States and Union*, Sept. 6, 10, 1860; Richmond *Examiner*, Sept. 6, 1860.

[25] New York *Herald*, Sept. 7, 1860.

[26] Baltimore *American*, Sept. 6, 1860.

[27] Montgomery *Weekly Advertiser*, Sept. 19, 1860.

assailed the silence of President Buchanan and Breckinridge, and declared that he was aware that his unqualified opposition to disunion was costing him votes in the far South.[28]

On October 20, the Senator was in another important border slave-state city, St. Louis, where his theme was the unity of the Mississippi valley. He complained that the Negro question monopolized all the time of Congress, and prevented a Pacific railroad, known to be desired by St. Louis. As for his favorite doctrine of Popular Sovereignty, Douglas said he could pardon his Eastern friends who denied the capacity of frontier men to govern themselves; but as the people of Missouri and Illinois had only recently cut through the forest, they knew of no people more capable of self-government.[29]

From this time till the end of the campaign, defying fire-eaters, Douglas spent his days on slave-state soil. After other speeches in Missouri, he concluded the momentous campaign in the far South. Ere this the omens of the October election results had determined him to go South to "try to save the Union." He was represented as believing that Lincoln was certain of election, but he would fight on.[30] When the Douglas speaking schedule was announced the Southern press once more reacted heatedly. Of course the few Southern Douglas papers were jubilant that their champion was coming South, and the Bell press was generally sympathetic. One friendly source predicted that there might be some disturbance "as there are Southern men who are afraid to hear the truth."[31] The fire-eating journalists gave vent to their wonted indignation. One of them doubted that Douglas would be permitted to complete his Southern tour, and hoped that he would be expelled from the South. Lincoln should not be allowed to spread his "damnable" doctrines; why should Douglas?[32] And another poured scorn on "an itinerant peddler of Yankee notions."[33] Be it

[28] Daily Louisville Democrat, Sept. 30, 1860. New York Herald, Sept. 30, 1860, reported that Douglas' train on the Nashville and Chattanooga railroad was thrown off the track by "a fiendish plot."

[29] Washington States and Union, Oct. 25, 1860.

[30] Milton, Eve of Conflict, p. 496.

[31] Augusta Daily Constitutionalist, Oct. 25, 1860.

[32] Petersburg (Va.) Bulletin in Lexington Kentucky Statesman, Oct. 30, 1860.

[33] Memphis Daily Avalanche in Richmond Examiner, Oct. 25, 1860.

noted, however, that one Breckinridge paper bespoke a calm and dispassionate hearing for an eminent national leader.[34]

But regardless of possible disastrous personal consequences, Douglas carried out his program as planned. At Memphis he was heard by an audience estimated by an anti-Douglas observer at 5,000, very few of whom came from outside the city, we are told.[35] After speeches at Huntsville in Alabama, Nashville and Chattanooga in Tennessee,[36] the Senator invaded Georgia, arriving in Atlanta on October 29. He was greeted there by the Stephens brothers, Alexander H. and Linton, the latter of whom took occasion to declare against secession merely because of "any man's election." The next day Douglas was presented to the audience by Alexander H. Stephens, whom Douglas told his hearers that he had been ready to support for the presidential nomination at Baltimore. It had been intimated that no person would be permitted to utter the Norfolk sentiments on Georgia soil, but Douglas' Atlanta address followed familiar lines. The "stern, humorless demeanor" of the speaker was noted, and a supporter could boast that "the man who faced abolition mobs in Chicago was not afraid to say what he thinks in Georgia." [37] Alexander H. Stephens accompanied Douglas to Macon, where they spoke to a large crowd. The Bell paper in Macon praised their addresses as "eminently patriotic and sound." The theme of both men was one of opposition to disunion for existing grievances, or because of Lincoln's election.[38] Douglas and Stephens made their final plea to Georgians at Columbus.[39]

With the election only a few days before him, Douglas turned to Alabama, the home state of the extremist William Lowndes Yancey and the heart of the cotton kingdom. The New York Times reported that there was strong prejudice there because of the Norfolk speech, that threats were made, and that "the

[34] Macon Daily Telegraph, Oct. 19, 1860.

[35] Memphis Daily Appeal, Oct. 25, 1860, has the text of Douglas' speech there. Douglas' procession was compared to Falstaff's army. Ibid.

[36] Nashville Republican Banner, Oct. 27, 1860; Huntsville Southern Advocate, Oct. 31, 1860, compared Douglas to Andrew Jackson.

[37] Augusta Daily Chronicle and Sentinel, Nov. 1, 1860; Augusta Daily Constitutionalist, Nov. 1, 3, 4, 1860.

[38] Macon Georgia Journal and Messenger, Nov. 7, 1860.

[39] Columbus Daily Times, Nov. 2, 1860; Macon Daily Telegraph, Nov. 1, 1860; Augusta Daily Constitutionalist, Nov. 4, 1860.

favorite indignities of the latitude went the rounds." But with the exception of an occasional egg-throwing, courtesy generally prevailed and Judge Douglas was permitted to speak to the citizens of Alabama from the steps of the capitol in Montgomery. A dramatic and ironic scene was described by the *Times* correspondent. Here the " Little Giant " was depicted as pleading for the Union, and " glancing over the heads of a hostile and impulsive crowd, beyond the city, his eye might follow the valley of the Alabama, for miles to the North, twinkling in the soft light of an autumn sun." Whether or not he won his audience on political issues, he was favorably received and went away popular, in the opinion of the same writer.[40] A few months later, Jefferson Davis would make his inaugural address near the spot where Douglas had pleaded for the Union and against a separate Southern nation.

The long and arduous campaign was ended in Mobile, a city in which Douglas' cause had received vigorous support from John Forsyth's Mobile *Register*. He arrived there on November 5 after a boat trip via Selma, and the Little Giant replied to a welcome, extended by former Governor John A. Winston, standing on an elevation of cotton bags. Later he formally addressed a large crowd in the final speech of what was to be his last quest for the Presidency. The Mobile *Daily Advertiser,* which supported Bell, characterized this finale as " a triumphant vindication of his consistency since 1850." [41] This last effort, made as it was on the day before the election and buried by the excitement of Lincoln's election, has been overlooked by historians, as indeed it was overlooked by contemporaries.

It was in the course of this address that Douglas was called upon by a writer in the Mobile *Mercury* to answer two queries. The " Mobile Questions " and Douglas' answers were as follows: 1. If the election goes into the House of Representatives and it were apparent that he could not be elected there, would

---

[40] New York *Times,* Nov. 9, 1860. For a repudiation of egg-throwing, see Montgomery *Daily Mail,* Nov. 2, 1860. See also David R. Barbee and Milledge L. Bonham, Jr., eds., " The Montgomery Address of Stephen A. Douglas," *Journal of Southern History,* V (1939), 527-532.

[41] Mobile *Daily Advertiser,* Nov. 6, 1860. Governor Winston nominated Douglas as standard bearer in 1864, " if in God's Providence there is another election." Huntsville *Southern Advocate,* Nov. 14, 1860.

Douglas advise his friends to vote for Lincoln or Breckinridge? 2. If Lincoln were elected, would Douglas accept a seat in his Cabinet? The Senator replied to the second question first by denouncing the " wretch " who could propound such a question, and then by a clear-cut statement " that in no event will I accept office under Mr. Lincoln or Mr. Breckinridge or any other sectional candidate who advocates the doctrine of Congressional intervention." And he added " that I would not surrender my seat in the Senate to accept any executive appointment under any man who may succeed to the Presidency in the present contest." To the first question he replied that " no event or contingency could possibly happen in which I would advise any friend of mine to vote for Abraham Lincoln or could any event or contingency possibly happen in which I would advise any friend of mine to vote for John C. Breckinridge." In Douglas' opinion the former represented the abolitionists and the latter the secessionists and disunionists. Furthermore he pointed out that an election in the House devolved upon the Representatives, that it was their duty to make a selection, and that he did not intend to interfere. As for his own candidacy if the election went to the House, he declared, " I shall not be a candidate there." He was unwilling to accept the presidential office unless chosen by popular vote, which would bring with it the " moral power to sustain me in the performance of my duties." In the course of this discussion he declared: " I scorn to accept the Presidency as a minority candidate." [42] In the company of editor Forsyth, Douglas learned of Lincoln's election from the dispatches which came to the office of the Mobile *Register*. After a futile discussion with Forsyth as to Alabama's future course, Douglas returned to his hotel, " more hopeless than I had ever seen him," an observer wrote.[43]

An epilogue to Douglas' unsuccessful trip remains to be written. In New Orleans, a city which had voted strongly for the

---

[42] Mobile *Register* in *Weekly Montgomery Confederation*, Nov. 16, 1860. This report inserted after Douglas' points in his address such comments as " tremendous applause " and " loud and long-continued applause." This is a fragmentary report. I have been unable to locate a complete text of this final address. Milton's *Eve of Conflict*, a detailed account of the period, omits the Mobile speech.

[43] Milton, p. 500.

moderate candidates, Douglas was received with enthusiasm, for which he thanked the crowd with the comment that the demonstration was more for his principles than for him. The arguments to be heard in the South within the immediate future were foreshadowed by Douglas' plea for peace and harmony, and by his emphasis on the fact that as Lincoln had both houses of Congress against him he was powerless to imperil Southern rights.[44]

How shall the historian evaluate this episode of Douglas' career? Students of the period have not hesitated to criticize his record in the fifties, but what shall be said of him in the crisis of 1860? To attempt such an evaluation involves a basic philosophy of history, on which it will be difficult to secure agreement. If the War Between the States was an inevitable event, an " irrepressible conflict " as the abolitionists believed, or an unavoidable contest between two conflicting economic and social systems as some students believe, then of course the efforts of Douglas and of all advocates of moderation were futile. Likewise, if it be maintained that in the long run the war was desirable in order to extirpate slavery—some have thought that the " peculiar institution " would otherwise have lived into the twentieth century—the middle-ground men were in an untenable position. If however, the thesis of an inevitable or of a desirable war be rejected, then it is possible to interpret Douglas' course in 1860 in an entirely different light. If the contemporary arguments of Douglas, Crittenden, and their like-minded allies be regarded as sound; if the belief that slavery had reached its natural limits of expansion in 1860 as one modern scholar has argued; if the war were " needless " as Douglas' biographer has contended; if it be held that in spite of Northern and Southern extremists of the era it were yet possible to adjust American problems by means other than resort to warfare, then indeed Douglas may appear in a different role. It should be emphasized that compromise measures came very close to acceptance. Perhaps it was worth while to strive to avoid war, a war which cost the victors 600,000 lives and five billions of dollars, and the vanquished 300,000 lives,

---

[44] It will be noted that Breckinridge polled about 25 per cent of the total in New Orleans. New Orleans *Commercial Bulletin*, Nov. 9, 1860.

four billions of dollars, and complete destruction of the civilization of the Old South.[45]   And historians now see as the most significant result of this conflict, not the freeing of the slaves, but the triumph of industrialization in the United States, a result it would be difficult to relate to humanitarianism.   In any event, Douglas' struggle for peace in 1860 may appear as one of the most courageous phases of his career.

[45] W. E. Dodd, *Expansion and Conflict* (New York, 1915), p. 328.

CHAPTER V

THE USES OF EMOTIONALISM

It has long been known that the John Brown raid of October, 1859, reverberated throughout the South, at the time and afterwards, as proof at last that the abolitionists were translating their hated theories into direct action, and that the Brown raid heralded the opening of the abolitionist offensive. But historians have neglected to describe the exact forms later assumed by the terroristic psychosis, nor have they adequately pointed out the relationship of terrorism and emotionalism to the presidential election of 1860.

With the horrible example of the Harpers Ferry incident before them, as the new year dawned, Southern editors in news columns and in editorials wrote excited warnings to their fellow-countrymen. The Atlanta *Southern Confederacy* was certain that a vile crew of abolition emissaries was being distributed over the South. Maryland, Virginia, Kentucky, and other border states were infested with " vipers," although an encouraging sign was the destruction of abolition "nests " in Missouri and Kentucky. North Carolina was urged to hang the Reverend Daniel Worth who had been recently arrested on the charge of circulating seditious documents and of having uttered words tending to incite insurrection of slaves.[1] It was now time that the South purge itself of all such dangerous incendiaries.[2] Indeed a group of antislavery people, known as the Bereans, had but recently been expelled from Kentucky.[3] Another Georgia paper, the Rome *Weekly Courier*, had learned of a man who drank a toast to John Brown, and who was allowed to escape without " just " punishment. When guilt was established in such cases, the offenders would be dealt with severely. In Tennessee, a " vile incendiary " was said to be prowling about.[4]

[1] Greensborough *Patriot*, Jan. 6, 1860, for Worth's difficulties.
[2] Quoted in New Orleans *Courier*, Jan. 17, 1860.
[3] See article " Those Bereans " from Cincinnati *Gazette* quoted in Nashville *Republican Banner*, Jan. 3, 1860.
[4] Rome *Weekly Courier*, Jan. 12, 1860.

In South Carolina, the Charleston *Mercury* suspected the presence of abolitionists in the Williamsburg district.[5]

On the Southwestern frontier similar symptoms were manifested. The Fort Smith *Times* linked the Republican party with violence, and favored the formation of a Southern Confederacy before the whole federal government should fall to the control of a party

who counsel, aid, and encourage treason, insurrection and bloodshed—who plot the destruction of the lives of the inhabitants of the South, and send out emissaries, and books, to poison the minds of the slaves, to murder our wives and children, and counsel the non-slaveholding population to aid in elevating the negro to be his peer and equal in all things.[6]

An excited state of mind was disclosed by public meetings in Palestine, Texas, at the close of 1859, when resolutions were passed relating to the " covert, dark, unholy, and fanatical, insidious " plot to abolitionize the South by means of ostensibly harmless peddlers, teachers, and books. Booksellers were warned, and a committee appointed to collect all said dangerous books for destruction by public burning. A number of vigilance committees were set up in the country to ferret out and dispose of abolitionists. The town merchants were requested not to purchase from antislavery Northern mercantile houses. Nor were teachers of Northern birth to be employed, " unless by long residence among us we know their soundness." Even music was declared to be incendiary, " dangerous to and subversive of the Constitutional rights and liberties of the South! " [7]

The truth was that in this situation Northern residents and itinerants in the South were objects of suspicion. In Mississippi it was said that if the excitement increased, all Northern-born people would be forced to leave the state, regardless of their position or length of residence. With some bitterness it was further stated that Northerners would not be received socially, and that the people of the South had a higher regard for Englishmen or foreigners than for Yankees. However, this

[5] Jan. 6, 1860.
[6] Jan. 12, 1860.
[7] Palestine *Trinity Advocate*, Jan. 4, 1860. Northern book agents were resented in Alabama, where it was proposed that they be taxed. Carrollton *West Alabamian*, Feb. 8, 1860.

ungracious sentiment was contradicted by another observer in the same state.[8] But elsewhere hostility was noted. The Savannah correspondent of the New York *Herald* wrote on January 28, 1860, that the spirit of retaliation and a disposition to lynch all Northerners suspected of abolitionism were rampant in Georgia. A vigilance committee there was reported to have shipped the captain and several members of the crew of a Massachusetts schooner because they were accused of having used seditious language in the presence of slaves. Of course the distribution of tracts and the Helper book was another cause of the application of tar and feathers.[9] Linton Stephens, brother of Alexander H. Stephens, rejoiced every time a Yankee abolitionist received the last-named treatment and was sent home.[10]

Yet a large section of the Southern press was silent on the subject in the spring of 1860, and some minimized the danger. The New Orleans *Daily Crescent* thought that good would ultimately emerge from the John Brown episode by the stimulation of home manufacture and direct importation, and indicated that the North had lost trade in both Virginia and the Carolinas, a fact of which the North was said to be painfully aware. Thus it was hoped that the North would be taught to respect Southern rights.[11] Another and reassuring view was that although cases had occurred where individual slaves attempted a massacre, it was said to be against the nature of the Negro to engage in such violence. Negroes would fight for and not against their masters, if a test came.[12]

In the same period occasional alarmist references were made to the "nefarious" activities of the enemies of the South, thus keeping the embers of hatred glowing. The Memphis *Avalanche* reported a case in Ashley county, Arkansas, where Negroes had been incited by an abolitionist to kill their overseer, an event which produced "intense excitement."[13] Some disturbances were reported in Dallas, Texas, where a Negro woman was

---

[8] Oxford *Mercury* in Jackson *Daily Mississippian*, Feb. 11, 1860.

[9] New York *Herald*, Feb. 12, 1860.

[10] James D. Waddell, *Biographical Sketch of Linton Stephens* (Atlanta, 1877), p. 199.

[11] Jan. 10, 1860.

[12] LaGrange (Texas) *True Issue*, Feb. 3, 1860.

[13] Quoted by Charleston *Mercury*, March 6, 1860.

detected in a third attempt to burn her master's dwelling. Of
course she was linked with other conspirators more sinister and
diabolical.[14] The public repose was disturbed by the detection of
a consignment of 150 copies of the Helper book at High Point,
North Carolina, which was followed by a bonfire of this literature in the public square.[15] And in an adjoining state, more
Helpers were burned in front of the courthouse of Greenville,
South Carolina, before a large crowd, the books being ignited
by a colored boy " who seemed to be as much in earnest as
anyone present." [16] But there was not enough of this kind of
thing, said the Montgomery *Daily Mail*, too little fear and
emotion in a South which this journal called " comatose."
" It does not startle her to hear that Redpath is organizing
another Harper's Ferry Raid—that he is listened to approvingly
by thousands when he makes his vaunting declarations to that
effect." [17] Possibly the attention of the Southern papers was
largely absorbed in the old game of presidential nominations;
but whatever the explanation, it is a fact that almost nothing
was publicly said of the work of incendiaries from late in April
till the end of June. This was but the calm before the storm.

After the several national party conventions had concluded
their deliberations—while a political situation had developed
which was distinctly unfavorable to the South—the Southern
press returned with zest to the " hellish " machinations of the
abolitionists, and from that time till after Lincoln's election
there was no surcease from hysteria, the high point of which
was reached in that episode which contemporaries called the
" Texas Troubles." [18] Few newspapers in any section of the
United States failed to inform their readers of the latest blood-
curdling outrage from Texas, and it may be observed that even

[14] Palestine *Trinity Advocate*, March 7, 1860.

[15] Wilmington *Daily Journal*, March 16, 1860.

[16] Greenville *Patriot* quoted in Grove Hill (Ala.) *Clarke County Democrat*,
April 26, 1860.

[17] April 20, 1860.

[18] It is interesting to note that " Texas Troubles " occurred in the fall of 1856,
and that other wild stories of slave insurrections were reported in the Southern
states during the last half of 1856. A recent student of the subject noted that
it was a presidential year, but concluded that some of the reports were genuine.
Harvey Wish, " The Slave Insurrection Panic of 1856," *Journal of Southern
History*, V (May, 1939), 206-222.

papers of the most conservative character, the Alexandria *Gazette* for example, apparently accepted these reports at face value.[19] And while Southern men read of these distant but fearful events, they became increasingly apprehensive as to their own safety. A wave of terrorism was reported throughout the South.[20]

In general, the " Texas Troubles " may be summarized from the numerous, repetitious and sometimes conflicting reports as follows: Texas, a lawless frontier state in 1860, the southwestern outpost of slavery, was considered to be of great importance in the extension of slavery. In August and September, abolitionists were accused of having unsuccessfully plotted a gigantic servile uprising, when at a given signal, the slaves would rise against their masters, burn towns and dwellings, and murder their owners and families.[21] The harrowing tale was told in part by a contemporary, the Houston *Telegraph*: " Poisoning was to be added, and the old females slaughtered along with men, and the young and handsome women to be parcelled out amongst these infamous scoundrels. They had even gone so far as to designate their choice, and certain ladies had already been selected as the victims of these misguided monsters." [22]

A systematic division of the counties was made for purposes of massacre and arson; prominent citizens were to be assassinated as they fled from their burning homes, and " further particulars of the Abolition Plot in Texas," revealed that " burnings and hangings are the order of the day." [23] A letter was discovered six miles west of Fort Worth, which was purportedly written by one W. H. Bailey, Denton Creek, Texas, July 3, 1860, and

---

[19] Alexandria *Gazette*, July 27, 1860.

[20] Rome (Ga.) *Weekly Courier*, Sept. 7, 1860, said that scarcely a newspaper reached the office but carried an account of abolitionist trouble. A month later the Waynesboro *Independent South*, Oct. 3, 1860, noted that its exchanges were filled with accounts of insurrections, revolts, and a spirit of insubordination among the slaves.

[21] Details may be found in the following: Richmond *Examiner*, Aug. 6, 1860; New York *Herald*, July 29, 1860; Knoxville *Whig*, Sept. 1, 1860; Dover, *Delawarean*, Aug. 25, 1860; Lexington (Va.) *Gazette*, Aug. 16, 1860; Rome *Weekly Courier*, Aug. 24, 1860; Marshall *Texas Republican*, Aug. 11, 18, 1860; Houston *Weekly Telegraph*, July 31, Aug. 14, 1860.

[22] Quoted in New York *Times*, Aug. 4, 1860.

[23] Richmond *Examiner*, Aug. 6, Sept. 4, 1860.

which revealed the progress of "our glorious cause." He alluded to the initiated, who understood the "Mystic-Red." If the abolitionists could gain control of trade, preaching, and teaching, Texas would be won. Lincoln would win the election, he wrote, and the Indian nation would also be won, which would then create a link of freedom from the Great Lakes to the Gulf. Slavery would thus be estopped. Bailey also alluded to the necessity of night meetings with Negroes, in order to impress the grandeur of freedom upon their "clouded intellects." But more agents and incendiary materials were needed to assure final victory.[24] A Negro woman was hired to burn the town of Henderson; Mt. Vernon was in flames; and a plot to burn Sulphur Springs was uncovered. A correspondent from San Antonio wrote the New York *Herald* that "abolition scoundrels" were being hanged all over the state, but regretted that those in the North who were "behind all this" could not be treated likewise. Large quantities of strychnine were allegedly found in the possession of Negroes, fortunately before the drinking water and food of Texas masters had been poisoned. Finally slaves were equipped with pistols and bowie knives with which to complete the fiendish work.[25]

Professor C. G. Forshey became so much alarmed by the news that he hastened home to Rutersville, Texas. He described the situation for a friend in Louisiana: "The scoundrels of abolitionists had disseminated their devilment far and wide." Many attempts, and successful ones, he said, were made on or about August 6—election day—to burn homes and destroy masters. The local armory, he feared, might have tempted the terrorists, but because it had been well patrolled, all "villainous" Negroes were caught and whipped—or worse. One runaway Negro, who had long been away from that vicinity, was detected

[24] Waynesboro (Ga.) *Independent South*, Sept. 26, 1860. Whether the letter was genuine is a matter for speculation. Its authenticity was sworn to Aug. 10, 1860, *ibid*. It is interesting to note that this matter was given publicity by a rural Georgia paper weeks after its occurrence. The New York *Tribune* (semi-weekly), Oct. 23, 1860, asserted that no such person as "Wm. H. Bailey" was known.

[25] New York *Herald*, Sept. 3, 1860. The Baltimore *Clipper*, Sept. 10, 1860, cited Helper chapter and verse as advising the use of strychnine, and declared that it was but the Helper policy which was being applied in Texas. Helper's reference to strychnine, *The Impending Crisis of the South*, p. 139, seems twisted by the *Clipper*.

skulking about; it was suspicious that his former master's barn and gin were set on fire, and a horse was missing. The patrol scented his trail, pursued and overtook him near Columbus, Texas, and upon the fugitive's refusal to surrender, shot him dead. Professor Forshey also recounted the details of the poisoning of a family, which, however, was believed not to be a part of " the plan." The vigilance committee discharged some suspected Negroes, for lack of evidence, but Forshey thought that a Negro cook and her husband would be hanged " in a quiet way." He further reported that " there was a widely diffused notion among the negroes that they were to be freed & go to Mexico." Happily, quiet had been re-established, and the few whites involved were being rounded up, and if the evidence against them was strong, they were to be strung up " like dogs." " Strolling preachers & book pedlars are the rascals very often." [26]

In such manner was the vast state of Texas, believed by slaveholders to be the bulwark of the " peculiar institution," to be made a free state. Northern settlers and Negroes were to take over the state, just as the first named had recently won Kansas for the cause. The San Augustine *Red Land Express* interpreted the issue as a final death struggle between the abolitionists and the South.[27] In a letter to the *Texas Christian Advocate*, R. S. Finley of Rusk explained the " failure " of the abolition plot in August. Through a misunderstanding, the poisoning and murders which were not to have taken place till the presidential election in November were attempted in August.

But in Finley's mind all these matters proved that a crisis was at hand:

The designs of the abolitionists are no longer matters of doubt—they are lettered poison, fire, and blood—and visible from Maine to Mexico: and he who fails to read them is either to be pitied or censured; and he who, in the coming election, aids by his suffrage to place in the hands of an abolitionist the reins of his government, gives his approval not only to this fiendish warfare, but to a dissolution of the Union; as certainly no one but a madman can bring himself to the belief that the

---

[26] C. G. Forshey to St. J. R. Liddell, Aug. 18, 1860, MS, St. J. R. Liddell Papers, Department of History and Archives, Louisiana State University. Forshey was a professor and writer on ethnology.

[27] New Orleans *Daily Picayune*, Sept. 29, 1860; San Augustine *Red Land Express*, Aug. 18, 1860.

South embracing fifteen States, will doggedly submit to a continuation of these thieving, murderous insults, and repeated attempts to invade her territory, to disfranchise her of her rights, and deluge her in blood and flame. It is no longer safe to tolerate any one, in Southern society, who in any wise affiliates with the abolitionists.

Nor should any one properly make the charge of " lynch law " against Southerners.

A people who would lie supinely upon their backs until their enemies had burned down their towns and houses, murdered by poison or abolition pikes and spears, their wives and children, and force their fair daughters into the embrace of buck negroes for wives, and plead the absence of a *protective law* . . . deserve to be enslaved.[28]

By a number of influential Southerners these lurid accounts were accepted without question, but there were others who were openly skeptical and who believed that the " Texas Troubles " were imaginary or exaggerated.[29] The latter suspected political implications, and it is a fact that the skeptical were usually, though not always, supporters of Bell or Douglas. Those prone to accept the atrocity stories were in most cases identified with the Breckinridge candidacy. A press supporter of Douglas in Georgia pronounced the accounts of terrorism in the South to be " wholesale lies," and in the same state their purpose was believed to be the " firing of the Southern heart " for revolution.[30] From the scene of the alleged difficulties came a protest, which asserted that there had been only two fires in the past summer, at Dallas and Henderson, which possibly had been caused by carelessness with fire combined with a very hot summer.[31] E. W. Cave, Secretary of State in the Houston administration in Texas, noted that Alexander H. Stephens and his brother, Linton Stephens, had alluded in speeches to the " pretended insurrections in Texas," and that the Stephens brothers had been attacked for doing so. Cave sent Stephens copies of the Austin *Southern Intelligencer,* a paper which had combated

[28] Quoted in Waynesboro *Independent South*, Sept. 26, 1860.

[29] New Orleans *Picayune*, Sept. 8, 1860, said in a deprecating article: " Texas, like all of our frontier States, has been the point where desperate men have congested, and her whole history is full of violence and outrage inflicted by the foes of society." Quoted by New York *Tribune* (semi-weekly), Sept. 18, 1860.

[30] Augusta *Daily Constitutionalist*, Aug. 28, 1860.

[31] Marshall *Harrison Flag*, Sept. 22, 1860. They may well have been " hot weather stories."

the ludicrous stories, " which have so much inflamed the public
mind in Texas and elsewhere." His " gallant old Chief," Sam
Houston, was much pleased with Stephens' attitude against
secession. " We have in Texas a set of disunionists who have
used these reports to good advantage. A reaction is now taking
place." [32] And the *Louisiana Baptist* declared that more than half
of the " confessions " obtained from Negroes, on which the case
rested, were untrue or exaggerated but thought there was some
truth in the " Texas Troubles." As befitted a religious paper,
the principle of hanging people first and trying them afterward
was condemned.[33]

Furthermore, the picture painted in the national press of the
state of Texas was believed in some quarters to have damaged
the good name of the Lone Star state. If people believed the
extravagant accounts of insurrections, fires, murders, and rob-
beries, they would hesitate to come to Texas. " That most of
the accounts we have received from the Northern part of the
State are falsehoods and sensation tales, is too evident to every
well informed man to need contradiction." It appeared that
fear had seized some.[34] Negro insurrections were got up for
political purposes prior to the presidential election in the opinion
of the conservative Vicksburg *Daily Whig*.[35] And another Bell
paper in Mississippi agreed that there was no basis for the
reports; they were circulated to affect indirectly the election.[36]
As election day approached, a writer from Lamar county, Texas,
wrote that the fires had not in a single case been connected with

[32] Cave to A. H. Stephens, Austin, Texas, Sept. 20, 1860, MS, Stephens
Papers, Library of Congress. Governor Houston, in an address at Austin, Sept.
22, 1860, flayed the "whipsters and demagogues" who sought to mislead the
people. He reviewed the stories of terrorism, which he minimized almost to
the vanishing point. "We all know how every occurrence has been magnified
by the disunion press and leaders and scattered abroad, and for no other purpose
than to arouse the passions of the people and drive them into the Southern
Disunion movement. . . ." Houston inquired as to who the people were circulating the alarming reports: ". . . examine the matter and it will be found
that by far the large majority of them never owned a negro, and never will
own one." Amelia W. Williams and Eugene C. Barker, eds., *The Writings of
San Houston, 1813-1863* (8 vols., Austin, 1943), VIII, 155-156.
[33] Quoted in Memphis *Daily Appeal*, Oct. 10, 1860.
[34] LaGrange *True Issue*, Oct. 18, 1860.
[35] Oct. 18, 1860.
[36] Raymond *Hinds County Gazette*, Nov. 7, 1860. Yet this paper had been
worried about Texas.

an abolitionist emissary. Scheming politicians were responsible.[87] Yet occasionally even the cautious were impressed, such as the Macon *Georgia Journal and Messenger,* which published little on the subject but discerned restlessness and insubordination among the servile population. "Negroes are huzzahing for Lincoln." [38]

Less than a month before the election, and in spite of criticism, some remained of the same opinion and declined to be "muzzled." Unrepentant, the Montgomery *Daily Mail* intended to continue, because "if Alabama could be kept ignorant that strychnine and arsenic were prepared for the tanks and wells of Texas and Mississippi—*then,* Abolitionism would have received a great, efficient and *cheap* advantage." [39] Nor did denials and skepticism deter Southern orators, campaigning on the hustings for Breckinridge, from citing the "existing" insurrections as proof that Lincoln intended to reduce the South to the condition of Santo Domingo. So William L. Yancey argued at New Orleans on October 29.[40] Senator Louis T. Wigfall of Texas protested at Huntsville, Alabama, on October 10 that the "miserable, tory, and submission" Bell and Douglas papers had said that the Texas plot had been trumped up to beat Sam Houston. The Senator naively asked whether men would resort to such extremes to win elections. He was an eye-witness: on his return to his state for a rest, he found Texas a military camp, and fourteen towns burned. As a result, he complacently concluded, Bellism and Douglasism were entirely dead there.[41] Senator Albert G. Brown of Mississippi, an extremist, alluded to John Brown and the Texas Troubles in the same breath before an audience at Crystal Springs in his home state.[42] Representative J. W. H. Underwood of Georgia, in a calendar of Northern crimes against the South, included the horrible Texas fires and insurrection.[43] Henry A. Wise of Virginia advised Texans to hang all invaders they could catch.[44] James L. Orr

[87] Baltimore *American*, Nov. 1, 1860.
[38] Sept. 5, 1860.
[39] Oct. 18, 1860.
[40] New Orleans *Daily Delta*, Oct. 30, 1860.
[41] Jackson *Semi-Weekly Mississippian*, Oct. 23, 1860.
[42] *Ibid.*, Sept. 11, 1860.
[43] Rome *Weekly Courier*, Sept. 14, 1860.
[44] New York *Times*, Sept. 10, 1860.

of South Carolina referred in a letter to the " untiring fanatics "
who came South, teachers and preachers, and to recent events
in Texas, where " abolition fiends " had destroyed one million
dollars worth of property, and barely failed in the execution of
a " hellish " conspiracy.[45] And finally, the Southern candidate
for President himself, John C. Breckinridge, in his principal
campaign address at Ashland, included in a list of Northern
encroachments, " arson in Texas." [46]

The Governor of Arkansas, Elias N. Conway,[47] became
alarmed at the activities of terrorist agents in Texas and in his
state, and prepared for distribution among the people a mani-
festo concerned with the subject. Unlike his contemporaries
above quoted, Governor Conway did not believe that Northerners were the real villains of the piece. His was the original
discovery that British agents were responsible, and he darkly
declared that if all the facts relating to them could be made
public and documented, the patriotic people of the United
States would be astonished,

. . . and that having discovered the real author and instigator of the
mischief, all discord between the Free States and Slave States would at
once be allayed . . . and that they would become fraternally and more
firmly united; and that . . . the indignation . . . of the whole Union
against the British government and its agents and emissaries would be
so great that war would be declared against the British government in
less than twelve months.[48]

The Conway thesis was not adhered to by many Southerners,
but it may be noted in passing that he expressed the essence of
Seward's famous memorandum of April Fool's day, 1861,
" Thoughts for the President's Consideration." [49]

But the main point to be emphasized is that terrorism continued to be paraded through the columns of the Southern press,

[45] New York *Tribune* (semi-weekly), Sept. 25, 1860.

[46] *Ibid.*, Sept. 7, 1860.

[47] *D. A. B.*, IV, 361-362.

[48] New York *Herald*, Oct. 6, 1860. The text of the Conway pamphlet may
be found in the Little Rock *Arkansas True Democrat*, Sept. 29, 1860. Samuel
A. Cartwright of Louisiana wrote Governor Conway that he had the proof of
British machinations, which he had assembled over a period of twenty years.
Cartwright to Conway, Oct. 10, in Little Rock *Arkansas True Democrat*, Oct.
20, 1860.

[49] Rhodes, III, 341-342.

in the form of alleged new discoveries of the latest activities of mysterious and malignant foes, until election day and after. As stated above, the furor was frequently related to the presidential canvass, with the twofold purpose of discrediting the moderate candidates, John Bell and Stephen A. Douglas, and of further arousing hatred against Lincoln and his party, who were charged with the ultimate responsibility. The character of the terrorist propaganda in the period immediately before the election must be further described, at the risk of repetition, if a complete picture of the situation is to be drawn.

Citizens of northern Alabama read a warning of dark suspicions. " Who knows but what some deep-dyed villain under the guise of friendship to our institutions, may be at this time tampering with our slaves, and furnishing them with arms and poisons to accomplish their hellish designs." [50] In mid-September the same community was told from another source that " . . . we are in imminent danger—danger of the most revolting character—hence this article—hence our alarm." The South was " over-run with unqualified, unprincipled, absurd, mendacious, low-lived, hypocritical scoundrels," accomplished in the arts of Negro-stealing and of underground railroad management. " Students " of the Greeley-Seward-Gerrit Smith-Beecher-Cheever-Garrison-Helper-John Brown " school " pursued various callings. Clericals, doctors—" with large M. D's after their names," mechanics who unfavorably compared work done in the South with that of Ohio, so-called gentlemen, peddlers, even the " hypocritical music-maker and his nobler companion "—all believed to be agents of insurrection.[51]

If " proof " was needed to establish these generalizations, a half dozen or more cases were listed for perusal. At Coffeeville, Clarke county, Alabama, a party of Gypsies requested a master to lend some Negroes to assist in a burial. The next day a Negro informed his owner of the extraordinary weight of the coffin, which on investigation was found to contain ammunition and arms. At Columbus, Mississippi, a planter named John Kelley was killed by one of his slaves, and at the same place a planter who stripped a Negro before whipping him, discovered a large

---

[50] Tuscumbia *North Alabamian*, Aug. 31, 1860.
[51] See article " Read and Reflect," Tuscumbia *States Rights Democrat*, Sept. 14, 1860.

knife on his person. Inquiry revealed that twenty others were likewise armed, and that abolitionists had furnished the weapons and instructions as to their use. This information came from Negro testimony. At Alexandria, Louisiana, a man was arrested for tampering with slaves; the charge against him was that he had told a Negro that although Fremont had been defeated, Lincoln would win, and that he would be free. And on August 28, the repose of the village of Talladega, Alabama, was disturbed by the detection of a plot that would have utterly destroyed that place. So the story went. Two white men and eight Negroes were arrested. Let the violent words of a contemporary tell their fate.

On the same night a posse of citizens went to the jail and forced the keep from the jailor—took the black-hearted scoundrel and the white-livered rascal out—adjusted a cravat of Southern style around his swan-like neck—passed an end over the limb of a tree—and made him dance a fancy dance between heaven and earth until his face resembled the color we painted his heart—he quit dancing—to dance no more on this side of eternity.

Similar troubles were reported in Florida, and to close this catalogue of horrors, insurrections in the whole state of Texas and in Georgia were briefly mentioned. What was needed to put an end to all this was first, a more stringent slave-code, and second, severe treatment for suspicious characters—probably a euphemism for hanging.[52]

A few weeks before election a " diabolical " plot was discovered at Plattsburg, Winston county, Mississippi, as usual with these matters, mercifully in time to prevent its execution. According to the Louisville (Miss.) *Central Enquirer,* a Mr. D. Kelly flogged his cook so severely that she promised to reveal a secret, if he would desist. Her confession pictured whites as distributors of poison among Negroes; as proof she displayed some in her possession. Mr. Kelly then assembled a committee of " sober-minded " men to conduct an investigation, and more details of the affair were learned. On the morning of election day, Negro cooks were instructed to include strychnine and

---

[52] Tuscumbia *States' Rights Democrat,* Sept. 14, 1860. For the Talladega episode, see account of the Talladega *Reporter* in Augusta *Daily Chronicle and Sentinel* Sept. 4, 1860. The Negroes there were said to believe that a " black Republican " President meant a Negro, who would set them free.

arsenic in the planters' breakfast diet, after which their homes were to be burned. (This was the same formula used in Texas.) A suspicious Northerner was arrested, a vigilance committee was appointed, and a tribunal of twelve persons set up which was given power to try suspects, black and white, and to punish them.[53]

Occasionally examples of activity of abolition emissaries were reported in Virginia. One such case was at Bowling Green, where a vigilance committee waited upon a suspect, but the proceedings of the committee were interrupted by two men evidently opposing the committee's action. Another meeting was held, and the interrupters were requested to leave the county. A significant resolution condemned "any attempt to array one class of the community against the other, regarding as we do the mechanic and the farmer as mutual helpers, the one of the other." [54] And in Richmond one Thomas O. Quillan was fined in Hustings Court for tampering with slaves. He defiantly proclaimed himself to be an abolitionist, a believer in John Brown's martyrdom, and supporter of Lincoln. He was also imprisoned in jail one year.[55] A melee was caused at Sperryville in October by suspicious characters—Northern itinerants —one of whom was " awfully whipped." [56]

The press ground out more of the same kind of atrocity story; the reports emanated fom Alabama, Georgia, Mississippi, Arkansas, and Louisiana. The Montgomery *Daily Mail* in October declared that the South was " infested " with hundreds of abolitionist agents, whose business was to prepare Southerners to accept the rule of Lincoln. An alleged incendiary caught in Marengo county, Alabama, bragged of the achievements of his

[53] Quoted in Jackson *Semi-Weekly Mississippian*, Oct. 9, 1860; also Richmond *Examiner*, Oct. 23, 1860, and Charleston *Mercury*, Oct. 23, 1860. Early in the summer, the *Meridian* of Meridian, Mississippi, reported a serious disturbance among planters of that region. A group of abolitionists were discovered, who defied public opinion. A vigilance committee waited upon them and were met with resistance. An old man named Gilbert and a preacher named McDonald were the ring-leaders, and were connected with John Brown, it was thought. Negroes had been congregating with them at night, so one testified. "One of the negroes was taken up, and confessed this under the lash." Quoted in Waynesboro (Ga.), *Independent South*, July 20, 1860.

[54] Richmond *Examiner*, Aug. 31, 1860.

[55] *Ibid.*, Aug. 15, 1860.

[56] Petersburg *Express* quoted in *ibid.*, Oct. 24, 1860.

friends with fire and poison in Texas. Of a fire in Opelika, Alabama, a published letter said: "It is believed to be the work of a *black-hearted Yankee*. If we catch the rascal we will *hang him* higher than old John Brown ever hung." [57] In glee the *Mail* exclaimed, after announcing the detection of a man in the act of tampering with slaves, "... *he is to be hung at Auburn today*! Let him swing high and long." [58] The towns of Dalton and Marietta in Georgia and the railroad which connected them were imperilled by an abolitionist "plot" which, as always, was uncovered before the damage was done. Thirty-six Negroes were arrested and great quantities of ammunition taken from them. Of course it was said that "demoniac" white men were the impresarios, but none was apprehended.[59] And in Scriven county, Georgia, "insurrectionary developments" were reported by the Waynesboro *News*. A box containing dirks, Sharpe's rifles, several swords, and portraits of "Old Brown" was discovered on "Parson" Wade's plantation. Moreover, his brother-in-law, a native of Massachusetts had just returned from a visit to the state.[60] This man had taught several slaves to read, and had given them incendiary documents. One fire-eating journal of the region pointed the moral: "The development is but another warning to our people. They will not be convinced that they are slumbering over a volcano, whose smoldering fires, may at any quiet, starry midnight, blacken the social sky with the smoke of desolation and death." A vigilance committee should be created to hang forthwith, without benefit of laws, such "abolition villains." [61] The same message was delivered to the voters in western Georgia by the Carrollton *Advocate*:

The abolition incendiaries who have caused the slaves in Texas to conspire against their masters, applied the torch to their dwellings, and sought to deprive them of their lives by poison, are but the forerunners of the vast hordes that will be poured upon us in case their friends, the Black Republican party, get control of the government.[62]

[57] Montgomery *Daily Mail*, Oct. 24, 27, 30, 1860; Waynesboro (Ga.) *Independent South*, Nov. 7, 1860.

[58] Montgomery *Daily Mail*, Nov. 2, 1860.

[59] Columbus *Sun* in New Orleans *Daily Delta*, Sept. 5, 1860.

[60] Waynesboro *News* in Waynesboro *Independent South*, Sept. 14, 1860.

[61] Waynesboro *Independent South*, Sept. 14, 26, 1860.

[62] Carrollton *Advocate*, Sept. 7, 1860. Under this title, "The Irrepressible

A few weeks later, forty or fifty Negroes were discovered near Waynesboro, Georgia, in the presence of Peterson B. Cochrane at the store of John Hart. Cochrane told the Negroes that they were as good as whites. The Negroes were said to have been intoxicated and in an excited state of mind. Upon learning of this incident, a committee of sixteen " gentlemen of the highest character " assembled and resolved that the guilty whites depart from the county by the first train, or be lynched by the committee. It was reported that Cochrane left, but the local paper expressed regret that he was not put to death, or at least treated to fifty lashes on the bare back.[63] And just at election time, an itinerant piano tuner asserted tartly that Lincoln was a good man, which infuriated Georgians.[64] At the beginning of September the people of Harris county, Georgia, were warned against slave insurrections and urged to watch strangers. About a month later, a well-digger named Parker, working at Georgetown, Georgia, became the center of a disturbance. When an overseer corrected a Negro woman, Parker sympathized with her and said that she was as good as a white. It was reported that he was pursued by hounds, and that he would probably be hanged.[65] Yet in the same state, there were those who continued to attribute these incidents to politics.[66]

Likewise, bad reports emanated from Louisiana and South Carolina.[67] In the latter state, the Marlboro local paper gave an account of incendiary incidents in a nearby community, where resided a newcomer, one James K. Hitchens. Rumors followed him from North Carolina, a vigilance committee was formed, and Hitchens and his son were arrested. Pistols and bowie knives were found in their possession and a letter from an agent of the Hartford Fire Arms Company, stating that a shipment of firearms valued at $300 had been shipped to him. Also letters

Conflict in Georgia has already Begun," the Athens *Southern Banner*, Sept. 6, 1860, described a plot in Floyd county near Adairsville and Dalton to " murder and burn," and warned: " If such things come upon us with only the *prospect* of an Abolition ruler, what will be our condition when he is *actually in power?* "

[63] Waynesboro *Independent South*, Oct. 3, 1860.

[64] *Ibid.*, Nov. 7, 1860.

[65] Hamilton *Harris County Enterprise*, Sept. 6, Oct. 4, 1860.

[66] Athens *Southern Watchman*, Sept. 6, 1860; for character of the evidence in these matters, see Macon *Daily Telegraph*, Oct. 13, 1860.

[67] Memphis Morning *Enquirer*, Oct. 30, 1860; New Orleans *Daily Delta*, Sept. 5, 1860.

were detected addressed to Seward. The Marlboro county paper said laconically that there seemed to be a disposition to give him a fair trial by those who arrested him, but if guilty he would be summarily dealt with as a warning to others.[68] A resident of the vicinity wrote that he had seen the guns and pistols shipped to Hitchens and he was convinced of his guilt as an abolitionist emissary, and that he was a part of the " irrepressible conflict." The same writer was certain that the Union was as good as dissolved.[69]

Simultaneously, William S. Pettigrew of North Carolina took cognizance of a letter of warning he had received that was intended to prepare him " to encounter the fruits of the teachings of our Northern enemies." Pettigrew was pleased to note that neither his Negroes nor his brothers were implicated; nevertheless he was " glad that the whites have manifested such commendable energy." [70] Thus examples may be multiplied, but enough has been set forth to demonstrate this particular phase of emotional propaganda in the campaign of 1860.[71]

One may well raise the question, in considering the subject of terrorism in the presidential election, as to whether these atrocity stories sank in the consciousness of Southerners, or whether they were dismissed as campaign devices. Clement Eaton has recently shown that the fear of a servile insurrection had long been a very real one with Southerners, and it seems unlikely that Southerners of 1860 could read day in and day out of the outrages which were allegedly occurring in the South without reacting to such news.[72]

R. S. Holt of Yazoo City, Mississippi, wrote his brother Joseph Holt, shortly after election, and the depth of his feeling may be gathered from his words:

In the heart of the planting States we have constantly a foretaste of what Northern brother-hood means, in almost daily conflagrations & in discovery of poison, knives & pistols distributed among our slaves by

[68] Clipping, Gourdin-Young Papers, Emory University Library.

[69] Allan Macfarlane to R. N. Gourdin, Cheraw, Oct. 18, 1860, MS, Gourdin-Young Papers.

[70] William S. Pettigrew to Josiah Collins, Oct. 18, 1860, Pettigrew Family Papers, Southern Historical Collection, University of North Carolina.

[71] For examples in Arkansas, see Little Rock *Arkansas True Democrat*, Sept. 22, 1860; Van Buren *Press*, Aug. 31, 1860.

[72] Clement Eaton, *Freedom of Thought in the Old South* (Durham, 1939), pp. 89-117.

emissaries sent out for the purpose by openly organized associations. I suppose there cannot be found in all the planting States a territory ten miles Square in which the foot prints of one or more of these miscreants have not been discovered.

Holt thought that " Miracles & Providence " had directed attention to them before their " hellish " work was done, and that the " Army of Associations " at the North must number thousands. Indeed, strychnine and arsenic had been delivered in such great quantities that the factories must have worked overtime to meet the demand. In spite of evidence to the contrary, Holt was sure that Postmaster General Holt knew nothing of the " Conflict," because " only one in ten of these terrible things gets into the press." Yet he could say that " I have read of twenty three of these wretches being hanged in the last three weeks." [73] Along the same line, the Charlestonian Alfred Huger indited a fierce denunciation of Seward, whose emissaries had " outraged, invaded, murdered and poison'd . . . ." [74]

South Carolina extremists, moreover, pointed to the reports of terrorism as confirmation of their worst apprehensions. Congressman Laurence M. Keitt, a foremost fire-eater, wrote Senator Hammond: " I see poison in the wells in Texas—and fire for the houses in Alabama. Our negroes are being enlisted in politics—with poison and fire—how can we stand it?" Keitt was very much alarmed if Northerners secured access to " our negroes to advise poison and the torch. We must prevent it in every way." He complained bitterly that Southerners were " blind." [75] And the secessionist Charleston 1860 Association made use of the Texas reports in a pamphlet which paraded the alleged operations of " demons of hell," and earnestly requested that " husbands, fathers, and brothers " read and ponder. One

[73] R. S. Holt to Joseph Holt, Nov. 9, 1860, MS, Joseph Holt Papers, Library of Congress.

[74] Alfred Huger to Joseph Holt, Nov. 12, 1860, MS, *ibid.* John D. Ashmore told a Northern inquirer: " Treason, insurrection & murder has [*sic*] been perpetrated upon quiet unoffending fellow citizens because they have defended & sustained these [Southern] rights & institutions." Events of the past twelve months had satisfied him for the first time that the Union was doomed. Ashmore to Horatio King, Anderson, S. C., Nov. 5, 1860, MS, Horatio King Papers, Library of Congress.

[75] Keitt to James H. Hammond, Sept. 10, 1860, MS, Hammond Papers, Library of Congress. Perhaps Keitt had good cause for alarm. His brother, William J. Keitt, of Ocala, Florida, had been murdered by his slaves while ill in bed. R. B. Rhett, Jr., to W. P. Miles, MS, Miles Papers.

letter, dated Marshall, Texas, August 12, after remarking that only ten Northern Lincolnites and about sixty-five Negroes had been burned to death or hanged, predicted that the Union could not possibly survive a single day after " Abe Lincoln has been declared President. . . ." [76]

During the summer of 1789, a vague feeling of unrest swept the rural provinces of France, where it was said that " the brigands are coming." It seems that some kind of similar feeling existed in the states of the old South in the summer and fall of 1860, a feeling of tenseness which led Southerners to hang peddlers and piano tuners, and to see abolitionists swarming everywhere. Charles L. Pettigrew analyzed this point in a letter to a relative: " I really see no reason to apprehend any difficulty among the negroes: It is mainly resulting from the panic on the part of the whites. I think there is a profound agitation in the South, a feeling as if something was going to happen, if not that which each one thinks, then something else." [77] And a Georgia paper discerned the same thing: " There seems indeed to be a sort of smothered sentiment everywhere that this is a desperate if not a final struggle." [78]

Since the Texas troubles and other alleged incendiary incidents had been fully reported in the Southern press, it is of interest to note the reactions of Northern papers, especially as many of the Republican journals carefully followed affairs in the South from their Southern exchanges. Of the most extreme variety of Republicanism, " Long John " Wentworth's Chicago Democrat was an example. The Democrat interpreted the Texas situation as but an earnest of future events, and professed to believe that the only certain way to prevent a fearful uprising of slaves lay in the preservation of the Union under Republican auspices. In any event, slavery would be terminated in a peaceful manner in a few years everywhere. The situation in the border states was desperate, and a bloody insurrection was only prevented there because of fear of the federal government. The Democrat drew the moral for Southerners: Let them eschew secession, or be faced with a horrible servile uprising, the lurid details of which were described, which would of

[76] John Townsend, The Doom of Slavery in the Union: Its Safety out of It.
[77] Charles L. Pettigrew to Johnston Pettigrew, Mt. Carmel, N. C., Oct. 20, 1860, MS, Pettigrew Family Papers.
[78] Waynesboro Independent South, Oct. 3, 1860.

a certainty follow an attempt to break up the Union. Nor could it be expected that Northern men would not assist the slaves. It would all be a terrible retribution for slaveholders, who for years had beaten, robbed, and cruelly treated four millions of blacks.[79]

Horace Greeley's New York *Tribune,* the bellwether of Republicanism in 1860, alluded on several occasions to the Texas troubles, and to reports of servile difficulties in the South. Assuming that the insurrections had been " invoked " by Southerners for ulterior purposes, the *Tribune* declared: " Nothing is easier than for them to create a panic of insurrection, and the unreasoning multitude may be led to believe that such will be the result of a Republican ascendancy in the North, and that their only safety is in immediate disunion." But such incitement carried with it real dangers, and the four millions of blacks might some day rise in fearful revolt. Continued the *Tribune*:

Beginning in Texas nearly three months ago, the attempt is made to create the panic of insurrectionapartly, no doubt, to influence, in some inconceivable way, the pending election; partly in the vain hope of inspiring a sincere and earnest desire for disunion among the Southern people; and partly to arrest the nascent Anti-Slavery feeling which, it is useless to conceal, is growing at the South.

The Texas situation was but an effort to destroy a class of settlers, antislavery Northern Methodists and their preachers, the *Tribune* believed.[80] Of course, when such words as these from Northern presses were in turn quoted in the South, they enraged the already outraged Southerners, and were equated with the sentiments of Lincoln.[81]

[79] Quoted in St. Louis *Daily Bulletin,* Aug. 11, 1860.

[80] See " The Reign of Terror," New York *Tribune* (semi-weekly), Oct. 23, 1860. For an amusing apportionment of motives, see letter from Nacogdoches, Texas, Oct. 5, 1860, which challenged: " Do gentlemen, let us have one case, if it is only a pretended one, where somebody has suffered beside a negro, a Yankee school-teacher, or a preacher! " *Ibid.,* Oct. 26, 1860. See also *ibid.,* Sept. 11, 18, Oct. 19, 1860.

[81] The Montgomery *Mail* condemned the Bell press for sneering at the Texas insurrections, and because they said, along with the New York *Tribune,* " that the rumors of the burning of towns are all gotten up for political effect—to scare the people—and are a complete hoax." (Quoted in New York *Tribune* [semi-weekly], Sept. 14, 1860.) Yet during the Civil War, when conditions might have been propitious for servile revolts, difficulties with slaves were infrequent. For explanation of this situation, see Bell I. Wiley, *Southern Negroes, 1861-1865* (New Haven, 1938), p. 84.

A wide survey of the uses of emotionalism in the election of 1860 discloses that the Breckinridge men, the "United Southers," and the secessionists were not alone in the employment of "startling disclosures" and of deep-laid plots. Indeed the Bell and Douglas forces bombarded the newspaper public with documentary "proof" of the wily machinations of their political opponents, the Breckinridge men. If there was lethargy extant in the South during the campaign, all sides did their best to dispel it with excitement. One of the most widely copied documents of this type was a lengthy indictment of Yancey and Jefferson Davis as conspirators in a scheme to destroy the Union, which first appeared in the Nashville *Patriot,* a supporter of John Bell. Yancey's speech of May 10, 1858, at the Southern Convention in Montgomery, his much-quoted "Slaughter Letter" of 1858, his alleged relationship with the League of United Southerners, indeed his course through the Charleston and Baltimore conventions—were viewed with profound suspicion. The first pretext of the conspirators was the demand for the reopening of the foreign slave trade, but when that was found to be unpopular, the doctrine of Congressional Protection of Slavery in the Territories was substituted. The climax of the conspiracy was to be brought about by the election of Lincoln: before March 4, 1861, revolution would be precipitated, and a Southern Confederacy established. This document was widely used by Bell newspapers, and repeated efforts were made to associate Breckinridge with disunionism.[82]

Another sensational and unique charge exploited by several Unionist journals was that which linked the Breckinridge candidacy with a secret-military-filibustering organization known as the Knights of the Golden Circle. This order, so characteristically American, was equipped with passwords, grips, degrees, secret signs, and enjoyed a momentary notoriety throughout the South during 1860-1861. The founder and principal protagonist was the Virginia-born adventurer, the amazing George W. L. Bickley, self-styled "General" of the K. G. C.[83] A pamphlet setting forth the objectives of the Knights, undoutedly written by the fluent Bickley, came to the attention of the ardent

[82] Nashville *Patriot,* July 11, 1860; Memphis *Daily Appeal,* July 19, 1860.
[83] For a description of the Knights of the Golden Circle's activities as a Southern filibustering organization, see Ollinger Crenshaw, *American Historical Review,* XLVII, 23-50.

Douglas paper, the Louisville *Democrat*. Seeing the political possibilities of the pamphlet, the *Democrat* reprinted copious excerpts with the following comment on the mysterious order:

There is no knowing who belong to this secret order, unless they choose to proclaim it. It professes not to have political objects, or, at least party aims. It calls on the whole South for Union. It is, however, plain that the whole purpose is political. . . . Whilst its members, no doubt, ostensibly belong to open political parties, their acts are controlled by secret obligations, which, to outsiders, produce unaccountable results. Who broke up the Charleston and Baltimore Conventions? What produced the strange actions of prominent men in those bodies? Secret oaths and obligations; the members of the new secret order, who saw that the existence of a national party was incompatible with their purposes, and that the first great object to be accomplished was to break it up. . . . Mr. Yancey knows more about it than he chooses to tell, and so do others, no doubt. How many of these delegates were Knights of the Golden Circle, and sacrificed their obligations to the party they represented to their duties to a secret order? [84]

By another critic the K. G. C. was thought to be the same as " Billy " Yancey's " Southern Leaguers " by another name. The Chattanooga *Gazette* denounced the order as a " hellish conspiracy," and pleaded that in " the name of our sacred institutions, we appeal to the people to forsake for once in their lives their party leaders who are acting in concert with such an order as the K. G. C. and consign these infamous conspirators to an inglorious defeat." [85] The Montgomery *Daily Mail* vigorously denied that Breckinridge was affiliated with the K. G. C. Such a story was branded a " roor-back." [86]

Although the sinister importance of the organization was probably exaggerated to secure political effect, it was true that General Bickley was campaigning for Breckinridge in Texas during October, and seeking recruits for his movement. This adventurer, an elusive figure in American history, found the Texans responsive to his proposals, especially his plans to seize Mexico. Only the minority remnant of old Whigs there opposed the Knights.[87] Whatever the real role of this cabalistic order in

[84] *Daily Louisville Democrat*, Sept. 2, 1860.

[85] Quoted in Athens *Southern Watchman*, Oct. 11, 1860. Bell papers chided Democratic papers, which had been severely critical of Know Nothingism, for not assailing the Knights of the Golden Circle. *Ibid.*, April 5, 1860.

[86] Montgomery *Daily Mail*, Oct. 8, 1860. Nashville *Union and American*, Oct. 11, 1860.

[87] Charleston *Mercury*, Nov. 1, 1860.

the election of 1860, its very existence was useful to those who sought Breckinridge's defeat by labelling him as a secessionist conspirator.

One may be permitted a further observation as to the thesis of the Nashville *Patriot*. Here was ready-made a theory, earlier formulated by abolitionist writers, and accepted by post-bellum historians, the theory that a Southern clique had plotted secession for several decades before the outbreak of the Civil War. The point to be noted is that in 1860 Southerners had formulated the charge of conspiracy against other Southerners; when secession came and the moderates went into the Confederacy, the conspiracy thesis was ready for appropriation by Northerners. Very little which harsh historians later said about the political activities of ante-bellum Southerners had not already been said by Southerners themselves in the campaign of 1860. The " aggressive slavocracy " thesis found wide acceptance by writers on the Civil War, and it was not until the twentieth century that it was disposed of by historical research.[88]

Near the end of the presidential campaign, an observer in the far South concluded " that the minds of the people are aroused to a pitch of excitement probably unparalleled in the history of our country. . . ."[89] If this was not altogether accomplished, at least such a condition represented a goal towards which many strove during the last half of the year 1860. As Professor Craven has suggested, after the John Brown raid profound apprehensions and resentment seized the Southern people. "Fear and hate had taken charge."[90] It was in this atmosphere that the election of 1860 was conducted in the South.

[88] Chauncey S. Boucher, "*In Re* that Aggressive Slaveocracy," *Mississippi Valley Historical Review*, VIII (June-Sept., 1921), 13-79.

[89] Natchez *Daily Free Trader*, Nov. 2, 1860.

[90] Avery O. Craven, "Coming of the War Between the States: An Interpretation," *Journal of Southern History*, II (Aug. 1936), 303-322. Inevitably the excitement continued, or reappeared, after election. Late in the year, Justice John A. Campbell noted "rumors of insurrectionary attempts & conspiracies promoted by white men, suspected of being sent to the South for the purpose. I suppose that many of these rumors have no foundation at all, & that all the facts of any case have been exaggerated. But no community can exist & prosper when this sense of insecurity prevails." Campbell to Franklin Pierce, Dec. 29, 1860, MS, Franklin Pierce Papers, Library of Cogress. For a different viewpoint of the whole subject, see Herbert Apthaker, *American Negro Slave Revolts* (New York, 1943).

CHAPTER VI

THE CAMPAIGN OF 1860 IN THE BORDER SLAVE STATES AND UPPER SOUTH

MARYLAND

Early in the year 1860 Governor Thomas H. Hicks of Maryland had declined to participate in the convention of slaveholding states which had been proposed by South Carolina. He had supposed that it was to be a secession convention, and despite the denial of Governor William H. Gist of South Carolina, the Governor of Maryland reiterated his belief that such a convention was unnecessary.[1] Maryland's attitude throughout the campaign was one of moderation, with but few voices counselling the state to cast her political lot unreservedly with the South. Even the tenor of the Breckinridge press, while tinctured with sympathy for the South, was one of Unionism. Indeed, toward the close of the canvass, which had aroused passion elsewhere, it was noted that Maryland citizens were apathetic, because it was believed that they were powerless to prevent Lincoln's election.[2]

The case for Breckinridge may be summed up briefly. It was said that a vote for him would unite Maryland with the South, would give notice that the border states rebuked fanaticism—" the radical and inflammatory theories " of the Republicans on the slavery issue. Moreover, if the state went for Bell, such an act would be interpreted as segregating Maryland from the Southern people. By supporting Breckinridge, Maryland would retain her influence in the South, especially during the critical days which were expected to follow Republican victory. No

[1] Gist to Hicks, Feb. 3, 1860; Hicks to Gist, Feb. 11, 1860; Alexandria *Gazette*, Feb. 16, 1860.

[2] Baltimore *Daily Exchange*, Oct. 31, 1860; *Daily Baltimore Republican*, June 6, 1860, regretted the existence of even a few ultra men and journals in the Democratic party; conciliation and compromise must displace the suicidal spirit. Later this paper spoke against secession, but insisted that the Union be voluntary and just. It predicted that the policy of the abolitionists must end in dissolution. *Ibid.*, Sept. 14, 1860.

" overt act " would ever materialize if Lincoln were given to understand that the slavery agitation had been " pushed quite as far as is safe to carry it." Pleas for the Union were made in behalf of Breckinridge, and his candidacy was dissociated from the South Carolina ultraists.[3] Little attention was directed to the doctrine of Congressional protection by the Breckinridge press, although party orators—some of whom were from other states—pledged fealty to it.[4] An especial appeal to the city of Baltimore was made, in which it was argued that Baltimore's commercial interests in the South would best be served by voting the Breckinridge ticket.[5] The regular party organization backed Breckinridge in Maryland, and the Douglas faction was but a small fraction of the normal Democratic vote.[6]

The Constitutional Unionists, strong numerically and supported by a considerable press, were made up of the residue of the old Whig party.[7] There were several shades of opinion in this party, two groups of which seem to emerge: the conservative faction, which favored the economic policies of the old Whigs, was friendly to the South and to slavery, and execrated the Republicans; and that wing led by Congressman Henry Winter Davis.[8] In general it was agreed by Bell men that sectionalism was dangerous, that the territorial question was of

[3] Baltimore *Daily Exchange*, Oct. 31, Nov. 2, 1860; Easton *Star*, Sept. 25, 1860, spoke of the moral effect at the North if the " solid South " voted for Breckinridge—such would " paralyze the ' Black ' Republicans."

[4] Baltimore *American*, July 7, 1860. Humphrey Marshall of Kentucky and Senator L. T. Wigfall of Texas were examples. *Daily Baltimore Republican*, June 28, 1860, dismissed Popular Sovereignty as unimportant and Congressional protection as of no value.

[5] *Ibid.*, Nov. 5, 1860.

[6] Levi K. Bowen to Jeremiah S. Black, Baltimore, April 27, 1860, MS, Black Papers, Library of Congress.

[7] John P. Kennedy was an enthusiastic Union worker. Kennedy to J. J. Crittenden, March 5, 1860, MS, Crittenden Papers, Library of Congress.

[8] Friction developed at the state convention in April between the Americans and the old Whigs. The former seemed to dominate proceedings. Governor Thomas H. Hicks was critical of the Whig element, he believed that Americans should direct the campaign, and he disliked the Union party idea. Hicks suggested that the Opposition party in Maryland adopt neutrality, in case the Republicans refused to accept the Opposition nominee, or perhaps join the Republicans. " I was greatly surprised to hear him talking so much nonsense." John P. Kennedy's " Journal," XII (April 19, 1860), 100-102, MS, Kennedy Papers, Peabody Institute Library.

no signifiance,[9] and that a protective tariff was of prime importance. A banner in a Bell parade which was held just before election day read, "We are for the Protection of American Industry." [10] It would be accurate to say that, so far as Maryland was concerned, the term "protection" in the election of 1860 referred far oftener to American industry than to slavery in the territories. The Baltimore *Clipper* supported Bell and declared its loyalty to the South and to slavery, but opposed secession.[11] And there were shades of opinion among the Constitutional Unionists in their attitude to the Republicans. Some were hostile to Lincoln, some moderate, and others seemed to be prepared to engineer a fusion of the Bell party with the Republicans, after the election of Lincoln.

Although the *Clipper* recognized that there were two wings of the Republicans—the Seward-Sumner-Lovejoy-Phillips-Giddings group of extremists and the conservative element which merely opposed the extension of slavery—it declared that the former controlled the latter and concluded that Lincoln was the "zealous endorser of Sumner." [12] Others in the Bell party called attention to the moderation of the Lincoln press, which, it was pointed out, relegated antislavery diatribes to the background. The Republicans were described as busy with tariff schemes and other matters which were inserted to divert attention from the supposed weakness of their platform. Northern concern over the defeat of the Morrill bill was cited as proof of basic Republican interests. Moreover, Lincoln was represented as loving the South, but the Southerners were blind to it. Such was one view of Republican "amiability." [13]

In reply to the Breckinridge argument addressed to the special interests of the city of Baltimore, Bell men argued that propertied and business men should realize that their best Southern customers were not among the violent, blatant disunionists, but among the real business men and large slaveholders, who

---

[9] Baltimore *American*, July 19, 1860. J. Dixon Roman of Washington county opposed Democratic policies and could not ignore the millions which went to foreign workmen. *Ibid.*

[10] Baltimore *American*, Nov. 2, 1860.

[11] Baltimore *Daily Clipper*, Sept. 18, 1860, which also said: "Thirty thousand native born voters uphold slavery."

[12] *Ibid.*, Sept. 21, 1860.

[13] *Ibid.*, Sept. 15, 1860.

were conservative Unionists.[14] To the contention that Maryland should vote for Breckinridge in order to have influence at the South and thus exercise it to restrain that section from violence in the event of Lincoln's election, it was countered that the ultraists would give such a vote a very different interpretation indeed: they would say " if Maryland was truly opposed to disunion, she should have voted so." [15]

The exposed position of Maryland as a border state which might bear the brunt of war in case of secession and coercion, seems not to have been stressed by the Union orators in this state during the campaign. However, the Port Tobacco *Times* expressed the hope that the South would give Lincoln a chance, and inquired of those rash secessionists if they had reckoned the cost. What would become of Maryland, northwestern Virginia, Kentucky, and Missouri in case of war? The " chivalric " states of Alabama and South Carolina were far from harm, but border-state soil would be the battle field. The "foe" would be near at hand, ready to confiscate property, and to enslave women and children. Let there be peace and union, that Maryland might escape the curse of war. [16]

It was the faction of the Constitutional Unionists led by Congressman Henry Winter Davis,[17] a member of the American party and a " suspect " supporter of Bell, that was closest to the Republicans. Because of his vote for Pennington in the Speaker's contest early in the year, he had been overwhelmingly censured by the lower house in the Maryland legislature.[18] It was reported that the Congressman had been burned in effigy in several places at the South.[19] Davis was suspected in 1860 of being a " missionary of the Republican church." [20]

---

[14] *Ibid.*, Nov. 5, 1860.

[15] *Ibid.* After the election, the *American* continued to call for moderation and an end to sectionalism. "While we are Mr. Lincoln's masters, and he has to account to us for all his acts," there was no cause for secession. *Ibid.*, Nov. 8, 1860.

[16] Quoted in Augusta (Ga.) *Chronicle and Sentinel*, Oct. 16, 1860.

[17] *D. A. B.*, V (New York, 1930), 119-121; B. C. Steiner, *Henry Winter Davis* (Baltimore, 1916), pp. 144-171.

[18] *Daily Baltimore Republican*, Feb. 10, 1860.

[19] Easton *Star*, Feb. 21, 1860.

[20] By W. Price, a Bell elector, who objected to the association of Lincoln's name with that of Henry Clay. Baltimore *Clipper*, Oct. 2, 1860.

Suspicion of Henry Winter Davis was accelerated by the sentiments he expressed in an address at Baltimore on September 27. With obvious relish, the speaker, who had been accused of fierce hatred of the Democrats, described the unhappy condition of the once potent Democratic party. He had only passing praise for his party's nominees, Bell and Everett, and that because they were old Whigs. A change was what was necessary at Washington, and to prove it he listed many shortcomings of the party in power. The Democrats were not " fit " to be entrusted with the power of the sword, nor should they be allowed to direct foreign and commercial policy. The Democrats were corrupt, a charge which he substantiated by reference to the Fort Snelling report, the Willett's Point report, and of course, the Covode Committee report. He denounced political brokerage for contracts, the use of patronage, the management of the Navy Yards, and the subsidization of the press.[21]

Warming to his subject, Davis waxed bitter as he flayed the Kansas policy of the Buchanan adminstration. He charged that the interests of the " agricultural classes " had been ignored by the veto of the Morrill bill, by which the state of Maryland had lost $150,000 with which to endow her recently established agricultural college. With regard to the tariff, Davis asserted that the Democrats refused to remodel it so as to protect the varied American industrial interests. Was it not clear that a " new deal " was needed? Restore to the commerce of the United States the protection of the federal government, write a protective tariff, build the Pacific railroad, develop internal improvement over the entire country, and build up the army and navy, he enjoined his hearers.[22]

The Democrats " howled " about the Negro question to keep themselves in power, but it should be minimized. " Salutary " economic changes could never come about as long as the Democrats were in Washington. " Our political friends everywhere are striving to give John Bell the glory of doing these things." Boldly describing himself as fearless, he boasted that he was no " child " in politics, and that he would leave nothing undone to defeat the Democrats. It was unfortunate that the opposition to

[21] New York *Times*, Sept. 29, 1860.
[22] *Ibid.*

the Democrats was divided. His desire was to fuse the anti-Democratic forces, because either Bell or Lincoln would need national support as President. Therefore, he maintained, let the old party lines be obliterated, that men who think alike could act together. A great national party could hold together for a generation, he believed, if only slavery were eliminated as an issue. He foresaw the Republicans in that role, but feared the tenor of present political controversy: a state of feeling might develop that would get beyond control. To illustrate this he condemned attempts to depict the Republicans, not as political opponents, but as traitors to the Constitution and inciters of servile insurrections. Such tactics were deliberate misrepresentation which played into the hands of Southern disunionists. The slavery question was but an abstraction, which in his opinion was settled.[23]

In conclusion Davis passed judgments on Douglas, Breckinridge, and Lincoln. Although critical of Douglas, he praised the introduction of free discussion in the South. Breckinridge was characterized as " the most extreme, untenable and dangerous of all; his election will mean perpetual strife in Congress over Slavery in the Territories." Lincoln was not radical on the subject of slavery. Of course, a search into a candidate's record for the past twenty years would disclose some obnoxious sentiment or objectionable vote. But the Maryland Congressman recommended that a man be judged on what he would likely do as an administrator, and not as a theorist. In any event, he reassured those concerned over various aspects of slavery. The interstate slave trade and slavery in the District of Columbia would be safe under Lincoln, and Lincoln would enforce the fugitive slave law. Lincoln's views on slavery were similar to those held by Henry Clay in 1850. He closed his Baltimore address with a plea for silence as a cure of the slavery agitation, which was good Constitutional Union doctrine, and with a denial that there was danger of a dissolution of the Union.[24]

From this vigorous exposition it was obvious that Henry Winter Davis' second choice was Lincoln. It was obvious that

[23] *Ibid.*

[24] *Ibid.* Davis and Montgomery Blair disagreed on slavery in territories. W. E. Smith, *The Francis Preston Blair Family in Politics* (2 vols., New York, 1933), I, 488-489.

if the slavery question were removed, identity of economic objectives would lead to a merger of the Republican and the Constitutional Union parties. Northern approval of the Davis speech was noted in Maryland, where it was suspected that Davis, known throughout his career for his ambition, wished to cast himself in the role of leader of such a party in the South.[25]

The Baltimore *American* observed that it was " A Lincoln pronunciamento in Bell clothing, or rather an eccentric Republican sheep with a Union Bell on its neck." [26] The election of Lincoln and the coming of the war made Davis a stormy and notorious national figure, but events did not afford Davis the opportunities he had outlined in the Baltimore campaign address. After a brief support of Lincoln, he became a bitter foe of the war President as an arch-Radical Republican.

An insight into the thinking of a Bell-Everett leader in Maryland may be had from a letter of John Pendleton Kennedy, Baltimore novelist and brother of Senator Anthony J. Kennedy of Maryland, written at the end of the campaign. He described the nation as torn by faction and excited to a pitch of frenzy; the extremists of both sides were hastening large masses of people into civil war. " Bell and Everett have now become the objects of actual derision in both sections of the Union because they represent peace and lawful rule and right supremacy!" He expressed himself as deeply disturbed at the prospect of " mischief " as a result of the campaign. He foresaw the secession of South Carolina and predicted that others would be drawn to her support, until the complex situation would become unmanageable. Kennedy was convinced that the disunionists were proceeding in " orderly conspiracy," and he correctly discerned that they rejoiced in the coming emergency. Separation had

[25] *Daily Baltimore Republican*, Oct. 3, 1860.

[26] Baltimore *American*, Oct. 1, 1860. This paper did not share Davis' view of Lincoln; it feared that the Republicans would be worse than the Democrats in national control. (*Ibid.*) It may be remarked that Davis was not one of those who cloaked their economic objectives behind a crusade against slavery. Perhaps because Davis lived in a slave state, he found that strategy unnecessary or undesirable. He frankly set forth his economic hopes during the campaign of 1860. The Baltimore *Clipper*, Aug. 31, 1860, desired a political party in the South based on Clay's " American System," and hoped Bell and Douglas would crush the " anti-progressives " or " disunionists."

long been planned, and the Democratic party, especially its
" fiercer section," was plotting continued supremacy in a Southern confederacy. The novelist characterized the agitators as
" traitors," and their grievances " ridiculous." The world would
laugh at them. All the fury was, according to Kennedy, " one
of the most inexplicable phenomena of history." [27]

During the campaign of 1860 the Republican party in Maryland was very weak numerically. But it was the center of furious
onslaughts which included physical violence, and as it was the
party most receptive to " advanced " ideas, and because it was
destined by events in the immediate future to assume a vastly
more important position in the state, the Republicans deserve
examination. In April, the first Republican state convention to
be held in Maryland assembled in Baltimore. The convention
elected Montgomery Blair to preside, and, after a preliminary
unpleasantness in which a mob broke up the meeting, reas-
sembled at a private residence to name delegates to the Chicago
convention.[28] On April 26, Montgomery Blair enunciated Republican principles in an address to the convention. He pleaded for
moderate and circumspect conduct by members of his party,[29]
because of the " violent misrepresentation made by our enemies."

Blair mentioned two great measures for which the Republicans stood: (1) a Homestead law, which would prevent the
Africanization of the territories, and (2) the colonization of
free Negroes, on what he termed " Jefferson's plan," in an
undetermined area near the United States.[30] He wished it to be
understood that the Republicans did not favor equality of the
races or amalgamation, and that the Republican was pre-eminently a white man's party. Assuming the role of prophet, he
predicted that the day would come when Maryland would

---

[27] Kennedy to R. C. Winthrop, Oct. 20, 1860. This eighteen-page letter also
contains a long harangue against Lincoln and Breckinridge. (MS, Letter Book,
John P. Kennedy Papers.) The press teemed with disturbing reports of Southern
disaffection. John P. Kennedy's " Journal," XII, 195, 199, 203.

[28] J. T. Scharf, *History of Baltimore City and County* (Philadelphia, 1881),
pp. 126-127.

[29] N. Burnheim wrote from Charles county that although Republicanism could
not be professed openly in 1856, he felt safe in 1860; he added that some Bell
voters secretly were for Lincoln. Burnheim read the Republican platform in a
store crowded with "chivalry." Burnheim to M. Blair, Oct. 29, 1860, MS,
Gist Blair Papers, Library of Congress.

[30] Smith, I, 443-452, for details of what was a family project.

emancipate her slaves as Pennsylvania had done. But the Republican party had nothing to do with such a process. The party should nominate a Southern man at Chicago in order to reassure the South that the party would not touch slavery in the states. Blair knew of such a man—no doubt Edward Bates.[81]

The " rotten borough " system in Maryland was opposed by the Republican party, the speaker said. Calvert county had representation in the state senate equal to that of Baltimore city. Northern and western counties of Maryland were also discriminated against in the distribution of seats. The rotten borough system was needed, according to Blair, to protect slavery. The southern counties were the slaveholding counties. Slavery was an evil, but the Republican party was not making war on anybody. The convention instructed the Maryland delegates to the Chicago convention, which included the Blairs, to work for the colonization scheme.[82]

In midsummer the Maryland Republican Central Committee issued a circular which stated the " great question " of the fight: " Shall slavery be nationalized and extended, or shall it be limited?" The charge that the Republicans proposed to abolish slavery by force, and to elevate the Negro to a social equality with the whites, was denounced as ignorant and malicious. To the contrary, it was emphasized that the Republican party in Maryland was a white man's party, whose object was to protect and " ennoble " free labor. Other objectives were the Homestead law and " judicious import taxes to develop and foster industry and bring revenues." Buchanan's economic program was condemned by the circular. Let Marylanders fear no " novel-

---

[81] Reinhard H. Luthin, " Organizing the Republican Party in the ' Border Slave ' Regions: Edward Bates's Presidential Candidacy in 1860," *Missouri Historical Review*, XXXVIII (January, 1944), 138-161.

[82] New York *Tribune*, May 11, 1860. It may be noted that Blair's attack on the rotten borough system appealed to a sectional feeling within the state of Maryland, a situation which was to be found in many other states. As late as the twentieth century, H. L. Mencken of Baltimore ridiculed the system which discriminated against the city. Blair's ideas may be followed further in a speech delivered Oct. 13, 1860, at Iddins' store, Montgomery county. There he stressed freedom of speech, condemned Yancey and Breckinridge, and opposed the conversion of the U. S. government " into a despotism wielded by nine Judges." Blair declared that judges should carry out the popular will; that Taney himself had been placed upon the court for that purpose. Slavery was not consonant with popular rule, he asserted. MSS, Gist Blair Papers.

ties " from the Republicans, because they had proposed nothing which Pinkney and Chase would not have accepted.[33]

Rowdyism, which had plagued the city of Baltimore in the fifties and which was to give the city unenviable notoriety in 1861, characterized some aspects of the campaign of 1860. It had been employed to disrupt the Republican state convention in April, and it was directed against that party throughout the canvass, with increasing virulence as election day approached.[34] The Wide Awakes, famous for their activity in Northern cities, held a parade in Baltimore on November 1, during which they were stoned and pelted with rotten eggs. Feeling was intensely bitter, but no one was killed or seriously injured. The German " Turners " joined the Wide Awakes.[35] A Republican orator, the Reverend French S. Evans, spoke with great difficulty in the midst of hissing, laughter, shouts, nose-blowing, and the hurling of rotten eggs. " What, I ask, is the Republican party? A voice —' Niggers '—and great laughter." The scene was one of wild disorder, and the Wide Awakes were protected from further attacks of the mob only by police intervention. The press accounts of this incident were unsympathetic to the Republicans, and included the observation, " The association of the Republican party with negroes was quite evident." The Republicans were tormented by this issue. The Reverend French S. Evans was asked if his sister were not a Negro.[36]

The Republicans of 1860 in Maryland were negligible in number, but they were hardy pioneers who suffered the hatred of their neighbors, and who were persecuted with the zeal which Americans have sometimes visited upon unpopular minority political groups. But the coming of war in 1861 gave great impetus to the Republican party and it was not long before it became numerous and respectable in the state, and Montgomery Blair became a member of President Lincoln's cabinet.[37]

[33] New York *Times*, July 24, 1860. Yet manufacturers in Maryland threatened to dismiss laborers who voted for Lincoln. W. E. Smith, I, 502.

[34] Scharf, pp. 786-788.

[35] The " Turners " were members of the Turnverein, a German organization.

[36] Baltimore *American*, Nov. 2, 1860; Baltimore *Daily Exchange*, Nov. 2, 1860. Evans was editor of the Baltimore *Patriot*, and was aligned with Henry Winter Davis. It was also reported that C. C. McTavish, grandson of Charles Carroll, described as a large planter and owner of sixty slaves, was a Lincoln man. Wilmington (N. C.) *Daily Journal*, Oct. 10, 1860; Smith, I, 489.

[37] *Ibid.*, I, 501-502. Privately Republicans prophesied that after Lincoln's

DELAWARE

In this small, northernmost slave state, close to Pennsylvania, three of the four presidential tickets had a sizable following.[38] The Democratic organization, led by Senator James A. Bayard,[39] supported Breckinridge as a party matter, but it was doubtful whether there was much real concern even in that party for the doctrine of Congressional protection of slavery. In fact there were articulate groups, which ultimately supported Bell or Lincoln, which were far more interested in the protective tariff, and which were more friendly to the North than to the South. That the Census of 1860 revealed a recession of slavery in the state, while the white population increased, was a matter of comment. Within a few years the state would be free, it was predicted. State laws restricted the buying and selling of slaves,[40] and the nominal character of slavery in Delaware was conceded by observers North and South.[41]

Breckinridge propagandists accepted the Southern platform on slave extension and the need for Congressional protection. One Wilmington paper went the whole way with the Southerners in demanding an outlet into which the South could pour her invaluable laborers. This outlet was in the direction of Central America. The same exponent proclaimed slavery the " pioneer " which would blaze the trail for the white farmer, and demanded the reopening of the slave trade. " Open the Southern gate for the African." [42] The same paper had earlier committed itself to the Southern interest, which it thought would be imperilled by an " abolitionizing " opposition. Negroes, who were now

election it would be possible for those working covertly to come out in the open, and that then the American Bell party would come over to them. W. L. Marshall to M. Blair, May 27, 30, 1860; Jos. M. Palmer to M. Blair, Oct. 22, 1860, MSS, Gist Blair Papers.

[38] New York *Times*, July 16, 1860.

[39] *D. A. B.*, II, 66-67.

[40] Wilmington *Delaware Gazette*, Aug. 7, 1860.

[41] Jackson *Daily Mississippian*, Feb. 21, 1860. The New York *Tribune* (semi-weekly), Nov. 2, 1860, pointed out that there were only four slaves in the city of Wilmington, while the total number of slaveholders in Delaware was 615. The *Tribune* calculated that only one man in 165 was a slaveholder. Delaware would not go Republican in 1860, but would in the near future.

[42] Wilmington *Delaware Gazette*, Aug. 3, 1860.

benefiting the world by cotton, rice, and sugar production, would be transformed into vagabonds and vagrants.[43] Nor was it considered inconsistent for the same advocate to champion a protective tariff. The thesis of Seward, that there was an irrepressible conflict between "capital" states and "labor" states, was expressly refuted. Instead it was believed that the two systems were complementary and harmonious.[44] W. G. Whitely, Democratic member of Congress from Delaware, had recently voted for the tariff, and it was predicted that the United States Senators would also support protection for industry. Indeed, the protective tariff was essential to Wilmington's industrial development.[45] Senator Bayard blamed the party's difficulties on Douglas, but was himself assailed for having "sold the State to Slidell, Yancey & Co." [46]

William L. Yancey, the famous Alabama ultra, whose name was so frequently denounced by Unionists in the border states, spoke in Wilmington for the Breckinridge cause on September 27. In an address, notable for its restraint, he stressed the argument that Delaware, of all states, should stand with the South to guard the "equality of the States." The issue of the campaign was the preservation of the Constitution, by which the speaker meant the Constitution as interpreted by himself and his section. Yancey pronounced the Republican party the "mulatto" party, and identified Douglas with them on that issue. Douglas was the exemplar of the "Divine right of majority rule." Yancey was for checks and balances. Doubtless with the pro-tariff sentiment of Delaware in mind, Yancey was mild in reference to that question.

All we ask of the North is that they shall leave us to our industry. Though we are required to pay an unproportionate taxation, we will not complain. Although tariffs are made discriminating largely in favor of the North, we will not complain. But when they come to take away our tools then we do complain, and bitterly too. When they come to interfere with our Negro, who is the tool of our industry, the source of our prosperity and yours, then we do complain.

The man who was so violently condemned as a disunionist

---

[43] *Ibid.*, Feb. 17, 1860.
[44] *Ibid.*, March 19, 1860.
[45] *Ibid.*, May 25, 1860.
[46] *Ibid.*, July 10, 1860; New York *Times*, July 16, 1860.

conspirator, concluded the Wilmington speech with a humorous allusion to himself, " as a disunionist, twenty seven feet high, weighing three thousand pounds and eating a little nigger broiled every morning for breakfast and a roasted Union man for dinner . . . ." On the contrary, Yancey said, the " nigger " was fed and fattened, so that his worth would be increased. It was obvious that the fire-eating Yancey had toned down his utterance to suit the latitude in which he spoke, because the Breckinridge party in Delaware, while sympathetic towards the South, was hostile to secession.[47]

The opposition to the Breckinridge Democrats in general looked to the North for economic guidance and was sharply critical of slavery and the South. Early in the year, one observer rebuked extremism in both sections, and appealed to patriotism in the crisis.[48] The South was criticized for intolerance and censorship, which did not prevail in Delaware. White laborers of the North were asked if they agreed with Senator Albert G. Brown's view that the four million slaves were better off morally, socially, and intellectually than they were.[49] One critic placed the onus for the slave agitation on the South: the " slave oligarchy " made demands, which if not granted, led extremists to blame Northerners as agitators. It was time to employ moral courage with which to stop the " blighting extension of slavery." [50] If the state wished retrogression, then let her join the South, from which there was little gain. If she cut off from the North, labor and capital would go elsewhere, and Delaware's lands would decline in value and her population would shrink.[51] Those interested in securing a protective tariff were warned to eschew the Democratic party, lest the trickery of the campaign of 1844 once more deceive them.[52]

Some weeks before the national conventions there was discussion as to whether the People's party, which was composed of anti-Democratic elements, should send delegates to the Republican convention at Chicago, or whether it should adhere to the incipient Constitutional Union movement. It was feared that the latter course might result in the election of the nominee

[47] Wilmington *Delaware Gazette*, Sept. 28, 1860.
[48] Wilmington *Delaware Republican*, Jan. 12, 1860.
[49] *Ibid*., Jan. 30, 1860.   [51] *Ibid*., March 15, 1860.
[50] *Ibid*., Feb. 9, 1860.   [52] *Ibid*., Feb. 27, 1860.

of the Charleston convention, and that it was the wise course for all to support Chicago. However, objection was made to the Republican convention's call which had omitted reference to the protection of labor: it was all about slavery, and the people of Delaware were not interested in that. Others were concerned for the election of local tickets, a more important matter to some than the fate of the national nominees, as Delaware was unlikely to be a decisive factor in the presidential election.[53] The division of opinion in the People's party led to representation at both the Republican and Contitutional Union conventions. Lincoln's nomination was praised by an important Wilmington paper, which identified him with Clay and the tariff. The same source also praised Bell but criticized him for vagueness, because he was said not to speak for the South on the slave question, and because he was unlikely to carry a single school district north of Delaware.[54]

Finally, at a convention of the People's party agreement was reached that all factions should unite in support of a Congressional ticket, and that the members be left free to vote for Bell or Lincoln.[55] This group expressed resentment at the term "black Republican," and with heat repelled the aspersion. Far from being the "black" party, it was argued that the party which favored the preservation of territory for white settlers, and was opposed to the extension of "niggers and niggerdom," was assuredly the white man's party. It would be more appropriate to refer to the "black Democrats."[56] Thus the Bell and Lincoln parties were very close together. As was the case in Maryland, on economic matters they were in complete accord. Although the New York *Tribune* predicted electoral victory for Breckinridge in Delaware because of the large slaveholding Sussex county, the future was with the Lincoln party.[57] To complete the political picture in Delaware it should be men-

[53] Wilmington *Delaware Republican*, Feb. 6, 1860. It was claimed that the overwhelming majority of the party in New Castle county, which contained the city of Wilmington, was for cooperation with the Republicans. *Ibid.*, April 5, 1860.

[54] *Ibid.*, May 3, 14, June 4, 1860.

[55] *Ibid.*, July 30, 1860.

[56] Wilmington *Delaware Republican*, May 14, 1860.

[57] New York *Tribune*, Aug. 17, 1860.

tioned that the faction which supported Douglas was strongly Unionist, as indeed were all parties.[58]

VIRGINIA

In this large and important state, discussion during the campaign of 1860 centered not only on candidates, immediate issues, and such matters, but on the ultimate course of Virginia in the months and years following the presidential election, which might involve secession and civil war. As in other border states, the argument was most heated on the question as to whether Virginia should face southward, or whether through a moderate course she should strive to cooperate with her neighboring border states, as well as with the North and West.

Such men as Edmund Ruffin and Henry A. Wise were foremost counsellors of a strong Southern policy for Virginia. Ruffin held that slavery was beneficial to the South, that more of this type of labor was needed, and covertly favored the reopening of the African slave trade—though in this stand he was supported by but few Virginians.[59] He was an advocate of Southern territorial expansion, which was much discussed in the year 1860. He did not take William Walker seriously and apparently ignored the flamboyant Bickley, but he believed that Central America and the Isthmus of Panama were desirable objectives of annexation—preferably after the South had quit the Union, but immediately if necessary. This expansion was put on the ground of duty to civilization. Ruffin predicted the triumph of the Black Republicans in 1860, who would speedily put an end to minority rights. It was his duty to rouse the South to such a danger. Presidents Pierce and Buchanan were regarded by Ruffin as weaklings, chosen because of their ability to get Northern votes. It galled him that Southerners were barred from the presidential office. And in common with other Southern radicals, he entertained a furious contempt for New Englanders and the Personal Liberty Laws of Northern states.

[58] Wilmington *Delaware Inquirer* in Wilmington *Delaware Republican*, Aug. 13, Oct. 29, 1860. The *Delaware Inquirer* supported Douglas. James Montgomery to Stephen A. Douglas, Jan. 9, 1860, MS, Stephen A. Douglas Papers, Library of the University of Chicago.

[59] See E. Ruffin's article, "The Effects of High Price of Slaves," *The Southern Planter* (August, 1859) in A. H. Stephens Papers, Vol. III, Library of Congress.

These were some of the sentiments of Edmund Ruffin in the decade before secession. He was discouraged at his lack of progress as he awaited the election of 1860. At the end of the year 1859, however, the John Brown raid enabled him to send pikes to Southern governors. Momentarily Governor Wise was strengthened politically, wild rumors circulated throughout the South, and men like Wise held the entire Republican party responsible for the attack.[60]

Like R. Barnwell Rhett of South Carolina, Ruffin had long hoped for the disruption of the national Democratic party. Events at Charleston encouraged radicals in all sections: of course Ruffin was jubilant, and later at Baltimore he urged the Southern delegates to secede. His biographer has noted the rising dominance of radicalism in both sections.[61] But there was still a large portion of " sanity " left in his own state, as the campaign of 1860 would demonstrate.[62]

At the close of 1859, the Central Southern Rights Association of Virginia presented a memorial to the General Assembly of the state, which embodied a statement of grievances and suggested remedies. It contained a fierce denunciation of the " wicked excesses of the North," for which moderate men were to blame. There could be no peace until the " panderers to public demoralization and crime " should be ejected from office, until their legislatures repeal the unconstitutional laws, and until the invaders of the South be punished. This organization demanded that Virginia take the lead: " With oneness of purpose and concert of action, Virginia and the South are invincible, in the Union, or out of it." For the same purpose, let Virginia establish economic and cultural independence.[63]

[60] Avery O. Craven, *Edmund Ruffin, Southerner* (New York, 1932), pp. 143-170; 178-180. Ruffin to James H. Hammond, May 4, 1860, MS, Hammond Papers, Library of Congress. Wise believed that a wide and fanatical sympathy existed for Brown in the North. He was disturbed by a proposal originating in Boston to arrange an " excursion " to Charleston to witness the hanging of Brown. Wise to James Buchanan, Nov. 12, 1859, MS, James Buchanan Papers, Historical Society of Pennsylvania.

[61] Craven, *Edmund Ruffin*, pp. 182-183.

[62] Ruffin analyzed the campaign in Virginia. He predicted Bell would carry the state by a plurality. Ruffin to John W. Ellis, Aug. 29, 1860, MS, Ellis Papers, Southern Historical Collection, the University of North Carolina.

[63] Richmond *Whig and Public Advertiser*, Jan. 6, 1860, which also contains the constitution of the Central Southern Rights Association of Virginia.

The new Governor of Virginia, John Letcher, who assumed office in January as the successor to Wise, summarized his view of the troubled times in his first message to the legislature. He advocated the calling of a national convention, under Article V of the United States Constitution, in which the sectional controversy should be thrashed out, and a working agreement reached. If such proved to be impossible, there should be peaceable secession. Letcher recommended the appointment of Commissioners to each state which had opposed the execution of the fugitive slave law, and these representatives were to insist, in the name of Virginia, that the offensive Personal Liberty Laws be repealed. If the aggressions against the South were climaxed by the election of a sectional Republican to the Presidency, Letcher declared " it cannot and will not be submitted to." It would be intolerable to permit a man like Seward to control the country's armed forces and the appointing power. Darkly the Governor urged military preparedness on the people, and commended liberal appropriations for the Virginia Military Institute.[64]

The stormy John Minor Botts,[65] an ambitious and articulate leader who had long been associated with the old Whigs, and active in the ranks of the Opposition party, took a contrary view. Writing ten days after Letcher, he expressed his disbelief that any " respectable portion of his fellow-countrymen had any direct or indirect participation in the John Brown Raid . . . ." No proof had been adduced, but Botts knew that there was widespread belief in Virginia of the complicity of hundreds of thousands of Northerners in the John Brown raid. The writer dissociated himself from the abolitionists, as well as the secessionists, and took pains to deny the expediency and legality of secession. At the time, Botts was mentioned for the presidential nomination of the gathering Constitutional Union party, and he even hoped for a fusion with the Republicans.[66]

With regard to Helper's *Impending Crisis* which was the subject of confiscation and book-burning, Botts said that, while far from endorsing the volume, he did not overlook the fact that

[64] Norfolk *Southern Argus*, Jan. 11, 1860.

[65] *D. A. B.*, II, 472-473.

[66] Baltimore *Clipper*, Jan. 2, 1860, carried the name of Botts for President.

Helper correctly quoted hostile opinions of slavery held by eminent eighteenth-century Virginians. And while he did not approve the Personal Liberty Laws, they did not justify the " grim jest " of offering rewards for the heads of Republican leaders, which he said had been recently perpetrated in the Richmond press. Nor could he approve what he termed the " lynching " of Northerners in the South.

On economic matters, Botts proclaimed himself to be a supporter of Henry Clay's " American System " of protection of home industry. He warned that not till Virginia adopted such a program would the state be enabled to cope with the manufacturing states. Botts' condemnation of the extension of slavery in the territories, by force or by national legislation, and his espousal of the Henry Clay system, placed him very close indeed to the hated Republicans. As in the case of Henry Winter Davis of Maryland, Botts was a potential leader for a future fusion of Republicans, old Whigs, and Unionists. And in spite of aberrations, an influential Virginia organ characterized his letter as " able, straightforward, and manly." [67]

William C. Rives,[68] a distinguished Virginian, and old-line Whig, surveyed the situation of his state early in the year and offered counsel. At the outset of his public letter, Madison's biographer admitted the gravity of the times. He condemned abolitionists, the Helper book, and the Sherman candidacy for Speaker. He recommended military and economic measures of state defense. But Rives saw encouraging signs in the Union meetings in the North, and he would not exacerbate Northern opinion by agitation of the slavery-territorial question. He would not engage in demands for " new and untenable pretensions," such as a slave code.

Let Virginia reject the invitation of South Carolina for a Southern conference, which Rives thought tantamount to a secession meeting. Whatever such a conference might do—and he believed that it could accomplish nothing—it would surely meet with the disapproval of Virginia's neighbors, to whom she

[67] Richmond *Whig and Public Advertiser*, Jan. 20, 1860; Baltimore *Patriot* in Wilmington *Delaware Republican*, Feb. 2, 1860; *Alexandria Gazette and Virginia Advertiser*, Jan. 21, 1860. Of course some thought Botts was as bad as Helper. Norfolk *Southern Argus*, Jan. 26, 1860.

[68] D. A. B., XV, 635-637.

was bound by many ties. Rives had been considering the matter of secession since 1844, with particular reference to his state's economic position. He could not follow the arguments of men like Ruffin, who wished to bind Virginia to the lower South.

Rives cautioned the Old Dominion against the acceptance of a " King Cotton " commercial policy, which under a Southern confederacy, would throw open Virginia ports free to foreign manufacturing and other products. He subjected Virginia's agricultural products to examination. Unlike " King Cotton," they were grown in " every clime," and tobacco was heavily burdened with taxes by foreign nations. He favored diversification of Virginia economy and the development of industry. Some advocated this policy to increase Virginia's independence of the North, and to strengthen Southern nationalism. This was not Rives' attitude: he saw Virginia linked to Maryland, Delaware, Pennsylvania, New Jersey, New York, the West, and the Mississippi Valley. On the South she was bound to the "Union-loving and conservative" states of Tennessee and North Carolina. " These border states are naturally . . . the conservators of the Union." Rives rejected the " beau ideal " of the South Carolinian, George McDuffie, who had proposed in 1844 that there should be three great Confederacies: a Northern [manufacturing], a Western [farming], and a Southern [planting]. The folly of man could not destroy natural boundaries, Rives insisted.[69]

Professor John B. Minor, of the University of Virginia Law faculty, disturbed by the critical situation late in 1859 and early in 1860, sought the views of former students, friends, and relatives. Minor took firm Union ground, but his replies included various shades of opinion. William M. Blackford of Lynchburg favored waiting for an overt act, although he feared that many would stigmatize him as a " submissionist." Blackford was no fire-eater, but he did desire that the North know

[69] Rives' letter, dated Castle Hill, Jan. 27, 1860, appeared in the Richmond *Whig*, and was reprinted in the Lexington *Gazette*, Feb. 9, 1860. Rives, as Minister to France following the revolution of 1848, was said to have been much impressed with the horrors of civil war, which he desired his country to avoid. (*D. A. B.*, XV, 635-636.) After the Charleston rupture, Rives wrote that that event had demonstrated the Democratic party's impotency in national affairs. (Rives to J. J. Crittenden, May 5, 1860, MS, Crittenden Papers, Library of Congress.)

of the serious danger in Virginia. By warning the North he hoped that the Conservatives there would show their hand. In response to Minor's prophecy that rupture of the Union would mean political destruction, Blackford declared that he knew that "unnumbered calamities" would follow secession. He painted a dreary picture: "The work of disintegration would be progressive, and before ten years there would be half a dozen confederacies, or single States playing the part of independent nations—then wars of course—conquests—consolidation and military despotism." But he endorsed military preparation for Virginia, and he viewed the prospect of a three-month balloting for Speaker with grave misgiving.[70]

Another to reply to Professor Minor was Frank V. Winston of Louisa Court House, who wrote, he said, not as a politician but from sincere conviction. Winston took a pessimistic position. His hopes for resisting aggression were slight: the single principle of the Republican party was hostility to "an institution which is the basis of society, prosperity, and wealth," in fifteen states. After all, the federal government only had been of threefold negative benefit to the South up to 1860: it had given prestige in foreign policy, peace at home, and a freedom from standing armies. To be sure, these were important benefits; but they were vitiated by the operation of the central government which took "money out of our pockets and put it into theirs." Nor did he doubt that the Republicans would attack slavery in the states. To Winston, submission was worse than plunging into the abyss of disunion, "or into the still more dread abyss of civil war." If he had to choose between the rule of a "Southern King" and Northern "Mobocracy," he indicated strong preference for the former. The Union's days were numbered, Winston predicted.[71]

Professor Minor characterized the Southern extremists in a letter to his daughter.

I trust, however, Lamar, & Keitt & Edmondson, & Hindman, & Tombs [sic], are not fair samples of the Southron in Congress. Otherwise the world might well esteem us at a stage of civilization inferior to the

---

[70] William M. Blackford to John B. Minor, Dec. 5, 1859, MS, John B. Minor Papers, Alderman Library, University of Virginia.
[71] Frank V. Winston to John B. Minor, March 10, 1860, MS, *ibid*.

Muscovite, or even the Hindoos. Men who thus, by their unbridled insolence, bring reproach upon a whole section, & condemn the peace of the Country, deserve the severest censure, and sooner or later will receive their desserts.

But he thought that the Republicans were even " meaner " than the " bloated bullies from the South." [72]

Thus in the months before the national conventions assembled, there was a searching discussion by men of all parties to ascertain where the true interests of Virginia lay. Nor did the end of the presidential campaign terminate the argument, which continued till April, 1861.

The projected Southern conference, initiated by South Carolina, met a cool reception in Virginia, where it was predicted that not a single border state would send delegates to such a meeting. Delaware, Maryland, Kentucky, and Missouri would not touch the proposition "with a forty foot pole." Virginia's interests were with her sister border states—for " weal or woe." The recent legislative junket of the Kentucky and Tennessee legislatures was noted with approval in Virginia. Indeed, this point of view may be summed up in the words of a leading Richmond paper: Virginia's policy should be one of " wise and masterly inactivity." [73]

An eminent Virginian, Alexander H. H. Stuart,[74] wrote Henry C. Carey and others concerning a theme much discussed by historians—the supposed divergence of labor systems of North and South. Stuart thought that no such clash existed, that the economies of the sections were harmonious. His chief regret was in the abandonment of the national policies of Webster, Clay, and Everett. He was alarmed at certain signs— " only yesterday the Virginia House passed an appropriation of $500,000 to arm the State." Another bad sign was the presence

[72] John B. Minor to Mary L. Minor, April 6, 1860, MS, *ibid.* See also letter from " A Slaveholder " to John Sherman, Lynchburg, Va., Dec. 10, 1859, MS, John Sherman Papers, Library of Congress.

[73] Richmond *Whig*, Feb. 3, 1860. This paper flatly opposed the objects of such a conference. It argued that whatever aggression against Southern rights existed had been committed long before John Brown's raid, which incident did not justify secession. The eminent scientist, Matthew F. Maury, analyzed the South's grievances and favored a Southern council of " sages " to define Southern rights. Maury to Bishop J. H. Otey, Dec. 30, 1859, Jan. 16, 1860, MSS, M. F. Maury Papers, Library of Congress.

[74] *D. A. B.*, XVIII, 160-161.

in Richmond of a South Carolina Commissioner: it all boded "a bloody future." [75]

There was a distinct consciousness of Virginia's position as a border state, and a realization that in a Southern confederacy she would be in a most dangerous strategic location. This attitude was expressed a few years earlier by a perspicacious youth, A. H. Jackson of Weston, Virgina, Valedictorian of the graduating class of 1857 at Washington College. The youthful speaker exhorted the college graduates to remain in the ancient Commonwealth, against which charges had been brought of decline in wealth, population, and civilization. These charges were not true, he declared. But with dark and accurate prophecy the young Virginian warned that there was another reason why those who wished to serve Virginia should remain. "And remember, that if it ever comes to pass that the difficulties between the North and the South are to be settled by the sword, this will be the battle ground; so, if you are patriotically inclined, you can have an opportunity of dying for the rights of the South, not in Kansas—but in Virginia. . . ." [76]

This theme was reiterated during 1860. The Richmond *Whig* predicted that Virginia would be the greatest sufferer in the event of a dissolution of the Union.[77] One of the most eloquent statements containing this viewpoint was made in the Virginia Opposition convention by John S. Pendleton. He asserted that Virginia must speak out emphatically. She owned more Negroes by far than any other state, and because of this fact and her long, exposed frontier, she was therefore far more concerned than any other state in the enforcement of the fugitive slave laws. With sarcasm, Pendleton affirmed that Virginia should be the judge of her grievances, "quite as well as even South Carolina." Moreover, he was entirely satisfied with the fact that Virginia was at that time the center of the "freest, greatest, best government on earth." Pendleton graphically described the plight of Virginia after disunion. In the new scheme of

[75] Richmond *Whig*, Jan. 31, 1860. "You see Memminger is here. For God's sake give us a rallying point or disunion may follow." A. H. H. Stuart to J. J. Crittenden, Jan. 22, 1860, MS, Crittenden Papers.

[76] Lexington *Gazette*, July 9, 1857.

[77] Ruffin was incensed at the course of the Richmond *Whig*, which he deemed submissionist. Craven, *Edmund Ruffin, Southerner*, p. 190.

things the once powerful Commonwealth would sink to the status of " a miserable border province of a third rate Confederation." Virginia would be comparable to the German municipalities, in that she would become a battleground for years, perhaps centuries. " In the name of God, can any man tell me what Virginia is to gain by disunion? " The duty of Virginia was first to herself, and then to the North as well as the South, according to his analysis. And it was ironical that the border slave states, which had the largest material interest in the matter of the fugitive slave law, " were of all the Southern states most opposed to disunion." [78]

This side of the debate was presented emphatically after the presidential nominations had been made, usually in behalf of John Bell's candidacy.[79] Unionism and moderation were the keynotes of the Constitutional Union party, and because that party was numerically strong in Virginia and other border slave states, it may be of profit to consider further the arguments set forth in Bell's interest. Although many names had been suggested as agreeable to the party in Virginia, such as Everett, Scott, Bell, Hunt, Crittenden, Rives, Graham, Stuart, Winthrop, Fuller of Pennsylvania, Thompson, Summers, and Goggin (the name of Botts was pointedly omitted), when Bell received the nomination he was cordially supported by the party press.[80]

The heaviest fire from the Constitutional Unionists was directed against Breckinridge. By far the stronger of the two Democratic candidates in Virginia, he was linked with the disunionists of the lower South—Yancey, Rhett, and Keitt. Copious quotations from Breckinridge supporters in the far South were reprinted in the Bell papers to " prove " the charge. An example of this strategy may be cited in the publication of

[78] Richmond *Whig*, March 9, 1860.

[79] Occasionally a Bell supporter expressed the view that Lincoln's election would be a menace to the South. The Lynchburg *Virginian*, Aug. 7, 1860, said: ". . . we could not long endure the reign of a party whose existence would be ' a standing proclamation of Southern inferiority,'—a party, led and controlled by such political knaves and fanatics as Horace Greeley."

[80] Richmond *Whig*, May 1, 1860, for suggested candidates. That rare specimen of 1860, a neutral journal, congratulated the Constitutional Union party on the high character of the nominees, Bell and Everett. Richmond *Daily Dispatch*, May 11, 1860.

the Montgomery *Mail*'s "formula" for breaking up the Union: first divide Lincoln's opposition by placing three candidates in the field, which would assure his election; the South would then refuse to permit his appointment of federal officials; the United States would attempt to enforce the laws; somebody would be shot, and civil war would then envelop the land.[81]

Though the historian of West Virginia has written that citizens of western Virginia were unimpressed by the possibility of secession as demonstrated by the heavy Breckinridge vote,[82] one John S. S. Herr of Taylor county, wrote the Attorney General of the United States that prosecutions for "high misdemeanors" against secessionists were in order. He forwarded an enclosure from the Raleigh *Register,* a Bell paper, of quotations from Yancey, John T. Morgan, George Gayle, David Hubbard, Robert D. Gayle, and George D. Johnson, which he believed was proof of conspiracy and meditation of conspiracy. Under the precedent of the John Fries case, 1798, Herr asked Attorney-General Black to take action against these incipient secessionists of the lower South.[83] The attitude of the Bell men towards Douglas was one of increasing cordiality as the campaign progressed, especially after it became clear that their Unionist views were identical.[84]

The Bell press stressed border-state psychology in their appeal for a ringing Union declaration by Kentucky, Maryland, Missouri, and Virginia on election day. It was hoped that such an emphatic vote would produce a strong moral effect on the lower South—an effect which might "stay them in their mad course." If South Carolina should secede, the quiet man in his home who had not bothered about politics would be jolted severely. Let Virginia answer the Breckinridge demand for a "united South"

---

[81] Alexandria *Gazette,* Aug. 3, 1860.

[82] C. H. Ambler, *West Virginia, The Mountain State* (New York, 1940), p. 301.

[83] John S. S. Herr to Jeremiah S. Black, Aug. 2, 1860, MS, Black Papers, Library of Congress.

[84] Alexander H. H. Stuart to Blanton Duncan, Aug. 23, 1860. Stuart wrote editorials in the Richmond *Whig* to establish an *entente cordiale* between the Bell and Douglas parties. He noted with pleasure the bitter schism in the Democratic party. Stuart made the interesting prediction that Douglas would become the leader of the Union party, after he had supported Bell in the electoral college. MS, John Bell Papers, Library of Congress.

by voting for a Union man. The question was put to the " propertied, solid men " as to what they had to gain from a secessionist policy. War? The Bell press rang the changes on the theme that Virginia would be the battleground of civil war, that every hill and valley would run red with blood of Virginians. But if the state voted for Bell the cotton states would be discouraged.[85]

From western Virginia came a pessimistic appraisal of the situation of the border land in a cotton confederacy. This writer feared that property in Negroes would be lost—they would run away or would be sold South at ruinously low prices. Virginia was not a cotton-growing nor yet a manufacturing region. In the event of secession, " None dreams of a peaceful division." Border-line incidents and psychology were not wanted by Virginians, who would run all the risks and bear heavy expenses of war, and who would obtain none of the advantages deriving from such a conflict. Indeed, the border would become comparable to " bleeding " Kansas. The cotton states were the villains of the piece: they knew of the strong arms and resources of the border states, but for Virginia the outcome of cooperation with them would be prostration.[86] Francis H. Pierpont of Fairmont, a representative of northwestern Virginia, industrial-minded and hating the " slaveholding oligarchy," supported Bell and Everett.[87]

Perhaps the most articulate and unorthodox of the supporters of John Bell in Virginia was John Minor Botts, whose two addresses delivered in October contained ideas not frequently expressed in the Virginia of 1860. No prominent Virginian assumed a more uncompromising and even bitter Unionist position than he did.[88]

As Virginians prepared to go to the polls to cast their votes, they were solemnly informed that voting in this election was likely to be the most important event in their lives. " If you desire to avert dire calamities and nip treason in the bud, vote for Bell." So voters were instructed by the leading party organ.

[85] Richmond *Whig*, Oct. 19, 1860.
[86] Kanawha *Republican* in Alexandria *Gazette*, Nov. 8, 1860.
[87] C. H. Ambler, *Francis H. Pierpont* (Chapel Hill, 1937), pp. 65-70.
[88] For Botts' speeches, see *Daily Richmond Enquirer*, Oct. 4, 1860; *New York Tribune*, Oct. 31, 1860.

If the state should go for Breckinridge, " we will be compelled to look the frightful question in the face." Every man was urged to weigh his present advantages against the future. This election was the greatest contest in American history, said the Richmond *Whig*. Lest Virginians forget, it was again pointed out to them that if a southern confederacy were formed, Virginia would, as a border state, have all the fighting to do—all to gratify the " whims of the Cotton States." Slavery would best be preserved by voting the Bell ticket.[89] ·Other Bell journals were prepared for the worst, but before election day urged that Virginia give Lincoln a chance.[90] Thus did the Constitutional Union party present its case to the Virginia electorate.

It will be noted that the destruction of the slave trade was predicted in the event of secession. Virginia would be adversely affected. The Lynchburg *Virginian*, a Bell paper, condemned secession on the ground that the African slave-trade would be reopened and that Virginia's trade with the South would be ruined. It was pointed out that Virginia Negroes were sent each year in large quantities to the cotton and rice states. Clearly Virginia's interests and those of the lower South did not coincide in this matter.[91] Governor John Letcher's political organ argued along much the same lines. The Lexington *Valley Star*, which supported Douglas, assailed the Yancey disunionists because it believed that they would reopen the slave trade, and by importation from Africa secure slaves at $200 to $300 instead of paying $1000 to $1200 per head for Virginia Negroes. The scheming and mercenary secessionists were ready to pocket the difference in prices. This was condemned by the " lofty " Virginia paper. " What is there in such a policy for slave-holders of Rockbridge? For several years the

[89] Richmond *Whig* in Alexandria *Gazette*, Nov. 3, 1860.

[90] Charlottesville *Review*, Nov. 2, 1860. The Staunton *Spectator*, Oct. 23, 1860, pointed to a probable anti-Lincoln majority in Congress. " To break up the Government under these circumstances, simply because Lincoln should be elected, would be adding madness to treason." Lincoln would be unfortunate, but the cotton states a greater force for evil. Bell would avoid disunion and civil war. General Winfield Scott, a native Virginian, urged Virginia not to fly to unknown evils. He dismissed the territorial issue as impractical. General Scott was for Bell. Winfield Scott's " Memorandum," New York, Oct. 29, 1860, MS, Buchanan Papers, Historical Society of Pennsylvania.

[91] Lynchburg *Virginian* in Washington *National Intelligencer*, Nov. 1, 1860.

State Revenue of the county has been paid by the sale of her slaves. Open the Slave Trade and what will our negroes be worth?" The only reason a Southern confederacy was desired was to secure higher cotton and cheaper labor. The *Valley Star* assailed those who, to gain " filthy lucre," would break up the " fair Union." [92] The prices of Negroes were already declining, from 24 per cent to 50 per cent caused by the uncertainty of the future.[93] This pro-Union argument, while not based on the highest ethical principles, was an eminently practical matter, and was doubtless understood by slaveholding Virginians. Thus both the interstate slave trade and the " peculiar " institution itself would be much safer inside the Union than outside.[94]

It now remains to describe the Democratic campaign in Virginia. The state's role in the Charleston and Baltimore conventions was complicated by the conflicting ambitions of Henry A. Wise [95] and Robert M. T. Hunter,[96] the former having gained strength because of his activity in the John Brown episode. Wise was a militant advocate of Southern rights in general and Congressional protection to slavery in particular. Hunter's faction espoused a moderate position with regard to the sectional issue; the lapse of time obscured the Brown raid, and by clever manipulation thirty-five delegates to Charleston were chosen favorable to Hunter's candidacy. Douglas hoped that the Virginia delegation would eventually support him, and, conversely, it was expected that after the elimination of Douglas, Hunter would be the legatee. Although a majority of the delegation was for Hunter, some of his supporters were lukewarm, and other members favored Douglas from the outset.

At Charleston the Virginians, after a caucus, agreed to support the lower South's territorial demands, an action which was contrary to the Virginia state convention's earlier reaffirmation of the Cincinnati Platform. After the secession at Charleston, most Virginia delegates remained, hoping for a compromise on the basis of the Tennessee Resolutions and a Southern nominee. Nor was there much enthusiasm among Virginia Democrats

[92] Lexington *Valley Star*, Sept. 13, 1860.
[93] *Ibid.*, Oct. 11, 1860.
[94] Lynchburg *Daily Virginian*, Oct. 27, 1860.
[95] *D. A. B.*, XX, 423-425.
[96] *Ibid.*, IX, 403-405.

for the Seceders' Convention in Richmond, and some bitterly condemned it. Hunter's position at Baltimore was difficult, inasmuch as he sought the nomination and endorsed the demands of the lower South at the same time. The failure of the Baltimore convention to seat the seceders from Alabama and Louisiana was the cause of the withdrawal of the Virginia delegation, which joined the Seceders' Convention in the same city, and participated in the nomination of Breckinridge and Lane.[97]

Virginia's course in the Democratic conventions was reviewed critically by R. H. Glass, editor of the Lynchburg *Republican*. He declared that before the Charleston convention most of the Virginia Democratic press had endorsed a restatement of the Cincinnati Platform of 1856. Wise and his friends took a contrary attitude, demanding Congressional protection to property in the territories. Upon that clear issue the Virginia delegates were chosen, and at least two-thirds of them favored the Cincinnati Platform. At that time, wrote Glass, Douglas was the leading candidate and was expected to win the nomination. For two days at Charleston the Virginia delegation held to that

[97] Henry T. Shanks, *The Secession Movement in Virginia* (Richmond, 1932), pp. 103-109. See also " Journal and Debates of the Virginia Delegation at Charleston," which disclosed that Virginians voted to consult with the Southern delegations, and Lewis E. Harvie represented the delegation. Harvie reported back that he had told the conference that Virginia was ready to unite with the South to protect her rights inside or outside the Union. R. H. Glass fought the slavery-protection plank, and also opposed further consultation with Southern states. He feared that unless the platform was sufficiently broad, that the party and the Union would be dissolved. Muscoe R. H. Garnett favored quitting the convention on April 30. " We have waited, and submitted, and dilly-dallied long enough. We have already been subjected to a John Brown raid. I don't want to submit to a Northern Democratic raid." To which Barbour replied that Virginia had not been sent to form a new organization. He denied that a Southern candidate could be elected. He opposed making the territorial issue. But he and others were in the minority of the delegation. (Richmond *Examiner*, Aug. 15, 16, 1860. See also, C. H. Ambler, ed., *Correspondence of R. M. T. Hunter, 1826-1876, A. H. A. Report*, II, 280-337.) Hunter, who had the active or passive support of many prominent Southerners, including Toombs, Hammond, and A. H. Stephens, alienated the radicals by his course at Charleston. (R. B. Rhett, Jr., to W. P. Miles, May 12, 1860, and W. H. Trescot to Miles, May 8, 1860, MSS, Miles Papers, Southern Historical Collection, University of North Carolina.) "M. H. G[arnett]." was in a quandary after Charleston. He considered Seward's election a certainty, but meanwhile did not know with what faction to act. He was bitter against Wise's " agents," whom he charged with breaking up the party at any cost, to defeat " Robert." (To R. M. T. Hunter, Jr., Loretto, Va., May 11, 1860, MS, R. M. T. Hunter Papers, Alderman Library, University of Virginia.)

position, and then to Glass' "astonishment," reversed themselves. He could not accept this change, even to aid Hunter's candidacy. Virginia remained after Alabama had left the Charleston convention, and balloted fifty-seven times for a candidate "*upon the Cincinnati Platform.*" It was his opinion that Virginia's shift on the platform issue had encouraged the cotton states to secede, in the belief that Virginia would follow. Glass condemned the vacillation of the Virginia delegation, which " lost her influence and prestige and precipitated a disruption of the Party, which might have been averted." [98]

In summary and conclusion of his lengthy letter, Glass severely criticized recent events in the Democratic party. Although he did not hold Douglas and his faction blameless, he asserted:

I give it as my deliberate opinion that the Democratic party has been wantonly and recklessly broken up, and I believe the scheme had its origin among certain disunion politicians in Alabama, and its consummation in Senatorial intrigues in Washington. It has been broken up, not upon any principle, because that was not involved in Baltimore, but mainly because the disorganizing and disunion delegations from two states were not admitted to seats upon the floor of a Convention from which they had wantonly, factiously severed their connection in Charleston, and whose disruption they desired in Baltimore.

This sharp critic found the party's errors irremediable. The only hope lay in an election in the House of Representatives, to achieve which Douglas must carry the North, while Breckinridge must receive the solid electoral vote of the South. Otherwise, Glass accurately forecast, both would be hopelessly beaten. To accomplish this purpose Glass supported the Breckinridge-Lane ticket, as best able to carry Virginia. He urged a single Democratic slate of electors, who were to be left free to cast the vote of the state as the best interests of the party and country required. [99]

Indeed, there were others who expressed regret that an issue

[98] New York *Herald*, May 5, 1860, agreed that the Virginia delegation abandoned principle by vacillation on this issue.

[99] Richmond *Examiner*, July 10, 1860. In commenting on this plain-spoken letter, the *Examiner* editorially said that Glass had used too strong language, and that he harmed those whom he professed to support. (*Ibid.*) Charles W. Russell of Wheeling, Va., a delegate to Charleston, wrote that he condemned the seceders. (Russell to R. M. T. Hunter, May 19, 1860, Ambler, *Correspondence of R. M. T. Hunter, A. H. A. Report*, II, 328.)

had been raised between the Gulf states and Douglas. Said the Richmond *Examiner*: "We thought that the election of Douglas was far better than the election of Lincoln, even with his position; and we thought that the catastrophe of a Black Republican election would be rendered more probable by raising the issue." The border slave states were thus forced to choose between the "united Democracy of the South" and "the powerless and yielding conservative minority in the North." [100]

It appears that there had existed some tendency among Virginia Democrats to accept Douglas as the party candidate, but after the emergence of two party nominees, most of the leaders and party presses swung sharply to Breckinridge. However, there was a minority faction which stood by Douglas to the end. Among them was Governor John Letcher, who greatly deprecated the party division,[101] and Congressman W. G. Brown, who recommended "great forbearance" on the part of all, in case of Lincoln's election.[102] Efforts to harmonize the factions failed, and a Douglas convention met in Staunton, August 16, which placed a slate of electors in the field, and expressed a preference for Bell over Breckinridge.[103] Support for Douglas proved to be sporadic and geographically scattered. His strength was located in the cities, in a part of the Valley of Virginia, and in a few trans-Allegheny areas. The Douglas campaign was dramatized by the appearance of their principal for addresses in Norfolk, Petersburg, Richmond, and points in the Valley.[104]

But the issue was clarified. Henceforth no more wavering was discernible among the Breckinridge partisans, and throughout the remainder of the campaign the *Examiner* became quite uncompromising. Senator R. M. T. Hunter, before the Breckin-

[100] Richmond *Examiner*, July 27, 1860.

[101] John Letcher to Benjamin Crawford and M. G. Harman, Aug. 22, 1860. Richmond *Examiner*, Sept. 3, 1860. Letcher to Messrs. McNulty, Beach, *et al.*, Oct. 21, 1860. Washington *States and Union*, Oct. 31, 1860. But an observer wrote from Letcher's home town that he did not believe the Governor's avowal of Douglas to be important. J. W. Massie to R. M. T. Hunter, Aug. 28, 1860, MS, R. M. T. Hunter Papers.

[102] Baltimore *American*, July 16, 1860. Congressman John S. Millson supported Douglas. He favored acquiescence in Lincoln's election. Washington *National Intelligencer*, Oct. 11, 1860.

[103] Richmond *Examiner*, Aug. 20, 1860.

[104] Douglas had the support of both Harrisonburg papers, and carried Rockingham county by a large vote. New York *Herald*, Aug. 14, 1860. For Douglas' vote in Virginia, see Shanks, p. 117.

ridge state convention, August 17, at Charlottesville, summed up the possible results for the South should any of the three opposing forces be victorious. The Republican party he characterized as undisguisedly and relentlessly opposed to slavery. Their future attacks on the institution would be abetted by a loose construction of the Constitution. If Bell should win, it would mean but a temporary check to the Republicans, because his party's consolidationist Constitutional ideas would ultimately be useful to Free Soil majorities. Douglas' election would be an endorsement of his territorial views, and would proclaim the impotence of the Constitution to protect property in the territories.[105]

The advocates of ultra Southern rights of course warmly supported the Breckinridge-Lane nominations. The Richmond *Daily Enquirer* militantly defended the " noble and gifted" William L. Yancey. It was ridiculous to charge him with disunionism—if " equal rights " prevailed. But Yancey as the "bold and powerful champion of the rights, property, and lives of the Southern people, will prove a veritable ' Moses to the second exodus.' " These words surely could not have convinced many of Yancey's Unionism. Southern unity in the face of peril was the argument most emphasized in the closing weeks of the campaign. Henry A. Wise wrote that only the Breckinridge ticket could be considered pro-slavery; the Douglas ticket was splitting the majority in the South, and was a short-cut to Republicanism. Wise warned Virginians that the South would soon have a " Black flag hoisted over our heads," and his answer was unification of the slave states. The former Governor would not " concede, nor secede "; he would resist—in the Union. First he would appeal to Virginia; if he received no response, he would appeal successively to North Carolina, South Carolina, Georgia, and the other Southern states—he was ready to enlist with " Little Florida " to resist " black " Douglas' promised coercion. Let each state jump into the fray. Wise foresaw a widespread civil war, with the North combating Southern sympathizers there, while the South would battle " traitors in our midst." He was frankly concerned for his Negroes, his property, and his political rights.[106]

[105] Richmond *Examiner*, Aug. 25, 1860.
[106] Wise to C. B. Harrison, *et al.*, Sept. 1, 1860. Augusta (Ga.) *Daily*

A fairly complete picture of the Virginia extremist position may be derived from the files of the Richmond *Enquirer*. The political organ of Henry A. Wise, it often paid its respects to Northern "philanthropists—honest, but crazy fanatics," to the "agrarians" who wished to seize the "fair Southern fields," to the "anti-slavery Political Economist" and the "Irrepressible slavery demagogue." [107] The *Enquirer* pronounced the presidential election "the most important and exciting . . . in which American citizens have ever participated . . . ." The South would be embittered against Virginia if the Old Dominion should cast her vote for Bell. The spectre of civil war within her confines was conjured up, a result which would follow willingness of Bell men to take up arms for Lincoln.[108] What would Lincoln do in office? As argued elsewhere, the *Enquirer* attributed Machiavellian powers to the Republican candidate. He would insidiously employ the federal patronage to build up in every state a powerful Republican party, which would soon openly champion abolition. Lincoln would convert the border slave states into free states, a fate worse than rapine and war.[109]

Hardly less violent was the Richmond *Examiner*, formerly a mild exponent of Southern rights, which interpreted the October elections in the North as proof of the strength there of the "ruthless majority of Free-Soilers." The unfortunate trend in the North was encouraged by the political divisions at the South. The *Examiner* heard Bell men praising Republicans, and sorrowfully observed Bell and Douglas men recommending submission: worst of all, they sustained "one of the candidates in insolent threats to coerce the South." All this had an effect at the North, which would cost Douglas the Northwest.[110]

Economic issues were involved in the Breckinridge candidacy.

Constitutionalist, Sept. 29, 1860. His views were set forth in detail in a speech which filled thirteen columns of the *Daily Richmond Enquirer*, Oct. 10, 11, 12, 1860. His biographer commented: "The views of Wise were considered peculiar, as he favored neither secession nor peaceable acquiescence in the triumph of the antislavery and sectional party." Barton H. Wise, *The Life of Henry A. Wise* (New York, 1899), p. 267. The New York *Tribune* (semiweekly), Oct. 26, 1860, alluded to "Furioso" Wise.

[107] Richmond *Daily Enquirer*, Sept. 29, 1860.
[108] *Ibid.*, Oct. 30, 1860.
[109] *Ibid.*, July 10, 1860.
[110] Richmond *Examiner*, Oct. 12, 1860. An allusion to Douglas' Norfolk doctrine.

Virginians were urged to vote for those who had given them the " most lucrative commerce the world ever saw," for those " who freed the government from a corrupt alliance with banking and manufacturing." The Democratic party had developed agriculture and commerce, had protected capital from a " meddling Federal government," and labor from the " blighting touch " of the Opposition's policy. Douglas and Bell were respectively recent and old advocates of the " hateful and ruinous protective policy." A vote for Breckinridge was a vote for free trade, antibank and " State Rights Democracy." [111] One of the speakers at a Douglas rally in Richmond was reported to have warned the working classes that they would have no place in a Southern slaveholding confederation. Thus it appeared that for the first time, in addition to sectional warfare, a war of classes was to be inaugurated in Virginia.[112]

At the last minute bold-faced warnings appeared against " Roorbacks." People were advised to " Trust nobody disseminating anti-Southern rumors and apologizing for the Black Republicans." [113] A vote for either Douglas or Bell was a vote for surrender to Lincoln: " For the first time in history a Presidential election will not quiet the country." A defeat for Breckinridge in Virginia will be taken at the North " as an abandonment of all thought of ever using State authority to stay Federal oppression." Breckinridge alone directly opposed Lincoln in principle. Disturbances were feared at the South, and a conference of Southern states was urged. If Virginia refused to lead, she would be " dragged along and forced to follow." [114] Henry A. Wise declared that Lincoln's election would serve notice on the South that Constitutional rights were to be disregarded. Wise offered a set of resolutions calling for the creation of local committees of safety, in each magisterial district, and for the calling of a state convention immediately

[111] Richmond *Examiner*, Nov. 2, 1860. John Tyler, Jr., wrote that he was working for Breckinridge, but Lincoln's election would " throw off the Planting States." Tyler was in reduced financial condition. Could he not have an " agency " in the office of the Postmaster General? He conceded he had been addicted to the " bottle," but had " sworn off." This was difficult because he lived among extremely " sociable " folk. Tyler to Joseph Holt, July 21, 1860, MS, Holt Papers, Library of Congress.

[112] Richmond *Examiner*, Aug. 4, 1860.

[113] *Ibid.*, Nov. 5, 1860.

[114] *Ibid.*, Nov. 6, 1860.

following the announcement of Lincoln's election. These " Princess Anne " resolves, which were adopted by the meeting, were denounced by the Richmond *Whig* as the recommendation and beginning of revolution in Virginia.[115] The Norfolk *Southern Argus* reprinted with approval an editorial from the Montgomery *Mail* which declared that every aggrieved state should withdraw at once from association " with the despicable hounds that bark at her . . . . " [116] The Breckinridge press answered the question, " Where Shall Virginia Go? " in clear language —with the South.[117] But Edmund Ruffin was discouraged over the prospects in his native Virginia, where he found too many who were willing to accept " Black Republicanism, the tariff, and the nigger." [118] And Wise's biographer has written that " the vast majority of the people of the State . . . deprecated war in any event; and who were, moreover, opposed to anticipating any overt act on the part of the Federal Government." [119]

While that may have been true, Virginia authorities were preparing for any eventuality. In his first message to the legislature, Governor Letcher had recommended appropriations for military preparedness of the state.[120] The General Assembly had complied with his request by the passage of appropriations for that purpose.[121] In May the Governor and Colonel Francis H. Smith of the Virginia Military Institute were reported to be in Springfield, Massachusetts, on business related to the arming of the state.[122] In the fall, the Clarksville *Tobacco Plant* described the organization of the " Roanoke Guards," which were to combat the " crouching beast " and the " fell spirit of fanaticism." [123] At the end of October, Governor Letcher announced that ninety companies of cavalry were reported to him as nearing readiness, and that four batteries would be at Richmond within the week.[124]

[115] B. H. Wise, p. 266; Shanks, p. 125.
[116] Norfolk *Southern Argus*, Oct. 27, 1860.
[117] *Ibid.*, Oct. 29, 1860.
[118] Avery Craven, *Edmund Ruffin*, p. 185.
[119] Wise, p. 266.
[120] Lexington *Gazette*, Jan. 12, 1860.
[121] *Acts Passed by the General Assembly of Virginia, 1859-60* . . . (Richmond, 1860).
[122] Alexandria *Gazette*, May 3, 1860.
[123] Quoted in New York *Tribune* (semi-weekly), Sept. 18, 1860.
[124] Washington *States and Union*, Oct. 30, 1860.

These "warlike" preparations on Letcher's part did not escape notice in the North. The hostile New York *Tribune* said: "He affects to deprecate and deplore the course of the Southern secessionists, but says that Virginia must be ready to make common cause with them if they are pushed by the General Government." [125] Henry A. Wise's activity in the organization of Committees of Safety occasioned a difference of opinion between him and his successor, the New York *Tribune* noted. Both influential Breckinridge journals in Richmond discussed the imminence of war. The *Examiner* descanted upon the beauties of the drawn sword, with the hilt in the hand. This paper believed the days of the Union were numbered.[126] Virginia would be powerless to prevent a catastrophic civil war if Lincoln won. The *Enquirer* advised the lower South to strike early, and to have no fears regarding Virginia's course.[127]

At the extreme opposite pole from the Breckinridge party in Virginia was that handful which composed the Republican party. The Republicans were execrated by the press above all others. In general it may be said that the Republicans of 1860 were no more welcome in Virginia than the Communist party of eighty years later, and were accorded about the same degree of toleration. The Republican State Convention assembled in Wheeling, May 2, despite the bitter denunciation of the Virginia press,[128] to appoint delegates to the national convention and to adopt a platform. The argument against undiversified economy paralleled closely that of William C. Rives, but was couched in less guarded phrases. The cotton and sugar planters had a monopoly and a market abroad for their products. They had

[125] New York *Tribune* (semi-weekly), Oct. 30, 1860.

[126] Richmond *Examiner*, Oct. 3, 16, 1860.

[127] *Daily Richmond Enquirer*, Oct. 15, 1860. T. L. Hunter of King George Court House wrote just before election that he had always had hard times—the hardest under Buchanan, and he did not dread Lincoln, revolution, and secession. His more prosperous neighbors were more concerned than he. "But there is no danger of more stirring times. Virginia is prepared to submit." Hunter to R. M. T. Hunter, Nov. 2, 1860, MS, R. M. T. Hunter Papers, University of Virginia.

[128] Richmond *Examiner*, April 27, 1860, hoped that the people of Wheeling, for the honor of the state, would not allow "a convention of conspirators against our institutions to meet in that city." This was compared to John Brown's raid. The Richmond *Whig*, May 8, 1860, promised tar, feathers, and rope, for the Wheeling "nigger-worshippers"·should they attempt to hold their 1864 convention in Richmond.

made war on the manufacturing interest of the non-cotton and non-sugar growing states, in order to compel them to grow foodstuffs for cheap sale in the far South. The Virginia Republicans condemned such a system. They favored a fair reward for white labor, and a development of the "mechanic arts" by a "judicious" tariff on foreign products. A tariff would also aid the producers of wheat, corn, oats, and stock, by creating a demand for their products.

The real cause of the unhappy condition of the country was the aggression of "slave capitalists" against white labor and rights. The Republican party would protect personal as well as property rights, a slogan heard much in twentieth-century politics. The oft-discussed sectionalism of Virginia manifested itself in the Republican platform. Non-slaveholding farmers of western Virginia, mechanics, and poor laborers were burdened with taxation which benefited the eastern Virginia slaveholders. Capital, in the form of slaves, rendered but $300,000, under the system in force; if slaves were taxed as other property $1,300,000 would be yielded. Moreover, tobacco, corn, wheat, and oats—products of slave-labor—were exempt from taxation; but cattle, hogs, and sheep, produced in the non-slaveholding portion of Virginia, were heavily taxed. Eastern Virginia had built canals and railroads in that section to facilitate the transportation of their products to the seaboard market; in the west oats and wheat must be converted to stock, which again was heavily taxed. A slave under twelve years of age went untaxed, whatever his worth, but lambs and calves were not exempt. If a bull or a steer be adjudged a menace, the state might kill the dangerous animal without compensation; but if a Negro were killed by the state, his owner was reimbursed. Because of slaveowning, it was estimated that ten thousand eastern Virginians were equal to forty thousand western Virginians, so far as repesentation in the legislature was concerned. The Republicans protested that these "outrages" had been perpetrated in the name of democracy. The Republican party was much needed, to rectify these abuses. It was conserative, Union-loving, and construed the Constitution as had the founders.

The attitude of the Republican party of Virginia was anti-slavery in tone, but not abolitionist. Slavery was recognized as under the sovereignty of the states; it was a local and not a national problem. The territories should be free. As to the specific question of slavery in Virginia, it was recognized as property, but the Republicans believed that public morals and prosperity were " deplorably injured by slavery . . . ." The Augusta county memorial of 1829, which declared that slavery's effect was injurious, was quoted with approval. The decline of Virginia was a corollary of slavery, and " . . . until we make some provision for the gradual riddance of this consuming evil, we never will regain our natural position as a State of the confederacy." But as long as slavery was law, it should be upheld. One of the planks of the platform endorsed the plan, espoused by the Blairs, for colonization of free Negroes in the American tropics, where a strong Negro colony might interchange products with the United States. Thus white Americans would be relieved of competition with blacks, and advantage accrue to all. The Republicans placed themselves on record as for equality under law, free opinion and speech, and against discrimination in favor of privileged property.[129]

As a bitterly hated minority group in Virginia, the Republicans might well champion freedom of discussion.[130] One of the most widely publicized incidents of the campaign was that of the Occoquan flag-pole, which ended " happily." It appears that on July 4, a group of " black " Republicans, who lived in the vicinity of Occoquan, erected a flag-pole and raised a flag bearing the names of Lincoln and Hamlin. The Republicans, who were said to number sixty in the community, defied public opinion by asserting that none was brave enough to lower their flag. An indignation meeting was held, which decided to destroy the pole, whereupon the Republicans appealed to the Governor for protection. Although cavalry was dispatched to the village, it did nothing when James Jackson of Fairfax and others solemnly chopped down the pole. It was reported that some heckling accompanied the act, and as the pole fell, the

---

[129] Wheeling *Intelligencer* in New York *Herald*, May 5, 1860. M. Blair spoke to this " first great demonstration of the Republican party in Virginia."

[130] A Pennsylvanian, Albert Patterson, was reported to have attended a wood-chopping in Marshall county, Virginia. Patterson said that " old Brown was a fool and Governor Wise no better." " Let's hang him," cried a group of enraged Virginians. Fortunately he was rescued by some Pennsylvanians. Montgomery (Ala.) *Daily Confederation*, Feb. 23, 1860.

crowd gave three cheers for Lincoln and Hamlin. This incident was widely reported by the newspapers, and although a small matter, it irritated both sides of the sectional controversy. The New York *Herald* believed it was a trap by which "good people" were to be goaded into violence, on which the Republicans could capitalize in the North.[131]

John C. Underwood of Clarke county had desired in 1857 to colonize Virginia with free labor and to industrialize the state, and the project of the famous Eli Thayer in Virginia was along the same line.[132] In the campaign of 1860, Underwood made stump addresses for Lincoln in Virginia. For example, at Bellton, October 17, Underwood advocated organized, concerted immigration into Virginia. He depicted, in terms suggesting the Helper thesis, the blessings of free labor, which would operate with especial efficacy in western Virginia.[133]

---

[131] Alexandria *Gazette* in Richmond *Daily Examiner*, July 30, 1860. The Boston *Courier* declared that the Occoquan incident made votes for the Republicans, and urged moderation on the South. Quoted in the Lynchburg *Daily Virginian*, Aug. 6, 1860, which replied that when passions were inflamed, it was difficult to restrain men, and recalled that United States officials once were murdered in Boston when performing their constitutional duties. Later, in friendly Wheeling, another Republican flagpole was erected. Richmond *Daily Examiner*, Aug. 9, 1860. The New York *Tribune* (semi-weekly), Oct. 26, 1860, boasted of three "Wide Awake" clubs in Wheeling, with 375 members, in spite of violence.

[132] George Winston Smith, "Civil War Pressure Groups," MS, doctoral dissertation, University of Wisconsin, 1939.

[133] New York *Tribune*, Oct. 23, 1860. Henry C. Carey congratulated Underwood for this speech. (Carey to Underwood, Nov. 1, 1860, MS, John C. Underwood Papers, Library of Congress.) No doubt Virginians would have been further enraged had they known of Underwood's other activities. He was engaged in correspondence with some of the most execrated Northerners. Charles Sumner sent Underwood moral encouragement but no cash in the "glorious contest for Freedom in Virginia." (Sumner to Underwood, May 8, 1860, MS, *ibid.*) Hinton R. Helper urged Underwood to campaign in New York, where "Your voice, as one of the persecuted and proscribed whites of Virginia, would . . . be heard with interest and profit. . . ." (Helper to Underwood, Oct. 22, 1860, MS, *ibid.*) The viewpoint of one abolitionist, Mrs. L. Maria Child, was set forth with engaging frankness: "My zeal is exceeding great to convince the South that immediate, unconditional emancipation would be conducive to their safety and their prosperity." She requested a list of Virginians to whom she could send her antislavery tracts. She already sent her tract, "The Patriarchal Institution," to Governor Wise and Virginia editors. "I hope you will not think me very unamiable, if I confess that I a little enjoyed annoying them by the presentation of a mass of Southern evidence, so little to their liking." (L. Maria Child to Underwood, Oct. 20, 1860, MS, *ibid.*)

Although the Republicans usually met proscription and sometimes violence, and in most counties Lincoln received a blank ballot, occasionally Virginians spoke of him in a rational way. Thus William L. Goggin, candidate for Governor in 1859 and prominent in the Bell party, said of Lincoln in a campaign speech: " . . . I must say that I have ever known him to be a gentleman." He had known him as a member of Congress, and thought Lincoln had been an industrious and respected Representative. "His private as well as public character was free from stain or blemish." [134] Botts had likewise refused to denigrate Lincoln, and occasionally a Virginia newspaper—usually a Bell supporter—had a kind word for the Republican nominee.[135]

Thus the Virginia Republicans were closely related ideologically to their fellow party members in the border states. All placed emphasis on economic development, all stressed that theirs was a white man's party, and all relegated slavery to a place of secondary importance. In Virginia, however, the cleavage on the question of slavery was perhaps more distinct than in Delaware and Maryland.

In connection with the Republican party, the situation in western Virginia during the election of 1860 should be noted. It was generally held in the North that western Virginia was distinctly antislavery, and much sympathy was expressed for the suffering free-soilers there. Persons moving into that section in former years had doubtless brought with them ideas antagonistic to slavery.[136] Yet they were not in evidence during the campaign or at the polls. The correspondent of the New York *Herald* wrote from White Sulphur Springs, Virginia, an analysis of the situation in the western part of the state. He ascertained a grand emancipation scheme, at that time in embryo,

[134] Goggin's speech at Petersburg, New York *Tribune* (semi-weekly), Sept. 7, 1860.

[135] Lynchburg *Daily Virginian*, Aug. 3, 1860, conceded that Lincoln was " a man of talents and character."

[136] One man wrote from Clarksburg, Virginia: " Situated as we are on the borders of two free States, we have some trouble to keep a proper sentiment on the slavery question. We have a mixed population, many coming from free States bringing with them in many cases strong anti-slavery feelings." Gideon D. Camden to R. M. T. Hunter, Feb. 14, 1860, Ambler, *Correspondence of R. M. T. Hunter*, A. H. A. *Report*, II, 291.

which was to be developed the coming winter in western Virginia and which was to be led " by a distinguished gentleman of eastern Virginia, not very sound on slavery."

According to the correspondent, the time for such a plan was propitious for the following reasons: (1) Political party feeling had kept down hostility to slavery, but the chaotic condition of parties minimized this factor; (2) opposition to bearing a share of the expense of defending slave property in the east; (3) completion of several internal improvement projects for which western Virginia had needed eastern support. According to this source, the movement was to be begun at the reform convention which was soon to assemble as required by the Convention of 1851. The same observer saw " demoralization " spreading in the non-slaveholding parts of western Virginia, because of the prestige of the Republicans, and the prospects of their controlling patronage; he found open expression of sympathy and good will for Lincoln's cause.[137]

Yet the historian of these critical years has only partially supported the above analysis, and has disagreed with the extent and depth of antislavery feeling in western Virginia. He has admitted the possibility that the *viva voce* method of voting kept some voices quiet, but has concluded that western Virginia was not sympathetic with antislavery.[138] As early as 1851 Webster warned western Virginia that it could not remain with Virginia if that state seceded. The arguments of Bell journals and orators concerning the exposed situation and isolation of that section had an effect there. Wheeling, the largest city in that area, was only sixty-six miles from Pittsburgh. Although Breckinridge polled many votes in western Virginia, and carried twenty-one counties, each by a majority, it was neither an index of secession nor of antislavery sentiment in western Virginia, where there was no secession party. What happened after 1860, in western Virginia, seems not to have been closely related to the election of that year. McGregor has characterized western Virginians as isolated from, ignorant of, and indifferent to the

[137] New York *Herald*, Sept. 6, 1860. The delegate from Brooke and Hancock counties declared early in 1860 that the people of the border counties would as soon fight against the South as the North, if the former were wrong. Richmond *Daily Dispatch*, Jan. 14, 1860.
[138] J. C. McGregor, *The Disruption of Virginia* (New York, 1922), pp. 66-68.

national political issues of the day. In his opinion, but for the activities of a small group of men in northwestern Virginia, the state might have remained undivided. Breckinridge's votes in western Virginia have been explained on the ground of party regularity. Events beginning in 1861 produced the Republican majorities in western Virginia, and the new state of West Virginia.[139]

KENTUCKY

This state's political complexion as well as its general civilization was largely molded by geology. That section known as the blue grass, which comprised about 5,000 square miles in the northern part of the state, was endowed with rich soil and limestone base. Lexington has been called its capital, and Louisville its metropolis. In the blue grass, a famous horse country, Virginian and English ideals prevailed. Slavery has been painted in its most attractive aspects in this plantation area, an area tied socially and commercially with the South. However, there were also similar links with the nearby city of Cincinnati, and opinion was more diversified in Kentucky than in Virginia. The carboniferous area which supported small farmers, stretched to the Tennessee border, and eastward were the mountains, whose inhabitants although perhaps of " purer " race, were less modified by outside ideas even than those of east Tennessee or western Virginia. Far westward in the triangle created by the Ohio and Mississippi rivers lived the small tobacco-growing planters, the " loud slavocracy " an eminent historian has called them.[140]

Thus it may cause no surprise to find many points of view among Kentuckians. Natives of the state had attained distinction in other parts of the United States. Lincoln and Jefferson Davis were examples, and varying political opinion at home was represented by such men as John J. Crittenden, John C.

---

[139] McGregor, pp. 66-76, 88-89; C. H. Ambler, *Sectionalism in Virginia From 1776 to 1861* (Chicago, 1910), pp. 330-338; Francis H. Pierpont kept to the fore the differences between East and West. Ambler, *Pierpont*, pp. 67-68.

[140] Carl Russell Fish, *The American Civil War*, ed. William E. Smith (New York, 1937), pp. 145-146.

Breckinridge, Robert J. Breckinridge, and Cassius M. Clay. It will be recalled that the eminent James G. Birney was a Kentuckian, and in the period under discussion a furor was created by the " Bereans," a group of militant antislavery men. A few samples of this diverse sentiment as it existed on the eve of the campaign may be helpful.

On December 21, 1859, John C. Breckinridge surveyed the political scene in a speech at Frankfort, Kentucky, which followed his election to the United States Senate for the term beginning March 4, 1861. In a dispassionate manner, the speaker reviewed the territorial question, which he thought was near to a conclusion. The Democratic party was not a great pro-slavery organization, and did not desire to employ patronage to propagate slavery. That party was a Constitutional party. No reasonable man wanted slavery in Nebraska and other northern territories, and as for the territories south " of a certain line," he did not doubt that climate, soil, adjacency to slave states, the Constitution and the Courts would uphold the South there. In this particular, it is significant that the man who would soon lead the Southern Democratic faction as its presidential nominee agreed with the contentions of Crittenden, Douglas, and others as to the effect of climate and soil on the territorial issue.

Yet the Vice President's tone did not continue in this vein. He warned against the Republican party, which he declared was an advocate of Negro equality, and whose goal was emancipation. It was useless to call for peace, when there was no peace. Holding aloft a copy of Helper's *Impending Crisis*, Breckinridge read excerpts to his Kentucky neighbors, and informed them that he feared " blazing border war." A stranger in Washington might mistake President Buchanan for the executive of two hostile Republics. Although the speech pointed to an imminent clash because of inevitable resistance to the Republican program, it closed with an eloquent appeal for the Union. Breckinridge condemned the African slave trade, praised Northern Democrats and minimized the differences between them and the Southerners: they agreed on vital things, in his opinion. It was " the first duty of all who love their country . . . to overthrow the Republican party." [141]

[141] Washington *Constitution*, Jan. 14, 1860.

On January 9, 1860, an open letter was written to John C. Breckinridge by his uncle, Reverend Robert J. Breckinridge, in which sharp exception was taken to some points made by the former in his Frankfort address. Dr. Breckinridge reminded his nephew of the distinguished heritage of the family. He then launched into a bitter and ably written condemnation of extremism and "madness" of parties. Kentucky saw nothing in disunion but calamity, and posterity would execrate any government which permitted secession. Civil war, he predicted, would fail to break up the Union, and declared the lives of "traitors" should not be spared. Further, he foresaw no peace, "along the frontier, along the slave line, or anywhere else." With regard to the Brown raid, its failure gave more security to the slave frontier than before: to any thinking man the incident demonstrated the value of the Union: the guilty were punished in due course of law, without recourse to war of any kind.

Slavery was well entrenched in Kentucky in 1860, said the writer. Yet he thought there were few who held extreme pro-slavery views; others merely tolerated it; while many believed that the growth of the white population would cause the black to fall into insignificance. Kentucky had a 700-mile exposed frontier, and was therefore in greater danger than all the complaining states combined. They had no such frontier. Yet his state had never resorted to threats, and entertained no thought of secession. "Kentucky sees no reason for dissolution of the country, none for secession, none for allowing the passions of the lower South or North to put her into an insecure position." Indeed, an opportunity existed for all the border slave states to act in unison: Maryland, Virginia, Kentucky, and Missouri had suffered losses, and would continue to bear the brunt of the fugitive slave problem. These states should throw their entire influence against rash action, and posterity would condemn them if they failed to do so. Surely the other slave states "ought to forbear what these States disapprove."

As to the dangers of the Republican party, Dr. Breckinridge believed that it was in power temporarily; it had been given power because of belief that the South dictated to the Union, and that the cotton states dictated to the South. Yet the South plus the Northern minority made for security of rights. On the other hand, if Southern ultras had determined to break up the

Union, the Republican party would serve as a pretext. But Republicans could be kept out of office, or held in proper bounds if in office.

The Dred Scott case enlarged the dispute—the result of turning over questions pre-eminently political to a tribunal wholly judicial. " In a high state of excitement," he wrote, " no more respect was held for infallibility of Judges, than of Senators, Kings, or Popes." Of the federal Constitution, he warned that " it was made for us, not we for it. . . ." A spirit of passionate nationalism pervaded the letter, and although Breckinridge admitted that the states were sovereign, he contended that " the American people [are] a people." Rome survived a thousand years and the Hebrew nationality four thousand. This nationalistic Kentuckian looked forward to the day when the United States would be an influential nation of one hundred millions.[142]

Cassius M. Clay, an outspoken antislavery man, had made his opinions known despite hostility of the press and many communities. In January he defined his position on slavery and the Republican party, which latter had been misrepresented by Governor Beriah Magoffin and John C. Breckinridge. Clay pictured the Republicans as by no means being " so desperate a set of scamps " as some believed. He denied the endorsement of or affiliation with the Berea abolitionists. Nor did he approve the John Brown raid, but challenged the world to prove that a solitary Republican had been connected with it. His doctrine was to prevent by all legal means the extension of slavery into free territories. None of the Republican platforms had favored the repeal of the Fugitive Slave law. At the time of this speech the possibility existed of merger of the Opposition party and the Republican, and Clay declared he would vote for Seward, Chase, Bell, Bates, and " most heartily " for John J. Crittenden.[143]

In spite of Clay's denial of sympathy for the Berea antislavery men, who were accused of being abolitionists, be became involved in a dispute because of persecution directed against these people. The Cincinnati *Gazette* spoke of the expulsion

[142] Robert J. Breckinridge to John Cabell Breckinridge, Jan. 9, 1860, Augusta (Ga.) *Chronicle and Sentinel*, Jan. 28, 1860.
[143] Frankfort *Commonwealth*, Jan. 17, 1860.

from Kentucky of the Bereans, natives of the state, the greater part of whom were young men, although there were some old men, women, and children. Reverend John G. Fee [144] was the leader and was described as a native whose father was and had always been a large slaveholder. He was the founder of several antislavery institutions, one of which was a seminary where antislavery doctrines were taught. Fee was, according to this account, a moral suasionist; but Kentuckians suspected him of subversive designs, and meetings were held at Richmond, Kentucky, in December, 1859, to consider the propriety of his deportation. The reasons given for the proposed action were: (1) Fee's associations were incendiary, and (2) his principles were not in harmony with those of the community and the best interests of society. The town of Berea was said to be connected with Brownism, and its strategic location for such purposes was pointed out. [145]

Evidently the expulsion of the Bereans had not been complete, for in March, 1860, Clay wrote a public letter to the citizens of Madison county in which he explained his part in the troubles with the radical abolitionists at Berea. He made it clear that while he was an antislavery man, he was a moral suasionist who did not advocate force; he upheld property, the Constitution and the laws, and majority rule. He denounced the radical abolition doctrines of Rev. J. G. Fee. But Clay could not countenance vigilance committee attacks. If Republicans were attacked because of their principles, he and they would defend themselves to the last. Clay was for peace; he stood by the Republican party everywhere and liberties inherited from 1776. Never would he submit to any " Revolutionary committee." He might be overpowered, but he " could never be driven from his duty." [146]

Shortly afterward, the Madison county committee explained the " dangerous, seditious Fee settlement, financed by the North." The committee had been appointed and vested with broad discretionary powers. There had been a " battle " at Berea, but the committee denied Cassius M. Clay's statement

---

[144] J. Winston Coleman, *Slavery Times in Kentucky* (Chapel Hill, 1940), pp. 231-235.

[145] Cincinnati *Gazette* in Nashville *Republican Banner*, Jan. 30, 1860.

[146] Louisville *Daily Courier*, April 4, 1860. Clay to Citizens of Madison county, White Hall, Kentucky, March 31, 1860.

that a sick man had been abused. The unanimous support of the county was claimed for the committee.[147] Clay was charged with ambition of seeking the Republican presidential or vice-presidential nomination. His qualifications included his Southern birth, which would please the conservatives, and his acceptability to Seward's *ultras*. His difficulties in Kentucky were widely circulated by Clay's letters to the Northern press.[148] The St. Louis *Democrat* was reported to believe that Clay's persecutors would yet make him President. Later, after Lincoln's nomination, an unsympathetic Louisville paper said Clay's friends were exceedingly anxious to make a martyr out of him. " If they could only goad the people of Kentucky into a deplorable act of madness by their perversions, misrepresentations, attacks upon slavery and slaveholding—this would increase Lincoln's chances for election and they would get drippings of Federal patronage." [149]

The Louisville *Journal* early in the year declared that the prospects were growing daily that the Union movement would gain such strength that before the Republicans met at Chicago, they would join the Union forces and yield their " distinctive " basis of organization. Kentucky was urged to facilitate this trend.[150] Just how much Crittenden worked for such support is not clear, but his " affectionate friend," Francis Preston Blair, Sr., wrote of the Republicans:

They will nominate some man from the slave states. If you should not be *selected*, I am sure it will at least be one with whom you can cordially unite in giving direction to the government. Let me beg, therefore, that in your speech you will lay down some broad platform on which the whole Union party of the nation can unite.[151]

But the proposed coalition of the " South Americans " and the Republicans would never materialize, the hostile Louisville

[147] Louisville *Daily Courier*, April 6, 1860.

[148] Clay informed friends in New York that he was in danger of being driven from the state, but that he and his family planned to remain to fight it out. A Republican ward club in New York City passed resolutions of sympathy. Alexandria (Va.) *Gazette*, April 5, 1860.

[149] Louisville *Daily Courier*, April 6, 7, 12, 13, June 9, 1860.

[150] Quoted in *ibid.*, Feb. 9, 1860.

[151] C. Coleman, *The Life of John J. Crittenden* (2 vols., Philadelphia, 1873), II, 186-187.

Courier predicted, because of fundamental differences on slavery.[152]

Before the Charleston convention, there had been mild rivalry between John C. Breckinridge and James Guthrie, the Louisville capitalist. Guthrie received the vote of the state at Charleston, but Breckinridge eventually received the nomination of the Southern group at Baltimore. Crittenden was not nominated by the Constitutional Union party, but Bell was supported vigorously by the party press, the leader of which was George D. Prentice's Louisville *Journal*. The Louisville *Democrat* led the Douglas forces, and the Louisville *Courier* and Lexington *Kentucky Statesman* were the most important Breckinridge organs.[153]

The Breckinridge case was presented by press and party orators, the candidate himself making an important statement in his Ashland address in September. As usual, it was the rule to claim everything for the candidate, but one Breckinridge journal frankly confessed the party's weakness. The storm which burst at Charleston and Baltimore had made the party the laughing stock of the nation. Never were party prospects darker. " We may not hope for the success of our candidates in this election, but they are tried and true men . . ." [154] A much bolder tone was assumed by the Louisville *Courier*. This paper stressed the right of the slaveholder to remove to the territories with his slaves. This right must never be surrendered; it must be maintained " at all hazards, and regardless of consequences." [155] An attack was made on Douglas and Bell, in an effort to drive a wedge between them. Breckinridge had been charged with being a secessionist. By an appeal to the " record,"

[152] Louisville *Daily Courier*, Feb. 9, 1860. The Louisville *Journal* characterized the Constitutional Unionist party as neutral concerning the use of the power of the central government either to extend or stop the spread of slavery. Prentice's paper appealed to the Republicans to come to the Unionists; if Chicago ratified the Union nominees, it would ensure the defeat of the Democrats. Quoted in and endorsed by Nashville *Republican Banner*, April 17, 1860.

[153] The editors of the *Democrat* and the *Courier* exchanged bitter letters; the latter challenged the former to a duel which was declined. Louisville *Daily Courier*, June 21, 1860. W. N. Haldeman of *The Courier* was Surveyor of the Customs at Louisville.

[154] Madisonville *Southern Kentucky Register*, June 30, July 7, 1860.

[155] Louisville *Daily Courier*, June 15, 1860.

the tables were turned, and by lengthy quotations from the speeches and writings of W. B. Gaulden of Georgia, the Atlanta *Southern Confederacy,* Pierre Soulé, Herschel V. Johnson, Alexander H. Stephens, H. S. Foote, R. J. Walker, John A. Winston, Miles Taylor, John Forsyth, Governor John Letcher, J. P. Hambleton, Robert C. Wickliffe, and E. C. Cabell—Douglas emerged as a secessionist! [156]

In order to arouse Kentuckians, it was necessary to recall the days of 1824-1828, when John Bell was said to have accused that "noble God-like statesman," Henry Clay, of a "corrupt bargain." Efforts were made to prejudice the mountain people against Bell.[157] As for Douglas, he would repeal the fugitive slave law, the neutrality laws, the Compromise of 1850, and would reopen the African slave trade.[158] Attack was evidently considered to be the best defense. By October every Southern state was claimed for Breckinridge—except Kentucky, and she surely would not desire to remain aloof from her Southern sisters. Southern unity was the best guarantee against Northern aggression.[159]

Humphrey Marshall in a Breckinridge speech at Covington, Kentucky, repelled the charge of disunionism which the Bell and Douglas press had levelled against his party. "We are asked if Lincoln succeeds do you propose disunion? I would answer emphatically no! It is a remedy for no evil under heaven. It would be a political suicide, and Kentucky would be the very last state to give up the union." He concluded, "But the party did and does intend to fight for its rights inside of the union [cheers]."[160] And the Kentucky *Statesman* used harsh words. There was "absurdity, mendacious malignity and despicable hypocrisy in the disunion howl cunningly gotten up by the dough-faced submissionists, free-soil squatters, and unprincipled adventurers . . . ." Granted that Yancey and Keitt and the Charleston *Mercury* did support Breckinridge, it was recalled that they had formerly supported Polk, Pierce, and Buchanan.[161]

---

[156] *Ibid.,* July 31, Aug. 23, Sept. 27, 1860.
[157] *Ibid.,* July 31, Aug. 23, 1860.
[160] Richmond (Va.) *Examiner,* Aug. 14, 1860.
[161] Lexington *Kentucky Statesman,* Aug. 28, 1860

[158] *Ibid.,* Aug. 2, 1860.
[159] *Ibid.,* Oct. 11, 1860.

Although he was in the background during most of the campaign, John C. Breckinridge made one public appearance at Ashland, near Lexington, Kentucky, on September 5. He said that he did so first to repel charges that he was a disunionist and a traitor, and secondly to expound his constitutional views. Disclaiming intrigue and ambition, he declared that the presidential nomination came to him unsought. In fact he would have been content to serve in the Senate, to which he had already been elected, for the ensuing six years. But he upheld the regularity of his nomination, a matter of much dispute. A variety of charges needed to be answered. Breckinridge denied that he had requested the pardon of John Brown, or that he had supported Zachary Taylor for President in 1848. The speaker clarified his relationship to Dr. Robert J. Breckinridge, and distinguished between their views. That he had been a Know Nothing in 1855 he denied.

Then the candidate turned to the charge that in 1856 Buchanan and Breckinridge stood on the same platform as Douglas, namely, Popular Sovereignty. In that year he held to a different interpretation from that of Douglas. To Breckinridge, "nonintervention" meant that Congress *and its creature, the Territorial Legislature* must keep hands off. Misquotation was blamed by the speaker, and he sought to back up his contentions by reference to considerable counter-testimony. As for 1856, both sides had agreed to leave differences of interpretation to the courts. He then exhibited the discrepancy which existed between Douglas' position and that of the Supreme Court, and accused Douglas of repudiating an agreement on this issue. The Illinois leader was, in fact, moving in the direction of the " higher law." His hearers were given to understand that Webster and Henry Clay should be dissociated from Douglas.

It was the disunion charge which the speaker most desired to rebut, to answer " the large number of young gentlemen who are engaged in enlightening the people upon the Constitution of the country, by the ringing of bells, with tongues as long and heads as empty as the bells they ring, shout ' disunion.' " Breckinridge wondered how it was that in Kentucky where his antecedents were known, Crittenden could accuse him of being connected with an organization whose aim was disunion. And as for Joseph Lane, his running mate, the last act of treason which that individual had committed was the addition of another state to the Union. His opponents had insisted that the territorial question was an abstract one, but this was denied by Breckinridge, who asserted that on the contrary it was of vital importance, because it involved the equality of the states. But above all, he asked that his hearers judge him by what they knew him to be, and not by the fact that certain men elsewhere whose prinicples were unpopular in Kentucky were supporting him.

Later in the address, however, Republican principles were declared to be clearly unconstitutional, and if Lincoln attempted to carry them out, the Union would be destroyed. The remainder of his speech was given over to an attack on Douglas for refusing to cooperate in the fusion movement in the East, especially in Pennsylvania. Should Lincoln win, the blame must fall upon " the restless ambition and almost insane policy of one man and his violent adherents." [162] Although Breckinridge had omitted an answer to the "Norfolk questions" which Douglas had challenged him to answer, toward the end of the campaign his home paper took up the practical question, what would be the outcome if the South should secede? Delay was recommended. Lincoln would " Tylerize " his administration; that is, he would cut loose from the radicals and give a conservative and union administration. Yet it was also predicted that if secession should take place, the federal grovernment could do nothing. The army and navy would dissolve, the treasury would melt away, and finanical panic would follow Lincoln's election.[163] Such were the arguments presented to the electorate to persuade Kentucky to cast her electoral vote for John C. Breckinridge.

It will be convenient to consider the Bell and Douglas campaigns together, because probably nowhere was the *entente*

[162] Washington *National Intelligencer*, Sept. 18, 1860. Breckinridge, it was reported, was unwell when he delivered the address. The Charleston *Mercury* was displeased because Breckinridge took the stump, and promised not to repoit anything he said. (Charleston *Mercury*, Aug. 31, 1860.) In July, Breckinridge had been serenaded at Frankfort, and had made some remarks which shocked W. N. Beckham of Kentucky. (Beckham to Joseph Holt, July 19, 1860, MS, Holt Papers, Library of Congress.)

[163] Lexington *Kentucky Statesman*, Oct. 26, 1860.

cordiale more pronounced than in Kentucky. The keynote of both forces was ardent Unionism. There was little Southern ultraism to be discerned among any faction, as the secessionist Edmund Ruffin was astonished to learn when he visited Kentucky in the fall of 1860. Governor Magoffin, whom he thought radical, demanded an overt act.[164]

The Douglas campaign was led by the Louisville *Democrat*, a paper which printed pro-Douglas speeches and articles from newspapers in other parts of the country. It had supported Douglas at the Charleston and Baltimore conventions, on the ground that he was the only Democratic candidate with strength in the North. The Richmond meeting of seceders was dubbed a " Hartford Convention " because of the improbability that their demands would be secured in the Union.[165] In all the border states, on both sides of the slave line, the paramount issue was secession and preservation of the Union. The Douglas press insisted that no legal power of secession existed. If Mississippi and Louisiana should become foreign powers, the ten millions resident in the upper Mississippi Valley would find it imperative to conquer and annex them. The people of the great Valley would compel the federal government to assist them in this task. Peaceable secession was impossible, and the South must realize that war would be the result of such a policy. And it was suggested that secession might be effected peaceably with Breckinridge in office.[166]

The Douglas forces made capital of the famous " Slaughter Letter " of June 15, 1858, which was cited as proof of the treason of its author, William L. Yancey. It was captioned " An Arnold-Burr Document." [167] Humor did not often lighten the dreary millions of words emitted in political campaigns of that era, but an attempt was made with the large drawing which represented " The Piratical Craft Disunion," headed for " Salt River," with the following crew: "Owners—Honest Old Abe and Dishonest Old Jim; Captain Commanding—J. C. Breckinridge; Mate—Joseph (his x mark) Lane; Pilots—William L. Yancey of the Southern Confederacy and Henry A. Wise of

[164] *Ibid.*, Aug. 7, 1860. Craven, *Edmund Ruffin*, p. 187.
[165] *Daily Louisville Democrat*, May 5, 1860.
[166] *Ibid.*, Aug. 23, 1860.
[167] *Ibid.*, July 8, 1860.

Gizzard Fort; Engineers—Beriah Magoffin and Thomas P. Porter; Steward—James B. Clay; Boot-black—James Gordon Bennett; Freight—Humphrey Marshall." [168] Breckinridge would preach Unionism in Kentucky, but his supporters Yancey and Davis would advocate disunion farther South.[169] On September 2, the *Daily Louisville Democrat* printed copious portions of a pamphlet containing the objectives of the Knights of the Golden Circle. Although this order's primary aim was to secure lands in Mexico and the Caribbean area as an outlet for slave expansion, the pamphlet contained support for secession. The *Democrat*, a Douglas paper, linked the Knights to Yancey and the Breckinridge candidacy, and charged that they had deliberately broken up the Charleston and Baltimore convention. Let Kentuckians read and ponder these disclosures.[170]

But the people were too keenly aware of the evils which would befall them as a border state to be drawn into Yancey's scheme. Kentucky would fight all the battles and endure all the evils.[171] There were other aspects of the Douglas campaign, but Unionism was the main theme.[172]

Kentucky had long cast a large Whig vote, and in 1860 after the failure of the Constitutional Union convention to nominate Crittenden, the candidacy of John Bell was espoused by this large element. The efforts of Garret Davis and John J. Crittenden to demolish the doctrine of Congressional protection have been noted. Their efforts were in behalf of the Bell ticket. Others were not so clear-cut in their attitude. The Louisville *Journal* vacillated on the issue; it claimed that Bell was for the doctrine, but did not place it higher than the nation's existence. The Breckinridge party was accused of using the issue for the " infernal " purpose of wrecking the Union. Thus the more important issue obscured the lesser.[173] The objection often made during the campaign and since by historians, that Bell's

---

[168] *Ibid.*, Aug. 11, 1860. Frankfort *Commonwealth*, Aug. 14, 1860.

[169] *Daily Louisville Democrat*, Aug. 23, 1860.

[170] *Ibid.*, Sept. 2, 1860.

[171] *Ibid.*, Oct. 24, 1860.

[172] Douglas' alleged protective tariff speech at Harrisburg, Pa., was explained and defended. Pennsylvania would get only that protection which a revenue tariff would afford. *Daily Louisville Democrat*, Sept. 18, 1860.

[173] Quoted in Augusta (Ga.) *Daily Chronicle and Sentinel*, Sept. 16, 1860.

vague platform did not commit him to a definite line of administrative conduct with regard to slavery or anything else, was declared to be no objection at all, but an argument in his favor. The nation demanded peace, and Bell, a statesman of integrity and experience, was not bound by partisan dogmas. And had not Washington condemned partisan Presidents? [174]

In no part of the country did anyone assume a stauncher Unionist attitude than did the Louisville *Journal,* one of the most widely circulated and influential papers in the slave states. Prentice's forthright and grimly humorous views of a Carolina secessionist may be quoted: " We know Mr. Keitt. He is a warm-hearted man. He is a good fellow. He is a pleasant companion. We like him. We are sorry he is a traitor. When he is hanged, we shan't be able to look through our spectacles at that one. We shall turn our head away." [175] And near the close of the canvass, the *Journal* declared it had proved that the seceding movement was designed to bring about the election of the Republicans and to achieve union of the South to overthrow the government. If the Republicans were victors, and Breckinridge secured a commanding vote in the South, the conspirators would begin the work of revolution forthwith, trusting that such action would inflame and unite the South. Even if the Republicans were beaten and Breckinridge elected, it would not be long before the " cunning spirits " would " demand more and impracticable and unattainable concessions." A huge cloud of treason overshadowed all. Yet while these words were being written, the gaze of the civilized world was fixed upon the " noble efforts of Garibaldi." Did Americans dare to remove the light which guided him and all other oppressed peoples? [176]

How effective various campaign arguments were cannot be judged with complete confidence, but the testimony of a visitor to Kentucky in the summer of 1860 indicated that the disunion talk had made a profound impression there. He told Jeremiah S. Black to abandon hope for Breckinridge in Kentucky. " You can hardly imagine how strong a feeling is excited there on the *Union* sentiment. *That* is the rallying point. The thing that

---

[174] Louisville *Journal* in Augusta *Daily Chronicle and Sentinel,* Oct. 20, 1860.
[175] Quoted in the Alexandria *Gazette,* Aug. 4, 1860.
[176] Louisville *Journal* in Washington *States and Union,* Nov. 2, 1860.

damages Breckinridge there is the fact that the Southern *disunion talkers,* the Yancey men—the Richmond conventionists, are for him. This fatal fact will hopelessly kill him there." [177] A student of the period has called the Kentuckians of 1860-1861, the most pacific of Americans. The seven hundred miles of undefended frontier and the fact that the state was connected with the Ohio and Mississippi river systems had their effect. Disunion was " the greatest of evils and a remedy for none." [178]

Finally, Republican arguments may be considered. As in other border states, there was no deep chasm separating the Republicans and the Constitutional Unionists. But it was respectable to be a member of the latter group, and dangerous to join the former. Avowed Republicans were active in the counties along the Ohio river. On May 31 a small but determined body of Republicans met in Louisville, with Bland Ballard in the chair, to ratify the Chicago nominations, form a campaign club, and to invite Cassius Clay to address them. The committee urged a large Republican vote in the border slave states, where freedom of speech was not entirely stifled. It was predicted that 50,000 votes along the border would be polled by Lincoln, an augury which fell far short of fulfillment. Such a showing would add to the national character of the party. Kentuckians were reminded that Lincoln was a native of their state. The committee expressed abhorrence of disunion schemes, and endorsed the orthodox Republican view on the tariff and other issues. All opposing candidates were denounced, including Gerrit Smith.[179]

On November 1, the eminent Ohio Republican, Salmon P. Chase, addressed an audience of Kentuckians at Covington. He would reassure them as to the real purposes of his party. " I am a Republican and I intend to vote for Abraham Lincoln; but I would not be a Republican if I believed that the Republican party meditated hostile aggression upon the Constitutional

[177] Charles L. Loos to Black, Aug. 24, 1860, MS, Black Papers, Library of Congress.
[178] Mary Scrugham, *The Peaceable Americans of 1860-1861* (" Columbia University Studies in History, Economics and Public Law," XCVI, No. 3, Whole No. 219, New York, 1921), pp. 106-108.
[179] Signed by Lewis N. Dembitz, Edgar Needham, *et al.*, Louisville, Sept. 17, 1860; New York *Tribune*, Sept. 24, 1860.

rights of any State or any citizen of any State . . . ." Chase desired that the slavery question be settled permanently. He brushed aside the Calhoun-Breckinridge theory, the candidacies of Bell and Douglas, and neatly summed up the Republican plan: " It is non-interference by the federal government with Slavery in the states, and exclusion of Slavery from the sphere of exclusive Federal jurisdiction. This . . . will give peace." The Republicans were pledged to aid Kentucky's interests, and " . . . should invasion endanger us, Kentucky, as of yore, will send her sons to join us in repelling it." He hoped that the Ohio river would never run " with fraternal blood "; instead it should ever bind the states.[180]

MISSOURI

Economic changes had occurred in Missouri which Southern extremists had hardly observed in the two decades prior to 1860. Farm products in tobacco, hemp, and corn had vastly increased, and the values of improved farm lands had multiplied sevenfold. Diversification in farming was well along, and in these years iron and lead mines were developed, while the value of manufacturing products had almost doubled. Transportation routes had changed significantly: Missouri's products were by 1860 largely finding their way eastward via growing railroads. In general, the state's interests were no longer entirely bound up with the plantation system.[181] Missouri was a border slave state, and much of the campaign of 1860 was fought out in familiar arguments. But Missouri had the largest white population of any slave state, and economic factors were likely to be reflected in diversified political action in the presidential election.

During the months prior to the national conventions, much was heard in Missouri of a projected program which called for a merger of all anti-Democratic elements in the state and nation —Americans, Free-Soil Democrats, Whigs, and Republicans— into one great party. Although there were several possibilities for the leadership of such an organization, Missouri's interest

[180] Cincinnati *Commercial* in New York *Tribune* (semi-weekly), Nov. 9, 1860.
[181] Fish, *The American Civil War*, p. 135.

in the movement was quickened by the presidential boom for St. Louis' distinguished citizen, Edward Bates.[182] This plan would operate especially to the advantage of Opposition and Republican politicians in the border slave states, and was actively promulgated by the Blair family, Frank P. Sr., and Frank P. Jr., and Montgomery. The latter was active in Maryland politics, and his brother Frank P. Jr., was likewise engaged in Missouri.[183] Encouraged by this support, urged on by the editor of the Richmond *Whig,* and with some favorable newspapers in Maryland, Bates was optimistic concerning his chances to win the Presidency at the head of a formidable coalition.[184]

Late in 1859 the Opposition members of the Missouri legislature nominated Edward Bates for President,[185] and the following February the Opposition State Convention endorsed Bates, a protective tariff, internal improvement, a Pacific railroad, free homesteads, and condemned Democratic " heresies " regarding slavery in the territories.[186] A friendly paper said of Bates, " . . . ere the present year has closed, we shall behold in him the chosen Chief Executive of the Nation." [187] Bates had set forth his views on public questions in a letter to the New York *Tribune,* April 16, 1859, in which he had decried the continued agitation of the " pestilent " Negro question,[188] but it was again necessary that he specifically define his attitude on the leading issues of the day. Opportunity to do this arose in connection with the endorsement given Bates by the Missouri state Republican Convention.[189] A committee of the Republican group requested his views on seven direct questions, which were answered seriatim by the candidate.

Bates clearly replied as follows: 1. *Slavery—Its extension in the Territories*: In the American revolutionary era slavery was regarded as an evil, temporary and likely to disappear in time, but nonetheless an evil while it continued to exist. Here Bates

---

[182] Howard K. Beale, ed., *The Diary of Edward Bates 1859-1866* (Washington, 1933), xi-xvi. Hereafter referred to as *Bates' Diary.*
[183] *Ibid.,* pp. 80-81, 89; Smith, *Blair Family,* I, 461-469.
[184] *Bates' Diary,* pp. 94-95.
[185] *Ibid.,* pp. 84-85.
[186] *Ibid.,* p. 106.
[187] St. Louis *Daily Evening News,* Jan. 9, 1860.
[188] *Bates' Diary,* pp. 1-9.
[189] *Ibid.,* p. 108.

was in accord with the theory of the Republicans.[190] Nothing had since come to light to alter Bates' agreement with the nation's fathers on the subject.

Slavery is a social relation, a domestic relation. Within the States it exists by local law, and the Federal Government has no control over it there. The Territories, whether acquired by conquest or peaceable purchase, are subject and subordinate, not sovereign like the States. The nation is supreme over them, and the National Government has the power to permit or forbid slavery within them.

He thought that

the spirit and policy of the Government ought to be against its extension.[191]

2. *Does the Constitution carry slavery into the Territories?* His answer was no. The Constitution did not carry slavery anywhere, and Bates declared, that in his carefully considered opinion, the Supreme Court of the United States decided only one point of law, *viz.*, that Dred Scott could not be a citizen of Missouri, and could not sue in the federal court. He thought it unfortunate that the Court went beyond its jurisdiction in the discussion of political questions, which might set a dangerous precedent and lead to "conflict of authority among the co-ordinate branches of the Government." 3. *As to the Colonization of the Free Blacks.* He had long favored the objects of the American Colonization Society, but Africa was distant, and he believed that the American tropics were more suitable. Here the pet scheme of the Blairs received approval.[192]

4. *As to any inequality of rights among American citizens.* Bates had opportunity to attempt to satisfy the foreign voters, who were known to disapprove of his connections with the American movement. He declared that there was no distinction between native-born and naturalized citizens, that the government must protect all alike.[193] 5. *Am I in favor of the construction of a railroad from the Valley of the Mississippi to the Pacific ocean, under the auspices of the General Government?*

[190] W. G. Bean, "Anti-Jeffersonianism in the Ante-Bellum South," *North Carolina Historical Review*, XII (April, 1935), 103-124.

[191] *Bates' Diary*, pp. 111-112.

[192] *Ibid.*, pp. 112-113.

[193] *Ibid.*

None could doubt what his answer would be. As a resident of one of the greatest cities of " the great valley " he ardently favored this project as a means of increasing wealth and population of his home city and the Mississippi Valley; but also on the ground of national defense and the preservation of the " integrity of the Union." 6. *Am I in favor of the measure called the Homestead bill?* Yes, he was in favor of that policy which would actually place settlers on the land who would remain there and improve it, but he desired that the public lands be kept from speculation. And finally, 7. *Am I in favor of the immediate admission of Kansas under the Wyandotte Constitution?* The writer favored that policy, and would allow Kansas, like other states, to be " the sole judge of her own Constitution." [194]

The reaction to Bates' replies was generally favorable in the free states, but the difficulties inherent in the plan to fuse Northern and border state Oppositionists and Republicans became apparent in the hostile reaction in the Opposition ranks of Kentucky and Tennessee.[195] This Missouri leader saw the political situation with realism. He was convinced that his ultimate chance of success rested in his nomination by the Republicans and the Unionists. He was not interested in a third party; he did not want the Union party nomination alone. In Bates' opinion, Bell and Crittenden wished to get him out of the way.[196] In any event, the coalition plan, difficult at best, failed, and its failure was foreshadowed by the Democratic rupture at Charleston. It has been suggested that if Douglas had carried the day there, and had secured a united party, the movement to nominate a man of Bates' type would possibly have been strengthened. The Charleston explosion emboldened the Republicans, for they had no need of a moderate from a slave state. The Chicago convention passed over Bates and named Lincoln, and thus ended the coalition scheme.[197]

Bates reflected on the events which took place, and recorded his disappointment in his diary. Lincoln's nomination was " a fatal blunder "; " Lincoln was quite as *far North* as Mr. Seward

[194] *Ibid.*, pp. 113-114.

[195] *Ibid.*, p. 117; Memphis *Morning Enquirer*, March 28, 1860; Nashville *Republican Banner*, March 24, 1860.

[196] *Bates' Diary*, pp. 118-119.

[197] *Ibid.*, pp. 124, notes 92, 125.

is "; in Missouri it meant the total destruction of the Republicans, and would postpone indefinitely the conversion of the state to freedom. Yet Lincoln was an old Whig, and though he had uttered unfortunate phrases in discussing the Negro question, Bates would support Lincoln.[198] Though Bates denied pique at his failure at Chicago, one of his supporters said in protest against the treatment which Americans received:

Gov. Koerner of Illinois, Carl Schurz of Wisconsin, and other Germans, as exponents of that foreign element in the United States, at Chicago, formally waited on the Indiana delegation that was supposed to be favorable to Mr. Bates, and threatened the revolt of the whole German vote of the country, and the running of an independent ticket, in case Mr. Bates was nominated.[199]

Requested by Orville H. Browning of Illinois to take the stump for Lincoln, Bates declined to make a speaking tour, but wrote a cordial public letter in behalf of Lincoln's candidacy. He was not backing Lincoln because of the Republican platform adopted at Chicago, for he had no high opinion of party platforms.[200] At that, however, the Republican platform was better than anything the Democrats could produce, because their faculties were entirely controlled by Negro slavery. As for Bell and Everett, he had a high opinion of them, but they had no chance. The Democrats deserved condemnation for their neglect of protection of home industry. Lincoln deserved praise as a national, not a sectional candidate. He was a " Great Valley " man, and that Valley was indivisible: it was the body of the nation. The Valley was only then beginning to feel its power, and in the immediate future it would dictate the law of the land. Bates concluded with an expression of disgust at the " mad passions " of the times, but he was hopeful of " a new deal " at the hands of Lincoln.[201]

---

[198] *Ibid.*, pp. 129-131.

[199] St. Louis *Daily Evening News*, May 19, 1860.

[200] The fact is that Bates was privately displeased with parts of the Chicago platform. Unlike modern historians, who have considered the 1860 platform a retreat from the radical doctrines of 1856, Bates called it " defiant," and opposed the lugging in of the generalities of the Declaration of Independence. This was done to " insult " the Americans and please the Germans and abolitionists. *Bates' Diary*, p. 129.

[201] Edward Bates to Orville H. Browning, June 11, 1860. St. Louis *Daily Missouri Republican*, June 20, 1860.

The Douglas forces had the support of the influential St. Louis *Missouri Republican*, whose editorials set the tone of the Douglas campaign in the state and were widely quoted outside. Early in the year this paper had denounced South Carolina secession threats and had condemned the dictum of the Charleston *News* that the South had a " higher destiny," the settled policy of that state for the past ten years.[202] Likewise the Alabama Resolutions were disapproved as driving from the Democrats every free state, which would of course insure the victory of the Black Republicans. Throughout the Douglas arguments ran the most emphatic Unionism. The *Missouri Republican* said it preferred to ignore sentiment in the South, but it could not do so, because of the danger involved. Such danger was not realized; the United States as a nation was on the verge of " a hell of destruction." Therefore much activity was needed to check that " fiendish " work. A bloody collision between Southern and federal forces was warned against. Yet some at the South professed to believe that " the insane idea of . . . a Southern Confederacy would be a heaven on earth." This argument concluded with a passionate plea for the Union, and a fierce denunciation of the Breckinridge party and the secessionists.[203]

People who might be beguiled by the tariff plank of the Republicans were told that the latter were only using that to secure the votes of manufacturers and laborers. Especially was the tariff argument heard in the city of St. Louis. But the Douglas people insisted that the vague tariff plank adopted at Chicago was meaningless, and besides, Senator Hannibal Hamlin and William Cullen Bryant of the New York *Evening Post* were free traders.[204] The Douglas forces in Missouri were better organized and led than in perhaps any other slave state. The Democratic organization backed Douglas,[205] and the Democratic nominees for Governor and Lieutenant Governor, C. F. Jackson and T. C. Reynolds, announced for him. Jackson however, did not subscribe to Douglas' views when in conflict with the Democratic state platform adopted early in April,

[202] St. Louis *Daily Missouri Republican*, Jan. 24, 1860.
[203] Quoted in Washington *States and Union*, Oct. 30, 1860.
[204] St. Louis *Daily Missouri Republican*, Sept. 13, 1860.
[205] St. Louis *Daily Bulletin*, June 28, 1860, which urged a " purge."

which endorsed Congressional protection in the territories.[206] Listed as Douglas electors were such names as John B. Henderson and G. G. Vest.[207] And it will not be overlooked that the " Little Giant " personally campaigned in St. Louis and in the interior of Missouri.

The Constitutional Union campaign may be summarized briefly. That party seemed to be without important press support in St. Louis, although the *Evening News* was friendly. It had urged the coalition nomination of Bates, but that having failed, mildly advocated Bell and Everett. This paper was strongly Union and nationalistic in sentiment. It was also pacific, and on one occassion expressed wonder if the people stopped to count the cost of war. The people of the United States had at times clamored for war with some foreign country, whom they desired to " whip," and " pestiferous demagogues" in various sections of the United States had accustomed themselves to talking about fighting in or out of the Union. If those men would but consider the cost of war, " and the incalculable wretchedness, desolation, and misery that result from it, they would not be so eager to invoke the fearful calamities which a war involves." A case in point was the recent Italian Eleven Weeks' War.[208] An outside observer described the Bell party as composed of moderate Whigs in the interior of the state and of old Benton Democrats.[209] There was a keen interest in the West, as the region which would put an end to sectional bickering. Anent the passage of the Homestead bill, a contemporary predicted: "With population will come the *political power*, and when the mighty West—the Free West—gets control of our Government, the bickerings of the ' North ' and the ' South ' will be lost in the grand march of the Federal Union revolving around its Western Centre." [210]

In the Breckinridge campaign, on the other hand, Missouri voters were told of " the aggressive spirit of Northern fanaticism" and of " the just exasperation of the South." [211] All

[206] St. Louis *Daily Missouri Republican*, July 18, 1860.

[207] St. Louis *Sunday Morning Republican*, Sept. 23, 1860.

[208] St. Louis *Daily Evening News*, Feb. 9, 1860.

[209] New York *Tribune*, July 30, 1860.

[210] St. Louis *Daily Evening News*, March 13, 1860.

[211] St. Louis *Daily Bulletin*, June 1, 1860.

elements of strength were represented in Breckinridge and Lane. With considerable exaggeration usually found in national campaigns, the party organ in St. Louis prophesied: " They will sweep the country with the irresistible force of the whirlwind. They will contest successfully with Mr. Douglas even those States which he considers peculiarly his own." [212] Regarding the regularity of the nomination of Breckinridge, it was argued that he was chosen by those states which voted Democratic.[213] The Breckinridge Democrats welcomed the Constitutional Union nominations, because they believed that the Bell ticket would greatly weaken the " black " Republicans in the border states. They rejoiced at the collapse of the Bates movement, which perhaps would have been a threat even to the undivided Democratic party. To the Bell party's adherence to the Constitution, it was cogently stated that *all* parties adhered to the Constitution. It was the *interpretation* of the Constitution which was the important thing.[214]

One of the leading Missouri politicians supporting Breckinridge was James S. Green,[215] senior United States Senator, who regularly voted with the Jefferson Davis-Toombs-Slidell group in Washington. Another was Trusten Polk, his colleague in the U. S. Senate.[216] The St. Louis *Bulletin* and a large number of newspapers in smaller towns kept the Breckinridge case before the public. They, of course, advocated Congressional protection in the territories, and concentrated their fire on Douglas, who was accused of every political crime in the calendar. Bell was largely ignored. At times, indeed, the bitterness of factional warfare among the Missouri Democrats almost obscured the national campaign.[217] There were signs, subsequently borne out by the election returns, of marked weakness of the Breckinridge ticket in St. Louis. A Breckinridge meeting was disturbed there by what the *Bulletin* contemptuously dismissed as " levee rats " who were " soaked in whiskey." [218] And Edward Bates recorded in his *Diary* that there were but 275 " traitors " in St. Louis county.[219]

[212] *Ibid.*, June 25, 1860.
[213] *Ibid.*, June 27, 1860.
[216] *Bates' Diary*, p. 142.
[217] St. Louis *Daily Bulletin*, June-November *passim*.
[218] *Ibid.*, June 26, 1860.
[214] *Ibid.*, May 11, 1860.
[215] *D. A. B.*, VII, 549-550.
[219] *Bates' Diary*, p. 142.

Missouri was the one important slave state in which the Republican party made a sizable showing, and in which much activity was expended in behalf of Lincoln. In view of the fact that Bell and Lincoln electors ran separately, each ticket was doomed to defeat—as Blair and Bates had feared, although Bell almost carried the state. It has been seen that on such questions as free homesteads, hatred of secession, and the protective tariff, there was little difference between the Bell and Lincoln parties in Missouri. Greeley's *Tribune*, with possible wishful thinking, said of the situation: " The Americans sustain Bell for the time. Thousands of former freesoil Whigs and Benton Democrats will join the Republicans after the explosion of the Bell party." [220] Two matters in particular continued to irritate the Constitutional Unionists and Republicans in their relationship to each other. One was the slavery issue,[221] on which the Germans were radical, and the other was the persistence of the resentment engendered by the Nativist and Know Nothing movements.

The Germans, who it is agreed, composed the bulk of the Republican party in Missouri, complained at the " predominance " of former Nativists at the St. Louis county Republican Convention.[222] The St. Louis *Anzeiger* objected on the same score, and feared that such dissension would endanger the election to Congress of Frank P. Blair, Jr.[223]

Although it was reported that the Republican ticket had been voted for " freely " in all sections of the state in the August elections, it was true that there were difficulties which arose for Republican campaigners, as Frank P. Blair, Jr., discovered when he stumped the Missouri Valley region.[224] Hostile press accounts were blatantly unfair in reporting Republican meetings.[225] And when S. Harbaugh, who published the Lexington *Citizen's Public Advertiser*, hoisted the names of Lincoln and Hamlin, he was " waited upon " by fifteen of the staunchest pro-slavery men in town. They threatened violence, after which the editor

[220] New York *Tribune*, Aug. 23, 1860.

[221] O. Williams to Editor, *Missouri Republican*, Sept. 4, 1860, St. Louis *Sunday Morning Republican*, Sept. 1860.

[222] *Westliche Post* in St. Louis *Daily Missouri Republican*, July 11, 1860.

[223] Quoted in St. Louis *Daily Missouri Republican*, July 11, 1860.

[224] New York *Tribune*, Aug. 23, 1860; Smith, *Blair Family*, I, 498.

[225] St. Louis *Daily Missouri Republican*, May 23, 1860.

departed forthwith, leaving his printing press probably to be destroyed.[226]

The leading Republican in Missouri, Frank P. Blair, Jr., believed that he could obtain from thirty to thirty-five thousand votes for Lincoln.[227] If he could not deliver those votes, however, he secured his own election to Congress from the First District in St. Louis. During his campaign, Blair had stressed his opposition to slavery in the territories, and had pointed to under-representation of St. Louis in the legislature. After his election, Blair characterized St. Louis as " the banner city of Republicanism," and praised the solid " phalanx of German Republicans," [228] The rising German-American figure, Carl Schurz, took part in the Missouri campaign with speeches in German and English at St. Louis. Schurz called one of his speeches " The Doom of Slavery," in which he assailed slavery on economic grounds and declared that emancipation was the remedy for business and social evils.[229] The St. Louis *Anzeiger* applauded Schurz, who brought to the Republicans a real understanding of the depth which separated them from the Democrats.[230]

The party organ, the St. Louis *Missouri Democrat*, summed up the Republican argument. A vote for Bell, Breckinridge, or Douglas was a vote for the extension of slavery. Voters in St. Louis were urged to prove that theirs was one city " bold enough to rebuke treason." Free lands, a tariff, and more Republicans in the South were some of the results to follow Lincoln's election.[231] Lincoln was a conservative, whose inauguration would be followed by business revival. Moreover, " Lincoln's election means peace—peace at home and abroad, and a long period of unprecedented prosperity." Men of trade and business were asked to give a final *coup de grâce* to slavery. And

[226] Baltimore *American*, July 16, 1860.
[227] Smith, *Blair Family*, I, 497.
[228] New York *Times*, July 27, Aug. 17, 1860.
[229] C. M. Fuess, *Carl Schurz Reformer* (New York, 1932), pp. 76-77.
[230] In St. Louis *Daily Missouri Republican*, Aug. 6, 1860.
[231] See also Republican address of R. S. Hart, Oct. 16, 1860, at St. Louis. If Lincoln had designs against slavery in the states, Hart would oppose him. But Lincoln would be generous to the South. Hart was critical of slavery, and was opposed to filibustering and civil war. R. S. Hart, *Review of Politics and Parties* (St. Louis, 1860), Library of Congress.

what if the more powerful section of the nation did come to dominate? That was but an inevitable development.[232]

TENNESSEE

Although not a border slave state, Tennessee [233] was in some respects similar to Kentucky and Missouri. As in the former, the Whig party had been for a generation strong in Tennessee, and until 1860 the state had been largely free from secession advocates. There were occasional exponents of separation, such as the historian J. G. M. Ramsey and the fiery Memphis *Avalanche*. But geography, economics, and the social background of the people made secession unpopular. The political leaders generally were devoted to Unionism; John Bell and Andrew Johnson, although members of different parties, were in accord on that subject.[234]

Tennesseans were bound by their economic interests to the North as well as to the South, and this fact made the perpetuation of the Union desirable. Tennessee was not a typical cotton and plantation state. The ratio of white people to slaves was more than four to one, and this condition was said to be increasing. There were only 36,844 slave owners out of a total population of 1,109,801. Of these very few owned as many as a hundred slaves each. Livestock and food products were finding markets in the North and West as well as in the South. Projects for the extension of slavery and for the reopening of the African slave trade had scant support in Tennessee.[235] And it should be recalled that Memphis was a thriving river port, which was a unit in the great Mississippi Valley system. Long before the campaign began, the conservative Nashville *Republican Banner* warned the South of a conspiracy to " chloroform " her people with " sectional prejudice " in order to achieve secession.[236] Much of this argument was heard in behalf of Bell and Douglas in the presidential canvass.

[232] St. Louis *Daily Missouri Democrat*, Nov. 6, 1860.

[233] See Marguerite B. Hamer, " The Presidential Campaign of 1860 in Tennessee," *East Tennessee Historical Society Publications*, XXXI (No. 3), 3-22.

[234] J. W. Patton, *Unionism and Reconstruction in Tennessee* (Chapel Hill, 1934), pp. 3-4.

[235] Patton, pp. 4-5.　　　　　　　　[236] *Ibid.*

Early in 1860 a movement was launched to make Andrew Johnson,[237] United States Senator from Tennessee, the nominee of the Charleston convention. The Chattanooga *Advertiser* observed that the press of the Northwest was commenting favorably on Andrew Johnson's chances. He was able and fearless, and if chosen at Charleston would be elected. Moreover, the tone of the Southern press was said to be cordial to Johnson.[238] The organ of the Southern ultras in Memphis had high praise for him; although preferring Lane of Oregon, it would support the favorite son of Tennessee. In any event, there could be no doubt that Andrew Johnson, at no very distant day, would be President of the United States.[239] These words were written in spite of his activity in behalf of the Homestead bill, which was bitterly opposed by many Southern Democrats. It has been suggested that such a policy enhanced Johnson's popularity in the West, and that the friends of Douglas attempted to arrange a deal with Johnson, who probably would have been offered the Vice Presidency.[240] If the party had remained united, he might have accepted second place, despite his dislike of Douglas. In any event, the Homestead bill was supported in Tennessee by the Nashville *Union and American,* which claimed that the Republicans were pushing the bill because they had discovered that it was popular in the Northwest, " the debatable ground of the ensuing Presidential election." It was senseless for Southerners to oppose the Homestead bill merely because the Republicans were for it. Their " hateful fanaticism " should not blind Southerners.[241]

As was the fashion among politicians, Johnson wrote his son that he was not a candidate for President, but that he was for a Southern man. He desired the Tennessee state Convention to express a first choice for the nomination. To his son he repeated a conversation which he had recently had with his colleague, A. O. P. Nicholson. Although Nicholson professed to support

[237] *D. A. B.*, X, 81-90.
[238] Nashville *Union and American*, Feb. 19, 1860.
[239] Memphis *Daily Avalanche*, Jan. 24, 1860, a prediction which came true by circumstances undreamed of by this prophet.
[240] St. George L. Sioussat, "Tennessee in National Politics, 1850-1860," *Annual Report of the American Historical Association for 1914* (2 vols., Washington, 1916), I, 257-258.
[241] Nashville *Union and American*, April 4, 1860.

Johnson as the only man who could defeat Douglas, Johnson later learned that Nicholson was working against him in Tennessee. Nicholson desired the state's endorsement for himself, Johnson believed, and concluded: " *I fear Nicholson is by nature treacherous and by practice a liar.*" [242] Despite a hostile undercurrent, Johnson won the endorsement of the state Convention, the machinations in which were fully reported to him by faithful adherents who participated.[243] Nor did the Tennessee hopeful lack for candid, confidential advice as to strategy.[244]

In March Johnson significantly informed a correspondent that if Douglas were stopped, the latter's friends would turn to a Southerner.[245] A few weeks before the Charleston convention, he considered that his own chances were hopeless; but Douglas would dictate the nomination. Therefore, it would be advantageous to hold a position acceptable to him. Yet it was said in Washington that Douglas would make a desperate battle. Johnson complained of " these corrupt times." [246]

Sam Milligan, a home-town confidant of Andrew Johnson, became earnestly preoccupied with the promotion of Johnson's candidacy; he and other determined Johnson men attended the Charleston convention. There a tug of war developed within the Tennessee delegation between the real and the nominal Johnson delegates. Some of the latter wished to shift to Douglas. The Senator was notified of developments, and he advised the Tennesseans to hold on and to acquiesce in the nomination. The Douglas managers tried to ensnare Tennessee by dangling the Vice Presidency before Johnson. But Johnson refused to commit himself to Douglas, and the Douglas men were immov-

[242] Robert Johnson to Andrew Johnson, Jan. 10, 1860, reported to his father that Senator Nicholson had written to Tennessee that Johnson did not desire the Convention's endorsement. Andrew Johnson to Robert Johnson, Jan. 15, 1860, MSS, Andrew Johnson Papers, Library of Congress.

[243] Robert Johnson to Andrew Johnson, Jan. 22, 1860; John K. Howard to Andrew Johnson, Feb. 5, 1860, MSS, *ibid.*

[244] See especially, Sam Milligan to Andrew Johnson, Jan. 18, 30, Feb. 4, 8, March 4, 20, 1860. These interesting letters set forth Milligan's dissatisfaction with Buchanan's policy, his desire to restore the sectional equilibrium, without which slavery was doomed within ten years; his justification of slavery according to " natural laws "; and his desire to make Johnson president as a compromise candidate. MSS, *ibid.*

[245] Andrew Johnson to B. McDounel, March 24, 1860, MS, *ibid.*

[246] Andrew Johnson to Robert Johnson, April 8, 1860, MS, *ibid.*

able. Secessionist pressure, enhanced by " fire-eating " surround-
ings, almost succeeded in taking Tennessee with the Gulf states.
One Johnson man suspected that the Douglas people welcomed
the secession of the Gulf states, in the belief that Douglas could
win two-thirds of the remainder; but the border states insisted
upon two-thirds vote of the *entire* membership—and thus
blocked Douglas at Charleston.[247]

In spite of discouragements at Charleston, Milligan still
believed that Douglas could be beaten at Baltimore and Tennessee's favorite nominated. Douglas could be forced to withdraw or disrupt the party—which he would be loath to do.
Milligan favored the Tennessee resolutions, or something which,
in the weakest form possible, recognized the South's territorial
doctrine. Milligan pronounced the withdrawal at Charleston
" an irreparable error ": the South had gone so far that she
could not surrender everything. Meantime, Tennessee should
steadily vote for Andrew Johnson. But if, as was unlikely,
Virginia, Kentucky, North Carolina, and Missouri should go to
Douglas, then Tennessee should follow. The times were
perilous, and Andrew Johnson would go to Baltimore to do all he
could.[248] But after his failure before the conventions, and when
the party divided, Johnson gave his support to Breckinridge.[249]

The Breckinridge campaign may be briefly summarized.
Breckinridge had the backing of the party organization, of the
important leaders, and most of the Democratic press.[250] As in
other states of the upper South, various shades of opinion were
represented among the Breckinridge men. An occasional secession voice was heard. The Memphis *Avalanche* was " sick of
all this talk about Union," because it was through such that
the " black " Republicans expected to achieve their " hellish "
designs.[251] The Lebanon *Democrat* declared that Tennessee
was with the South " heart and soul," and criticized the state

[247] One may obtain a picture of the Charleston convention through the eyes
of Johnson sympathizers who were present. Sam Milligan to Johnson, May 7,
1860 (confidential); Robert Johnson to Johnson, May 8, 1860; W. C. Whitte-
horne to Johnson, May 8, 1860, MSS, *ibid.*

[248] Sam Milligan to R. Johnson, May 28, 1860, MS, *ibid.*

[249] R. W. Winston, *Andrew Johnson, Plebeian and Patriot* (New York, 1928),
pp. 147-148, indicates Johnson vacillated during the campaign.

[250] New York *Herald*, Aug. 8, 1860.

[251] Memphis *Daily Avalanche*, May 16, 1860.

delegation at Charleston because it did not secede with the lower South delegations.[252] It was a mistake to mislead the Northern people, who believed that in the event of Republican success, " a host of Bell and Douglas men would whip them [Southerners] into submission." Instead, moderate Northerners should be encouraged by the spectacle of a United South, especially business men at the North who were urged to shift to Breckinridge.[253]

On August 14, William L. Yancey spoke in Memphis. In his address he read what he said was the constitution of the much-discussed " League of United Southerners." He also inquired whether people judged Douglas by the fact that he was backed by the Atlanta *Southern Confederacy* and W. B. Gaulden of Georgia.[254] Yancey's more sensational appearance in the state was at Knoxville, where he crossed swords with Parson W. G. Brownlow. It seems probable that the Southern fire-eater won but few votes in this non-slaveholding area when he sneered at menial labor performed by Northern whites.[255] An interesting colloquy occurred when Brownlow and Yancey each stated his position on secession. The Parson said that when secessionists marched to Washington to dethrone Lincoln, " I am for seizing a bayonet and forming an army to resist such an attack, and they shall walk over my dead body on their way." To which Yancey retorted, " If my State resists, I shall go with her, and if I meet this gentleman (pointing to Brownlow) marshalled with his bayonet to oppose us, I'll plunge my bayonet to the hilt through and through his heart, and feel no compunction for the act, and thank my God my country has been freed from such a foe." [256]

And there were some Tennesseans who used fiery language. The Gallatin *Examiner* predicted that the South would soon be overrun by a Vandal horde from the North, who would chain Southerners to their " triumphant cars and make them objects of contempt to . . . the civilized world." It was recalled that

---

[252] Quoted in *ibid.*

[253] Nashville *Union and American*, Nov. 1, 1860. Bell was a " Political John the Baptist " to prepare the way for a quiet submission to Lincoln. Nashville *Republican Banner*, July 21, 1860.

[254] Memphis *Daily Avalanche*, Aug. 17, 1860.

[255] Patton, *Unionism and Reconstruction*, p. 4.

[256] Knoxville *Register* in New Orleans *Courier*, Sept. 26, 1860.

the Democratic party had long warned that the teachings of the Republicans " would culminate in war, bloodshed, and revolution." Whig papers were taunted for demanding a war-footing for the South.[257]

John H. Crozier, a resident of East Tennessee, similarly declared that though the South might be overpowered by numbers, he would never submit. If Lincoln were elected, he would stand an inch higher than before. He declined to be " a white nigger " an instant for the abolitionists. The moment Lincoln was inaugurated, Crozier would make war on him, and the milder his rule the fiercer would be the resistance, for tyrants always began their oppression with coolness, cunning, and stealth. It was true that there were few slaves in the region where he lived, and it would make no difference if owners were robbed of their slaves, but from duty he sympathized with his fellow-citizens. The slaveholders in the cotton states were fighting for their existence and for the security of their wives and children. Whatever they might decide, Crozier was with them.[258] A correspondent wrote from Knoxville, " Strange as it may appear, here in East Tennessee, where slaves are comparatively few, we are far sounder on the Southern Question than they are in West Tennessee, where most of the slaves of the State are held." [259]

On the other hand, Andrew Johnson did not share Crozier's views. Asked what course to pursue in the event of a Republican victory, he replied that he proposed to remain in the Union and there fight for Southern rights. All others should do the same.[260]

In bold-faced type the Memphis *Avalanche* accused Emerson Etheridge, member of Congress from Tennessee, of having read and defended the " Black " Republican platform at his home town of Dresden. It was emphasized that Etheridge was ostensibly a Bell man in the presidential election, but one who

[257] Gallatin *Examiner*, Oct. 20, 1860. Yet after Lincoln's victory, this paper did not urge secession. *Ibid.,* Nov. 10, 1860.

[258] Nashville *Republican Banner*, Sept. 13, 1860.

[259] New York *Herald*, Oct. 27, 1860. In a party sense only as post-election events would show.

[260] Winston, p. 147.

declared that the Republican platform would give peace to the country—assuredly " unsound " doctrine in Tennessee. On the other hand, he was represented as asserting that Breckinridge's election would destroy the Union.[261]

There is evidence that the campaign to attain unity in Tennessee, and a solidarity with the lower South, was not successful. This fact was discerned by observers in the far South. The Montgomery *Mail* chided Nashville editors because of their hostility to Yancey, and complained that they ignored sectional feeling except to condemn it in the South. The *Mail* denominated Lincoln as the leader of the " Ossawattomie " party. It could not understand Southern opposition to men who believed that there was a limit to oppression. It was a pity that such men lived in the South. And it was to be hoped that public opinion in Nashville was more " conservative " than it appeared.[262] On the other hand, Linton Stephens, writing from Tennessee late in the campaign, found public opinion alarmed over the prospects of Lincoln's election. It was believed that South Carolina would quit the Union, that coercion would follow, and the entire South would join South Carolina. Stephens agreed with this analysis.[263]

The campaigns of Bell and Douglas were conducted in Tennessee with coordination, and before election day it was apparent that these parties had a common objective—that of preserving the Union.[264] One Douglas supporter alluded to the seceders' fear that Bell would carry Tennessee, and declared that it would be far better to have that happen than to have the nationality of the Democratic party destroyed.[265] Bell himself was on record as preferring Douglas to Breckinridge, on the ground that

[261] Memphis *Daily Avalanche*, Aug. 9, 1860. Etheridge remained a Unionist, became a Republican, and served as Clerk of the U. S. House of Representatives, 1861-1863. *Biographical Dictionary of the American Congress 1774-1927* (Washington, 1928), p. 949.

[262] Montgomery *Mail* in Nashville *Union and American*, July 25, 1860. This was a loose usage of the word " conservative."

[263] Waddell, *Biographical Sketch of Linton Stephens*, pp. 235-236.

[264] An occasional note of rivalry appeared. A writer, " Memphis Mechanic," said that he heard it said of Bell: " Gentlemen, Bell was never guilty of an impulse in his life; a quart of brandy would not make his pulse beat oftener than ten strokes an hour; damn the cold-blooded, calculating trimmer, I want a man of nerve, of boldness. . . ." Memphis *Daily Appeal*, Oct. 5, 1860.

[265] Memphis *Daily Appeal*, Sept. 15, 1860.

he was the more national man of the two.[266] And with regard
to the slavery controversy, an authoritative party spokesman
declared: " Mr. Bell is neither the candidate especially of the
friends or especially of the opponents of slavery." If elected, he
would administer the government in such a manner as would
offend only disunionists in both sections.[267]

John Bell has been called the most popular man in the state
in 1860,[268] and with his long record of public service—marked
by manifestations of independence—the Whig strength in Tennessee, the ample press support, it is not surprising that his candidacy was formidable. Among his newspaper supporters were
the Knoxville *Whig*, the Nashville *Republican Banner*, the Nashville *Patriot*, the Memphis *Bulletin*, the Memphis *Enquirer*, and
many others. Among Tennessee politicians who actively worked
for Bell were Horace Maynard,[269] Emerson Etheridge, Jere
Clemens,[270] and Parson W. G. Brownlow.

Arguments in behalf of Bell and Everett included attacks on
the value of Congressional protection; a calculation based on
1856 figures that proved the impossibility of Breckinridge's
election; and a sensational document which sought to establish
a secessionist conspiracy of Breckinridge partisans to break up
the government. The conspiracy was heavily " documented "
and was widely circulated in the Bell press.[271] Parson Brownlow
in particular rang the changes on this thesis, contending that the
secessionist movement was merely an effort to create new offices
in a new government for " brokendown " politicians. There
was no Bell supporter more determined in his devotion to the
Union than the picturesque Brownlow.[272]

About a week before election, an organization appeared in
Memphis, known as the " Minute Men," which was promptly

[266] New York *Herald*, Aug. 8, 1860.
[267] Nashville *Republican Banner*, June 15, 1860.
[268] Patton, p. 1.
[269] *D. A. B.*, XII, 460-461.
[270] *D. A. B.*, IV, 191-192; Clemens heatedly retorted to Sumner's charge that
slave relations engendered " violent and bloody instincts." Letter to Editor, St.
Louis *Daily Missouri Republican*, June 13, 1860, St. Louis *Daily Missouri
Republican*, June 22, 1860.
[271] Nashville *Patriot*, July 11, 1860. This was circulated in pamphlet form.
[272] E. Merton Coulter, *William G. Brownlow Fighting Parson of the Southern
Highlands* (Chapel Hill, 1937), pp. 130-131.

branded by the Bell press as "a disunionist, Breckinridge" creation, as a South Carolina secret society.[273] Congressman R. B. Brabson of Chattanooga, wrote confidentially to one of the Bell managers that he foresaw the election of Lincoln, and inquired as to the future course which Constitutional Union men should pursue. They could not join the Republicans or the secessionists, without surrender of principle. In his view, revolution was inevitable, and he suggested that the people of the seven border Southern states meet in convention to decide policy. Brabson advocated a "neutrality" declaration by this convention, which would solemnly say to North and South, ". . . thus far shalt thou go, & no farther." He hoped that such action would check "mad" and "wild" schemes, and their "ruinous consequences." He thought that only the unlikely overwhelming rejection of Breckinridge by the South could avert the storm, while resistance to Lincoln would be war on the Constitution.[274]

After the election the Bell press continued to support the Union. A few days after Lincoln's election, the Memphis *Morning Bulletin* reminded its readers that a fair and full trial was allowed to the "meanest hogthief, assassins, murderers, cold and crafty rogues, [and] unprincipled forgers . . . ." Why not allow Lincoln the same chance? It was moral cowardice not to listen to his self-defense; and in order that Tennesseans and others be informed on Lincoln's views of slavery, the *Bulletin* published excerpts of his speeches and writings.[275]

The Douglas campaign may now be summarized. It will be recalled that the Illinois leader personally canvassed the state, and that his case was fully presented by the Memphis *Appeal*. The Unionist emphasis was as characteristic of the Douglas arguments as of those for Bell. Even if Lincoln were Buchanan's successor, no irremediable harm would be done, and it would

[273] Memphis *Morning Bulletin*, Oct. 30, Nov. 1, 1860. A citizen of Memphis described the "Minute Men," whose objects were not then clearly defined, but who were ready for "anything." The "Minute Men" might collide with the "Wide Awakes" of the North. J. W. Merriam to Horatio King, Oct. 31, 1860, MS, Horatio King Papers, Library of Congress.

[274] R. B. Brabson to A. R. Boteler, Oct. 15, 1860, MS, Boteler Papers, Library of Duke University.

[275] Memphis *Morning Bulletin*, Nov. 13, 1860. Just before election, it advocated prayer and fasting for the Union. *Ibid.*, Oct. 28, 1860.

not be necessary to coerce the seceders, who, it was predicted, would " come back " within six months. The Memphis *Appeal* affirmed that " we Tennesseans and Kentuckians " knew Illinois and Indiana, and that the majority were " sound " there. Classifying Tennessee with the border states, it wondered why the " rhodomontade " of secession and revolution should be confined to the lower South. For in the matter of slave losses caused by the operations of the underground railway, it was the border states which suffered most heavily. " We " lost a thousand as compared to ten of Alabama or South Carolina. In language similar to that employed in Kentucky and Virginia, the *Appeal* pointed out that "we " must first be overrun and " our " cities destroyed before the lower South should suffer. Thus the lower South ought not to act until the border states had made a decision. If the lower South should decline to wait on the border states, it would be apparent that they distrusted the " honor " of their neighbors. Unless Lincoln and other Republicans were madmen, they were incapable of harm.[276] However, Douglas was weak in Tennessee, a fact noted by several observers before election, except in Memphis, and the counties of Hardeman, Hayward, and Madison.[277] He had almost no strength in East Tennessee, the New York *Herald* correspondent reported.[278]

That the Bell-Douglas vote in Tennessee was an indication of staunch Unionist sentiment is as certain as any political generalization can be, but the impact of events in the ensuing five months altered the situation sharply. In the end John Bell himself announced for secession, and the Breckinridge counties of East Tennessee pronounced themselves for the Union.[279]

[276] Memphis *Daily Appeal*, Oct. 17, 1860.
[277] New York *Herald*, Aug. 8, 1860.
[278] *Ibid.*, Oct. 27, 1860.
[279] Patton, pp. 7-8, analyzes reasons for the shift. Coulter, *Brownlow*, p. 134. Votes of the three sections of the state follow:

	Breckinridge	Bell	Douglas
East	18,881	22,125	1619
Middle	33,789	27,152	2243
West	11,797	18,384	7548
	64,467	67,661	11,410

NORTH CAROLINA

This was a state which contained a large proportion of small farmers, and although there were counties in the eastern portion where the plantation system was well established, the former predominated.[280] Like all Southern states, North Carolina was disturbed at the trend of national affairs in the late fifties, a condition which was exacerbated by the John Brown raid in neighboring Virginia, and approached the election of 1860 in a state of mind hardly conducive to moderation. Conservatives in North Carolina, as elsewhere, tended to minimize the Brown raid and continued to work for friendly relations with the North.[281]

In spite of the alarm for Southern security which North Carolinians felt and expressed, there existed in the state a large moderate element. People of varying degrees of unorthodoxy were active in politics. John A. Gilmer, Congressman from Greensboro, prominent Opposition member who was considered for Speaker in the memorable contest of 1859-1860, although a slaveholder, was not considered to be " sound " on Southern rights.[282] And the Quaker settlements in Guilford, Randolph, Alamance, Chatham, and Surry counties were hostile to slavery.[283] It is true that patience was exhausted with the Reverend Daniel Worth, whose " subversive " activities in 1860 caused much adverse comment.[284] The notorious Hinton R. Helper, one of the most controversial authors of the age, was a native, if not a resident at this time.[285] But such tolerance did not extend to permitting a Republican electoral ticket to appear in 1860.

In January, the important Democratic organ, the Raleigh *North Carolina Standard*, edited by the active Democratic politician, W. W. Holden,[286] asked: " What will North Caro-

---

[280] Guion G. Johnson, *Ante-Bellum North Carolina* (Chapel Hill, 1937), pp. 468-469.

[281] Joseph C. Sitterson, *The Secession Movement in North Carolina* (Chapel Hill, 1939) is a scholarly monograph.

[282] *D. A. B.*, VII, pp. 307-308.

[283] Sitterson, pp. 16-17.

[284] Guion Johnson, pp. 347-348.

[285] *Ibid.*, pp. 567-568.

[286] *D. A. B.*, IX, 138-140.

lina do in the event of the election of a Black Republican to the Presidency?" This was, he thought, the most important question before North Carolinians since the Charlotte "Declaration of Independence" in 1775. The surest way to avoid dissolution was to prepare for it. The probabilities were that the Republicans would be victorious, which would in turn produce dissolution. The question so often asked in the South was, "Should the South await an overt act?" Holden declared that the very election of a Republican would constitute an overt act. He was concerned with the military preparedness of the South, and desired to be assured that the militia were in readiness and equipped with enough powder and guns. He feared that the "forms" of the Constitution would be employed to destroy the South. In the crisis North Carolina was associated with South Carolina and Virginia, and in the opinion of the *Standard*, "would go with the South." [287]

Governor John W. Ellis took advanced Southern ground in his address before the North Carolina Democratic state convention. In spite of the Governor's language and the convention's pro-Southern resolves, the delegates chosen to represent the party at Charleston were conservative. In the spring Holden shifted his position in the direction of moderation, and at the Charleston convention attempted to prevent radical action by the delegations from the lower South. [288]

Although the North Carolina delegation voted to sustain the majority platform at Charleston, they remained in the convention after the secession of the lower South. The North Carolinians strongly desired compromise, with a united party at Baltimore. Toward this end the *Standard* for a brief period favored Douglas, and Senator T. L. Clingman, who had made a Southern rights speech in the United States Senate, also hoped

[287] Raleigh *Semi-Weekly Standard*, Jan. 7, 1860.

[288] Sitterson, pp. 161-164, note 78, for analysis of Holden's change. Holden shifted to Douglas. "The choice is now between Douglas and defeat and national dissolution." W. W. Holden to T. G. Tucker, May 19, 1860; also Holden to S. A. Douglas, June 1, 1860. MSS, Stephen A. Douglas Papers, Library of University of Chicago. For pressure on Holden, see E. Cantwell and J. R. McLean to Joseph Lane, Raleigh, July 13, 1860. The Breckinridge National Chairman characterized the matter as "a subject of delicate and grave importance." Isaac I. Stevens to Jeremiah S. Black, July 13, 1860, MSS, Black Papers, Library of Congress.

for Democratic unity. However, after the Baltimore convention refused to seat certain seceders, North Carolina, with the exception of three delegates, withdrew and entered the seceders' convention.[289]

A majority of the Democratic press and the party organization favored Breckinridge; and Holden, who pledged that he would support that Democratic candidate supported by the party majority, eventually turned to Breckinridge.[290] There was some fear on the part of the Breckinridge men and hope among the Bell men that the party division would give the state to the latter. Efforts in North Carolina, as in all other Southern states, failed to bring about a fusion of electors.[291]

Voters were told that Breckinridge would be elected. An optimistic estimate gave him a far better chance than Lincoln. The entire South was assigned to the Breckinridge column, together with California, Oregon, New Jersey, and Pennsylvania.[292] Of course, the " records " of Southern Douglas men were displayed to prove them secessionists.[293] On September 6, Senator Clingman said at Raleigh that he had known Lincoln, and that " he was an obstinate, fanatical, ignorant, irrepressible conflict man." If such a man were elected President, there would be resistance, or social division. The issue might arise, he continued, over the refusal of Southerners to accept offices or to permit them to be filled by outsiders. At that juncture, D. K. McRae, a Douglas elector, interrupted the speaker. Clingman inquired if his interrogator would take office. To which McRae replied that he saw no reason for not doing so, if Lincoln clearly understood that the appointment was not to be used as " an instrument of aggression against the South." Clingman continued his condemnation of Lincoln, and urged that the time to resist Lincoln was before he got control of the United States army. Douglas' Norfolk speech was denounced, and John Bell was dismissed as having always advocated submission to the abolitionists. On the same occasion, former Governor Thomas Bragg asserted that no Breckinridge man in

[289] Sitterson, pp. 161-169.
[290] Ibid., p. 169.
[291] Raleigh Semi-Weekly Standard, Sept. 19, 22, 1860.
[292] Wilmington Daily Journal, Sept. 25, 1860.
[293] Ibid., Aug. 24, 1860.

the state would accept office from Lincoln, and A. W. Venable preferred to see the end of his country than to see emancipation.[294]

Yet Clingman was one of the few Breckinridge men who openly went so far as to advise resistance if the election went as many feared; the majority of Breckinridge campaigners extolled the Union.[295]

The Douglas campaign in North Carolina was ineffectual. A few meetings were held, and a Douglas convention was assembled at Raleigh to hear the nominee himself. Douglas' speech probably gained him but a few supporters because of its extreme nationalism.[296] There was, however, a cordial relationship between the Bell and Douglas campaigns in North Carolina.[297]

The Opposition state convention met in Raleigh, February 22, and adopted a platform mild in tone, one resolution of which stated: "That we yield to no portion of our fellow-citizens in our determination to maintain our common rights in slave property, and this can be better effected within the Union than by its destruction." Such events as Brown's raid were deplored, but the idea of converting the boundary of the free states into a foreign frontier did not appeal to the Opposition of North Carolina.[298]

The Opposition press, soon to support the Constitutional Unionist candidate, at the outset let it be known that " secession or a dissolution of the Union could not under any circumstances give advantages to the South which would not be greatly counterbalanced by other evils." This spokesman favored the development of Southern manufactures and trade, which would be useful weapons for a contest within the Union.[299] In general the Opposition was pleased with the Democratic split, and believed that Bell would surely carry North Carolina.[300] The

[294] *Ibid.*, Sept. 8, 14, 1860.

[295] Sitterson, p. 171.

[296] *Ibid.*, p. 170; W. K. Boyd, "North Carolina on the Eve of Secession," *Annual Report of the American Historical Association for 1910* (Washington, 1912), pp. 175-177.

[297] Wilmington *Daily Journal*, Aug. 30, 1860.

[298] *Weekly Raleigh Register*, Feb. 29, 1860.

[299] Hillsborough *Recorder*, Jan. 18, 1860.

[300] Fayetteville *Observer*, July 2, 1860.

idea that South Carolina could "hurry" Virginia and North Carolina out of the Union was decried by an influential old Whig paper, which opposed the attendance by North Carolina at the proposed Southern conference, because such an act might lead to disunion. The same source denounced the cry of "Southern Rights" raised by the Democrats, which term was translated to mean dissolution of the Union if the Democrats could not hold offices under it.[301]

Evidently the critical condition of the country did not prevent the most violent partisan attacks. The Wadesborough *North Carolina Argus* wondered whether it were possible that the people of the North and South could believe half the denunciations and assertions that each made of the other. The Whigs and Americans were superior to the Democrats and Republicans on that score. Later the same paper described Democrats as a "desperately corrupt, immoral, sacrilegious, blasphemous, and Heaven-daring faction," and added that they were "grasping, avaricious, unprincipled and insatiable. . . ."[302]

It may have been that some North Carolinians were pondering the value of secession and a Southern confederacy, but if the press, platforms, and orators were sincere in their protestations of loyalty, the Constitutional Unionist party was a unit for the continuation of the Union. From western North Carolina, the Reverend J. Buxton wrote a relative:

I believe the Disunion mania to be a practical blindness, and a Jereboam scheme against God and Man. Mr. Everett's Letter is a statesmanlike production, and is Washingtonian throughout. A sectionalized politican, on the " slavery question " pro and con, is my abomination, " object of my implacable disgust." We want breadth, patriotism, moderation, honesty, and my opinion is (which however I don't *preach*) that we won't find any of these things at large in either the Democratic or Republican Parties.[303]

An interesting evaluation of the party leaders and condition of the country was made by Samuel J. Johnston of Edenton, North Carolina. Johnston held the leadership of all parties in low esteem. Douglas was the greatest, next to General Scott,

[301] *Weekly Raleigh Register*, Feb. 8, 1860.

[302] Wadesborough *North Carolina Argus*, Feb. 22, May 3, 1860.

[303] J. Buxton to Ralph P. Buxton, Ashville, June 8, 1860, MS, Ralph Potts Buxton Papers, Southern Historical Collection, University of North Carolina.

but even he was but a dwarf in comparision with his predecessors. Bell was a " good respectable second rate man," nominated because of availability, but all things considered the best man in the race. Johnston hoped he would be elected, and that the people were " too great to be dashed to pieces by the folly or the madness of . . . politicians for their own personal agrandisement [sic]." [304] But later from the same area, Charles L. Pettigrew wrote: " All is prepared for secession in this part of the country in the event of the election of Lincoln." [305]

The Greensborough *Patriot* in a comprehensive article illustrated this devotion to the Union. A " terrible crisis " was approaching, North Carolinians were warned, and should Lincoln be elected " inconsiderate men would precipitate Slave States into disunion." The Southern Democrats were represented as ready to destroy the Union; Breckinridge and Lane were chosen at Baltimore as " blinds "; otherwise why were not more representative Southern men than they nominated? The belief that Breckinridge could be elected was ridiculed. Excitement was desired by " designing men," and the " pride and spirit of the South were to be played upon." This article accurately forecast that the conservatives, if in the minority, were to be subjected to a severe test after election, and that an era of civil strife and bloodshed was in the offing. The *Patriot* hoped for better times, but candor compelled a frank analysis.[306]

If further evidence be needed to prove the intensive devotion of the Bell party to the Union, the " Great Union Meeting " at Salisbury, October 11-12, may be noted. One who attended described the rally as " the largest meeting that has been held in North Carolina since the days of 1840." Zebulon Vance, William A. Graham, George E. Badger, William N. H. Smith, and John M. Morehead were distinguished party members who addressed the gathering in an orgy of oratory.[307] Graham declared that Henry Clay had once told him that in a critical hour he relied on Virginia, North Carolina, Kentucky, and Tennessee to preserve the Union. " If a Black Republican

[304] Sam. J. Johnston to W. S. Pettigrew, Aug. 1, 1860, MS, Pettigrew Family Papers, Southern Historical Collection, University of North Carolina.
[305] Charles L. Pettigrew to W. S. Pettigrew, Oct. 22, 1860, MS, *ibid*.
[306] Greensborough *Patriot*, July 20, 1860.
[307] *Weekly Raleigh Register*, Oct. 17, 1860.

President commit an overt act, rise and fight." This was Graham's advice to his fellow-citizens.[308]

It may cause no surprise to learn that the tone of the Salisbury assemblage was displeasing to the Breckinridge organ in that town, which termed it " that of utter, unqualified, unmitigated submission to Black Republican rule." [309] The Greensborough *Patriot* counselled that in view of the probability of Lincoln's election, " it behooves every man in the South to vote for Bell, so far as possible, to quell the disunion spirit at the SOUTH." [310] B. F. Moore wrote in October that he feared the continuation of the slave question after secession, which he predicted would lead to class conflict over the Africanization of the South through the reopening of the slave trade.[311] On another occasion, the same writer referred to " these traitors," an allusion to those advocating secession.[312] The great question to be settled at the polls in November, 1860, was put by the Raleigh *Register*: " Shall the Constitution and Union be maintained, or shall we break up the glorious Union and begin one of the bloodiest and most horrible wars of all times?" [313]

[308] Charlotte *Whig* in Fayetteville *Observer*, Oct. 22 1860; Sitterson, p. 174. For description of Bell rally at High Point, which reminded the writer of " the Log Cabin times," see H. H. Buxton to R. P. Buxton, July 21, 1860, MS, Buxton Papers.

[309] Salisbury *Banner* in Fayetteville *Observer*, Oct. 22, 1860; Charlotte *Western Democrat*, Oct. 30, 1860.

[310] Greensborough *Patriot*, Oct. 18, 1860.

[311] B. F. Moore to S. H. Rogers, Oct. 1860, Washington *National Intelligencer*, Oct. 30, 1860.

[312] Sitterson, pp. 173-174.

[313] *Weekly Raleigh Register*, Oct. 24, 1860. A few days after election, Miss A. N. Buxton wrote a relative in Fayetteville: " I suppose that your Union sentiments are at such a pitch at this present time, that you cannot view with a favorable eye, the result of the election. . . ." (A. N. Buxton to R. P. Buxton, Nov. 10, 1860, MS, Buxton Papers.) After election, the Bell press strongly recommended that the Union be continued. The Raleigh *Weekly Register*, Nov. 14, 1860, wanted to give Lincoln a fair trial. South Carolina was condemned. The Greensborough *Patriot*, Nov. 8, 1860, regretted Lincoln's election, but asked for tolerance and caution. Let people be slow to use the unpleasant word " traitor." The Hillsborough *Recorder*, Nov. 14, 1860, declared that Lincoln had been fairly and Constitutionally elected. The South had no right in advance to assume that Lincoln would not perform his duties faithfully. He was checked for two years: " Let us not anticipate evils which may not occur." The Fayetteville *Observer*, Nov. 8, 1860, believed that if the South were not to abide by the results of the election, it should not have taken part. Lincoln's party would disintegrate soon. The Whigs were " sustained by the more con-

SUMMARY FOR BORDER SLAVE STATES, TENNESSEE
AND NORTH CAROLINA

A survey of the campaign in the border slave states and upper South discloses that there existed in these seven states a distinct possibility of a fusion of old Whigs, Americans, and members of "the Opposition," with the Republicans. The Republicans had an organization and a small following in each of the border slave states. In St. Louis, thanks to the German population, the Republicans had a large membership. But in general, the border slave state Republicans were few in number and despised and persecuted. Nevertheless, ambitious men who braved the wrath of their neighbors to champion an unpopular cause in 1860, were rewarded with public office after 1861. Two such leaders, Edward Bates of Missouri and Montgomery Blair of Maryland, became members of Lincoln's Cabinet. In 1860, however, the possible merger of anti-Democratic elements and Republicans was prevented because of the real or supposed attitude of the Republicans towards slavery.

Such leaders as Henry Winter Davis of Maryland, John Minor Botts of Virginia, George D. Prentice, John J. Crittenden, and Garret Davis of Kentucky, Edward Bates of Missouri, Horace Maynard and Emerson Etheridge of Tennessee, and John A. Gilmer of North Carolina, as old Whigs were in substantial accord with the Republicans on economic policy. The division of the Democratic party in 1860 and the outbreak of the Civil War rendered first unnecessary and then impossible such a coalition. With Lincoln in office and America at peace, it is not fantastic to conceive of the eventual formation of such a party in the upper South. This very possibility perhaps haunted the Southern Democratic politicians, and may help to explain their actions of 1860-1861.

Certain it is that after war had disposed of the slavery

siderate and influential of the Democrats." The High Point *Reporter* did not consider Lincoln's election sufficient for action. (Quoted in Charlotte *Western Democrat*, Nov. 13, 1860.) The Raleigh *Press*, a Breckinridge paper, proclaimed the election of Lincoln the "death knell of the Union," and predicted that the Union would not last three months. (Quoted in *ibid.*) But the *Western Democrat* was cautious, and desired unity in North Carolina. (*Ibid.*)

13

question, many Southerners demonstrated that they were not antagonistic to capitalists and factories *per se,* although, of course, the bitterness engendered by war and reconstruction adversely affected the growth of the Republican party in the upper South. During and after the war, in Delaware, Maryland, Kentucky, West Virginia, and Missouri, the Republican party became an important factor, and had a considerable membership in Virginia, North Carolina, and Tennessee.

Another feature of the campaign in the border slave states was the common concern felt for their exposed geographical condition in the event of war. In language which despite politics appears to have been sincere, the horrors of a bloody war fought on battlefields among their homes were graphically depicted. This aspect was emphasized in the campaign by the Bell and Douglas orators. In view of the excellent showing of Bell along the border, and Douglas' victory in Missouri, it is clear that the great majority refused to heed the demands of Southern extremists. Moreover, the moderation of many Breckinridge voters, and the operation of party regularity in sections of the upper South in favor of Breckinridge, underscore this conclusion.

Five of these states were to some degree bounded geographically by free states, and it should be recognized that the Ohio and Mississippi rivers created special problems, which were sure to affect the political attitudes of the adjacent regions.[314] A distinguished historian has written of the Ohio Valley:

Welded into a decided unity among themselves by the difficulties of their adventure, they were distinguished from the people of the lake region by origin, from those of the South by their dislike of slavery; they were bound to North by love of free labor, to the South by kinship and tradition.[315]

Recognition of this fact was seen early in the year, in the meeting at Louisville, Kentucky, of good-will delegations from Kentucky, Tennessee, Indiana, and Ohio. At this festive occasion Union toasts were read, including the famous Jackson toast—in honor of Tennessee. Kentucky's toast was prophetic

[314] The Mississippi river appeared as a factor also in the election farther South, especially at New Orleans. See section below, "Louisiana," in chapter "The Campaign in the Lower South."

[315] C. R. Fish, "The Decision of the Ohio Valley," *Annual Report of the American Historical Association for 1910* (Washington, 1912), pp. 155-164.

of her neutral stand: " If treason to the Union shall prevail in the North or in the South, our noble State will stand between the two sections as stood the people of old between the living and the dead, to stay the progress of the pestilence." Governor Magoffin of Kentucky asserted that his state stood between the fanatics of the sections, and further said: " We are in the center of this Union, a rich country, highly conservative. . . ." Speaking to an audience from free and slave states, Magoffin would have slavery localized: if the people wanted it let them have it, and if not, slavery should not be forced upon unwilling people. Mexico and Cuba should be annexed as good Southern policy in the same manner as Louisiana, Texas, and Florida came to the United States.[316]

James A. Garfield, in responding to a toast to Ohio, predicted that the great name " the West" would eliminate sectional discord. The Mississippi Valley was the backbone of the country, and the future President assured his hearers that "the maturer voice of Ohio was for law, order, and the rights of states." All were invited in the name of the Governor of Ohio to visit the capital at Columbus. This, said Garfield, was the method by which people could understand each other.[317] The invitation was accepted, and after the conclusion of this legislative junket into " alien " land, the results were hailed with satisfaction by those who wished to conciliate the sections. The excursion to Columbus was described by one writer as " the best week's work they have done in a long time." It was intended to dispel the idea that the people of Ohio were their enemies, and the people of Tennessee should be satisfied that no irreconcilable enmity existed. Such representative Democrats as the Speakers of the Tennessee House and Senate did not hold Salmon P. Chase of Ohio to be a traitor and foe of the South. The delegations instead sat around " the festive board " clinking glasses with " Black Republicans," and all joined in patriotic toast to the Union.[318]

The situation in the border slave states was accurately discerned by the extremists in the lower South, who concluded that their neighbors to the north could not be depended upon.

[316] Louisville *Journal* in St. Louis *Daily Missouri Republican,* Jan. 27, 1860.
[317] *Ibid.*
[318] Nashville *Republican Banner,* Feb. 3, 1860.

Regarding Virginia's refusal to consider the proposal of a Southern conference, the Charleston *Mercury* concluded that no reliance should be placed upon the " frontier" Southern states to lead " the van of our resistance." Why had the South the right to expect such leadership from Virginia, Maryland, Kentucky, or Missouri? It was conceded that South Carolina was more interested in the struggle, because the border slave states might live with or without slavery, while " to us the institution is indispensable." And in any event, the *Mercury* was confident that Virginia would follow the South.[319] The same view was entertained by that other bellwether of radicalism, the Montgomery *Mail*, which described the upper South as being " too firmly caught in the meshes of a mis-called conservatism. . . ." There were few if any real state-rights leaders there.

Southern radicals often voiced alarm and fear for the future of slavery in the border states. The Charleston *Mercury* alluded to Maryland as that " quondam " slave state, and the Montgomery *Mail* observed: " *The institution* [slavery] *is even now in a tottering condition* in the border slaveholding states, where the people are constantly expecting fresh John Brown raids . . . ." [320] But another far Southern commentator asserted that the number of slaves in Virginia, Maryland, and Kentucky were " constantly increasing " in spite of drains by the cotton states.[321]

It seems clear, also, that if the Republicans wished to build up a party in the slave states, the border was indeed the proper place to begin. Southern secessionists painted graphic pictures

[319] Charleston *Mercury*, March 10, 1860.

[320] Montgomery *Daily Mail*, May 17, 1860. Edward Bates believed in 1859 that slavery would be extinguished in Missouri in the immediate future. *Bates' Diary*, p. 12. The percentage of slave increase in Kentucky between 1850 and 1860 was only 7 per cent, as against 15⅔ per cent 1840-1850. L. Collins, *History of Kentucky* (rev. by R. H. Collins, 2 vols., Covington, Ky., 1878), I, 84.

[321] New Orleans *Daily Crescent*, April 25, 1860. The condition of slavery in the border states on the eve of secession, remains a controversial point. The following table may be of interest:

SLAVERY IN THE BORDER STATES

	1850	1860
Delaware	2,290	1,798
Maryland	90,368	87,188
Virginia	472,528	483,993
Kentucky	210,981	225,490
Missouri	87,422	114,965

of the insidious methods of the Lincoln administration, if allowed to function under normal conditions, in employing power and patronage to create a formidable following there. Robert Toombs believed that under such a regime Maryland would be " abolitionized " within a year; in two years the party would be powerful in Virginia, Kentucky, and Missouri; and within four years there would be a free-labor party in the entire South. Thus the strife would be brought to Southern firesides. For that reason Toombs was not for awaiting an " overt act." [322]

Northern observers did not fail to assess the situation in the border states. The New York *Times* declared that the Bell party would not secede, nor would that of Douglas. The Breckinridge party " down to the thirty fifth parallel " would not.[323] On election day the New York *Tribune* was confident that the Union could not be overturned easily. " That question will be settled, not by power of the North, but by the people of Maryland, Virginia, North Carolina, Kentucky, and Tennessee." [324] And when the election returns were in, the New York *Times* interpreted the results, especially in the border states, as sufficient to dispel the danger of disunion.[325] A modern student has pointed to the fact that the " neutrals " had a majority in six out of seven states of the upper South, and in the other, North Carolina, the Bell-Douglas vote exceeded 45 per cent.[326] The returns from the seven states of this group were as follows:[327]

	BELL	BRECKINRIDGE	DOUGLAS	LINCOLN
	%	%	%	%
Delaware	3,864 (24.09)	7,337 (45.74)	1,023 (6.38)	3,815 (23.79)
Maryland	41,760 (45.15)	42,482 (45.92)	5,966 (6.45)	2,294 (2.48)
Virginia	74,681 (44.66)	74,323 (44.44)	16,290 (9.75)	1,929 (1.15)
Kentucky	66,058 (45.18)	53,143 (36.35)	25,651 (17.54)	1,364 (.93)
Missouri	58,372 (35.27)	31,317 (18.92)	58,801 (35.53)	17,028 (10.28)
Tennessee	69,274 (47.67)	54,709 (44.52)	11,350 (7.81)	
North Carolina	44,990 (46.75)	48,539 (50.44)	2,701 (2.81)	
Total	358,999	311,850	121,782	26,430

[322] Toombs to Alexander H. Stephens, Feb. 10, 1860, *The Correspondence of Robert Toombs*, ed., Ulrich B. Phillips, II, 462.

[323] New York *Times*, Oct. 4, 1860.

[324] New York *Tribune* (semi-weekly), Nov. 6, 1860.

[325] New York *Times*, Nov. 7, 1860.

[326] Scrugham, *The Peaceable Americans*, pp. 40-41.

[327] *The Tribune Almanac and Political Register for 1861* (New York, 1861).

Chapter VII

THE CAMPAIGN OF 1860 IN THE LOWER SOUTH

SOUTH CAROLINA

In this state, the well-spring of sectional discontent since 1828, the presidential election of 1860 was viewed by many with utter disdain, by some with a weather-eye to the federal patronage, and by others who desired a continued cooperation with the national Democratic party as in years past. Whatever the shades of political opinion, there were but few who dared openly to advocate Bell or Douglas, and after Breckinridge's nomination it became a foregone conclusion that the electoral votes of South Carolina, cast by the legislature, would be for him. And there was almost complete unity in attitude towards the " peculiar institution," and the election of a " black " Republican President. With a few exceptions to be noted, South Carolina by 1860 had secured for herself a large measure of that unity which many so ardently desired for the entire South. The overpowering question in the minds of most South Carolinians after the John Brown raid was the immediate attainment of Southern solidarity with which to resist aggression and to wring concessions from the North, within the Union if possible, without the Union otherwise.[1]

Governor William H. Gist,[2] in his message to the South Carolina legislature in 1859, employed strong language. Presenting certain antislavery resolutions of the legislature of Vermont, the Governor said:

These resolutions not only embody the opinions of Vermont, but of all the non-slaveholding States; and the signs of the times clearly indicate

---

[1] For a recent scholarly account of the activities of moderates in the state, see Lillian A. Kibler, " Unionist Sentiment in South Carolina in 1860," *Journal of Southern History*, IV (Aug., 1938), 345-366. It will, however, be noted that, with the exception of Senator James H. Hammond, the moderates in South Carolina, O'Connor, Orr, Perry, Petigru, Lemuel Boozer, and Simkins, either were out of office, or holders of minor offices. On the other hand, Governor Gist, Congressmen Miles, Bonham, Boyce, McQueen, Keitt, and Ashmore, spoke authoritatively for South Carolina.

[2] *D. A. B.*, VIII, 325.

an approaching crisis in the destinies of the South. The war so relentlessly urged against our institutions has assumed a form so menacing
that none but those who are wilfully blind can fail to see the dangers
that surround us, and the perils to which we are exposed.

Gist's indictment of the Northern people was sweeping. The
entire North was pledged to the destruction of the South, by
declining to admit slave states into the Union, by the establishment of underground railways, by the closing of the territories
to slaveholders, and finally by incitement of slave insurrections,
the most recent example being that at Harpers Ferry. The
Brown raid was but the first act in the drama. It was clear to
Governor Gist that the masses at the North approved this act,
and it was equally clear to him that it was of no avail longer
to rely upon the Democratic party. With regard to the impending presidential election, he said:

South Carolina should be careful not to commit herself, directly or
indirectly, to any presidential aspirant and be forced by party trammels
to support a party nominee. An open and undisguised enemy is infinitely preferable to a pretended friend. . . . We have sunk very low,
indeed, if our liberties are to depend upon the fortunate selection of a
candidate for the presidency, who on account of his popularity or his
mysterious manner of expressing his opinions, makes himself acceptable
to both sections, or what is generally termed available.[3]

Governor Gist admitted the difficulties which surrounded his
people, and confessed his inability to give right counsel as to
the proper course. But he recommended a Southern confederacy,
and gave it as his opinion that they could no longer live in
peace and security in the Union. The Governor recommended
that the legislature initiate a movement which would obtain
concerted action of the Southern states, in order to defend
Southern institutions against " black " Republican domination
of the federal government. He closed with an emphatic assertion of South Carolina's sovereign power.[4]

Measures to implement Governor Gist's recommendation in
regard to cooperation of the Southern states were immediately
passed by the legislature. Their author, C. G. Memminger, was
despatched by the Governor as commissioner to Virginia. His

[3] Henry D. Capers, *The Life and Times of C. G. Memminger* (Richmond,
1893), pp. 238-241.
[4] *Ibid.*

mission's purpose was to win the Old Dominion to the idea of a Southern conference, under Virginia leadership. The South Carolinians revealed their hopes and plans in letters to Memminger, who was received in Richmond with attention and official courtesy. He presented his plans privately to sympathetic Virginians, and publicly in a solemn plea to the Virginia legislature. But Virginia was cool to the conference proposal, and declined to participate. This action proved to be a bitter blow to Memminger and other Carolinians, some of whom concluded that, in the last analysis, South Carolina would be compelled to " lead off," to precipitate a crisis by separate state action, and thus to " drag" reluctant Virginia, and other states, into a Southern confederacy.[5]

There is a considerable body of evidence to demonstrate that some responsible South Carolinians were determined to dissolve the Union. Her Congressmen were in the thick of parliamentary battles in Washington. The fierce tension that existed during the session 1859-1860 has long been known, a condition which caused members to arm themselves and to maintain vigilance.[6] William Porcher Miles wrote: " When there is no telling when a collision may occur on the floor of the House—it would be rather awkward for any Southern men to be absent." [7] Alfred Huger wrote from Charleston that he daily expected the shedding of blood in the House of Representatives, nor was he averse to such an occurrence. He lamented that the proprieties of life had vanished, and that Americans lived like Comanches. " Indeed, I consider the Pistol as the only efficient Peacemaker, or remedy for the vulgarity which necessarily belongs to a democracy . . . ." Huger was violent in condemnation of the sixty-three " obscene" signers of the Helper book. He thought a good, rough, free-for-all in Congress would be most desirable.[8]

[5] For details of this episode see Ollinger Crenshaw, "Christopher G. Memminger's Mission to Virginia, 1860," *Journal of Southern History*, VIII (Aug., 1942), 334-349. Cf. above, Chap. VI, part 3.

[6] D. H. Hamilton wrote: " You give me great pleasure by telling me that you have consented to carry arms upon your person. . . ." Hamilton to W. P. Miles, Dec. 9, 1859, MS, Miles Papers.

[7] Miles to C. G. Memminger, Jan. 23, 1860, MS, Memminger Paper, Southern Historical Collection, University of North Carolina.

[8] Alfred Huger to Miles, Dec. 12, 1859, MS, Miles Papers. He was still

The fight over the Speakership was a matter of far more vital import to South Carolinians than historians have recognized. Of course any one of the endorsers of the Helper book was bitterly opposed by the Southern membership, especially John Sherman.[9] The South Carolina delegation in Congress was determined to defeat a Helperite at all costs, and evidently was involved in plans to withdraw from Congress and to break up the United States government. At a slightly later time, but while the Speakership contest still raged, R. Barnwell Rhett, Jr., referred to " . . . my proposition, that the Southern Representatives should withdraw from Congress in the election of a Black Republican Speaker. It was intended for other states than our own; and for effect with the people, not for Congress. Their minds should be familiarized with all forms of action, to be prepared for any." [10]

Governor William H. Gist's words are worth quoting fully in this episode. After asserting that, in his opinion, the South Carolina delegation would be sustained by the state in the event of withdrawal upon Sherman's election as Speaker, he added that he was less certain in the case of the election of a milder Republican, one " who had not committed such an overt act." Gist then alluded to a plan, of which he apparently had prior knowledge, to eject by force an offensive Speaker-elect.

If that plan was adopted a bloody revolution would be inevitable, and although I am prepared to wade in blood rather than submit to inequality & degradation, yet if a bloodless revolution can be effected, of course it would be preferable. If however, you upon consultation decide to make the issue of force in Washington, write or telegraph me, & I will have a Regiment in or near Washington in the shortest possible time.

Indeed, the South Carolina delegation could alone determine the state's secession on the election of Sherman. Let Congressmen lead: the public was waiting on them.

When I advise against the ejection of Sherman if elected I do not wish to be understood as not desiring the war to begin at Washington; but I would prefer it should begin in sudden heat & with good provocation,

---

lamenting the failure of Alexander Hamilton's senate-for-life proposal. Huger to W. P. Miles, Jan. 20, 1860, MS, *ibid.*

[9] Fite, *The Presidential Campaign of 1860*, pp. 33-46.

[10] R. B. Rhett, Jr., to W. P. Miles, Jan. 29, 1860, MS, Miles Papers.

rather than a deliberate determination to perform an act of violence which might prejudice us in the eyes of the world.

Governor Gist said the legislature would adjourn but that he would recall that body if the South Carolina Congressmen decided to take action.[11] It was rumored in Charleston that the Louisiana delegation in Congress would retire upon the election of Sherman.[12]

All ramifications of this scheme are matters of intense interest to the historian, and are proper subjects for further investigation, but it is certain that Governor Gist's letter presents proof that secession and war might have come late in 1859 or early in 1860, months before the presidential election. The letter also affords proof that the decision in this fateful affair was placed squarely in the hands of the South Carolina delegation in Congress. Historians have not usually considered the election of John Sherman as Speaker to be the cause of an immediate disruption, a *coup d'etat*.[13]

The situation presented apparent unity in South Carolina in 1860, and conservatives and radicals made an identical appeal.[14] A visitor there at the close of the campaign noted the unanimity of the Palmetto State, and ardently desired emulation by the

[11] William H. Gist to W. P. Miles, Dec. 20, 1859. Italics mine. His views were set forth " frankly & hastily," and he had no objection to " true " men seeing the letter (MS, *ibid.*). D. H. Hamilton declared: " Our people are ready for anything, and we shall hail with delight any measures which the Southern Members may adopt to bring this contest into some positive form of action." Hamilton to W. P. Miles, Dec. 9, 1859, MS, *ibid.*

[12] Alfred Huger to W. P. Miles, Dec. 12, 1859, MS, *ibid.*

[13] Mysterious communications from George N. Sanders of New York were sent to South Carolina Congressmen. See telegram of Sanders to Keitt and Miles, Dec. 16, 1859, and vague note telling Miles that " I'll return with you in one week & elect you Speaker *Sure*." (Sanders to W. P. Miles, Dec. 24, 1859, MSS, *ibid.*) Sanders as a Douglas man was anxious to hold the Union together. Early in February, Miles was seeking advice as to what Southern Congressmen could do. " We are constantly taunted with being ' behind the people ' . . . ." He asked what they could do to catch up with or surpass public opinion. (W. P. Miles to C. G. Memminger, Feb. 3, 1860, MS, Memminger Papers.)

[14] The Charleston *Mercury*, Aug. 2, 1860, boasted that not a single press in the state supported Bell or Douglas: " What has produced this unanimity in South Carolina? It is, because the Press and the public men of South Carolina have been more true and faithful to the rights of the South than they have been in other Southern States." Laura A. White, *R. Barnwell Rhett Father of Secession* (New York, 1931), pp. 172-173.

other Southern states of South Carolina's "dignified" position.[15] Rhett's scholarly biographer has written that the working agreement between Yancey and Rhett in 1859-1860 was formed to use the territorial question to destroy the national Democratic party. The Davis-Slidell faction joined Rhett-Yancey in order to defeat Douglas, and not primarily to destroy the Union. The nomination of a Southern man at Charleston would upset their plans, as it would make the platform less important. They achieved their ends by inflaming opposition to Douglas.[16]

An insight into the plans of the Rhetts may be gained from one of R. B. Rhett Jr.'s interminable letters to Congressman Miles. He thought that Miles distrusted the Southern people too much. " My belief is that the weakness is with the public men in the South, who themselves ' have no stomach for the fight.' " Rhett feared that they were not men who sought to direct public opinion. He recalled that the war of 1812 was brought on by a " . . . mere handful of fearless and patriotic Southern men, regardless of consequences, when their section was not the injured section and when a cowardly spirit was rife throughout the country." The spirit of the people in the cotton states was far in advance of that of their representatives, and the people would sustain " a bold and decided course."

It was their partisan contacts at Washington which sapped the boldness of Southern men.

The South must dissever itself from the rotten Northern element. After the Charleston convention we must have a Southern State-rights Democratic party organized on principles and with State-rights candidates upon whom to rally. This will insure the defeat of the double-faced ' National ' Democracy so called and make up the issue between the sections, with a resistance party already joined to meet the event of a Black Republican President elected by the North.

Rhett admitted that there was no chance for the state-rights wing to dominate the Charleston convention.

Hence the importance of attaining the secession of the Alabama and Mississippi delegations, on the issue of Squatter Sovereignty and the

---

[15] W. H. Babcock, a native of South Carolina, reported his observations of conditions in South Carolina, in his paper, the Fernandina *East Floridian*, Oct. 24, 1860.

[16] White, p. 163.

construction of the Dred Scott decision. If they will but do it, the people I am sure will come up to the scratch, and the game will be ours.

Indeed Rhett thought the idea of uniting the " *whole* " South on any resistance measure was absurd and unnecessary. Alabama, Mississippi, and South Carolina were the only Southern states of whom action could be expected. Georgia was held back, he believed, by Toombs, Cobb, and Stephens, but would act if other states did. These states were " quite enough to break down the spoils Democracy and, on the election of a Black Republican, to dissolve the Union."

Yet Rhett insisted that even in Alabama and Mississippi bold men must act, but he was not confident of their course. "It seems, however, unjust to lay the blame on the people, without giving them opportunities to sustain such movements." He reiterated his blame: " So far from stimulating, I believe the public men of the South are restraining their people—are obstacles in the way of reform." All his ideas were based upon his belief that South Carolina was ready, " . . . and should do nothing more than encourage other states to take the initiative." [17]

Thus Rhett adumbrated the events of the Charleston convention, and in view of the closeness with which the events actually followed Rhett's plan, gives some substantiation to the charges made during the campaign of 1860 by Unionists in the North and in the South, and especially by the Douglas Democrats, that the disruption of the Charleston convention was the result of a well-laid plan. The strategy outlined by Rhett two months before the assembling of the convention was followed almost to the letter.[18]

With the approach of the Charleston convention, the various political groups were wary lest there be an overturn in South Carolina politics as a result of the nomination of a man whom South Carolina could support. Some were opposed to the state's participation in the convention at all, and others were fearful that there existed a covert Douglas party. Robert N. Gourdin, a Charlestonian, wrote that he did not believe the rumor that

[17] R. B. Rhett, Jr., to W. P. Miles, Jan. 29, 1860, MS, Miles Papers.
[18] *D. A. B.*, XV, 527, says that the " Mercury Program " failed in South Carolina in 1860, but to Rhett Sr.'s " surprise," Yancey suceeded in breaking up the Charleston convention.

South Carolina would support Douglas even on a Southern platform. But he greatly feared that the South would compromise, which would seal the South's fate and lead to bloody revolution. " The result of the Charleston Convention will tell the future of the South for weal or woe." [19] D. H. Hamilton believed that there was a Douglas party in Charleston, and he predicted that the convention would develop a strong Douglas party in the state. The delegates chosen to the Charleston convention were " small fry " politicians. Hamilton thought there were men for Douglas " that you little dream of." After all, the Administration had done little to make friends in the state, because she would assuredly vote Democratic. " To be candid with you I believe that a large majority of the people of S⁰. C꙼. take but little interest in the Presidential question . . . ." [20]

John Cunningham of the Charleston *News* did not think that the state delegation would vote for Douglas in the convention. " But if he gets the nomination, they will probably support him." In common with R. Barnwell Rhett, Jr., he feared that the South Carolina delegation would not sufficiently back up the demand of Alabama and Mississippi for a territorial protection plank. " Among the Charleston gentlemen who participate in the Convention movement, there is much proclivity for Douglas." But he added: " In the country there is a general opposition to Douglas, and Orr cannot control it." [21] I. W. Hayne admitted that there was a Douglas fragment, but it was weak and would vanish. Some were playing up to Douglas to secure his support for a Southern candidate; they were playing a game, but Hayne absolved them from treachery to the South. He took consolation in the two-thirds rule, " the fundamental Constitution of the Convention System," which would defeat Douglas. After all, it would be good politics to conciliate him. [22]

[19] Gourdin to W. P. Miles, April 4-10, 1860, MS, Miles Papers.
[20] D. H. Hamilton to W. P. Miles, April 4, 1860, MS, *ibid*. See also clipping from Charleston *News*, April 7, 1860, " Douglas in South Carolina."
[21] John Cunningham to W. P. Miles, April 5, 1860, MS, *ibid*. R. B. Rhett, Jr., feared the " weak, spoils " party which would represent the state in the convention. R. B. Rhett, Jr., to W. P. Miles, March 2, 1860, MS, *ibid*.
[22] Isaac W. Hayne to W. P. Miles, April 11, 15, 1860, MS, *ibid*. One observer thought there was a group which would attempt to unseat Miles, if Douglas were nominated, but that the attempt would fail. William H. Trescot to James H. Hammond, April 28, 1860, MS, Hammond Papers, Library of Congress.

One careful observer reported, about two months before the Charleston convention, that the state was divided in opinion, but that he thought a majority ready to participate. And majority opinion was divided. Some thought the Charleston convention would be a Southern convention: that the South would name the candidate and write the platform. They felt bound to consult other Southern states as to what could be accomplished within existing political organizations. While not ready to follow Yancey, " . . . they hope either to give the Democratic party a Southern character or else having demonstrated that impossibility to be in position to ask for concerted Southern action as the only alternative." The other faction believed in national Democracy, and they would take any candidate, including Douglas and the Cincinnati platform. Trescot thought that this faction would win the day. This group was looking to the next administration.[23]

For months the Rhetts' Charleston *Mercury* had marshalled every argument to achieve the downfall of the national Democratic party. In one editorial the *Mercury* traced the history of the Democratic party to prove the Western faction " false " on the subject of internal improvements. On the tariff the Democrats had been false, particularly those of New York, New Jersey, and Pennsylvania. American historians might be surprised to learn that from 1816 to 1860, " . . . every Tariff passed by Congress has had Protection stamped on every line . . . ." Finally, the Democrats had been " false" on the subject of slavery. Even the Supreme Court was looked upon with suspicion by the *Mercury*. " There are those who with ' old John Adams ' declare the Supreme Court the final arbiter of Congressional legislation." Such were the " consolidationist" Democrats. Indeed the departure from " principle "was a prime requisite of a national Democrat. After all, the United States was not a nation, so far as internal affairs were concerned, but was a mere agent of the states.[24]

[23] William H. Trescot to W. P. Miles, Feb. 22, 1860, MS, Miles Papers. Trescot urged Miles to be aloof, and hoped he was not a secessionist. For an analysis of South Carolina's course, see also, same to same, March 10, 1860, MS, *ibid.*

[24] Charleston *Mercury*, Jan. 14, 1860. Regarding the tendency of men like Rhett to classify all Northern Democrats as depraved, it is interesting to note

According to the *Mercury,* it was the " trimmer," anxious to win a presidential nomination who prevented the South from securing her rights. The *Mercury* agreed with Memminger that the South's own worst enemies were her ambitious politicians.[25] Why should the South enter a convention in which Massachusetts, Maine, Vermont, Connecticut, Rhode Island—states unavailable for a single Democratic electoral vote—could outvote Georgia, South Carolina, Alabama, and Mississippi? [26] Noting the proceedings of the Mississippi state Democratic convention, the *Mercury* feared that she too might compromise, especially to gain Jefferson Davis' nomination for President.[27] One of the cardinal errors which had deluded the slave South was that " any party at the North is dependable." [28] Daily in the spring of 1860 the *Mercury* raged over some real or fancied injury. There was a bitter complaint at the loss of Kansas, " a fine hemp and tobacco country, with mines rivalling California." [29]

As the Charleston convention neared, the *Mercury* called for a resuscitation of the Democratic party upon principles. It advised that at the next presidential election, that the question be, not whether a Democrat or a Black Republican should be President, but one of Union or disunion. If believed at the North, that idea would win peace for the South.[30] On the eve of the meeting, the *Mercury* demanded a Southern Democratic organization to force the hand of the Democratic party to protect the rights of the South, and to save the Union, if that be possible.[31]

D. H. Hamilton wrote that a secession was expected at the

the comment of a member of a prominent Carolina family who visited New York early in 1860. " I went down there last night and met an Uncle of Mrs. N's. He is a warm Democrat and takes the Southern side of the great question that at present agitates the nation. He seemed greatly astonished when I told him that many people at the South thought the Democrats were no more to be relied on than the free soilers. . . ." The views of the uncle were reported to be all that any Southerner could desire. He said, " there always have been slaves and there always will be. . . ." Charles L. Pettigrew to Mrs. Charles L. Pettigrew, Jan. 11, 1860, MS, Pettigrew Family Papers.

[25] Charleston *Mercury,* Jan. 28, 1860.
[26] *Ibid.,* Jan. 21, 1860.
[27] *Ibid.,* Feb. 11, 1860. Davis was not enough of an extremist.
[28] *Ibid.,* March 13, 1860.
[29] *Ibid.,* April 3, 1860.
[30] *Ibid.,* April 16, 1860.
[31] *Ibid.,* April 26, 1860.

convention, " for how could they agree?" The South Carolina delegation was but a set of office-seekers, and were held in contempt by real Southerners. Douglas would be nominated after the secession, and he would attract a wide following of moderates. " The rascals" and "gulls" of the South would join him.[32] Alfred Huger described the conduct of the Douglas men, who " . . . came here rabid & reckless, like a gang of wolves or a flock of vultures bent on spoil, without compromise or alternative; their howlings are for blood. They were willing to give any platform that would insure them the carcass & they would do so . . . Douglas or nothing!" At the same time, Huger lamented the fact that if the sixty-five seceding votes had remained but thirty-six hours longer, the day would have been " ours." [33] And a member of the Pettigrew family wrote her Mother: " Well! the convention has broken up—a failure—the extreme South, & the Black Republicans seem to stand side by side in their equally unreasonable position. Charles & William [Pettigrew] are . . . Union men & this violent action gives a shock to their hopes . . . ." [34]

The *Mercury* rejoiced at the bursting of "the corrupt fungus," which was " . . . carried to Baltimore with its impurities to spread still wider the pestilence of its rottenness." Indeed, the Richmond convention was disappointing to the *Mercury*, which desired a convention of all Southern states. But it recommended sending a delegation to Richmond, because it was called by the cotton states, and its principles were clear.[35] Henry Gourdin favored sending delegates to Richmond as a convention whose platform was declared beforehand. He was against " irresponsible leaders " and meetings, who might desire to go to Baltimore.[36] After a spirited contest, the Rhett faction tri-

[32] D. H. Hamilton to W. P. Miles, April 26, 1860. MS, Miles Papers.

[33] Alfred Huger to W. P. Miles, May 7, 1860, MS, *ibid*. And about the same time, W. H. Trescot thought that the chance existed then, if ever, to show the South that its battle could be fought in the Union. Trescot to Hammond, May 12, 1860, MS, Hammond Papers.

[34] Mrs. Charles L. Pettigrew to Mother, May 8, 1860, MS, Pettigrew Family Papers. An insight into a Southern woman's mind is afforded by a letter of Mrs. Charles L. Pettigrew to her son, written during a visit to New York, June 5, 1860. *Ibid*.

[35] Charleston *Mercury*, May 5, 1860. W. E. Martin to W. P. Miles, May 9, 1860, MS, Miles Papers.

[36] Henry Gourdin to R. N. Gourdin, May 14, 1860, MS, Gourdin-Young Papers, Library of Emory University.

umphed at the Columbia convention in the election of delegates to Richmond.[37]

I. W. Hayne described events at this state convention, and remarked with disgust that Rhett and others like him would ruin any cause. " In case of *actual revolution,* already begun, no age or service exempts—but until that time, I am done." [38] The Richmond convention turned out to be another fiasco, as all the Southern states, except South Carolina and Florida, sent delegates to Baltimore. A member of the South Carolina delegation, A. H. Boykin, described the temper of that body: " But there are some very combustible materials with us, I fear they will put me down a real submissionist as I am obliged to urge moderation & patience with them all the time since I got here." The members were in a mood to quit Richmond in a huff and return home. Boykin agreed to assist them in gaining their objectives, provided they would acquiesce if beaten.[39]

B. F. Perry [40] of the Greenville *Patriot and Mountaineer* declared that outside pressure in Charleston had much to do with the secession movement, and he charged the state's delegates became much more fiery after their arrival.[41] He pointed out that the Columbia state convention had rejected the Alabama resolves.[42] Perry, one of the principal Unionists in the state, pronounced the secession a suicidal course. It was absurd, he thought, to repudiate Northern friends, and he saw no surrender of principle in what the North offered [43] J. P. Hunt, Perry's nephew, was in Charleston shortly after the convention, and heard much of the stand taken by his uncle. He reported

[37] Chauncey S. Boucher, " South Carolina and the South on the Eve of Secession," *Washington University Studies,* Humanistic Series, VI (April, 1919), 138.

[38] Hayne to Hammond, June 3, 1860, MS, Hammond Papers.

[39] Boykin to Mrs. A. H. Boykin, Richmond, Virginia, June 12, 1860, MS, A. H. Boykin Papers, Southern Historical Papers, University of North Carolina.

[40] *D. A. B.,* XIV, 483-484.

[41] R. B. Rhett, Jr., agreed that outside pressure brought about a change in the South Carolina delegation. " If they had not retired, they would have been mobbed, I believe." R. B. Rhett, Jr., to W. P. Miles, May 12, 1860, MS, Miles Papers.

[42] See telegram, R. B. Rhett, Jr., to Miles, April 17, 1860, which substantiates Perry's contention in this regard. Rhett lamented that the " Alabama resolutions " were rejected. " A packed jury trimming to keep in with Douglas." MS, *ibid.*

[43] Charleston *Mercury,* May 15, 1860; see also the defense of Douglas by Mr. Simkins of South Carolina. Mobile *Daily Register,* June 23, 1860.

that in the main it seemed unpopular, but Hunt's opinion was that he had acted "the part of a patriot." "I am glad to see you, as of old, still ready to face the current of popular opinion." [44]

R. B. Rhett, Jr., was busy writing and telegraphing in an effort to prevent the patching up of the disrupted party. On May 10 he wrote Miles to stop a possible appeal of Southern Congressmen to bring the seceders back to the convention at Baltimore. "I expect the Richmond Convention to be virtually a Southern Convention, though it should have been so in name and should have met at some city in the Cotton States." Rhett noted a "want of nerve in the management of the seceders here, and an evident want of leadership." He urged South Carolina to send a delegation which would "reaffirm the majority platform, nominate candidates and adjourn *sine die*." [45] The younger Rhett was much afraid that through pressure the Richmond convention would await action by the Baltimore convention, instead of making separate nominations and standing adamant. He feared that if Davis and Lane were named at Richmond that they might give way to a Baltimore ticket headed by Hunter. He was apprehensive that if the seceding movement should fail, "the South would be demoralized, and Seward triumphant." [46] Alfred Huger agreed with Rhett that Yancey's power was not secure, but he believed that cooperation between Richmond and Baltimore was desirable in order to combat the Chicago convention and Douglas. He still feared that South Carolina would not take the lead, nor did he think that the cotton states would take extreme action. [47]

Contrary to general belief, one Charlestonian complained at the divisions that existed at the end of May. "Union men say the state never so divided as now." He further reported discontent among less important politicians of Charleston, and that the "old submission" spirit which existed in Charleston since the days of Nullification and which educated our people

[44] J. P. Hunt to B. F. Perry, Sept. 16, 1860, MS, Governor B. F. Perry Collection, Alabama Department of History and Archives, Montgomery.

[45] R. B. Rhett, Jr., to W. P. Miles, May 10, 1860, MS, Miles Papers.

[46] Same to same, May 12, 1860, MS, *ibid*. E. W. Edgerton, a Charleston man, wrote pessimistically: "I have but little hope of a United South, and without it we can do nothing." Edgerton to Miles, June 6, 1860, MS, *ibid*.

[47] Alfred Huger to W. P. Miles, June 1, 1860. He deplored lack of leadership in South Carolina. MS, *ibid*.

for submission in 1850-1851 was still in existence.[48] But from Greenwood, James Gilliam reported that he had never before witnessed such unanimity as then existed. He hoped that firmness above all else would be adopted, " Come what may." [49]

After the four-party nominations, the political atmosphere was clarified. What hope did the Carolinians have for success of the party ticket? Although Rhett supported Breckinridge, he continued to indulge in fierce sectional diatribes. About a month before election, the *Mercury* indited a nine-fold indictment of the North, and concluded with a clarion call for a Southern Confederacy.[50] William M. Lawton, a planter of the Beaufort district, wrote that " . . . my Man for the Presidency is the most ultra Black Republican abolotionist [*sic*] to be found, hoping that in the event of his election, the Southern States may be forced, or kicked into an organization of such a Government, as I wish to see established." [51] Of course such an attitude was one of utter exasperation, and was not far from Rhett's position.

Indeed there appeared to be almost no belief among the South Carolina political leaders in the election of Breckinridge. Hammond alone seems to have been sanguine as to the success of the Southern ticket. But pessimism and confidence in Lincoln's election pervaded the private correspondence of the state's leaders. Thus J. D. Ashmore wrote that he would take strong secessionist ground in a speech, August 9, and promised to advocate a Southern confederacy, " in the event of Lincoln's election, which I regard as almost certain." [52] In describing politics to Hammond, Ashmore said: " We are almost unanimous for Breckinridge and Lane, & I have heard of three Douglas men in my Congressional District." He also planned to speak at Greenville on the eighteenth of July. In that speech, he would outline opposition to living under Republican rule, but would not " specify time or event when the final blow is to be struck, but advise preparation & harmony of action in order to meet the emergency." He would not favor separate seces-

[48] D. H. Hamilton to W. P. Miles, May 29, 1860, MS, *ibid*.
[49] Gilliam to Hammond, June 4, 1860, MS, Hammond Papers.
[50] Charleston *Mercury*, Oct. 4, 1860.
[51] W. M. Lawton to W. P. Miles, May 6, 1860, MS, Miles Papers.
[52] J. D. Ashmore to Miles, July 30, 1860, MS, *ibid*. Cf. above, Chapter III.

sion, or the placing of the state in the van. He would champion Breckinridge and Lane as one more attempt to save the Union. "But as I have no hopes whatever of success & believe that Lincoln and Hamlin will be elected I go for preparation first & dissolution afterwards on the first favorable opportunity." [53] At the end of the summer, Ashmore was annoyed by the question of separate state secession, which he would avoid as not germane to the subject before the people; it was ill advised to discuss it, and the time would come when it could properly be considered. He was still positive of Lincoln's election, but he did not publicly state it. [54]

A pamphlet of the Charleston "1860 Association" contended that it was futile to place faith in *any* President. Buchanan had been friendly to the South, but in reality ineffective and unsatisfactory. The writer poured ridicule upon the "Unionists" of 1860, who would, it was predicted, become the "abolitionists" of 1870. By that date, according to the "soul-confessions" of the quondam Unionist, the cry would be, "too late"—nothing awaited the South thenceforth but "submission forever." Union men in South Carolina and elsewhere in the South were but miserable "poltroons" and "traitors." [55]

Robert N. Gourdin wrote Miles that he hoped Georgia would secede in case of a Lincoln victory. [56] And Laurence M. Keitt summed up his ideas in a letter of October 3:

I suppose it is almost certain that Lincoln will be elected. I would like to escape the necessity; but I see no alternative but the sword. If we submit we are undone. The concentration of absolute power in the hands of the North will develop the wildest democracy ever seen on this earth—unless it should have been matched in Paris in 1789. What of conservatism? What of order? What of social security or financial prosperity can withstand Northern license?

He continued the jeremiad:

. . . the democracy, as a great party, is hopelessly divided, and if we submit to Lincoln, we substitute Republicanism for it at the South. The

[53] Ashmore to Hammond, July 10, 1860, MS, Hammond Papers. Miles saw no division in Charleston, and did not expect any. Miles to Hammond, July 10, 1860, MS, *ibid.*

[54] Same to same, Aug. 30, 1860, MS, *ibid.*

[55] John Townsend, *The Doom of Slavery in the Union: Its Safety Out of It.*

[56] Gourdin to Miles, Aug. 20, 1860, MS, Miles Papers.

truth is, I fear, a Union party at the South now means an abolition party—not at first it may be—but through quick transitions. . . .

Keitt went into this with the utmost seriousness, with determination to " peril all." In his opinion, South Carolina must lead, and not wait on Alabama, lest she wait " eternally." Alabam had no strong men. " But we must lead off!" [57]

Keitt told Hammond he had heard that the latter believed that there was a chance for the election of Breckinridge and Lane. Although Keitt hoped that was the case, he was certain that it was not. " I think that the events of the winter," he wrote in August, " are in sight & monstrous if we are to submit to Lincoln." Even Orr was for dissolution, Keitt had heard.[58] Breckinridge would not even take the election into the House, and would be badly beaten. If Bell won any cotton states, that would " hurt us badly." Keitt exclaimed, " Accursed be these dissensions among ourselves . . . ." This radical secessionist told Hammond: " I am in earnest. I'd cut loose, through fire and blood if necessary." [59]

I. W. Hayne was equally pessimistic. " Every day adds to the probability of Lincoln's election. I have myself, for a long time considered it *certain*." If South Carolina should fail to act in that case, it would entirely " demoralize those spirits who are earnest " and he feared that the public mind would be closed for all time. Let correspondence be opened with other slave states to learn sentiment. As many another had inquired, " Is there really an *action* party in Georgia?" [60] A. P. Aldrich preferred that Alabama and Mississippi retain the lead, but if they should back down, South Carolina could meet the issue. Aldrich believed that the election of Lincoln should produce dissolution, but feared it would not. His remedy was dissolution by the legislature, not by a convention.[61] Congressman W. Porcher Miles had given up the presidential election, and it was just a question with him as to whether South Carolina should act alone or in cooperation. As for himself, Miles desired to

[57] Laurence M. Keitt to Miles, Oct. 3, 1860, MS, *ibid.*
[58] Keitt to Hammond, Aug. 4, 1860, MS, Hammond Papers.
[59] Same to same, Sept. 10, Oct. 23, 1860, MS, *ibid.*
[60] Hayne to Hammond, Sept. 15, 1860, MS, *ibid.*
[61] Aldrich to Hammond, Oct. 4, 1860, MS, *ibid.*

break up things, which South Carolina could achieve.[62] Congressman Bonham considered the situation gloomy.[63]

Trescot called Miles' attention to a letter from W. W. Boyce recommending secession, published in the Charleston *Courier*, August 8.[64] Boyce favored the secession of the entire South; if that were not practicable, a portion of the South would suffice; and if South Carolina alone would secede, that should be done. He reviewed the character and principles of the Republican party in typical Carolina style. That party would first attack the " outposts " of slavery, before proceeding to assail slavery itself. Some of the border slave states might change their status, and the Republicans would surely use the patronage to infiltrate those states. Boyce declared that the North would be " master," the issue of Negro equality would be lost, and " the dogmas of fanaticism would become the decrees of the Supreme Court." To him the success of the Republicans in the presidential election " involved the necessity of revolution." It was for him a matter of the best timing: when the maximum of Northern sympathy and Southern unity could be achieved.[65]

It is interesting to note that the position of Senator James H. Hammond, author of the famous exposition of slavery known as the " mudsill " speech, was considerably " behind " these men.[66] As early as 1859 he wrote his novelist friend Simms that " things look gloomy." For this condition he blamed Southerners, who kept abolitionism alive by agitating a " slave code," or the reopening of the slave trade. With accurate prophecy he said: " Abolition will come into Supreme power with opinion all over the world to back it." He was bitter against Rhett, and it is significant that a Carolinian should make charges against him similar to those heard among Northern Democrats and Republicans.

They (the *Mercury* and politicians) think that a black Republican Pres. & the transfer of power to that side will produce disunion . . . on which

---

[62] Miles to Hammond, Aug. 5, 1860, MS, *ibid*.

[63] Bonham to Hammond, Sept. 26, 1860, MS, *ibid*.

[64] William H. Trescot to W. P. Miles, Aug. 10, 1860, MS, Miles Papers.

[65] W. W. Boyce to D. L. Provence and W. S. Lyles, Aug. 3, 1860, Fernandina *East Floridian*, Aug. 16, 1860.

[66] See Elizabeth Merritt, *James Henry Hammond 1807-1864* (" Johns Hopkins University Studies in Historical and Political Science," XLI, No. 4, Baltimore, 1923).

they will rise. Never were men so blind & besotted. If we are beaten
on the two issues I have named, America, the World, our *own South*
on the return of sense will admit & agree that we *deserved* it.

Hammond was ready to retire and let all " go to hell." For,
he inquired, " What . . . but ignominious submission to the
yoke our fire eaters & fools have constructed for us?" [67]

Although publicly he asserted, " Everyone knew that the
election of Lincoln will put the Union in instant danger," he
was careful to declare that he knew of no two men more
devoted to the Union than Breckinridge and Lane.[68] And
though he supported the seceders, in a letter on the South's
course, he remarked that the " . . . broadest and perhaps truest
policy of the whole country is to maintain the Union . . . ." [69]
The proper strategy for South Carolina in the election of 1860
Hammond outlined in a letter to Miles: " My opinion is that
So. Cª. should be quiescent as usual in the election & that every
blow she or any of her people strike for B. & L. will damage
them. I have reason to know that (*inter nous*) they *dread* the
support of the Mercury & Rhett, & want So. Cª. to vote quietly
as usual." He argued that such policy was sound and violated
no principle, and took occasion to defend James L. Orr as follows: " I think him an able, brave, & true man. *I would not
taunt him into doing wrong.*" [70]

[67] Hammond to W. Gilmore Simms, July 30, 1859, MS, Hammond Papers.
Hammond's central policy was " ' . . . the avoidance of side issues & the Union
of the South in the next Presidential Election.' " Such matters as disunion, expansion, slave trade were for the future. He would denounce the slave trade as
soon as possible. He was ready for " Union for a battle in the Union & for the
Constitution." One gets the impression in this letter, that in spite of all
Hammond's denunciation of political life, he had his eye on " the damn thing,"
the Presidency. (James H. Hammond to M. C. M. Hammond, July 23, 1859,
MS, *ibid.*) Sam C. Reid, Jr., of New Orleans, wrote that he had tried to
secure Hammond's nomination at Charleston. (Reid to Hammond, May 3, 1860,
MS, *ibid.*)

[68] New York *Herald*, Aug. 28, 1860.

[69] Hammond to H. D. Lesesne, May 15, 1860, Waynesboro *Independent
South*, June 1, 1860. In this letter he said: " Come what may, with our
surplus productions of cotton, rice, sugar, &c., and our substructure of black
slaves, *we are safe* against all the machinations of political intriguers from
abroad, and our demagogues at home."

[70] Hammond to W. P. Miles, July 16, 1860, MS, Miles Papers. The New
York *Tribune* (semi-weekly), Oct. 23, 1860, noted with satisfaction Hammond's
announcement for re-election to the United States Senate. Miles agreed that

An earnest of future events, and an indication of the conviction of South Carolinians that Lincoln was as good as elected, was the formation of the "Minute Men" in the state in the fall of 1860. The Columbia *Carolinian* noted 300 members of the order, each with a red scarf. It was an organization which was spreading over the South, designed to maintain the "interests" of the South, and to aid the formation of a Southern confederacy. "It will form an army strong enough to maintain any independence move by the South." [71]

While many journals commended the Minute Men, others viewed the organization as an irresponsible and dangerous development. The Charleston *Mercury* was pleased that a military body was formed, whose duty would be "to arm, equip, and drill, and be ready for any emergency that may arise in the present perilous condition of the Southern States." [72] One G. D. Tillman wrote Hammond describing the activities of the organization in the Edgefield district. The requirements for admission were: one dollar initiation fee, and pledge to furnish arms and to be prepared to march at a moment's notice to Washington to block Lincoln's inauguration. According to Tillman, the order at Edgefield had chosen officers, who included several members-elect of the legislature, and sundry fire-eaters. He thought the secret meetings of a sensational nature, where inflammatory speeches were made. "Champagne flowed freely at some of them at whose expense I know not." Four hundred had joined at Edgefield. Tillman suspected that James H. Adams, "Col. Pickens," and R. B. Rhett were behind the movement. This policy of employing revolutionary force against Lincoln in the Union, did not meet with the writer's approbation, and he warned Hammond that the order was active against him. [73] The New York *Tribune* took note of the order, and advised the South to use common sense, rather than blue rosettes and cockades, which could hardly afford adequate preparedness to the South. [74]

South Carolina should keep quiet, as she could not help Breckinridge and Lane. Miles to Hammond, Aug. 5, 1860, MS, Hammond Papers.

[71] Quoted in Fernandina *East Floridian*, Oct. 18, 1860.

[72] Quoted in New York *Tribune* (semi-weekly), Oct. 23, 1860.

[73] G. D. Tillman to Hammond, Oct. 9, 1860, MS, Hammond Papers. "Col. Pickens" referred to F. W. Pickens.

[74] New York *Tribune* (semi-weekly), Oct. 23, 1860.

Hammond's role in the crisis is difficult to estimate. He has been claimed for the Unionists, and indeed he often berated " big talk." In the spring, however, he had written his friend Francis Lieber concerning the possibility of war, a subject which had profoundly disturbed the philosopher.[75] To his relative, M. C. M. Hammond, he went far: " No two nations on earth are or ever were more distinctly separated & even hostile than we are here [Washington] . . . . How can the thing go on? One must succumb. *We* never can." [76] Yet his attitude caused criticism in South Carolina during the summer and fall. Several prominent Carolinians wrote to urge him to speak out, or to warn him that his conservatism would defeat his re-election to the Senate. Laurence Keitt wrote several times that the current was strong for dissolution, that the ultra spirit was rampant in South Carolina, and that if Hammond counseled " retreat," he would be beaten.[77] I. W. Hayne informed Hammond that there was much dissatisfaction at his and Chesnut's reticence. " It is said that you are opposed per se to any disunion movement, based on Lincoln's election." [78]

Hammond replied to the latter, September 19, with the assertion that all depended upon the presidential election. That would " determine the destiny of the country." He thought, however, that action based upon Lincoln's election the weakest possible strategy, unless the South and West showed otherwise by their votes. If South Carolina should act, he would back her, and if she must move, let it be by secession, and not by violent prevention of Lincoln's inauguration. " I wish therefore if we are to Secede, the Presidential Election had never been connected with the suggestion." As in divorce cases, incompatibility could be assigned for the secession, without specifying

[75] Lieber to Hammond, New York, April· 18, 1860, MS, Hammond Papers.
[76] Hammond to M. C. M. Hammond, April 22, 1860, MS, *ibid*.
[77] Keitt to Hammond, Aug. 4, Sept. 10, Oct. 23, 1860, MSS, *ibid*.
[78] Hayne to Hammond, Sept. 15, 1860, MS, *ibid*. William Gilmore Simms, who had earlier in the year demanded " thunderbolts " from Southern politicians, wrote: " One thing by way of prophecy. Be sure the South is waking up—& will go with a rush—possibly under the lead of Georgia even. The defeated Breckinridge party will be necessarily all Secession." (Simms to Hammond, March 21, Oct. 16, 1860, MSS, *ibid*.) John Belton O'Neall, however, commended Hammond's moderation. O'Neall feared an " act of folly." If the worst came, he would await Lincoln's course in office. (O'Neall to Hammond, Sept. 22, 1860, MS, *ibid*.)

further. Nor did Hammond think that South Carolina should lead off. The state was unpopular with the other Southern states. Had not Virginia rebuked her earlier in the year, and had she not stood alone at Richmond? But he was willing to concede that if the November vote showed Southern unity, then she might act. Although his opinion was that Unionist sentiment outside South Carolina was stronger than at any time since 1850, if it should come to pass that " a section is to govern," many would then be ready to face the issue of disunion. But the lack of Southern unity was obvious. Three parties were warring upon each other in the South. " Good God! What a prospect for a Southern confederacy." Hammond seemed to be balancing factors in his frank letter to Hayne. Above all, he desired to avoid an " abortion," which would be more disastrous than doing nothing. Yet if the South came up to " scratch " in the election, he would say, " Go ahead." The Senator had written out resolutions, but had not abandoned hope that " we will win." [79]

At other times, Hammond lapsed into a characteristic pessimism. It was a crazy age and generation, and the world had gone " daft." But if South Carolina should secede, he would go along.[80] Dr. J. F. Hammond, surgeon at West Point academy, wrote his brother that if Hammond could say what he was saying, the situation must be indeed desperate in the other portions of the South.[81] At the close of October, it is significant that James Chesnut, Jr., a colleague of Hammond's in the Senate, reported that his mind was " daily inclining to the necessity of trying the issue of secession & the doctrine of coercion—even by the solitary movement of this State." [82]

[79] Hammond to Hayne, Sept. 19, 1860, MS, *ibid*. He recognized the correctness of the advice he had received, as he wrote that the South was rushing to disunion. "Let her rip." Perhaps the Union might be reconstituted minus New England and New York. Hammond to W. Gilmore Simms, Oct. 23, 1860, MS, *ibid*.

[80] Same to same, Sept. 23, 1860, MS, *ibid*.

[81] J. F. Hammond to Hammond, West Point, New York, Oct. 16, 1860, MS, *ibid*. Dr. Hammond offered his services to the state before the election. (Same to same, Oct. 27, 1860, MS, *ibid*.) He advised South Carolina to act while Buchanan was President, in the belief that he would do nothing. (Same to same, Oct. 29, 1860, MS, *ibid*.)

[82] James Chesnut, Jr., to Hammond, Oct. 27, 1860, MS, *ibid*.

Indeed, some of the Union men of South Carolina had curious notions of methods of preserving it. James J. McCarter wrote that he had always been a Union man, " ... even now, I do not give up my hope that some fortunate person may find out some way of escape from the evils of a dissolution. But my fears are now greatly in advance of my hopes and I begin to think, the only chance of saving it, is to bring about some collision, which will shew us the strength of the conservative element in the North." If that group was not strong enough to keep the Democrats in power, then all hope was gone. He likened the situation to living on a volcano.[83] And A. H. Brisbane stressed Unionism, but in case Douglas pulled down " the temple," thus electing a " black " Republican by his " defection," he was certain that the states would demand " absolution of allegiance." For the South would not endure the rule of a government that despised " our Industrial institutions." Brisbane was for the creation of a " peace-making " armed force of 500,000 men, which would halt the " barbarians." [84]

Even James L. Orr,[85] the leader of the National Democrats, held out little hope against secession in a letter declining to run for the legislature. Orr lamented the condition of the Democratic party, " the last safeguard of the South." He had practically given up hope for the Union. " Let it suffice here for me to say, that in my opinion, the secession of the Southern delegates from the Charleston Convention was unwise and impolitic." Douglas was justly obnoxious to the South, but he could have been defeated in the convention, and Breckinridge nominated. If the latter had won at Charleston, Orr contended that his election would have been assured. When Lincoln was elected, the South should secede as a unit, not by individual states. After which, if satisfactory terms could not be made, a separate Confederacy should be organized. Orr warned against bitterness against the Southern Douglas men, who, he predicted, would join the others in the crisis.[86]

---

[83] James J. McCarter to Miles, Jan. 16, 1860, MS, Miles Papers.

[84] Brisbane to Hammond, June 12, 1860, MS, Hammond Papers.

[85] *D. A. B.*, XIV, 59-60. Orr, who had but recently, 1857-1859, been Speaker of the United States House of Representatives, was suspected of aspiring to the Presidency or Vice Presidency in 1860. I. W. Hayne to Hammond, April 20, 1860; Hammond to M. C. M. Hammond, April 22, 1860, MSS Hammond Papers.

[86] J. L. Orr to John Martin, *et al.*, July 23, 1860, Richmond *Examiner*, Aug.

While Orr acted in the course of the campaign in an entirely orthodox manner, the politicians had their eyes on him, lest he make some upsetting move. W. Porcher Miles wrote Hammond that Orr and friends contemplated breaking down Parish representation, and planned to transfer selection of presidential electors to the people.[87]

A more pronounced independent was B. F. Perry, whose course at the Charleston convention has been noted. It seems that Perry deserves to share with James L. Petigru, the sobriquet "Union Man of South Carolina." In a letter dated Greenville Court House, August 13, and printed in the Charleston *Courier,* Perry began by admitting that Lincoln would probably be elected. It was a terrible misfortune, but one that was brought on by Southerners themselves. Perry foresaw the triumph of the Republicans. He agreed with Orr that if the seceders had remained in place, Douglas would have been defeated. The adjournment to Baltimore was for the purpose of allowing the Douglas forces to replace the seceders. In Perry's opinion, no Douglas ticket should be run at the South, and no Breckinridge ticket in the North. While he opposed Douglas and condemned his course at Charleston, Perry said: "It would be much better to have Douglas in the Presidency than Lincoln." But Douglas could not be elected. For a South Carolinian, Perry went about as far as possible in urging the South to give Lincoln a trial. "It may be that 'Old Abe' will go out of office quite a favorite with the Southern people." It was beyond his comprehension that Southern Bell and Douglas men should cooperate in secession. It would be foolish to break up the Union on "a mere abstraction," and Perry pointed to checks on Lincoln.[88]

In another letter, republished in the North, Perry continued his line of moderate reasoning. He pointed to the condemna-

11, 1860. "Orr thinks it will be impossible for us to live under the Black Republican rule." Ashmore to Hammond, July 10, 1860, MS, Hammond Papers.

[87] Miles to Hammond, July 10, 1860, MS, *ibid.* This subject was not openly discussed in the campaign, though South Carolina was the only state which had not provided for popular election of presidential electors. For background of the problem, see Chauncey S. Boucher, "Sectionalism, Representation, and the Electoral Question in Ante-Bellum South Carolina," *Washington University Studies,* IV (Oct. 1916), 3-62.

[88] Quoted in New York *Herald,* Aug. 24, 1860.

tion of John Brown by Northern public meetings, and to the repudiation by Seward and Henry Wilson. " It became manifest that such fiendish sympathy and expression were confined to the rabid, fanatical abolitionists alone." Perry pointed to the hostile attitude towards Lincoln of such men as Gerrit Smith and William Lloyd Garrison. These matters were kept out of the Southern press. The abolitionists were right, he contended, in their assertions that the Republicans cared nothing for the Negro; that power was their goal, and when that was reached, the Republicans would say nothing more about slavery. It was all political and insincere. Indeed, nine-tenths of the Northern people were against John Brownism. The North had given no evidence of supporting " fiendish " doctrines, and until there was something tangible, he was unwilling to destroy the Union. Answering the charge that he was comparable to a Tory in the American Revolution, he denied that the situations were parallel, and compiled a list of advantages the South had won in the Union. His list included: The admission of nine slave states to the Union, with no slave state ever having been excluded; each new state decided for itself on the subject of slavery; the " odious " Missouri restriction, approved by a Southern President with Calhoun in his Cabinet, was now repealed; the fugitive slave law had been enforced by the federal government; and finally, the Dred Scott decision. " What more do we want? " And Perry concluded his letter by a quotation from Washington's Farewell.[89]

A Charlestonian wrote that he had become quite depressed, that he was " in despair." He had just read Seward's Boston speech, and B. F. Perry's letter. In his opinion, many in Charleston endorsed the sentiments expressed by Perry.[90] There was, however, scant public commendation in the South, but the New York *Times* praised Perry's common sense, " a novelty at the South." The *Times* said people there regarded Republicans as " devils," and advised Southerners that " men like Col. Perry are far wiser leaders than Keitt & Co." Some Southerners expressed regret that Perry's letters would aid the Black Republicans.[91]

[89] New York *Times*, Sept. 3, 1860.
[90] Robert N. Gourdin to W. P. Miles, Aug. 20, 1860, MS, Miles Papers.
[91] New York *Times*, Sept. 3, 1860.

More celebrated as a Unionist than B. F. Perry in South Carolina was James L. Petigru. During the canvass he was sanguine that even though Lincoln won the election, South Carolina would not secede. He wrote to Alfred Huger: " No possible issue could be more untenable than to make his bare election a *causus belli,* without any overt act against the Constitution or even the Dred Scott decision." He continued with some observations which seem to undermine the contention that the base of Carolina discontent was economic. " If our planters were in debt, or cotton was at 5 cents, as I have seen it, such a thing might be likely; but, our magnanimous countrymen are too comfortable for such exercise." Yancey was too much of a load for Breckinridge to carry at the North, Petigru believed.[92] Late in October, he wrote Edward Everett: " If Lincoln is elected it will give the Union a great strain; yet still I don't think that this State will secede alone; because the country is too prosperous for a revolution; and the same reason is likely to keep Alabama and Georgia from taking the plunge." [93] So staunch a Unionist was he that his niece noted after election that there was some talk about placing " uncle " (J. L. Petigru) in Lincoln's cabinet.[94]

Not all Carolinians agreed with the glowing pictures painted by Southern nationalists of a future under a new government. When the crisis approached, some bethought them of monetary matters and were deeply apprehensive. For example, J. Johnston Pettigrew of Charleston wrote his brother, a planter in eastern North Carolina, to borrow money with which to tide over the crisis. Lincoln's probable election would be followed

[92] Petigru to Huger, Sept. 5, 1860, in James P. Carson, *Life, Letters and Speeches of James Louis Petigru* (Washington, 1920), pp. 356-357.

[93] Petigru to Everett, Oct. 28, 1860, *ibid.*, pp. 359-360. On the point of the Southerners' being too prosperous to fight, see C. H. Trioleau's letter, Liverpool, Sept. 27, 1860, to a member of the Pettigrew family: " The people of the South are fickle and vacillating lazy and above all *rich*; they do not really *feel* the encroachments of the Republican party because they have increased the production of cotton alone a million and three quarters of bales in the last two years or in money 87 millions of dollars. A man will not fight if his belly & pocket are both full and he has to go and look for a row. If we could only have two successive failures of the cotton crop I should feel quite cheerful about Southern Rights." MS, Pettigrew Family Papers, Southern Historical Collection, the University of North Carolina.

[94] Mrs. Charles L. Pettigrew to Charles L. Pettigrew, Nov. 7, 1860, MS, *ibid.*

by revolution and panic. Although the writer was not a fire-eater, he was in accord with the idea of a united South's demanding new guarantees, which he optimistically believed would be granted. He was receiving letters from the cotton states urging South Carolina to take the lead and secede alone, and they would follow.[95] To which W. S. Pettigrew replied that he would have been startled upon learning of conditions in South Carolina had he not had acquaintance with the state. He could not lend the requested money. "Indeed, I am not without apprehension, that if the South secedes, we will all be plunged into a vortex of ruin, particularly those who may owe money." South Carolina was placing herself in a desperate position he thought.[96]

"I cannot but think that the State is . . . committing herself to a position that the whole South will have reason to regret. Indeed it does appear to me that such men as Keitt & Rhett are very unsafe guides in a time like the present, when coolness, calmness & wisdom are required. The South is surrounded with perils; both at home and abroad they are to be seen." Pettigrew could only rely on God to extricate the South.[97]

The day after Lincoln's election, Mrs. Charles L. Pettigrew wrote her husband that she was sending him a copy of the Charleston *Mercury*. "You see the Mercury glorifies itself hugely—it is the most incendiary paper, *publishing* constantly the *worst* abolition sentiments & speeches—in a word it is detestable, but it gives the present state of affairs of which I suppose it may be considered leader." She reported that John-

[95] J. Johnston Pettigrew to W. S. Pettigrew, Oct. 24, 1860, MS, *ibid*. At the beginning of November the all-engrossing subject was politics, Mrs. Charles L. Pettigrew wrote her husband, Nov. 2, 1860. She was surprised to find some "blood & thunder people backing down." One member of the family counselled everybody to stay at home, "'& spend no money, times are coming when all will be required.'" (MS, *ibid*.). The maneuvering by South Carolina and other states to persuade each other to lead off in secession continued. Governor William H. Gist wrote Governor John W. Ellis of North Carolina, Oct. 5, 1860, that South Carolina desired another state to secede first, or act simultaneously with her. South Carolina would secede alone, if she had assurances that others would follow. (MS, John W. Ellis Papers, Southern Historical Collection, the University of North Carolina.) Gist wrote simultaneous letters to all Southern Governors.

[96] W. S. Pettigrew to J. Johnston Pettigrew, Nov. 2, 1860, MS, Pettigrew Family Papers.

[97] *Ibid*.

ston Pettigrew had told the fire-eaters, " ' the Devil is unchained at last.' " He said that he feared " ' some fools may attack the forts . . . get somebody killed & have a great deal of mischief done.' " She thought that moderate men were willing to withdraw because of Lincoln's election, " but are not willing to rush headlong into frightful evils. The negroes are all of opinion that Lincoln is to come here to free them but they are perfectly quiet, & nothing is apprehended from them." [98]

A number of Southerners had boasted of the stringent financial conditions which would prevail in the North if a crisis came, but doubtless they had not forecast the same situation in the South. Mrs. Pettigrew described the money pressure in South Carolina. " I am going this morning," she wrote, " to get 100 from Butler & Bee & will ask for it in gold." She did not altogether agree with her pessimistic brother-in-law but there was no doubt that a crisis was at hand. Everybody was seeking cash. " The shopkeepers look sad enough, total ruin is before most people . . . ." [99] These views of the Pettigrew family, a non-political group, were about as far from those of Keitt, the Rhetts, Boyce, and others, as possible, and it would be of interest to determine if others entertained the same misgivings of the new venture undertaken upon the election of Lincoln.

Privately some Carolinians had not shared the enthusiasm of the politicians for a Southern confederacy, and long before the catastrophe of Lincoln's election, were weighing the advantages of a new government. Some thought the time was not yet ripe. Others believed the South unwilling or unable to create such an organization, or that the South was unprepared in every way to undertake it. Most significant was the fear that political and economic interests of the upper South might diverge from those of the cotton states, and that the conflict might merely be transferred to the South. These doubts were entertained by men who expressed themselves as not satisfied with the status quo.

D. H. Hamilton wrote:

The subject of a Southern Confederacy I have thought about ever since 1850, and for the life of me I cannot see what possible benefit

---

[98] Mrs. Charles L. Pettigrew to Charles L. Pettigrew, Nov. 7, 1860, MS, Pettigrew Family Papers.

[99] *Ibid.*

could accrue to the South from a Confederacy of the Southern States, for I agree with you that the Tariff question is at the bottom of the whole controversy; and with a Southern Union we should have the same question to fight in the midst of our own people. How long would it be after disunion before we should have the same hungry manufacturing population infesting the upper part of S⁰. Cᵃ., Cherokee Georgia, Tennessee, North Carolina (French Broad with its exhaustless water power) and even the upper portion of Alabama? Why not five years would elapse, before they would be setting their looms to work on every stream in these locations, under the impulse of occupation and the introduction of numbers, they would soon make their presence felt amongst a people who only need a market for their produce, to bring to them wealth and prosperity. A few years more and you would have a strong party of our own people in favour of a protective Tariff, and advocating all those extravagant expenditures for Internal Improvements, and nearer home we shall be compelled to fight that same battle which has continued in the present Union since 1824.

Hamilton was far from satisfied with the existing Union, and if he were convinced that better conditions could be found out of it, he would earnestly advocate a new government. But, he told Miles, " You have much more confidence in ' the common sense of the people of the South ' than I have—they do not know the meaning of such a quality." In Hamilton's opinion they had passed by many favorable opportunities to do battle, " but they have retreated from each position, to one of the greatest weakness, that which is based upon the question of Slavery, and in many cases, merely in the abstract." [100]

Moreover, basing the fight upon slavery carried with it danger from the Southern non-slaveholding population. " We must travel through blood and carnage to some better and stronger form of Government than that which can be controlled by a popular majority—a Government strong enough to protect each valuable interest, and to restrain that spirit of plunder which has distinguished the New England States from the inception of the Govt. to the present day." He refused to concede that slavery could ever be abolished, " but we have complicated this question and precipitated upon ourselves a condition of affairs, the issue of which must be bloodshed and revolution." He was sure of the coming of an " irrepressible

[100] D. H. Hamilton to W. P. Miles, Jan. 23, 1860, MS, Miles Papers.

15

conflict," sooner or later, and he urged a thorough preparation in organization and armament for that day.[101]

The situation was indeed desperate. Hamilton had been educated among the people of " that infamous old Roundhead spirit," of whom John Brown was an example, and he knew how implacable they were, " without humanity and without mercy." But he was ready to await events, and was " . . . ready to sell our lives and our prosperity at the expense of the lives of many of our enemies." For " the South is almost entirely hemmed in and nothing is left to us but desperate fighting. The sooner it comes the better after we are prepared for it. I only trust that it may not be precipitated upon us in our present condition of unpreparedness." [102] And Alfred Huger wrote Miles that he thought the secession movement premature, and recommended waiting four years longer before taking action. In his opinion the Southern people were far behind their politicians on this question.[103] Likewise, the weather-vane, Trescot, thought the signs unpropitious in February of 1860.[104]

In another letter, D. H. Hamilton scored the apathy of the Southern people, including those of his own state. He returned to the fear of internecine war among slaveholders and non-slaveholders. He feared that 360,000 could not dictate to 3,000,000, and mistrusted his own people far more than he feared the efforts of the abolitionists.

Then comes the conflict in which we shall fight with the knife at our throats, in this contest all Government of course will be at an end, and the issue is most likely to be that a Military despotism will take the place of the present form of our Govt. eventually to be modified by a Constitutional monarchy. And if we are the winners, so be it. . . .[105]

Again and again Alfred Huger expounded his thesis as to the real cause of all the troubles; it was not North against South, nor slave labor against free labor. The whole difficulty lay in extreme democracy. Huger feared the " absurd " suffrage laws, the " demoralizing effect " of equality, and corrupt voting.

[101] *Ibid.*
[102] *Ibid.*
[103] Alfred Huger to W. P. Miles, May 7, 1860, MS, Miles Papers.
[104] W. H. Trescot to W. P. Miles, Feb. 22, 1860, MS, *ibid.*
[105] D. H. Hamilton to W. P. Miles, Feb. 2, 1860, MS, *ibid.*

He bitterly opposed permitting penniless men the right to levy taxes upon property. And if a Southern confederacy were set up, these problems would be transferred to it. He wished every-one to understand that he was a "republican," not a Democrat or a monarchist.[106]

That action involved the problem of separate state secession, or cooperation, was understood. As the failure of Memminger's mission and the abortive Richmond convention demonstrated, if action were to be obtained, South Carolina had best act alone, always confident that her initiative would bring the others along. Carolinians therefore kept a weather eye on the other Southern states. Such qualms as some entertained as to a new Southern Confederacy were resolved by the election of Lincoln.

The activity of the state in arms appropriations, and the for-mation of the Minute Men were indications that war prepara-tions were being made. While some thought that the North would not fight, that her society would collapse in a time of crisis, the possibility or even probability of war was recognized. W. W. Boyce weighed two alternatives if coercion were em-ployed by the North. The loss of trade would so "convulse" the "artificial" Northern structure, as to cause a reaction against the abolitionists: "The first gun fired in civil war will cost them five hundred million dollars, and strikes will not be confined to shoemakers, but will become epidemic." But if no such reaction should occur, Boyce would "grasp the sword" to demonstrate that Southerners of 1860 were no degen-erates: they had as good chance of establishing winter quarters in New York as their adversaries had of capturing New Orleans. Let Southerners die if they must, but he had no fears as to the outcome of a military contest.[107]

---

[106] Alfred Huger to Robert N. Gourdin, Aug. 23, 1860 (?), MS, Gourdin-Young Papers, Library of Emory University. In this letter Huger thought England had been wiser in suffrage matters than the United States. He was violent against the masses. After the war, in the midst of Reconstruction, Huger at the age of 83 continued to rage against equal rights, suffrage, etc. Same to same, Sept. 23-25, 1868, MS, *ibid.*

[107] W. W. Boyce to D. L. Provence and W. S. Lyles, Aug. 3, 1860, Fernandina *East Floridian*, Aug. 16, 1860. The Charleston firm of Gourdin, Matthiessen & Co. sent out a circular shortly after election, addressed to England and Europe, dated Nov. 16, 1860. The circular informed foreign countries that the recent election of a President and a political party hostile to the South would lead to a Southern Confederacy. They were warned that if peaceable secession took place, all would be well. But if coercion were attempted, "civil war" would result.

After election the discussion was closed, and dissenting voices were few. D. H. Hamilton warned his fellow Charlestonian R. N. Gourdin not to associate with men who might be thought of as submissionists. The people were so far ahead of the politicians that Hamilton feared a popular attack on the forts, an event which might discredit the secession movement.[108]

GEORGIA

In the preliminaries leading up to the national party conventions, there were numerous county and several state conventions held in Georgia. Governor Joseph E. Brown towards the end of 1859 had bestirred himself to see that the state was properly armed, and the legislature had already appropriated money for that purpose. Brown believed that the best policy for the state was to arm for the "emergency," employing of course, arms of Georgia manufacture. "Recent events have, I think, satisfied the Southern people that it is wise for them to *arm*. I have but little confidence in high sounding speeches and resolutions. We must meet aggression in future by energetic preparation and prompt action . . . . ' The argument ' is already ' exhausted ' . . . ." [109]

And in the spring of 1860, military activity was noted in the Georgia capital: arms received by the Governor had been distributed to various companies throughout Georgia, and an observer added: " We learn, however, that the Governor has sent to Hon. Mark A. Cooper as agent, North, to purchase $50,000 worth of arms which will be distributed as soon as they arrive to all companies organized that are in want." A general encampment in the state was called for May.[110] Throughout

Already trade was deranged, and a money stringency existed, which would necessitate Europe's sending coin for cotton. "But revolution and civil war will make their condition worse." Broadside, Gourdin-Young Papers, Library of Emory University. See also the raging, defiant, war-like letter, John D. Ashmore to Horatio King, Nov. 5, 1860, MS, Horatio King Papers, Library of Congress.

[108] D. H. Hamilton to R. N. Gourdin, Nov. 26, 1860, MS, Gourdin-Young Papers, Library of Emory University.

[109] Milledgeville *Southern Recorder*, Jan. 10, 1860. For a brief survey of the campaign, see Ulrich B. Phillips, *Georgia and States Rights* (Washington, 1902), pp. 187-192.

[110] Milledgeville *Southern Recorder*, March 27, 1860. Earlier the Atlanta *Intelligencer* quoted an interview with Congressman J. W. H. Underwood of Georgia, who favored arming the South and, as for Georgia, a preparation for

the year similar references appeared in the public prints, and on October 1, Major General J. W. A. Sanford wrote Governor Brown to urge higher taxation in order to strengthen the state's military organization. In his report he told the Governor that, while there might be no war, rumors of it were heard and that one could not say that in the frenzied condition of public opinion it would not come. Sanford believed that the South had been prosperous so long that the section had become overconfident and careless. Because of the madness of the hour, Georgia should prepare for the worst.[111] Of course the John Brown raid, the tense political situation, and rumors of servile insurrection and war were responsible for the military preparations here as throughout the South.

The most recent historian of the state has noted the confusion in Georgia during the campaign of 1860, which he thinks was not quite so bad as elsewhere, mainly because Georgia only considered three of the candidates for President. It was incredible that Georgians should vote for the "black" Republican candidate, Abraham Lincoln.[112] Indeed, factionalism in the Democratic party resulted in the calling of two Democratic conventions, the first in December, 1859, and the second in March, 1860. The former endorsed Howell Cobb of Georgia for President, but this was withdrawn by the later meeting. Not too well concealed was a rivalry for national preferment between Alexander H. Stephens, who had "retired" from politics in 1859, and Secretary Cobb.[113] The former denied that he was a candidate for the Democratic presidential nomination, but evidence exists to show that he did not irrevocably close the door in the matter.[114]

the "Irrepressible Conflict" which must come. Rome *Weekly Courier*, Feb. 9, 1860.

[111] Milledgeville *Southern Recorder* in Augusta *Daily Constitutionalist*, Oct. 18, 1860.

[112] E. Merton Coulter, *A Short History of Georgia* (Chapel Hill, 1933), p. 296.

[113] Milledgeville *Southern Recorder*, March 27, 1860. The Opposition Augusta *Daily Chronicle and Sentinel*, March 17, 27, saw machinations by A. H. Stephens and Governor Brown on behalf of Douglas. Stephens was accused of working for Douglas in '60, and himself in '64.

[114] H. R. Casey, a delegate to the Charleston convention, wrote Stephens rehearsing a conversation "yesterday" on the subject of that convention: "When asked, 'will you accept the nomination if tendered to you at Charleston?' Your reply is 'I cannot undertake to give a *determined* and *irrevocable*

At the Charleston convention, although the majority of the Georgia delegation withdrew, a number of delegates remained, and participated in the debates, but the fragment was not permitted to vote. Henry L. Benning signed a statement issued for the majority of the delegation, which expressed the hope that Northerners would modify the platform as adopted, and that the state be represented at Richmond as well as Baltimore. Another state convention assembled at Milledgeville on June 4, which again demonstrated the cleavage among the Democrats, but also showed a disposition among the seceders to reunite the party. Hiram Warner, Alexander H. Stephens, and Herschel V. Johnson led the moderate minority faction, while Robert Toombs expressed the fear that the Union would survive the Constitution. Governor Joseph E. Brown decried the effort to inject the Congressional protection issue—in which he believed as an abstract right—as a new doctrine in 1860. It could all be patched up, thought Governor Brown. Feelings ran high, and a duel was fought over the actions of the " staying " delegates. The outcome was a split in the June 4 convention, because the minority refused to demand Congressional protection, and also declined to recognize the Richmond convention.[115]

This resulted in the choice of two full slates of delegates to Baltimore. The historian of this era of Georgia history wondered at the split, and concluded: " There can be but one explanation. There were enough disunionists to drive party disintegration as the sure agency of national dissolution." [116] Thus the wedge which had wrecked one national Democratic convention and would split another, operated in Georgia. The Baltimore convention seated the majority faction headed by Henry L. Benning and rejected that led by James Gardner, a

negative to that question now in advance of the action of that body. Because I can conceive of circumstances in which that nomination might be made and tendered to me wherein I would consider myself derelict of all duty and obligation which as a citizen I owe to my country were I to withhold my assent.' " Stephens also told Casey that he would do his duty as a soldier, but that he would gladly see another, Hunter or Breckinridge, nominated. If required to choose between the first and second places on the ticket, Stephens preferred the second, because the latter would be less of a strain. Casey to Stephens, April 4, 1860, MS, Stephens Papers, Library of Congress.

[115] I. W. Avery, *The History of the State of Georgia From 1850-1881* . . . (New York, 1881), pp. 115-119, 121-122.

[116] *Ibid.*, p. 122.

Douglas man. But because of the refusal of the Baltimore convention to seat the Alabama and Louisiana seceders, the Georgia delegation refused to participate, along with most other slave state delegations.[117] These, of course, assembled elsewhere in Baltimore and nominated Breckinridge and Lane. Avery says: "In the light of common sense the democratic division was a mad piece of folly, useless and destructive." [118]

Meanwhile, the Georgia Opposition enjoyed hugely the disintegration of the national and the partial breakup of the state Democratic party—the old enemy of a generation. Although this party was not well organized, it was a factor of importance, with its able leaders and numerous party presses. This party, which took the name Constitutional Union, held its state convention in Milledgeville, May 2, but with only 44 counties and 111 delegates represented. Resolutions in favor of territorial-slave protection and in support of the fugitive slave law were passed, and a delegation chosen to attend the national convention at Baltimore. After his nomination, the party vigorously sought the election of John Bell electors in Georgia. Benjamin H. Hill, Joshua Hill, A. R. Wright, and Thomas Hardeman, were among the Constitutional Unionist leaders in Georgia, and such newspapers as the Savannah *Daily Republican*, the Macon *Georgia Journal and Messenger*, and the Augusta *Chronicle and Sentinel*, pleaded the Bell-Everett cause.[119]

The least popular ticket in Georgia, despite the presence of former Governor Herschel V. Johnson on it, was that of Douglas. This minority faction included Alexander H. Stephens, Linton Stephens, Augustus R. Wright, E. A. Nisbet, and Hiram Warner. Only a few papers such as the Atlanta *Southern Confederacy*, the Rome *Southerner*, and the Augusta *Constitutionalist* were in the Douglas column.[120]

During the summer more state conventions were held by all parties, with oratory, resolutions, and the choice of presidential electors. Some thought that the canvass was dull in 1860, but a wide investigation in contemporary sources does not confirm this view, and it is the opinion of Avery that there never had been a time when more fiery and vehement oratory was heard.

[117] *Ibid.*, pp. 122-123.
[118] *Ibid.*, p. 123.
[119] *Ibid.*, pp. 119-120.
[120] *Ibid.*, p. 125.

" The whole tendency of the intensely heated canvass was to educate and drive the popular will to disunion if the Black Republicans succeeded." [121]

A few samples may be selected from the public statements, the editorials, and if possible from private comments of the partisans of each of the three candidates. As the majority of the newspapers supported Breckinridge, and as he was backed by the dominant element in the state, it will be appropriate to consider his campaign first. The defiant tone of the Breckinridge press was fixed long before his nomination. [122] According to one rural Georgia Southern rights paper, the Northern people had come to believe that either through ignorance or cowardice, the South would submit to domination by a " corrupt and unscrupulous majority . . . ." The Charleston convention inaugurated in American annals a new epoch. [123]

To one Savannah resident sentiment there seemed to favor a united South. Unfortunately this individual heard discouraging reports from Augusta and from North Georgia; submissionists appeared to be strong in those areas. He was alarmed when he heard men say that even the fearful election of Seward would be no cause for action. " In other words if I have been notified by a man that he will attack & kill me, the first chance he has, I must do nothing till he does attack me! " This writer was afraid that there would be no action this time: " We have too many timid men." [124]

Another Savannah citizen wrote a Charleston friend in September that he wanted action at that moment, and not to wait until Lincoln's election. He thought that the South should prepare with arms then, and especially did he deprecate the making of a loud noise which ended in nothing. The state must have saltpeter: indeed, there was not enough there to fire a salute in the event of Breckinridge's victory. Georgia was not really prepared for secession, and he doubted if South Carolina was. All Georgia had done thus far was to send a

[121] *Ibid.*, pp. 127-128.

[122] Columbus *Daily Times*, Jan., Feb., March, 1860, *passim*. See also Waynesboro *Independent South*, March 17, 1860.

[123] *Ibid.*, May 18, 1860.

[124] W. D. Duncan to James H. Hammond, May 9, 1860, MS, Hammond Papers, Library of Congress.

commission to various munitions centers. If the South should make a revolution merely upon the basis of a theory, and be whipped, he did not favor any action. Nor was he a *per se* disunionist, for he deplored disunion. But things had come to the point that the South must enforce her rights by the bayonet. In his opinion, this could be done, if only the South could organize. For the South could arm the entire white population, and not withdraw a single laborer. This the North could not do, because she could not withdraw her laborers from mills and mines and fields.[125]

All the state's Democratic Congressmen, Senators Iverson and Toombs, Governor Brown, and most newspapers were in the Breckinridge camp. Included in campaign arguments were the usual examinations of the records of Bell and Douglas to " prove " the former " a Southern man with Northern principles " and the latter an antislavery man.[126] To one journal the simple issue of the contest, " the alpha and omega," was to determine whether the states were equals.[127] A rural western Georgia paper, the Carrollton *Advocate,* calculated in September that Breckinridge would be elected; in any event, a strong tone would convince the Northern states that the South had rights, that property must be protected in the territories. Posterity would rightly scorn Southern men, unless they resisted Lincoln. The *Advocate* cited the activities of abolitionists and of alleged incendiaries to frighten Georgians as to their fate under Lincoln. " There is no way of escape for us from these dire calamities, but in dissolution or the election of Breckinridge and Lane." [128]

In the fall the Breckinridge press began to call for separation, and turned fiercely upon Georgians who refused to fall in line.[129] Such papers as the Columbus *Times,* the Waresboro

[125] E. C. Anderson to R. N. Gourdin, Savannah, Sept. 30, 1860, MS, Gourdin-Young Papers, Library of Emory University.

[126] Waynesboro *Independent South,* June 29, 1860, spoke of the Tennessee " trimmer " Bell and the Massachusetts " abolitionist " Everett, and declared that it would be a " criminal " consequence to vote for them. See speeches of Robert Toombs and Henry R. Jackson, Athens *Southern Banner,* Sept. 20, 1860. Also *ibid.,* Sept. 6, 1860.

[127] Columbus *Daily Times,* Sept. 4, 1860.

[128] Carrollton *Advocate,* Sept. 7, 1860.

[129] Waynesboro *Independent South,* Sept. 7, 1860, turned on A. H. Stephens

Forester, the Waynesboro *Independent South*, the Albany *Patriot*, the Savannah *Morning News*, the Atlanta *Intelligencer*, and the Carrollton *Advocate*, raged against Lincoln, the North, and the Southern submissionists. As election day approached the crescendo of rage intensified. In Waynesboro, Atlanta, Macon, and Columbus, "minute men" were formed during October.[130] It would be difficult to find a more extreme example than the following plea for resistance to Lincoln: " Sooner let devastation and ruin spread over all the land—sooner endure bankruptcy with its disastrous consequences aye rather *welcome* the bloodiest civil and most deadly internecine warfare than hear even, much less obey, the injunctions of base submissionists —the fears of dastardly and craven hearted cowards. . . ." The very election of Lincoln constituted the overt act; the South was urged to prevent his inauguration. If the South believed that slavery was recognized by the Bible, it was a Christian duty to attack and not wait for the invasion.[131] The Albany *Patriot* agreed with this line of action, and especially cautioned against the waiting till Lincoln had control of the army, navy, and treasury, and could employ these agencies to coerce and bribe traitors. The *Patriot* desired the chasm to be made so broad and deep between North and South as to produce an eternal barrier between the sections.[132]

After the Pennsylvania reverses, the Columbus *Times* wished to act before those who desired to annihilate slavery should be ensconced in power. The Republicans would gradually build up a free-soil party throughout the South. Therefore, the time had arrived for action to defend honor, liberty, equality, home, and fireside.[133] Such talk is generally the prelude to war. This same hotspur sheet rather crudely put the argument:

Whenever she [South] speaks about aggression, Washington's Farewell Address pacifies us. . . . When the South says protect us, the North turns around and says, look here, the Government wasn't made to protect niggers, and if you insist upon it, you will break up the Govern-

---

and asked if he had " not proved recreant to every trust and faithless to every friendship."

[130] *Ibid.*, Oct. 24, 1860; Avery, p. 129.
[131] Waynesboro *Independent South*, Oct. 31, 1860.
[132] Albany *Patriot*, Oct. 18, 1860.
[133] Columbus *Daily Times*, Oct. 13, 1860.

ment. It don't [*sic*] protect niggers. . . . Then, we say, let the Union go if it fails to give us protection.[134]

Accepting Lincoln's election and secession as fixed facts, a few days before the end of the campaign, the Carrollton *Advocate* predicted that "croakers" would say "we will submit," but that they should be silenced by the "brave" and "patriotic." "Cowards" would then follow. In 1776 the craven-hearted did not prevail, and the era of 1860 would be as great: "No period of the earth's history will be so grand and stirring. We pity the soul who fears to witness it." [135] To expressed fears concerning dissolution, revolution, taxes, standing armies, decline in Negro prices, the Columbus *Times* replied that these calamities might not come, but if they came, they would be no argument to halt a people fighting oppression. Now was the time, it said, to strike out for a "free, united, congenial people." [136]

The convert to the Breckinridge Democratic party, Francis S. Bartow of Savannah, made a fiery address before his fellow townsmen. He was weary of the controversy, he declared, and desired that the issue be made, while he was in the prime of manhood. Bartow was ready to peril all for Southern rights; there was nothing for the South to gain by waiting. With apparent sincerity he spoke of the greatness of the United States, the best nation on the globe, the haven of the oppressed. But he would peril *all,* before he would submit to an "unprincipled majority." [137] Howell Cobb forecast secession in a speech at Marietta in the closing days of the campaign.[138]

Fearing that the Bell and Douglas men would effect a fusion in Georgia, a Breckinridge paper appealed to Douglas Democrats, especially those of foreign birth, to remain out of the "Know Nothing" camp, and recalled the "butcheries" of foreign born in Baltimore, New Orleans, and Louisville.[139] No such fusion was accomplished, but the usual cordial relation-

---

[134] *Ibid.,* Nov. 3, 1860.

[135] Carrollton *Advocate*, Nov. 2, 1860.

[136] Columbus *Daily Times*, Nov. 6, 1860.

[137] Avery, p. 127. Bartow's wish was fulfilled, as he was killed at first Bull Run.

[138] *Ibid.,* p. 129.

[139] Athens *Southern Banner*, Sept. 20, 1860.

ship between the anti-Breckinridge forces was in existence in Georgia. While at first the Opposition rejoiced at the Democratic split and professed to see no difference between the factions, as the campaign waxed the Constitutional Unionists reserved most of their fire for Breckinridge. At first too, the old Whig remnants stood by in the hope that, if the Democrats accepted the Douglas candidacy and doctrine, they could then come forward as the champions of Congressional protection.[140]

The Opposition-Constitutional Union press in Georgia included such papers as the Augusta *Chronicle and Sentinel,* the Macon *Georgia Journal and Messenger,* the Milledgeville *Southern Recorder,* the Savannah *Daily Republican,* the Columbus *Enquirer,* and other smaller papers. The tone of the Bell press was distinctly pro-slavery, sometimes aggressively so, and at times bitterly anti-Northern and "black" Republican, yet on the whole calmer than the Breckinridge press.[141] Such a spokesman for the party as the Augusta *Chronicle and Sentinel* expressed pleasure when the projected Southern conference failed, because the people feared its purpose was disunion without sufficient cause. The Charleston *Mercury* and its ilk, by irresponsible talk, caused the South's troubles. This influential Georgia paper objected to committing the South to a dissolution of the Union in the event of Lincoln's election, and also to the idea of frightening the North into supporting a Democratic candidate. This paper held that a Republican could be regularly and legally chosen President, if he had the electoral vote, and any effort to prevent it must resort to force; in which case the Constitution was gone and the Republic at an end. Nor could the *Chronicle and Sentinel* understand how the interests of slavery could be better protected outside than inside the Union.[142]

After Bell's nomination, the vagueness of his platform permitted his followers to take diverse attitudes toward Congressional protection. Benjamin H. Hill at first sympathized with

[140] Augusta *Daily Chronicle and Sentinel,* April 17, 1860. But cf. *ibid.,* July 13, 1860.

[141] For example, the Savannah *Daily Republican,* July 24, 31, 1860, denied that Douglas men were no better than Republicans, and recognized their Northern strength.

[142] Augusta *Daily Chronicle and Sentinel,* Feb. 11, 14, March 14, 1860.

the Constitutional Democrats and urged the seceders not to back down. He evidently dallied with the idea of a fusion between the Georgia Constitutional Unionists and the Breckinridge Democrats.[143] But the Augusta *Chronicle and Sentinel* by July 13 had discovered that it was "wicked" and "foolish" of the Breckinridge Democrats to insist upon Congressional protection; as a party of peace, this paper opposed agitation on this issue. The slavery question was "settled." Moreover, this partisan paper also took a far more friendly attitude towards Douglas, whom it had earlier berated—he was now preferable to Breckinridge.[144]

Occasionally an Opposition paper expressed concern that perhaps changes should be made in order to beat Lincoln,[145] others carried on partisanship as usual. Thus the Athens *Southern Watchman* echoed the charge that Buchanan's administration was the "most profligate and corrupt . . . in our history." [146] As the campaign wore its way to the end, the Bell papers assumed, despite earlier assertions in the year, a marked Unionist position, tempered in a few cases by the realization that a storm would break after election. Said the Athens *Southern Watchman*: "We know that the people are not ready for a dissolution of the Union. We see them dragged on, blindfolded, to the consummation of the horrid act." [147] The Augusta *Chronicle and Sentinel* adduced a unique argument against secession and a cotton confederacy. It saw the hand of nature intervening to prevent such a development in 1860, for a drought had struck the state late in June. With a shortage of bacon and grain, it would be needful to secure these provisions from the hated squatters of the Northwest. The "wild disunionists" would bring the South to ruin, establish eleven petty despots in state

---

[143] See interview of Hill by the Editor of the Atlanta *National American*, *ibid.*, June 20, 1860.

[144] *Ibid.*, July 3, Aug. 9, 1860.

[145] On July 2, 1860, the Savannah *Daily Republican* proposed the withdrawal of Bell, and the substitution of Hammond for him on the ticket with Everett. Earlier the Macon *Georgia Journal and Messenger*, Feb. 29, 1860, had defined the big question as ". . . how can black republicanism be annihilated and forever?" It proposed a union of all conservative Democrats, Whigs, and Americans.

[146] Athens *Southern Watchman*, Aug. 1, 1860.

[147] *Ibid.*, Aug. 16, 1860.

houses, and erect a military despotism. A Southern confederacy would have the entire world against it, and slavery would
become less secure.[148]

Commenting on a report from Washington that Secretary
Cobb had returned from a trip to Georgia with the belief that his
state would secede in the event, by then a certainty, of Lincoln's
election, the Milledgeville *Southern Recorder* favored remaining
in the Union even if Lincoln won, for the people of Georgia
were not ready to quit the Union by the simple election of Lincoln.[149] The Augusta *Chronicle and Sentinel* put the query to
Georgians: Had they counted the consequences of disunion?
What if other states disagreed with the right to secede, and
applied coercion? If the South should secede, and sustain
herself by the sword, history would speak of her " glorious "
revolution. Otherwise Southerners would be traitors. This
paper hinted that those who opposed dissolution would be
branded as traitors, and would lose their property. Georgia
was not prepared for war, and finally, the middle classes would
be thrown into a sorry plight.[150] Although fighting hard for
Union, at times this paper wavered, as after the Pennsylvania
elections, when it conceded that the storm would soon break.
Madness ruled the hour; prosperous the South was, but con-
sumed with bitterness; indeed it was the very excess of prosperity which had made the South rebellious, concluded the
Chronicle and Sentinel.[151]

Benjamin H. Hill wrote in mid-October that the canvass was
nearly over and he feared that the Union was also. Yet he saw a
possibility of saving the Union, and criticized those who advocated that " palpable absurdity," Constitutional secession. He
believed in the right of revolution; his objection to Lincoln was
entirely because of slavery. His suggestion was that two of the
anti-Lincoln men—Breckinridge and Douglas—withdraw as
each had been associated with slavery agitation since 1854.
John Bell was not a sectional, slavery agitator, and he fulfilled
every requisite required by Lincoln's enemies. If the North
should reject Bell, then the Southern right to retire would be

[148] Augusta *Daily Chronicle and Sentinel*, Aug. 26, 1860.
[149] Milledgeville *Southern Recorder*, Aug. 28, 1860.
[150] Augusta *Daily Chronicle and Sentinel*, Sept. 18, 1860
[151] *Ibid.*, Oct. 13, 16, 1860.

recognized, he asserted. By this date Hill merely would rest upon the Dred Scott decision; and he reversed his earlier position by denouncing the Breckinridge platform as madness. Thus the Union might be saved by a concentration on Bell.[152]

Some Bell partisans continued to argue for Union after the election of Lincoln, a fact which indicates that their Union talk in the campaign was not insincere. Said the Athens *Southern Watchman*: " If, unfortunately, Abe Lincoln was elected President on Tuesday, we cannot perceive how the event can in the slightest degree endanger the institution of slavery during his Administration." " Old Abe " and his party could not begin to harm slavery as much in the coming four years as the Southern agitators had done in the past four weeks, this paper concluded.[153] Some Bell partisans flopped almost immediately into the secessionist camp, but some continued to battle for moderation until the state's decision was reached.

The Douglas wing of the party constituted a dissenting minority of the Democrats in Georgia, as noted in connection with the several state conventions, 1859-1860. Alexander H. Stephens was the most important national figure in Georgia to champion Douglas, which he did earnestly and publicly in the two months before election. Of Stephens' deep and sincere Unionism there can be no doubt, and perhaps the same can be said of many others among the Douglas Democrats of Georgia. But here and there a man or a newspaper backed Douglas and at the same time assumed a fiery secessionist attitude. W. B. Gaulden, who made the famous African slave trade speech at Charleston, and J. P. Hambleton's Atlanta *Southern Confederacy* were examples. It was possible for the enemies of Douglas to quote the utterances of these few Douglas extremists and " prove " that Douglas was a disunionist! On the other hand, such a paper as the Augusta *Constitutionalist*,

[152] Hill to the Savannah *Daily Republican*, Oct. 13, 1860, Savannah *Daily Republican*, Oct. 19, 1860. Hill's proposal was attacked by the Savannah *Morning News*, which feared the disruption of the state Democratic organization and that Hill's party would share the spoils. The Democratic unwillingness to aid in the patriotic cause of harmonizing the South for serious post-election events, was assailed by the Savannah *Daily Republican*, Oct. 20, 1860.

[153] Athens *Southern Watchman*, Nov. 8, 1860. The western Georgia Hamilton *Harris County Enterprise*, Nov. 15, 22, 1860, agreed, and desired that every effort be made for peace.

a militant Douglas journal edited by Stephens' friend James
Gardner, was a Unionist sheet.[154]

Alexander H. Stephens accepted appointment as elector on
the Douglas ticket, and though he had no illusions as to the
chances of his candidate's winning Georgia, publicly and privately he endorsed the Little Giant. He wrote his friend Dr.
Hambleton his confidential views on the situation, a letter filled
with Stephens' pessimistic reflections as to the disastrous course
of affairs, in which he warmly characterized Douglas as an
altogether sound pro-slavery man, who championed the institution in a Northern state in 1858, and who was indeed the most
effective exponent of Southern interests outside the South.[155]
Stephens' speeches in Georgia during the campaign were often
badly reported, or, in the case of the Breckinridge press,
ignored. He made a number of Douglas addresses in Georgia,
and personally welcomed Douglas to the state in October and
traveled with him until Douglas entered Alabama.[156]

On June 29, Herschel V. Johnson, in an address at Macon,
urged that in view of the census returns, the South cherish an
alliance with the West, which latter would at no distant date
give laws to the nation. Such new states as were to be admitted from that region should be made Democratic states, and
the South should support the great Western leader, Douglas.
He pointed to the danger of giving Congress " jurisdiction " in
the matter of slavery in the territories, and made out a case
for Popular Sovereignty. He correctly saw that the real contest was in the free states, and that the South was really out
of the fight—she might defeat Douglas, but could not elect
Breckinridge. Johnson concluded, however, with the assertion that if at the end these unwise policies came to prevail, he
would follow the South.[157]

By the close of the campaign, the Douglas supporters saw
that the catastrophe which they had fought to stave off was

[154] Augusta *Daily Constitutionalist*, Sept. 5, 1860.

[155] A. H. Stephens to Dr. J. P. Hambleton, July 2, 1860, MS, Stephens Papers,
Library of Congress.

[156] See account of Stephens' speech at Augusta, Sept. 1, 1860. New York
Tribune (semi-weekly), Sept. 4, 1860. An example of the " roor-back " was
printed in the Vicksburg *Weekly Sun*, Nov. 5, 1860, which declared that A. H.
Stephens had deserted Douglas for Breckinridge. This was false.

[157] Baltimore *American*, July 25, 1860.

upon them. On October 15, Linton Stephens told Professor R. M. Johnston of the University of Georgia that he was no longer fighting the election of Lincoln, but the precipitation of revolution, "which is intended to follow his election." The people were blind; Stephens deeply regretted that the best government on earth was about to be destroyed and without cause. "What a causeless catastrophe it will be! and how terrible its results!" [158]

On November 3, the Augusta *Constitutionalist* affirmed its belief in secession, but continued to express its view of Lincoln in moderation, proposed a state convention in event of a Lincoln victory, and declared the issue to be "immediate resistance" versus a violation of the "Georgia platform" or of the Constitution by the President or Congress. If these matters were adjusted and Georgia remained in the Union, this paper hoped that the South would learn a lesson not to divide on the eve of a contest or to allow abstractions, hate, and desire for power to come before patriotism.[159] This provided the cue for the moderates, when they did battle under the leadership of Alexander H. Stephens, against precipitate action in the months after election.

As some observers predicted, no candidate received a requisite majority in the balloting in Georgia, and eventually the state legislature, as provided by the law of December 23, 1847, cast the state's entire electoral vote for Breckinridge. But by that time such was of little importance, as graver questions absorbed the people and legislature of Georgia. Breckinridge's failure to win a popular majority in the Southern Empire state has been noted by historians, and the vote for the moderate Unionist candidates has generally been held to be significant. Some of the moderates of 1860 were waverers, to be sure, but it was the events of the post-election weeks which caused the triumph of the state's secessionists.

---

[158] Waddell, *Biographical Sketch of Linton Stephens*, pp. 233-234.
[159] Augusta *Daily Constitutionalist*, Nov. 3, 1860.

16

FLORIDA

This region was a rural frontier state in 1860, where out-lawry and violence caused considerable concern.[160] Even then Florida was aware of her salubrious climate, especially suitable to African plantation labor. But there was a disturbing exodus of planters westward—to Texas and the Southwest. One de-fender of Florida admitted that while more cotton could be made in the West, it was unhealthy there. The planter would be forced constantly to replace his labor. " It is proverbial that no Southern State is so well adapted to the full physical development of the African. Here he breathes almost native air, without its excessive heats or pestilential vapors; and in a climate so well adapted to the race their increase is a source of profit." [161]

Although Florida was the most youthful and the least populous of the Southern states, Governor M. S. Perry de-clared that there was no reason why the state's voice should not be heard, to inform the leaders that Florida was ready to resist aggression. In his message to the legislature, Governor Perry said: " I believe that her voice should be heard . . . in favor of an eternal separation from those whose wickedness and fanaticism forbid us longer to live with them in peace and safety." There were grounds for believing that the South would not permit the government to pass to the enemy; prep-aration would be made to meet the emergency—the presidential election.[162]

The tone of the Florida Democratic press closely resembled that of Governor Perry's address, and the newspapers often quoted with approval articles from the Charleston *Mercury*. Dire forebodings were expressed. The Quincy *Republic* pre-dicted that the convention at Charleston " . . . may be the last national convention to be held." [163] And the Fernandina *East Floridian* anticipated nothing but discord. However, let Florida

---

[160] For a recent survey of Florida history, see Katherine T. Abbey, *Florida, Land of Change* (Chapel Hill, 1941), especially pp. 262-263 for the political situation in 1860.

[161] Tallahassee *Journal and Floridian*, Feb. 25, 1860.

[162] Fernandina *East Floridian*, Dec. 15, 1859.

[163] Quoted in *ibid.*, Jan. 11, 1860.

be represented. The Democratic state convention endorsed slavery, the Davis resolutions, and repudiated Douglas' doctrine. R. M. T. Hunter and Alexander H. Stephens each found newspaper support in Florida.[164]

The *East Floridian's* first reaction to the secession at Charleston was that the seceders' ticket could not succeed.[165] Later the opinion was expressed that the Democratic party was irrevocably destroyed. No regret was expressed, and it was hoped that the South would make no concessions. Florida should only send a delegation to Richmond.[166] In the interval between the Charleston and Baltimore meetings, there was much defiant sentiment in Florida. The movement at Charleston was not a disunion course; it was rather to unite the " real union loving Democratic conservative men." If the South should assume a firm position, it was contended, " the people of the other sections cannot, if they love the Union . . . persist in an unjust and unconstitutional course." It was right that the South test the issue, to determine her real position, which, if decided against her would enable her to take appropriate action.[167]

Some were ready to act without further ado. L. A. Hardee thought the crisis had fallen upon the Southern people. He ardently advocated the seceders' cause at Charleston. Hardee penned a fierce indictment of the North, and issued a " clarion call " for volunteers to join him in a cavalry corps which would be offered to the first Southern state to quit the Union.[168] County meetings endorsed secession,[169] and J. P. Hunt wrote from Lake Butler that extremism was rampant among the Florida planters.[170] Senator David L. Yulee of Florida [171] considered the big issue in the Democratic conventions to be " the right of colonization " or, as he preferred to phrase it,

[164] *Ibid.*, Jan. 11, Feb. 23, April 19, 1860. Tallahassee *Floridian and Journal*, April 7, 1860.

[165] Fernandina *East Floridian*, May 3, 1860.

[166] *Ibid.*, May 31, 1860.

[167] *Ibid.*, May 12, 1860.

[168] See Hardee's letter, " God and our Rights," Rural Home, Florida, May 8, 1860. *Ibid.*, May 17, 1860.

[169] Duval county and other Democratic county meetings endorsed secession. *Ibid.*, May 24, 1860.

[170] J. P. Hunt to B. F. Perry, Sept. 16, 1860, MS, B. F. Perry Collection, Alabama Department of History and Archives, Montgomery.

[171] *D. A. B.*, XX, 638.

"the Liberty of Growth." Yulee admitted that the future condition of all the existing territories was settled. Yulee advised against sending a delegation to Baltimore, but urged that Florida support the nominee of that convention, if he was regularly nominated. He summed up the twofold program of the Republican party; no more slave states and civil equality of the blacks. His advice was against the destruction of the party, as he thought the nominee of Baltimore would render a satisfactory type of administration. But if the Republicans won, it would be the duty of the South to secede and to demand new terms of Union; if that failed, then a Southern confedracy should be created.[172]

Unqualified Unionists were scarce indeed in the Breckinridge party, and not too numerous anywhere in Florida. The *Floridian and Journal* made a neat distinction. Though there were disunionists in the Breckinridge party, they also existed in the Opposition party.

We are willing to stand by the Constitution as long as it is carried out in its true spirit. We want the Union as it was established—we want the substance and not the shadow . . . God forbid that any Southern party should be willing to sacrifice their rights to maintain the Confederacy. Our rights first, the Union afterwards.[173]

Much discussion favorable to secession appeared in the press. A long letter advocating a Southern confederacy appeared in the *East Floridian*, which concluded: "There might be a civil war, but it would terminate in less than six months."[174] Minute Men and vigilance committees were in process of formation during the last weeks of the presidential campaign. Let Florida and all the South emulate South Carolina in her dignity and unanimity. Thousands of sons of South Carolina would fly to her protection if the "minions" of a "black"

---

[172] D. L. Yulee to C. E. Dyke, May 26, 1860. Fernandina *East Floridian*, June 14, 1860. Florida joined South Carolina in boycotting the Baltimore convention. Yulee, then in New York, later wrote: "My letters from the South evince a growing anticipation of unavoidable civil commotion in the event of the anti-slavery triumph." D. L. Yulee to Joseph Holt, Oct. 4, 1860, MS, Horatio King Papers.

[173] Tallahassee *Floridian and Journal*, July 7, 1860.

[174] Fernandina *East Floridian*, Oct. 18, 1860. After election, a letter appeared attempting to prove that the South would gain by a civil war. *Ibid.*, Dec. 12, 1860.

Republican President should attack her. Vigilance and military preparedness should be watch-words because the election of Lincoln would " embolden" his " emissaries." Let the scoundrels who tamper with slaves be exterminated.[175]

The St. Augustine *Examiner* declared that Southerners would never acquiesce in abolition. Time was precious, and as eventual unity was sure to come, why not act immediately? " We are defeated in the Union, but out of it we are still masters of the world, for we are a *necessity* to that world." In the opinion of this paper, there would be no sanguinary conflict, at least not for the present.[176] Finally, Senator Yulee declared that the South would soon be forced to weigh her position in the Union. Yulee still desired new guarantees in the Union, a rearrangement to enable the South to live " in peace." [177]

The Bell campaign in Florida did not command an impressive press or other support. The decline of the Whigs left only a remnant to champion Bell. Although Bell people pointed an accusing finger at the " disunionists," their opponents countered by characterizing the Bell men as " submissionists." [178] The Tallahassee *Sentinel* was represented as seeing no reason why Southern men should not hold office in the Lincoln administration.[179] G. T. Ward wrote that while he supported Bell, he would vote for Breckinridge if that would secure a " united South." He had no doubt that the Republicans intended to pass laws which would strip the South of her rights, as soon as there was a President who would not veto such laws.[180]

An interesting and misunderstood position was that held by Richard K. Call, a foremost citizen of Florida.[181] As a supporter of Bell, he was supposed to be a Unionist. But Call had the fixed belief that a Republican President could not serve both the Constitution and his party. The Republicans would, faced with this alternative, abrogate the Constitution, in which case Call would be for disunion. He hoped that a united South and West behind Douglas would solve the problem.

[175] *Ibid.*, Oct. 18, 24, 1860.
[176] Quoted in *ibid.*, Oct. 21, 1860.
[177] D. L. Yulee to W. H. Babcock, Oct. 18, 1860, *ibid.*, Oct. 31, 1860.
[178] Tallahassee *Floridian and Journal*, July 28, Sept. 22, 1860.
[179] *Ibid.*, Nov. 3, 1860.   [181] *D. A. B.*, III, 422-423.
[180] *Ibid.*, Aug. 11, 1860.

During the canvass, Call and the Breckinridge press had a colloquy as to the former's position on secession. On August 23, Call wrote from Lake Jackson that he opposed secession. His contention was that Lincoln could not administer the government and its functions would be suspended. He would resist Lincoln, like Henry A. Wise of Virginia, in the Union. Lincoln would be but the president of a faction, a mere usurper, and Call endorsed commercial and social non-intercourse.[182]

The Douglas campaign was extremely feeble in Florida. One observer noted that most of the Douglas activity and support seemed to be confined to Pensacola and Jacksonville.[183] The Jacksonville *Republican* displayed resolutions adopted by the Florida legislature in 1847 which endorsed Douglas' doctrine.[184]

When the returns came in, it was seen that Florida had gone by a majority for Breckinridge,[185] and Governor Perry's outgoing message to the legislature was a stirring secession document. The election of Lincoln was the terrible culmination of forty years of Northern " aggressions and insults " at the expense of the South.[186] And a few days after election, the *Floridian and Journal* inveighed against the idea of awaiting an " overt act." If the " blacks " could safely pass the danger of immediate resistance, the future would be used to achieve their " objects." But it would not be surprising if Bell, Crittenden, or William Cabell Rives should become Lincoln's Secretary of State. It would require no overt act to swamp South Carolina with " Sewardites," or to appoint an " incendiary " Postmaster General. No overt act would be required to establish and enforce freedom of speech and liberty of the press in the South; no overt act would be necessary to encompass the gradual downfall of the entire social system. The *Floridian*

[182] See statements of Call's attitude written by himself, Tallahassee *Floridian and Journal*, March 24, Sept. 1, 1860, and report of his remarks at a Bell rally, *ibid.*, Nov. 3, 1860.

[183] Quoted in Fernandina *East Floridian*, Oct. 27, 1860.

[184] Douglas men were in Pensacola and Jacksonville, but there were not " enough of them to serve as mile posts on the line of the Florida Railroad." *Ibid.*, Sept. 20, 1860.

[185] Breckinridge, 8,543; Bell, 5,437; Douglas, 367. *Tribune Almanac . . . for 1861* (New York, 1861), p. 63.

[186] Governor Perry's message was delivered Nov. 26, 1860.

and Journal took no stock in the plea made on behalf of Lincoln, "that a President *elected* is a very different man from a *candidate for election*." [187]

ALABAMA

Early in 1860, the Democratic state convention adopted the famous "Alabama resolutions," which demanded that the Charleston convention endorse the doctrine of Congressional protection to slavery in the territories. If this demand should be rejected, the Alabama delegates were instructed to retire from the convention. William Lowndes Yancey and his followers were in complete control of the party's state convention, but they were challenged by a determined minority led by such men as former Governor John A. Winston, J. J. Seibels of the Montgomery *Confederation,* and John Forsyth of the Mobile *Register*. The minority was favorable to Douglas and was disinclined to exact a definition of Southern territorial rights at that time.[188] Forsyth wrote his paper that the Democratic convention by a large majority had adopted a "violent, disruptive platform." According to him, Alabama had ordered the delegates to quit the Charleston convention, and the resolutions overturned the Compromise of 1850. They would lead to revolution if other Southern states took similar action.[189]

The state legislature, by an all but unanimous vote, followed up the action taken by the Democratic convention, with the passage of resolutions calling for elections to a state convention in the event of the election of a "black" Republican President. This was construed as being tantamount to the calling of a secession convention. Thus the stage was set for the dramatic events in the spring of 1860, in which Alabama politicians played a leading role. The story of the break-up at Charleston and the epilogue at Baltimore has been told many times, and cannot be rehearsed here. In general it has

[187] Tallahassee *Floridian and Journal*, Nov. 10, 1860.
[188] James L. Murphy, "Alabama and the Charleston Convention of 1860," in *Transactions of the Alabama Historical Society 1904* (Thomas M. Owen, ed., Montgomery, 1906), V, 239-266. C. P. Denman, *The Secession Movement in Alabama* (Montgomery, 1933), pp. 79-86.
[189] Quoted in Paulding (Miss.) *Eastern Clarion*, Jan. 18, 1860.

been assumed that events at Charleston and Baltimore played into Yancey's hands, and repeatedly it was charged during the campaign that the outcome was precisely what he had planned long in advance. Recently it has been suggested that Yancey hesitated to withdraw Alabama and the cotton states after the failure of the majority platform, because such action would aid Douglas' candidacy. But the refusal of the Baltimore convention to seat the Alabama and Louisiana bolters slammed the door in Yancey's face and irreparably divided the party.[190]

Governor A. B. Moore privately informed Governor William H. Gist of South Carolina that he favored waiting till after the Charleston convention for "action," or, if that went well for the South, till after the presidential election. Moore told Gist what the latter desired to hear: that a crisis was approaching. Alabama, South Carolina, and Mississippi had taken "high ground" from which there could be no retreat.[191]

The dominant Yancey faction in Alabama Democratic politics had with finality rejected Stephen A. Douglas. In the midst of the stormy days of the spring of 1860, the Carrollton *West Alabamian* asserted:

We must have a man above suspicion. We must have a candidate who *has never betrayed* the South. Douglas is not that man. In our time of need he joined our enemies and waged a bitter war against Mr. Buchanan, the Kansas Lecompton constitution and the South. Had he proved true, Kansas today would be the sixteenth slave State.[192]

While a recent student of the subject has expressed doubt that a majority of the people in the state regarded the Breckinridge party as synonymous with disunion, the overwhelming majority of extremist newspapers and orators adhered to that party. The ultras were contemptuous alike of Southern "trimmers"—Bell and Douglas men—and the detested abolitionists and "black" Republicans. Although he held no office at the

---

[190] Austin L. Venable, "The Conflict Between the Douglas and Yancey Forces in the Charleston Convention," *Journal of Southern History*, VIII (Feb.-Nov., 1942), 226-241. The standard account is in J. W. DuBose, *The Life and Times of William Lowndes Yancey* (Birmingham, 1892), pp. 439-540.

[191] A. B. Moore to W. H. Gist, April 2, 1860, MS, Miscellaneous Papers of A. B. Moore, 1859-1861, Alabama State Department of History and Archives, Montgomery.

[192] Carrollton *West Alabamian*, May 30, 1860.

time, the eloquent William L. Yancey's fame had spread to every state during the campaign. He toured North and South where he spoke frequently in behalf of Breckinridge. Yancey speeches and activities for some years past were frequently cited by Republicans, Douglas Democrats, and Constitutional Unionists to establish his " incendiary " intentions. Two days after Lincoln's election, Yancey wrote to a one-time fellow Democrat turned "black" Republican: "'You shall have Lincoln or Douglas & no other' said one or two of Douglas' leading friends to me at Charleston & Baltimore. We have Lincoln! The bitter cup is at our lips! *Will we drink it?* . . . I have done my duty by the Union—I shall do it by my State."[193] Many charged that Yancey deliberately plotted to bring such a situation to pass.

The Breckinridge press and orators breathed fire throughout, and voiced chagrin at the " timidity " and submissionist attitude of the South. Johnson J. Hooper's Montgomery *Mail*, a whilom Oppositionist sheet, led the " States Rights " Opposition element into the Breckinridge ranks, and it took ultra Southern ground.[194] An example of the *Mail's* exasperation was the account it printed of one General Cornelius Robinson's attitude to the sectional controversy. That worthy was preparing to sell his valuable plantation and Negroes. Chagrined at the " submissionist " policy of the South, he was determined " to sell out and leave." Hundreds of others, reported the *Mail*, " good and true men," would do likewise if Lincoln were elected, rather than have their children reared in a " subjugated " section.[195] Men like Robert G. Scott, David Hubbard, John T. Morgan, and George Gayle of the Cahaba *Slaveholder*

[193] W. L. Yancey to J. W. Forney, Nov. 8, 1860, MS, Autograph Collection, Historical Society of Pennsylvania. The real story concerning Yancey's activity, 1859-1860, is veiled by absence of manuscript evidence.

[194] J. E. D. Yonge, "The Conservative Party in Alabama, 1848-1861," *Transactions of the Alabama Historical Society 1899-1903* (Montgomery, 1904), IV, 518-519. Congressman George S. Houston of Athens, Ala., wrote that the ultras among the old Whigs had " gone to Yancey," and that those who remained were conservative. G. S. Houston to A. H. Stephens, Aug. 2, 1860, MS, A. H. Stephens Papers, Library of Congress. For exchange of hostile views between J. J. Hooper and Jere Clemens, see Little Rock *Arkansas State Gazette*, July 21, 1860.

[195] Quoted in Augusta (Ga.) *Daily Chronicle and Sentinel*, Oct. 10, 1860. The *Chronicle and Sentinel* commented in this issue that such talk was " alarmism."

represented the ultimate in Alabama extremism, and quotations from them were employed in other states to damage Breckinridge.[196]

William F. Samford of " Sunny Slope," near Auburn, Alabama, the defeated ultra candidate for Governor in 1859, and " penman " of the secession movement, was active during the campaign of 1860.[197] He wrote, August 11, that he could not see why " reasonable " men should vote for Bell. To Colonel Samford, the Douglas and Bell parties were " semi-abolitionist." [198] Again on October 18, he declared that even the victory of Bell, Breckinridge, or Douglas would not avert post-election difficulty. Samford, an ordained Methodist minister-lawyer-journalist-politician, had reached a grim conclusion: " There is no arbiter but *the sword*, these fanatics will respect—the ' steel whips ' with which tyrants have to be scourged." [199]

As the campaign closed, the secessionists became feverishly active. Mrs. C. C. Clay informed Postmaster General Holt that Senator Clay " will probably resign " if Lincoln be elected.[200] The Montgomery *Mail* urged the arming of every county. A few weeks before election, it declared that vile abolitionism was at the threshold, " with torch and knife " in hand. General L. P. Walker was " out for disunion " and was ready to fight. According to this account, Alabama was thoroughly aroused. An old man came up to Walker and expressed the desire to fight.[201] This picture was confirmed in a letter to President Buchanan from Mobile. T. Sanford described public opinion as " much excited " at the prospect of Republican victory, and forecast that the convention to be

[196] George Gayle and his Cahaba *Slaveholder* have become obscure, but deserve investigation.

[197] George Petrie, " William F. Samford, Statesman and Man of Letters," *Transactions of the Alabama Historical Society 1899-1903* (T. M. Owen, ed., Montgomery, 1904), IV, 465-485.

[198] Little Rock *Arkansas True Democrat*, Sept. 1, 1860.

[199] Montgomery *Daily Mail*, Oct. 24, 1860. Samford had favored Henry A. Wise for President. N. B. Drake to A. H. Stephens, Glennville, Ala., Dec. 6, 1859, MS, Stephens Papers.

[200] V. C. Clay to Joseph Holt, Oct. 20, 1860, MS, Joseph Holt Papers, Library of Congress.

[201] Quoted in Fernandina *East Floridian*, Oct. 31, 1860.

called would not be controlled by the conservatives.[202] A Virginian, teaching school at Clayton, Alabama, wrote a candid letter on the situation there. Three days after Lincoln's election, Eugene Blackford wrote Mary L. Minor: " They [Alabamians] are all violent Fire Eaters, are for dissolution to a man, and speak of any one, who professes the smallest love of the Union, as a traitor to his country, namely the South. Up to the 6th instant, every one old and young, wore the blue cockade (resistance to Lincoln). . . ." The parties were united, he noted, and continued: " The cause of half of the violence in public opinion here is their ignorance of politics; they never see any papers except the local papers, and the ' Charleston Mercury.' " [203]

The Minute Men with their blue cockades, which Blackford observed, were believed to be forming to resist Lincoln's inauguration.[204] A few days after election, the Auburn *Sketch Book* assayed the situation in excessively intemperate language. " What *right* have we that has not been *violated*? " It enumerated eight " rights " which North had denied South. The Constitution had been defied; they, Northerners, " steal our slaves shamelessly "; " angry contention and agitation " have been made to displace Southern peace and security; the North had not respected Southern " honor," instead " they have persistently thrown contempt upon us as vile Slaveholders! "; the North had denied Southerners a " good name." " These false brethren have slandered us as brutal and ungodly, polygamous and Polyphemean monsters, and made the ear of Europe ache with the ceaseless iteration of lying stories of our cruelty and crimes. Whatever character we have as a civilized people, we have in spite of their slanderous vociferations and malignant inventions." [205]

The *Sketch Book* continued its tirade. Southerners had a right to " respect . . . the purest women on earth." But " The

[202] T. Sanford to James Buchanan, Oct. 31, 1860, MS, James Buchanan Papers, Historical Society of Pennsylvania.

[203] Eugene Blackford to Mary L. Minor, Clayton, Alabama, Nov. 9, 1860, MS, John B. Minor Papers, Alderman Library, University of Virginia. This letter contains an amusing passage describing wherein the people of Alabama differed from Virginians.

[204] Augusta (Ga.) *Daily Chronicle and Sentinel*, Nov. 4, 1860.

[205] Auburn *Sketch Book*, Nov. 9, 1860.

infernal Devil himself inspired these painted hypocrites to deny and denounce the virtue of our wives, our mothers and our daughters!" Moreover, the right of life and security had been trampled.

These saintly, benevolent, puritanical brothers of ours, sacredly sworn in the Constitution to the maintainance [*sic*] of "domestic tranquility" '. . . have armed servile hands, with the bowl of *poison* for our boards —the incendiary torch and pike for our houses and throats; and stimulated them to hellish rape and plunder and murder! Midnight *raids* and mid-day *ravages* and *ravishments*, are the scenes in which they delight to contemplate us!

After such a catalogue, denial of equality in territories came as an anticlimax, but the *Sketch Book* concluded, as a final horror, that now Lincoln was victorious on a platform which "proclaims the negro our equal. . . ." [206] In view of such sentiments and the general character of the Breckinridge campaign, it is not surprising that, as Breckinridge received a majority of the popular vote in the election, Alabama soon moved to join South Carolina in the secession movement.

The campaign for John Bell in Alabama was conducted by such old Whig leaders as Jere Clemens of Huntsville, Thomas H. Watts, Henry W. Hilliard, and the Mobile *Advertiser*. In general, the Alabama Constitutional Unionists took a strong Unionist position, although Watts' Unionism was of a distinctly limited variety. He advocated the Breckinridge doctrine of Congressional protection to slavery in the territories, and ascribed it to Bell.[207] But the bulk of the Bell party was "conservative." Certain it is that Clemens assumed the most uncompromising Unionist ground. In a speech before his fellow townsmen at Huntsville, August 6, he assailed the legislature's action in pledging the state to resistance in the event of Lincoln's election. This was a bad principle, by which a minority dictated to a majority. Republicanism might be the cause in 1860, but it might be "a tariff, a bank, or some other cause tomorrow. Once in our history a Tariff was invested with this importance. It may be again."

[206] *Ibid.*

[207] Thomas H. Watts to Daniel Sayre, Sept. 21, 1860, Montgomery *Daily Mail*, Sept. 27, 1860. In this statement, Watts favored secession in event of Republican

Continuing, Clemens left no doubt as to his attitude to secession. Foreseeing a return to feudalism, he predicted that " soon counties, neighborhoods, or even individuals will be setting up castles! " With impatience, he exclaimed: " Go out of the Union because a Republican is elected President? Good God! Where is this to end? and what party is to be next proscribed? " As other Unionists did in this crisis, Clemens quoted Andrew Jackson with approval. Not only did he oppose the legislative resolutions of February 25, 1860, but he objected to the military resolutions, and to the granting of so much power to the " secession " Governor as to enable him to " railroad " the state out of the Union. It all had but one object, as Clemens saw it, and that was disunion. There was indeed a chasm between Clemens' analysis and that of the Breckinridge men. He saw peace, plenty, and freedom in the Union, " all around you." He concluded: " If you are pre-pared to exchange all this for the horrors of Civil War, pos-terity can only say such madness came as a result of excess of happiness." [208]

On October 1, Clemens penned a detailed county report of the campaign in Alabama to John Bell, who had a hard race to make. He referred to " our Douglas *cousins*," and described a vote for Douglas as " half a vote for us." Clemens' hatred and suspicion of Buchanan were intense. He informed his candidate: " I believe the old scoundrel would rather burst this government into pieces than see either Bell or Douglas in the White House." Developing his low estimate of President Buchanan, Clemens made more serious charges against him: " His late shipment of 17,000 stand of arms to Fort Moultrie, where in the event of civil commotion they would be certain to be seized by the authorities of So: Carolina looks to me as if he was encouraging them to make the experiment of dis-union." [209]

---

victory. See also, E. B. Culver, "Thomas Hill Watts, A Statesman of the Old Regime," *Transactions of the Alabama Historical Society 1899-1903*, IV, 415-439.

[208] Mobile *Daily Advertiser*, Sept. 5, 6, 9, 1860. The Louisville *Journal* reprinted excerpts of this address, and made it the occasion to deliver a homily on the monstrosity of secession doctrine. Quoted in St. Louis *Daily Missouri Republican*, Sept. 28, 1860.

[209] Jere Clemens to John Bell, Huntsville, Oct. 1, 1860, MS, John Bell Papers, Library of Congress.

Two weeks later, after the election of a Republican Governor in Pennsylvania, Clemens again reported to his chief. "The contest in Alabama is close & doubtful, & a small matter may turn it either way." He then gave an optimistic report on each Congressional district, and expressed the belief that if Douglas men in south Alabama voted for Bell, the state would go for him. Clemens commented upon Yancey's tour of the East, and favored Bell with a characterization of the eminent secessionist: "With all his speaking talent he has not one particle of common sense, & if he went North for any other purpose than that of helping the Republicans it must have been under the influence of a weak & childish vanity of which a lunatic ought to be ashamed." [210]

Complicating the national campaign in Alabama was the injection of the note of sectionalism within the state. This factor appeared in a "Letter from an Old Man in the Country to 'Young America,'" which expressed the attitude of many in north Alabama. This writer was opposed to "insolent infidelity" towards government. He warned impetuous Southerners that they could not live independently, and that "nature never intended that you should." As it seemed to be impossible to have manufacturing in the South, Southerners were urged to make slavery profitable to the North, and to ignore John Brown and other abolitionists. He continued:

I know you are a hot blooded young fellow: That you live down South and eat and drink all manner of inflammable things. . . . But all this will not inflame the blood of the people of the Tennessee valley. You are for war: we are for peace. . . . Look at us. We are cut off from you of the South, by cold, bleak mountains forever facing the North wind, and the wintry skies. Through the enterprize of Tennessee, Georgia, and Mississippi, we can visit New York and New Orleans, for half the expense, and in less than one half the time in which we can go to our own capital [Montgomery]. You give us no Railroads to draw nearer the ties that bind us to our own State.

This writer favored a regularly nominated Democratic candidate, and warned of an "avalanche" of votes from the northern part of Alabama.[211]

[210] Same to same, Oct. 14, 1860, MS, *ibid*.
[211] Huntsville *Southern Advocate*, Feb. 22, 1860. For other Unionist expres-

S. D. Cabaniss, a prominent citizen of Huntsville, wrote Governor Moore just before election a confidential survey of political feeling in the Tennessee Valley section. This letter was written in an effort to guide Governor Moore in order to secure unity of all factions after the election of Lincoln. Cabaniss thought that the Bell-Douglas parties had a majority in each of the counties of the Valley, excepting Jackson and perhaps Morgan. Notwithstanding the existence of a profound difference between the Bell and Douglas parties concerning the powers of a territorial government, Cabaniss noted a " very cordial sympathy between them." The bond which held them together was their conviction that it was the " settled purpose " of the Breckinridge party to " precipitate " a revolution. The Bell-Douglas leaders pointed to the conduct of the Breckinridge party at Charleston, the military bill passed at the last session of the legislature, and the resolution of February, which called for the elections to a state convention—" a conspiracy." Cabaniss thought that the Tennessee Valley folk feared that under the existing ratio a minority could gain control of the proposed convention, and force the state into a bloody war.[212]

Moreover, Cabaniss told Governor Moore, these leaders had, " by unmeasured eulogies upon the Union," led their followers to a theory of government which in 1799 would have been " rank Federalism." The Bell-Douglas leaders declared that the only remedy was revolution, and that " success " only could save those participating in it from " a traitor's doom." Cabaniss echoed the " Old Man in the Country " when he said that many in north Alabama were comparing the county's relation to the state with the latter's relation to the Union.[213]

A few days before writing the letter, Cabaniss heard the leading Douglas man in the Valley say that " if the people of South Alabama should succeed in putting the State out of the Union, he favored putting the Valley out of the State, contending that secession would operate as an utter annihilation of all

sions, see Tuscumbia *North Alabamian*, July 13, 1860, and Tuscumbia *States Rights Democrat*, Oct. 5, 12, 1860.
[212] S. D. Cabaniss to A. B. Moore, Oct. 29, 1860, MS, Alabama State Department of History and Archives, Montgomery.
[213] *Ibid.*

government within the borders of the state and that the people in this section could set up a government of their own." With this in mind, Cabaniss doubted if any state-rights men could be elected from most of the Valley counties. Therefore he suggested that Governor Moore call the legislature which would submit to all voters the question, " Convention or No Convention." He knew voters among the Breckinridge men who favored cooperation first. In a postscript, Cabaniss urged that the border slave states unite with other Southern states to demand the calling of a general national convention of all states, which he hoped would win pledges from the North " to abstain from all acts disturbing tranquility." This would build up an opposition party in the North, he argued, but admitted that this plan was dubious and that if it failed, there was scant hope of preserving the Union.[214]

It is probably true that the Unionism of the Bell men in central and southern Alabama was less adamant than that of the Tennessee Valley. The Montgomery *Mail*, which desired it to be the case, declared that it was a great mistake to assume that the supporters of Bell in Alabama would transfer to Lincoln after his election. The *Mail* believed that the majority of Bell men in Montgomery favored secession. Of course, the case of Thomas H. Watts, a Bell supporter, attracted attention, and was often cited by the radicals. The Southern people were divided as to men, said the *Mail*, but few " will submit to free negro

[214] *Ibid.* Cabaniss' analysis of the situation in the Tennessee Valley counties of Alabama may be compared with the election returns:

County	Bell	Breckinridge	Douglas
Lauderdale	444	706	790
Limestone	368	522	325
Madison	400	591	1300
Jackson	130	1760	565
Marshall	165	441	763
Lawrence	525	370	576
Morgan	144	549	545
Franklin	715	902	460
DeKalb	204	849	202
	3095	6690	5526

Cabaniss' prophecy thus was proved to be accurate. Bell-Douglas had a majority in every county save Jackson and DeKalb. The Douglas vote in this section was heavy.

domination." [215] In Mobile, however, the Bell paper hammered away with denunciations of disunion.[216]

The Douglas campaign was conducted in Alabama by three strategically located newspapers, the Mobile *Register*, the Montgomery *Confederation*, and the Huntsville *Advocate*. Forsyth and Seibels, editors of the first two papers respectively, were determined contestants against the Yancey wing, and the personal altercation between Yancey and Seibels caused some comment.[217]

John Forsyth, former Minister to Mexico and state representative from Mobile, and others were in touch with Douglas early in the campaign.[218] The tone taken by the Mobile *Register* was that the South should consult with Northern leaders, rather than to repel and reject them. Though he mentioned ex-President Pierce, Forsyth was thinking mainly of Douglas. Granted that such men were few, everything should be done to assure their cooperation in the battle against the "black" Republicans. The *Register* could not see how principle or Constitutional right could be vindicated or secured by turning over the national government for four years to the Republicans. The Montgomery "demands" could not be met, except at the expense of the destruction of the South's Northern friends. No answer was forthcoming from the fire-eaters as to the proposal first to beat back the common enemy, save that employed by "one of the Mirabeaus. . . . ' Let discord reign forever! ' " [219]

Former Governor John A. Winston [220] charged that the Alabama platform was but a plot to "precipitate revolution." He said after returning from Charleston: "Gentlemen might not admit it here, they might talk gingerly about it, but it was talked plainly in Charleston, and meant dissolution of the Union and nothing less. When the bolt was completed a

[215] Quoted in Richmond *Examiner*, Oct. 24, 1860.
[216] Mobile *Daily Advertiser*, Aug. 21, 1860.
[217] New York *Times*, Aug. 31, 1860.
[218] Austin L. Venable, "The Conflict Between the Douglas and Yancey Forces in the Charleston Convention," *Journal of Southern History*, VIII, 234.
[219] Mobile *Daily Register*, Jan. 21, 1860.
[220] Winston had been charged with Machiavellian conduct at Charleston. The evidence is inconclusive. Venable, *Journal of Southern History*, VIII, 239-240.

number of Alabama delegates exclaimed, ' thank God, the National Democratic party is broken up at last.' " Winston's twenty years in politics enabled him " to smell several rats," and he noted that Yancey " strutted " in Charleston as a man who had accomplished his purpose.[221]   The territorial question was unimportant to the Douglas men in Alabama, who were willing to await a future court decision as to an exact definition of slavery's status in the territories.[222]   A number of others, not all of whom supported Douglas, were skeptical of the Alabama platform.[223]

The election of Lincoln had the effect of moving the erstwhile Unionists in the direction of secession.   Even Douglas himself could not dissuade John Forsyth from writing a secessionist editorial for the Mobile *Register*.[224]   The former Unionists of north Alabama demanded immediate and separate secession.[225]   Three weeks after election, a correspondent informed Professor Minor of the University of Virginia that he had never seen such unanimity of opinion as in Alabama.[226]   And a month afterward, Henry W. Hilliard could only mourn at the " truly deplorable " state of the country.[227]

MISSISSIPPI

In this state, the epitome of that rural-plantation civilization which was characteristic of the ante-bellum lower South, the

[221] Mobile *Daily Register*, May 21, 1860.

[222] Venable, *Journal of Southern History*, VIII, 234.

[223] Yonge, " The Conservative Party in Alabama, 1848-1861," *Transactions of the Alabama Historical Society 1899-1903*, IV, 508-510.

[224] George Fort Milton, *The Eve of Conflict*, p. 500.

[225] T. K. Hobbs to John B. Minor, Athens, Ala., Nov. 22, 1860, MS, John B. Minor Papers, Alderman Library, University of Virginia. Circular of Citizens of Huntsville, Alabama, Nov. 19, 1860. Jere Clemens was a signer of the paper, which called for a conference of Southern states. MS, John J. Crittenden Papers, Library of Congress.

[226] N. Lockett to John B. Minor, Marion, Ala., Nov. 20, 1860. Lockett urged Virginia to act; if she does, there will be no war; if she vacillates, there would be war, and on Virginia soil. In this connection, T. K. Hobbs disagreed with Minor that secession would " destroy " the border slave states. He warned that slavery would be doomed in Virginia and Maryland if those states submitted to " black " Republican rule. Hobbs to J. B. Minor, Athens, Ala., Nov. 22, 1860, MSS, John B. Minor Papers, Alderman Library, University of Virginia.

[227] Hilliard to J. S. Black, Dec. 5, 1860, MS, J. S. Black Papers, Library of Congress.

contest was largely between the forces which ultimately supported Breckinridge, and those old line Whigs, Americans, and Oppositionists, who formed the Constitutional Union party. The Douglas wing of the Democratic party was extremely weak in the state, in party organization as well as in newspapers.[228]

The Opposition State Central Committee Address, issued late in 1859, expressed some of the lingering partisan hostility to the Buchanan administration. Among other things, that regime was " corrupt "; and under it " positive evils," strife and civil war raged. Yet in the face of this, some desired the acquisition of more territory, in order that the United States should witness further contention and bitterness. This Address deplored slavery agitation. True, none would deny that the South should have " a perfect equality in the territories, but our politicans have surrendered that right by the Kansas Bill." Thus the South had long ago lost an important point, and by the Popular Sovereignty of the Kansas-Nebraska bill, the North gained all. There was no use in quibbling further. Another matter of concern was the retreat of American nationalism before sectionalism, a trend which the Mississippi Opposition felt should be arrested. The formula, heard elsewhere, that the " great conservative majority " in all sections must be united, was endorsed. Moreover, the exacerbation of sectionalism was charged to Southern politicians, who kept the Brown raid alive. Finally, it is interesting to note, it was still possible in the state of Reuben Davis and Jefferson Davis, for a political faction to endorse a protective tariff and internal improvement by the federal government.[229]

Both before and after the nomination of Bell, the columns of the Vicksburg *Whig*, edited by Marmaduke Shannon, were crammed with the most uncompromising Unionism. At the outset of the canvass, the *Whig* condemned the resolutions of the Mississippi legislature, which provided " dissolving the

[228] For a recent scholarly account of the election in Mississippi, see Percy Lee Rainwater, *Mississippi, Storm Center of Secession, 1856-1861* (Baton Rouge, La., 1938), pp. 114-160.
[229] Richmond *Whig and Public Advertiser*, Jan. 17, 1860; see also union meeting at Raymond, Hinds County, which endorsed a tariff. Vicksburg *Daily Whig*, Feb. 10, 1860.

Union without even a violation of the Constitution." Nor did it favor the proposed Atlanta Southern Convention, which would " officially declare the weakness of our section. . . ." [230] This stern Union organ compared such a meeting with the notorious Hartford Convention, " now damned to everlasting fame." It would be deplorable indeed should Mississippi be represented at a convention where the states of Kentucky, Missouri, Maryland, and Delaware would be absent; states which suffered far more from " supposed encroachments " than all the other Southern states combined. And it was doubtful if Tennessee, North Carolina, and Virginia would be represented. Indeed, the *Whig* quoted with approval the Louisville *Journal*'s suggestion that if and when the proposed convention should assemble the members should be arrested for treason.[231]

Although the *Whig* entertained only contempt for abortive Southern conventions because they were controlled by fire-eaters, it did believe that the time was ripe for the South to launch new commercial policies, not as first steps toward secession, " but for our own protection." The suggestion was made that one-third or one-half of Southern capital be withdrawn from agricultural operations and invested in cotton factories. Such action would advance the price of cotton because of the curtailment of the crop. Cotton manufacturing could be carried on as profitably in Mississippi as in Massachusetts, the *Whig* maintained. The few factories which existed in Mississippi proved that manufacturing yielded from 10 per cent to 20 per cent each year. This policy should be accompanied by diversification of agriculture, and the " mechanic arts " should be encouraged. In this connection, the sentiment " labor is honorable and dignified " should be fostered. And finally the South must engage in the direct import and export trade.[232]

Indeed the *Whig* paid its respects to the fire-eaters of the state. They were " impulsive, chivalrous Southrons," who were always angry and excited, full of " sound and fury." These men considered themselves as the especial guardians of the honor and interests of the South. According to the *Whig*,

[230] Vicksburg *Daily Whig*, Jan. 28, 1860.
[231] *Ibid.*, Feb. 10, 1860.
[232] *Ibid.*, Jan. 18, 1860.

they were always ready to combat "an imaginary army of abolitionist invaders." And there was another group of the party, which outwardly professed deep regret at the coming dissolution, but who were insincere in reality, and were "cold" and "calculating." Such was a hostile critique of the elements which subsequently supported Breckinridge.[233]

To these people, the *Whig* posed the question: "In what way will a dissolution of the Union advance pro-slavery interests?" Slavery was better protected in the Union than outside, and the South was warned that the abolitionists would be more free than ever to attack slavery in case of dissolution. "Disunion will sound the knell of negro slavery in America." [234]

Another matter which disturbed the *Whig* was the indiscriminate proscription of people of Northern birth, resident in the South. The Oxford *Mercury's* attitude was but "foolhardy bigotry," and the *Whig* ironically inquired of its contemporary, if extremists boycotted Northern men, who would lead them? General John A. Quitman had "committed the crime" of Northern birth, and the president of the recent Vicksburg Southern Convention was a native of Ohio.[235]

In reply to a question raised by the Oxford *Intelligencer*, whether a "true" Southerner could hold office under the "black" Republicans, the Vicksburg *Whig* would not question the "fealty" of a man, "otherwise sound, merely because he accepted office under Lincoln." It would be unwise to stop the operation of government because of such an adamant position.[236] This paper went further and unqualifiedly denounced the validity of the secession doctrine. It is interesting and not a little startling to find, at this juncture, an important newspaper following closely Websterian Constitutional interpretation. The Compact theory was rejected *in toto*. Louisiana was a case in point. Purchased and later admitted into the Union, other states were therefore involved in the future of the state of Louisiana. They were interested in and entitled to the use of the Mississippi river and its outlet. If Louisiana should secede, what would be the fate of these rights and

[233] *Ibid.*, Jan. 10, 1860.
[234] *Ibid.*, Jan. 10, 1860.
[235] *Ibid.*, Feb. 18, 1860.
[236] *Ibid.*, Oct. 10, 1860.

privileges? Without doubt, the United States government would be called upon to enforce them, and the result would be civil war and revolution. Neither Louisiana nor any other state had a right to secede.[237]

Although the depth of the Union feeling among the Bell rank and file has been questioned, there is no doubt as to the lengths to which Bell orators and presses went in protesting their devotion to the Union and their abhorrence of secession. W. A. Lake, for example, went far in his " submissionist " and " appeasing " words in a campaign speech at Natchez. He was for Bell on the Compromise of 1850, and though he condemned Douglas' doctrine, he had a few friendly words for Douglas. According to Lake, when the Mississippi Platform of 1851 was violated, it was time to rebel. Said he: " I will not submit to outrage, but will not rebel until outrages are attempted to be inflicted. The election of no one, in conformity with the Constitution, is ground for disunion. The Cotton States are not endangered, when Maryland and Virginia, Tennessee, Kentucky and Missouri—States which lose slaves, while we do not—call on us, we will rally to a man." Mississippi suffered but little in comparison, and, while the border states believed in the Union, it did not become the lower South to complain. Slave property, Lake asserted, was in 1860 quite secure.[238]

An insight into the motives and real beliefs of the Bell managers in Mississippi may be gained by a confidential letter from a Union committee to Alexander R. Boteler, national campaign leader of the Constitutional Union party. In mid-September they reported a desperate situation. " We do not deceive ourselves: The party to which we are opposed is fatally bent on mischief in the event of the election of the Black Republican candidate for the presidency." The only event which would give the extremists pause in Mississippi would be a great vote for Bell. " Our friends " were " true " to the cause, but they knew that a crisis was at hand. One desirable factor would be the appearance of clear evidence that Northern moderates were enthusiastically cooperating. They wished to know if a sincere effort were being made by the Northern " brethren " to assure

[237] *Ibid.*, Oct. 19, 1860.
[238] Natchez *Daily Courier*, Sept. 13, 1860.

Southern rights.   In the opinion of the committee, such a conviction would sweep disunion out of existence.   If however,
this did not materialize, the Bell people in Washington could
rest assured that "we will be absolutely paralyzed."   "Let us
hear them [Northern speakers] *here*, for *here* they will speak
to the Southern heart and mind, and *here* if *at all* in the heart
of Southern Sentiment." [239]

The "plot theory" was publicized in Mississippi by the
Vicksburg *Whig*, which asserted that a diabolical secession
plot was in existence, and that President Buchanan along with
the Breckinridge leaders was involved.[240]   Another Bell journal,
the Natchez *Courier*, sought to prove the point by quotations
from the Charleston *Mercury*, from John Tyler Morgan,
George Gayle of the Cahaba *Slaveholder*, and R. G. Scott of
Alabama.[241]   And at the close of the campaign the *Whig* was
still flaying the fire-eaters.   As elsewhere, resentment was felt
against efforts "to cast suspicion on those not following the
zealots."   Most large slaveholders were conservative and believed that their property would best be protected in the
Union.[242]   Outside the state the staunch Union attitude of the
editor of the *Brandon Republican* was noted.   He would remain in Mississippi if all others departed.   Semihumorously
he averred that once a week he would read Washington's
Farewell Address, Andrew Jackson's Farewell and Nullification
message.[243]

Such were the principal campaign arguments presented to
Mississippi voters in behalf of John Bell.   The Douglas forces

[239] F. Anderson *et al.* to Alexander R. Boteler, Jackson Miss., Sept. 15, 1860,
MS, Boteler Papers, Library of Duke University. See also F. Anderson *et al.* to
John J. Crittenden, Sept. 14, 1860, MS, Crittenden Papers, Library of Congress.
[240] Vicksburg *Daily Whig*, Oct. 30, 31, 1860.
[241] The Charleston *Mercury* was quoted: "As the Democratic party goes to
pieces these will form the nucleus of a Southern organization." J. T. Morgan:
"If I had the power, I would dissolve this Government in two minutes." George
Gayle: "Let us break up this rotten, stinking, and oppressive government."
R. G. Scott: "Protection or Blood." See other quotations from Southern
extremists, Natchez *Daily Courier*, Oct. 6, 1860.
[242] Vicksburg *Daily Whig*, Oct. 24, 1860. A. G. Brown represented the poorest
elements. "Again it was shown that those who had the least property in
slaves were the most ardent and aggressive supporters of the slavery system."
Ranck, *Albert Gallatin Brown*, p. 199.
[243] LaGrange (Texas) *True Issue*, April 20, 1860.

in the state were very weak, and such following as the Little Giant had was located in the counties of northern Mississippi. The second choice of Douglas men was Bell, and it was reported that many would actually vote for the latter, for the reason that " the contest was one of Union or disunion." [244]

As to be expected, the Breckinridge men took the opposite position on every important issue from that enunciated by the Bell-Douglas orators and presses. The reverse of such attitudes as described above, Unionism, calmness, cooperation with Northern moderates, was maintained by the majority, the Breckinridge Democrats. There was some difference of opinion among Mississippi Democrats as to the character of the demands, such as pertained to the immediacy of the application of the doctrine of Congressional protection of slavery in the territories. The two United States Senators, Jefferson Davis and Albert Gallatin Brown, agreed in principle, but the latter demanded immediate application of the doctrine, while the former was content by his famous " Davis resolutions " to insist merely on the right. Davis was considered as the leader of conservative Democratic opinion in the state, while Brown's biographer has labelled him as a typical " radical Southern nationalist." [245]

[244] Natchez *Daily Courier*, Oct. 10, 1860. The situation through the eyes of a Douglas man who finally shifted to Bell may be followed in three letters of James S. Thompson of Ripley, Mississippi, to his father. In January he analyzed the situation: " One half of the talk here is disunion & it is my opinion a majority of the people of Mississippi are in favor of the South Seceding immediately." The confused situation in Congress caused gloom. " The people of this State will not suffer the inauguration of a Black Republican President." (Thompson to Solomon Thompson, Jan. 22, 1860.) In May he wrote: " You know that Miss. is noted for being a Secession & disunion State; but I am proud to say that we have some conservative men here, though they are in a considerable minority." Thompson was still for Douglas, who in his opinion was most available and sound on slavery. If the seceding party secured support, it could only result in Republican victory and make the more certain the resistance of Mississippi. (Same to same, May 13, 1860.) Finally he announced his shift to Bell, because Douglas had utterly no chance in Mississippi. " A great deal depends upon this presidential election. This Union is no longer a Union if Lincoln is elected." (Same to same, Oct. 11, 1860, MSS, Frank Nash Papers, Southern Historical Collection, University of North Carolina.)

[245] See Ranck, esp. pp. 183-200. For Jefferson Davis' position in the campaign, see R. McN. McElroy, *Jefferson Davis; the Unreal and the Real* (2 vols., New York, 1937), I, 192-224. By the close of the campaign, however, Davis asked the South to close ranks behind Breckinridge. He expressed complete belief in the idea that the Republicans planned an attack upon slavery in the

The fire-eating brand of politics was represented by the appropriately named Oxford *Mercury*, which replied to the Opposition address analyzed above. It was not possible to interest fifty persons in the state, under prevailing conditions, in the tariff or internal improvement. The *Mercury* felt the charges of corruption against the Buchanan administration to be of scant moment in the emergency. "Why haggle over sixpences when the robber Black Republicans are at hand, reeking with the gore of our fellow-citizens in Virginia. . .?" Indeed, the advice of the Opposition to dismiss discussion of slavery as the work of a few fanatics in each section, and their suggestion that the wildest abolitionists did not speak for all Northerners, were emphatically rejected. For according to the *Mercury*, the Republicans were "whetting their knives." It was nonsense to argue that such men could be trusted, and that they would obey the letter of the Constitution. Seward would approve the Opposition position: what more conclusive proof was needed of the unsoundness of the Opposition? [246]

Hatred of the Yankee Puritan occasionally appeared in the writings of fiery Mississippi editors. After descanting upon the lush richness and beauty of the Southland, one such declared that "our Northern enemies" were casting covetous glances at the South's wealth. Lincoln had told them in his Springfield speech that some day they would possess it.[247] Moreover, anyone acquainted with the essential character of the Puritan knew that they "would deluge the land in blood to achieve their aims." The utter loathing of the writer for his subject was clear: "They are a grasping and avaricious race, and are never half satisfied unless engaged in a strife with their neighbors. They left England because they had not the privilege of burning witches, cropping Quakers' ears, and hanging Catholics." It was not slavery which was the greatest curse to the nation, but the Puritans. At no distant day, it was plain to see, the Northern people would subjugate the South. Let the South prepare to resist.[248]

states. The issue was, said Davis, one of Constitutional government against the "votaries of mob rule, fanaticism and anarchy." Dunbar Rowland, ed., *Jefferson Davis, Constitutionalist*, IV, 540-541.

[246] Oxford *Mercury* in Jackson *Daily Mississippian*, Jan. 31, 1860.

[247] Cf. Lincoln's words in his Springfield speech.

[248] Natchez *Daily Free Trader*, June 13, 1860.

Much was heard of the United South argument in Mississippi, and apparently more interest was directed to defiance than to political strategy to win the election. If Lincoln attempted to reassure the South, nobody would believe him, even if he " solemnly swore to hold sacred every right of the South, including African slavery." [249] How this unity was being secured was reported with grim humor by the Vicksburg *Sun*. A Lincolnite, who had freely aired his views in Vicksburg, was well tarred and set afloat in the Mississippi river. He was last heard of twenty miles south, " slowly progressing towards New Orleans." A " stout cord " and a " strong limb " were recommended for such incendiaries.[250]

The state of mind of one Breckinridge orator may be learned from a campaign address delivered by Richard T. Archer, August 10, 1860, at Port Gibson, Mississippi. He paid his respects seriatim to the three opposing candidates. The Republican party's purpose was to destroy the labor system of the South and to incite servile rebellion. Lincoln was ineligible for the Presidency, he contended, for " no majority of electoral votes can make him President *de jure* of the United States. He is an enemy, he is therefore an expatriated foreigner for all purposes of the Constitutional Union." Nor was Douglas one whit better. That " arch fiend " of " squatter sovereignty " incited people in the territories to rebel against the " sovereign rights of the States," and supported bigamy and turpitude in Utah; John Bell was a political " Judas Iscariot " who had opposed the repeal of the " infamous " Missouri Compromise.

During the speech, a Bell elector inquired if the orator advocated dissolution if Lincoln were elected. Archer replied that he would not overthrow the national government, but as the election of Lincoln would be " an usurpation," it would become the duty of all the states to overthrow the " usurper." He would gladly assist in that process. Although participating in the presidential canvass, this fiery Mississippian added: " I am in favor of separation from the Northern States for ample and patriotic reasons." The Union was "fettered antipathies." [251]

[249] Jackson *Semi-Weekly Mississippian*, Oct. 23, 1860.
[250] Quoted in the Louisville *Daily Courier*, Sept. 5, 1860.
[251] *Speech of Richard T. Archer, Esq., Aug. 10, 1860 at Port Gibson, Miss.* (Port Gibson, Miss., 1860), Library of Congress.

The situation, as it appeared to a resident of Yazoo City, Mississippi, was reported in two interesting letters from R. S. Holt to his brother Joseph Holt, a member of Buchanan's Cabinet, and later known as an ardent Unionist. The future was bright, wrote R. S. Holt, save for the " gathering storm of social and political revolution." He feared that his eminent brother did not read the Southern papers enough to grasp the popular mind in the South. " If Lincoln is elected, rely upon it, that there will not be a single gulf or Atlantic Coast State represented in the next Congress." Entirely identified with the South, he declared the destruction of the Federal System was inevitable.[252] And after the fearful calamity had occurred, the same correspondent revealed his convictions: " . . . his [Lincoln's] election is a declaration by Northern people individually & collectively through the ballot box of a purpose to emancipate the slaves of the South, and to involve Southern States in all the horrors which that event would plainly entail." Should the Senate stand in their way, they would " reform " it, and likewise the United States Supreme Court, if necessary.[253]

Governor Pettus during the campaign coupled demands for commercial non-intercourse with the prediction that Mississippi would act with those ready to dare and hazard all to prevent the state from becoming a " black " Republican " province." Pettus had no faith whatever in Republican promises. They could be trusted to about the same degree as Comanches.[254]

Several weeks after election, a Mississippian wrote from Holly Springs that although he was himself a conservative, the state was ready for precipitate action. He returned to Memminger's project of a Southern conference, with Virginia in the lead; in that case it might be possible for Virginia to calm the radicals.[255]

Thus the election demonstrated a not inconsiderable minority of sincere Unionists in Mississippi. The enormous pressure upon the Unionists by the secessionist Democrats weakened the

[252] R. S. Holt to J. Holt, Sept. 28, 1860, MS, J. Holt Papers, Library of Congress.

[253] Same to same, Nov. 9, 1860, MS, *ibid.*

[254] Fernandina *East Floridian*, Oct. 31, 1860.

[255] John W. C. Watson to John B. Minor, Nov. 23, 1860, MS, John B. Minor Papers, Alderman Library, University of Virginia.

former, and eventually engulfed them, but it remains true that the people were of various opinions as to the effect of Lincoln's election upon slavery. The propertied classes along the Mississippi river seemed ready to prefer experimental " submission " to Lincoln than to face war.[256]

LOUISIANA

In this state the Democratic party was rent between the Slidell faction, which favored Senator John Slidell for President, and was pro-Southern rights, pro-administration, and favored Congressional protection of slavery in the territories, on the one hand, and the smaller Douglas wing, which endorsed Popular Sovereignty, nationalism, and the Illinois senator for President, on the other. The Douglas group numbered such men as Pierre Soulé, the fire-eater of 1850, and Miles Taylor, who was prominent in the direction of the national campaign of Douglas after the conventions. In general, the former faction comprised the bulk of the party in Louisiana, but Douglas followers were numerous in New Orleans and in a number of the parishes. After the Charleston and Baltimore conventions, the campaign resolved itself into a threeway contest between Breckinridge, Bell, and Douglas.[257]

The Breckinridge forces had powerful press support which included the New Orleans *Delta* and the New Orleans *Courier*,

[256] Percy Lee Rainwater, " The Autobiography of Benjamin Grubb Humphreys August 26, 1808—December 20, 1882," *Mississippi Valley Historical Review*, XXI (Sept., 1934), 231-255. See also, P. L. Rainwater, " An Analysis of the Secession Controversy in Mississippi, 1854-1861," *ibid.*, XXIV (June, 1937), 35-42. Benjamin L. C. Wailes was an old Whig, who looked to Washington as the capital of his country. He detested the secession movement and the Democratic leaders who led it; he heartily disliked Governor Pettus and Jefferson Davis. Ultra conservative, he opposed the fundamental philosophy of democracy. Wailes was apprehensive of the situation in 1860, but felt he could not stop the trend. He was bitter against the Breckinridge leaders, and wrote after election that so determined were they, that even the election of their candidate would not prevent secession. Charles S. Sydnor, *A Gentleman of the Old Natchez Region* (Durham, 1938), pp. 291-294.

[257] For a recent study of the election in Louisiana, see Willie M. Caskey, *Secession and Restoration of Louisiana* (University, La., 1938), pp. 1-15; for a different point of view, see Roger W. Shugg, *Origins of Class Struggle in Louisiana* (University, La., 1939), pp. 157-161. See also J. K. Greer, " Louisiana Politics, 1845-1861," *The Louisiana Historical Quarterly*, XIII (July, 1930), 462-483.

and the backing of Senators John Slidell and Judah P. Benjamin,[258] of the state's Congressmen, and the party machine. William L. Yancey was brought to New Orleans by enthusiastic admirers, but his speech there received mixed response, according to the partisan journalism of the age.[259]

The Breckinridge campaign argument in Louisiana was, as elsewhere, devoted to " arousing " the South to impending dangers, and to the securing of political unity. To achieve the latter objective it was necessary to denigrate the candidacies of Bell and Douglas, and to impugn the motives of their followers. After the October elections had placed Indiana, Ohio, and Pennsylvania in the Republican column, the New Orleans *Delta* conceded that the Presidency was lost and defined the issue from that point as the unification of the South and the determining whether the South would submit to " Abolition masters." [260] Attacks were made on Bell and Douglas men as " submissionists," who, by their Union talk, " egged on " the "black " Republicans to disregard Southern threats of disunion, and who were thus responsible for the October victories of the Republicans.[261]

A " mysterious circular " appeared in the New Orleans *Bulletin*, which declared that a vote for Bell or Douglas was a vote for abolition, and that Lincoln, who at least had the merit of being an open and declared enemy, was preferable to a " traitor." [262] A citizen of Terrebonne Parish, R. R. Barrow, wrote, September 17, that he had penetrated farther than most into the realities of the situation. It was his theory that the Abolition " conspiracy " was of the same origin which produced the Federalist party, a party which had contempt for the people and hatred for the laboring classes. The abolitionists wished to degrade the white laborer and to elevate the Negro to his level. All of which was consistent, he contended, with schemes of special privilege.[263] Barrow pronounced Bell and

---

[258] *D. A. B.*, II, 181-186.

[259] Caskey, p. 9.

[260] New Orleans *Daily Delta*, Oct. 11, 1860.

[261] " Old Line Whig " turned Breckinridge Democrat, *ibid.*, Oct. 13, 1860.

[262] New York *Times*, Aug. 22, 1860.

[263] Cf. speech of Reuben Davis, Charles A. and Mary R. Beard, *The Rise of American Civilization* (2 vols., New York, 1927), II 3-6.

Everett the candidates of the abolitionist-special privilege groups, and denounced Douglas as more dangerous than the abolitionists. He favored the establishment of direct trade with Europe, and advocated the " cheapening " of slave labor, for the reason that slavery might thus be " preserved " in Virginia, Kentucky, and Maryland. The state of the writer's mind may be judged further by his recommendation that vigilance committees be established to rid the South of spies, and that Northern pedagogues who " poisoned " the minds of Southern children be eliminated.[264]

Durant Da Ponte, speaking on behalf of Breckinridge at New Orleans, declared that Douglas was as bad as Lincoln, and that the Bell party was worse than the " black " Republicans. The speaker asserted that the Union was not worth the invasion of " our homes by Abolition armies," the burning of dwellings, and the assassination of Southern wives, parents, and children. This speaker employed violent sarcasm in attacking the Bellites, whom he characterized as " fanatical and hideous Union-savers." [265] Thus the Breckinridge campaign depicted their opponents as base submissionists, " appeasers," as abolitionists at heart.[266]

On the other hand, there was a large segment of voters in Louisiana who were not affiliated with either faction of the Democratic party. Early in 1860, the New Orleans *Picayune* expressed the moderate position in opposing the call of South Carolina for a Southern convention, on the ground of expediency rather than Constitutionality, and approved the declination of Virginia to participate.[267] Although on occasion the spokesmen for the old Whig or Opposition party tempered their Unionism with apprehension concerning the Republicans,[268] and the New Orleans *Crescent* declared itself opposed

[264] New Orleans *Daily Delta*, Sept. 26, 1860.

[265] Jackson *Semi-Weekly Mississippian*, Nov. 2, 1860.

[266] Shortly after election Slidell wrote Buchanan that the Douglas vote in New Orleans was made up of Germans and Irish, whom he termed abolitionists at heart. Louis M. Sears, *John Slidell* (Durham, 1925), p. 174.

[267] New Orleans *Daily Picayune*, Feb. 10, March 16, 1860.

[268] See *ibid.*, July 18, 1860, for an attack on "Lincolnism." William Lloyd Garrison, the "blatant negro" Fred Douglass, Sanborn, and Senator Henry Wilson were discussed under that term, and Charles Sumner was alleged to have said in a speech at Cooper Institute that Southerners regularly roasted

to unqualified submission,[269] in general it may be said that during the campaign the Constitutional Union party press and orators staunchly defended the Union. The New Orleans *Bee* surveyed American history and concluded that in sectional clashes the South had triumphed nine out of ten times, and inquired: " Wherein then has the South suffered real detriment, loss or humiliation from the fanatical doctrines prevalent with a majority of the people of the North? " The case of Kansas was cited and dismissed. Climate and soil of that territory were to blame for free soil there: if slavery were profitable in Kansas, it would have become a slave state. It would be about as profitable to grow bananas in Massachusetts, the *Bee* noted. Nor had the abolitionists as yet done much harm. While the *Bee* did not repose much faith in the Republicans, it predicted that " their bark was worse than their bite," and the South was too necessary to the North's prosperity. It was concluded that, for this reason, the avaricious Yankees would let slavery, and not the Union, " slide." [270]

Indeed, the Bell press resented and repelled the attempts of the Southern Democratic faction to obtain unity in the " crisis." Such tactics constituted political proscription, and spirited objection was offered to a " dead sea of political uniformity which the Breckinridge crowd seeks to secure under the cry of a United South." What would come after secession? The disunionists were silent on that question, which the *Picayune* answered in two words: " the deluge." [271] This influential paper disposed of the tariff and the territorial question as dead issues, and quoted the hated Seward in support of the latter contention.[272] The Bell press argued that the country was prosperous and the blessings of the Union were great. Restless Southern politicians were sharply criticized, and no need for alarm was seen. Moreover, it was asserted that it was impos-

Negroes alive. The *Picayune* wondered if these were not Lincoln's views. The Illinois press was radical. *Ibid.*

[269] Quoted by New Orleans *Daily Delta*, July 21, 1860.

[270] New Orleans *Bee*, July 27, 1860; New Orleans *Daily Delta*, July 28, 1860.

[271] New Orleans *Daily Picayune*, Oct. 21, 1860; the secession movement was one of " dictation and proscription" to force unity of sentiment. *Ibid.*, Nov. 1, 1860.

[272] *Ibid.*, Oct. 3, Nov. 2, 1860.

sible to unite the South on such an issue as the election of a Republican as President. Finally, peaceful secession was an impossibility, Louisiana voters were told.[273]

With the Unionism of the Bell forces, the Douglas press and orators were in accord. No unbridgeable chasm existed between them, and although there were differences of opinion relative to some issues and details, both groups were " animated by profound love and attachment for the Union." [274]

The special arguments addressed by the Bell and Breckinridge parties to the city of New Orleans, as a great commercial port, and the dire or roseate predictions concerned with the issue of dissolution of the Union and the fate of the great city in the future, have been discussed elsewhere.[275] An interesting and significant article appeared during the campaign under title, " The West, Its Power and Influence." Long before the publication of Frederick Jackson Turner's famous essay, the New Orleans *Picayune* considered in Turnerian terms the growth of the West and its future reaction on the older sections of the United States.[276] Of course, New Orleans was deeply interested in the development of the West, situated as she was at the mouth of the great Mississippi River system.

In this philosophic and prophetic essay, the ultimate transfer of political power west of the Alleghenies, and even west of the Mississippi River, was predicted. Nor would the West be a " mere reflection of New England, New York, or the Atlantic States." Of course, the West would receive from the older states some " moral and intellectual impulse," but

on the broad prairie, in the mighty wilderness, by the side of majestic rivers, in the shadow of gigantic mountains, and on the margin of widespreading lakes, the people of the West have received an expansion of

[273] Oct. 24, 1860. New York *Times,* Oct. 18, 1860, noted this Unionist sentiment.

[274] Quoted in New Orleans *Daily Delta,* July 26, 1860.

[275] See O. Crenshaw, " Urban and Rural Voting in the Election of 1860," in *Historiography and Urbanization,* ed. E. F. Goldman (Baltimore, 1941), pp. 43-66.

[276] New Orleans *Daily Picayune,* Oct. 7, 1860, also reprinted in Washington *National Intelligencer,* Oct. 27, 1860. Earlier in the year, the New Orleans *Daily Crescent,* April 19, 1860, had commented upon the " astonishing gains by the Northwest." The South rejoiced in the achievement of Anglo-Saxon energy, but asked if the political power of this new region would be used to oppress the South. *Ibid.*

thought, a liberality of views and a broader and more marked character than the stock from whence they sprung. Their influence already begins to react upon the older States. Brought into constant intercourse with the more stationary populations of the East, they begin to harmonize them with themselves. New York and the New England States derive their sustenance and the life of their trade from the West. They must ultimately receive from the same quarter their intellectual and moral impulsions.

This, said the *Picayune*, was too often overlooked by the Atlantic seaboard statesmen. In the South, it was asked, "What States are peculiarly Southern?" Kentucky, Missouri, Tennessee, and portions of Louisiana and Arkansas were more Western than Southern.[277]

All of which demonstrated the futility of finding a boundary for a proposed Southern confederacy. Western political opinion was more moderate than that of the East: there was a softening down of Eastern prejudices and New England ideas. Thus the westward movement had brought about better interchange of ideas, which built up a nationality of character. Time only was needed to settle the "vexed conditions of the Republic." The West was not negrophile, Southerners were told. Extreme measures were not only unnecessary, "but singularly suicidal." In time, the West would unite the nation.[278] Indeed, the people of Louisiana might well ponder their decision because of economic ties to the Union. A recent student has pointed out that commerce entirely and agriculture to a great extent depended on the state's connection with the nation.[279] This the Bell-Douglas forces emphasized as an issue in the campaign of 1860 in Louisiana.[280]

[277] New Orleans *Daily Picayune*, Oct. 7, 1860. Cf. F. J. Turner, *The Frontier in American History* (New York, 1920), pp. 1-38.

[278] New Orleans *Daily Picayune*, Oct. 7, 1860.

[279] Shugg, pp. 157-158.

[280] Some recent scholars have minimized the sincerity of the Unionism of Bell-Douglas forces, and have referred to it as "lip-service." Perhaps they do so in order to explain the shift to secession in 1861. Yet the eloquent appeals and heated language in 1860 seem sincere enough; the argument of Caskey, pp. 14-15, that Bell ultimately turned to the Confederacy seems unconvincing, as applied to 1860. A new situation had arisen in 1861. The Executive Committee of the Constitutional Union party of Rapides Parish wrote Alexander R. Boteler, a national manager, Aug. 25, 1860, warning against a possible fusion between the Bell and Douglas forces. They said they had every reason to believe that Douglas men would vote with them; and also many old Whigs, who hated

ARKANSAS

During the early weeks of the year 1860 a considerable hostility towards the North was manifest in the press of the frontier state of Arkansas. Even the conservative Little Rock *Arkansas State Gazette* employed strong language against conditions which it professed to see in the North. A crusade, the aim of which was the annihilation of slavery, was spreading rapidly over that section, aided by the " treasonable doctrine " contained in the Helper book. The paper continued: " There is but one saint known to the Northern calendar, and that is John Brown. According to abolition faith, John Brown and Jesus Christ occupy the same platform. His name is their watchword, and his example their emulation: and we fervently pray that his doom may prove their destination! " While the entire North was being united, the South was far too indifferent, its press too calm and moderate, and Southern patience was translated into " a tame and cowardly submission! " The North was said to regard the South as " standing self-accused before the judgment-bar of God! " In such a situation, the *Arkansas State Gazette* could only conclude that the South must prepare " as if an armament were being fitted out against us in a foreign port." [281]

Shortly afterwards, this journal warmly endorsed the policy

Democracy all their lives, would suspect the honesty of the movement. " Let the democrats come to us; we cannot ever go to them." (MS, Boteler, Papers, Duke University Library.) For an explanation of a citizen of New Orleans, recently removed to that city from Kentucky, of his vote for Douglas, see J. O. Harrison to Joseph Holt, Nov. 16, 1860. In this letter Harrison declared his personal preference for Breckinridge, which he cast aside to support Douglas. He believed the tendency of the Breckinridge party was to disunion, and " that there was no safety except in the Principle of total non Intervention by Congress." The breakup at Charleston had been deliberately achieved by disunionists. Even at the date of writing, Harrison urged a course of " masterly inactivity " on the Buchanan administration, with no coercion by either Buchanan or Lincoln. He concluded that the " South is strong in the number of its conservative men. . . ." (MS, Joseph Holt Papers, Library of Congress.) But see W. H. Paxton to Joseph Holt, Dec. 14, 1860, who claimed that secession sentiment in the Gulf States was so strong that no conceivable concession by the North would stop disunion. (MS, *ibid.*) M. Gillis to St. J. R. Liddell, New Orleans, Nov. 10, 15, 1860, predicted secession, and difficulties ahead. MSS, Liddell Papers, Louisiana State University.

[281] Little Rock *Arkansas State Gazette*, Feb. 4, 1860.

of commercial discrimination against the North as a weapon to compel abandonment of antislavery tactics there, and rejoiced that Northern trade and manufactures languished, and that " she is in imminent danger of a financial revulsion." It observed that the firm of Stewart & Company of New York had discharged over fifty clerks since the beginning of the year because of the decline in Southern trade, and that many other firms had been forced to curtail their activities for a like reason. It was noted further that workers' wages in various parts of the North had decreased as much as 75 per cent during the past three months.

Moreover, Northern business men were said to be thoroughly aroused and eager to prove their loyalty to the South.

One business firm in New York procured a special edition of the New York " Express," containing a detailed account of the " great Union meeting," for distribution at the South. Manufacturers are stamping their fabrics with symbols of clasped hands, and various other Union mottoes and devices, all with the view of conciliating and retaining the Southern trade. They are beginning to realize that Cotton is King, and Southern alienation the bane of their prosperity.

All this was well and good, thought the *Arkansas State Gazette*, but it warned the South to continue restrictive commercial policies until it was certain that the North was sincere in dropping her aggressive attitude, and was willing not to interfere in Southern domestic institutions.[282]

On another matter, the ardent Southern rights Democratic paper, the Little Rock *Arkansas True Democrat*, hurled defiance at the North. The legislature had, at an earlier time, passed a statute which expelled free Negroes from the state, for which Northern presses vigorously attacked this action as inhumane. According to the *Arkansas True Democrat*, enough time had elapsed by March, 1860, to permit a " test " of the operation of this act. The free Negroes had tried out life among the " freedom shriekers " of the North, and it was most agreeable for this paper to record that, from all viewpoints, this statute—which made of Arkansas a truly slave state—had

[282] *Ibid.*, Feb. 11, 1860. The Northern commercial and financial interests were disturbed during 1859-1860. Philip S. Foner, *Business and Slavery* (New York, 1940). It should be noted that the *Arkansas State Gazette* was the old Whig and Union party organ in the state.

demonstrated its value. The temper and conduct of the slave population had improved since its passage, and it could be recommended to other slave states. After all, the abolitionists had forced the state to pass this law, and thus had practically forced many free Negroes to return to slavery. A number had returned from "freedom" to selected masters in Little Rock and in other communities. All these were said to have left Arkansas with "plenty of money," but a brief sojourn among the abolitionists reduced them to beggary, and they returned to Arkansas and slavery, where the lot of the slave was better than that of the free Negro in the North.[283]

But as the year wore on, and after the party conventions had made their nominations, a furious battle raged in Arkansas between the champions of Bell, Breckinridge, and Douglas. During the presidential canvass, spokesmen for Bell and Douglas took strong Unionist ground, while the radical, positive action men supported Breckinridge.

In mid-July, the *Arkansas State Gazette* carried a conciliatory editorial in which it suggested that a conference of Bell, Douglas, and Breckinridge electors meet to devise the best method of rebuking "black" Republicanism. According to this old Whig and Unionist paper, it would soon develop that the contest was between Bell and Lincoln, and therefore the South should rally to the support of the former. The Union party desired free and thorough discussion, "for it may be that the fate of the country depends upon the result of the present election. : . ."[284]

Yet the suggested harmony of all parties failed to materialize, and the leading Bell journal proved to its own satisfaction that the Constitutional Unionist candidate was the only man in the race who had a chance to beat Lincoln, and "proved" by repeated references to Bell's "record," that he

[283] Little Rock *Arkansas True Democrat*, March 7, 1860.

[284] Little Rock *Arkansas State Gazette*, July 14, 1860. In this issue it was predicted that the presidential canvass would not begin until the state elections were out of the way. The Democratic party was divided into factions which were contending for the Governorship in 1860. One wing was led by Congressman T. C. Hindman, and the other by Senator R. W. Johnson. The Johnson family was wealthy and was said to have "monopolized" the state offices. L. H. Mangum to Willie P. Mangum, Harrisburgh, Ark., April 8, 1860, MS, Willie P. Mangum Papers, Library of Congress.

was the only entirely sound Southern rights man before the public. Said the *State Gazette*: " What excuse shall a Southern man render his conscience and his country for refusing to vote for John Bell? " [285]

At the end of September, the same organ waxed bitter in denunciation of the disunion tendencies of the Breckinridge party. This old Whig paper thought that the defeat of both Democratic candidates in itself would be cause for rejoicing, because " the incubus upon the country " would be removed. But the real objective of the Breckinridge wing was dissolution of the Union. " Hence they continue to support Mr. Breckinridge in full view of the foregone conclusion of his defeat, with no other end or object than the hope that, by dividing and distracting the South, they may be instrumental in electing Lincoln, the Black Republican candidate, when they intend making another desperate effort to dissolve the Union." According to this analysis, the disunionists did not hazard the nomination of William L. Yancey, " to effect their treasonable ends; for they knew that he could not get an electoral vote." [286]

Continuing in this vein, a few days before election, the *State Gazette* denounced a proposal of the Montgomery (Ala.) *Advertiser* to break up the Union, and effect an alliance with France or England. As this Alabama paper was a prominent supporter of Breckinridge's candidacy, declared the *Arkansas State Gazette*, it committed " the Breckinridge party, as far as it can, to its own view of the difficulty and the solution of it." To the *State Gazette*, there were three objections to such a plan. First, until all other remedies had been tried and exhausted, and until the people resorted to their " inherent right," the move would be " treason." Second, it would be folly for slaveholders to abandon the protection and guarantees of their own government and to place themselves under the control of the British government, the foremost abolitionist nation in the world. Third, America's opportunities would be poor indeed under a government based upon " *the divine right of kings*." But it was the sheer desperation to which the Breckinridge wing was reduced which the plan laid bare. " Determined to

[285] Little Rock *Arkansas State Gazette*, Sept. 22, 1860.
[286] *Ibid.*, Sept. 29, 1860.

rule or ruin, in the North they [the Breckinridge men] attach themselves to, and cooperate with, the Black Republicans, and in the South, with disunionists and monarchists; and the tendency of their movement, North and South, is the disruption and breaking up of the Government." So spoke the most eminent Bell journal at the campaign's climax.[287]

The case for the staunch Southern rights Democrats was presented in Arkansas through the columns of the Little Rock *Arkansas True Democrat*. In March this paper printed a discussion of the right of secession, which recalled the justified American and Texan revolutions, and continued:

So far as resisting tyranny and oppression, and protecting their lives, their liberties and their property, we believe every people have the right to do so—call it what you may, secession, revolution, rebellion or what not. When the Union ceases to subserve its end, and its tyranny becomes unendurable the question will not be of *right*, but of *might*. The awful awful day of dissolution, should it ever come, will not be ushered in by the discussion of the *right to secede*, but by an appeal to arms.[288]

Concerning the rupture at Charleston, the *True Democrat* placed the blame upon Douglas and his popular sovereignty dogma. There could be no peace until he stepped out of the picture, and it was hoped that his friends would be " patriotic " enough to withdraw him. This paper interpreted the secession at Charleston as likely to arouse the Northern Democrats to the necessity of protecting Southern rights. At that, however, it believed that the " matter has gone far enough for the present." This journal hoped that matters could be adjusted at Baltimore, the South given complete justice, and the breach closed.[289] Several of the Arkansas delegates to Charleston seceded reluctantly, and announced themselves in favor of compromise at Baltimore.[290]

Meanwhile, this Democratic organ paused to comment upon

[287] *Ibid.*, Nov. 3, 1860. It will be recalled that Governor Elias N. Conway of Arkansas had recently circularized his state with a blast against British abolitionists " emissaries " and the " machinations " of the British Government. O. Crenshaw, " Governor Conway's Analysis and Proposed Solution of the Sectional Controversy," *Arkansas Historical Quarterly*, II (March, 1942), 12-19.

[288] Little Rock *Arkansas True Democrat*, March 24, 1860.

[289] *Ibid.*, May 19, 1860.

[290] *Ibid.*

the nominees of the Republican and Union parties. Dismissing the Bell-Everett ticket as not having "the ghost of a chance" and as significant only in that it might assist the election of Lincoln by drawing away some votes from the Democrats in a few states, the *True Democrat* devoted considerable attention to Lincoln and Hamlin, both "ultra abolitionists and irrepressible conflict Helperites." It continued with a grudging admission that Lincoln was a man of "coarse ability" and that he was effective on the hustings. But Lincoln was by no means a statesman, and Hamlin was an abler man. More important was the *True Democrat*'s assertion that if the Democrats could unite with an acceptable candidate and platform, the Republicans would be beaten. However, if this were not done, the election of Lincoln would be followed by disunion.

We do not believe that Lincoln, or any other abolitionist can ever be President of the *United* States. The fourth of March that sees him inaugurated will see two empires where there is now one confederacy. . . . It [the Democratic] is the only party that can hope to contend against the hosts of black Republicans. . . . But with a democratic candidate at the North and one at the South, the latter still further divided by having a so-called Union ticket, Lincoln and the North will conquer. Then will follow disunion, civil war and its attendant horrors.[291]

This realistic and accurate prophecy was made during the interim between Charleston and Baltimore, but after the seemingly irrevocable split of the party, the *True Democrat* warmly championed Breckinridge and Lane. In July, it forecast with optimism that Oregon, California, and Pennsylvania, and "a united South together with the power of the administration in Northern States may force, not only the Douglas men, but the Union men of all parties to support Breckinridge." [292] Frequently, this organ argued fiercely against the Bell and Douglas parties. At the same time, it desired to dispose of the charges of disunion often hurled against Breckinridge. Yet in the manner of doing so, the *True Democrat*'s Unionism seemed to stop at Lincoln's election. The Douglas party was a do-nothing party: it proposed to wait till the foe invaded Southern hearths, as he was reported to be doing at the moment in Texas. The

[291] *Ibid.*, May 26, 1860.   [292] *Ibid.*, July 14, 1860.

Bell party was no better than the "black" Republican: their insistent cries of disunion were senseless; it was indeed even worse, for Southern attacks upon Breckinridge were virtual invitations to the abolitionists to make further aggressions. The New York *Herald* knew well enough that the South was "terribly in earnest," and that metropolitan journal's campaign to alarm the manufacturing and commercial interests of the North was noted with approbation. This Arkansas paper heartily endorsed the strategy which would touch the pocket nerve of the North, and asserted that if the North could be made to understand that the South was sincere in her threats of secession, Lincoln would "sink." But as long as the North observed the "puling and cowardly sentimentality of the *Southern Union croakers*," which emanated from the Bell men, that section could point to Southern Unionists as proof that nothing would happen in the event of Republican victory.[293]

According to such reasoning, it was the Bell men who were the "disunionists." The *True Democrat* uttered ugly words in this respect: "We have said and we repeat it that the Southern cry against disunionism is only the bugle blast of the traitor that summons the enemy into our camps. The fear of disunion is all that has restrained the Attila spirit of abolitionism." [294]

This Arkansas Breckinridge spokesman in mid-October interpreted a Bell victory in the South to mean an endorsement of the protective tariff policy, the reception of abolition petitions, and an acceptance of the most extreme Northern demands. It would also mean surrender of the territorial principle and indeed more: "In the first place the question of slavery is a practical issue—a *vital issue* for the South—if not why oppose the election of Lincoln? If the question has no *vitality* the election of Lincoln would be a desirable result—it would prove the question defunct and stop the agitation." Nor was it true that either Breckinridge or Lincoln men desired disunion. As for the latter, their object was clear to the *True Democrat*: "The palpable, avowed, and manifest purpose of the black republicans is to subjugate the South, to circumscribe slave territory, to foist upon the cotton-growing States, with the aid

[293] *Ibid.*, Aug. 25, 1860.   [294] *Ibid.*, Sept. 22, 1860.

of the Bell men, a protective tariff, scarcely less odious than a slavery restriction, and to do all this *in the Union*." [295]

As if to document the assertion concerning the alleged subjugation of the South by the Republicans, the *True Democrat* published a dispatch from Washington which described the activities of the " Wide Awakes." According to this account, the people of Arkansas were gravely informed that while ostensibly the Wide Awakes merely existed to create demonstrations during the campaign such as torchlight processions, it had been learned that actually it was a secret, military organization. The Wide Awakes, said to number 500,000, intended to aid Lincoln in coercing the South, assisted by the abolition incendiaries, who would swarm over the slave states. Echoes of Douglas' Norfolk doctrine were heard when the *True Democrat* placed the Douglasites alongside the Wide Awakes and abolitionists in a horrendous coalition, and queried: " With such evidences before them, it is mortifying that the Southern people should be divided in this contest." [296]

But despite the Breckinridge appeals for unity in the election, divisions continued to the end, with a segment of Democratic politicians and newspapers supporting Douglas. Among the latter were former Governor Thomas S. Drew,[297] Congressman Albert Rust, and T. B. Flournoy. The Van Buren *Press* and the Fort Smith *Times* editorially championed the Little Giant's candidacy. Representative Rust, in a speech in Congress, cited reasons why his state opposed the reopening of the foreign slave trade, and declared: " Arkansas . . . can herself supply more land of inexhaustible fertility than can be fully developed and cultivated by all the labor of that character now devoted to agriculture within the present slave States of this Union. Arkansas, sir, can, with the requisite labor, supply the present demand of the whole world for cotton." In his opinion, slavery would go where it would be profitable.[298]

In an address to the people of Arkansas in June, Rust

[295] *Ibid.*, Oct. 13, 1860.
[296] *Ibid.*, Oct. 20, 1860.
[297] See Thomas S. Drew to Editors, Jan. 21, 1860, in which he sympathetically interprets Douglas' territorial doctrine. Memphis *Daily Appeal*, Feb. 3, 1860. See also Thomas S. Drew to S. A. Douglas, Ft. Smith, Ark., Jan. 7, 1860, MS, Douglas Papers, University of Chicago.
[298] *Congressional Globe*, 36th Cong., 1st sess., p. 272.

announced his candidacy for the United States Senate to succeed R. W. Johnson. He denounced secessionists in general and Yancey in particular, and characterized their objectives as " mischievous, unpatriotic, and criminal. . . . " Southern interests would be entirely safe under Douglas, and his election would vanquish abolitionists at the North and disunionists in the South.[299]

T. B. Flournoy, a Douglas supporter who attended the Charleston and Baltimore conventions, addressed an appeal to the people of Arkansas in behalf of Douglas. He interpreted the assigned reason for the secession at Baltimore as the pretext; the real reason, according to Flournoy, was that it had become clear that the Yancey doctrine of slavery in the territories would be rejected and, moreover, that Douglas had a majority in the convention. He continued:

We are now, in my judgment, at the most memorable epoch in our national history. The indications are, that the coming election will decide the existence of the present Union of the States, for with scarcely an exception, the seceding delegates and their sympathizers are of opinion that the election of Lincoln justifies disunion and civil war. Should Lincoln be elected, we may reasonably expect all these gentlemen to use their influence to effect a revolutionary movement that is to plunge the land in strife and bloodshed. To divide the Democratic party at a juncture like this, is paving the way simply to disunion. It is merely electing in advance the black Republican candidate for the presidency, and furnishing a reason . . . for precipitating the country into internecine war.[300]

Taking a geographical view of the Democratic party, and breaking down the total cast in the election of 1856 for Buchanan, the pro-Douglas Van Buren *Press* demonstrated that the Northern wing of the party constituted more than two-thirds of the popular vote. This paper was ready to surrender any private preferences and to assist Douglas, who fought for Southern security and rights.[301]

Such were the main ideas expounded in behalf of the three parties during the campaign of 1860. Inasmuch as the sincerity

[299] Little Rock *Arkansas State Gazette*, June 9, 1860.

[300] " An Address to the Democracy of Arkansas by T. B. Flournoy," July 14, 1860, Little Rock *Arkansas True Democrat*, Aug. 11, 1860.

[301] Van Buren *Press*, July 27, 1860.

and depth of Unionism of the Bell and Douglas men in the South has been questioned, it may be of interest to note the attitudes of several representatives of those groups in the days following Lincoln's election. Three days after that event, the Bell organ, the *Arkansas State Gazette* discussed fully the implications of the presidential election. The legal and Constitutional choice of Lincoln as President was no basis on which to destroy the Union, this paper served notice to all Southern parties. The chances were that Lincoln would prove to be an honest, conscientious, and Constitutional executive of the entire country. Should this prove not to be the case, the proper remedy lay in the impeachment process; only after this shall have been tried and found wanting should the South take matters into her own hands.[302]

In the face of the deplorable national calamity, the *State Gazette* yet hopefully pointed to the Union party as the nucleus of a powerful opposition party to the Republicans which could defeat them in 1864. It would be a mistake to dissolve the Union, moreover, because " the burthen of expense and difficulty, and the field of war, will be on and in the frontier slave States of Maryland, Virginia, Kentucky, and Missouri." It would be rash and cowardly of the lower Southern states to take action which would immediately affect the border slave states. If grievances were so serious as to justify revolution, it was suggested that the border states take the lead, and the lower South might then follow such a lead.[303]

Indeed, the thought of a civil war deeply disturbed the editor of this Bell journal: " War between different races and nations is a terrible calamity—war between the people of the same country—between friends, relatives, brothers is too shocking to contemplate. . . . We know not what change may be wrought in our mind by time or circumstances; but now we could not charge cowardice on any one who would avoid doing a soldier's duty in such a war." These words went far towards that submissionism which the extremists so much deprecated.[304] Likewise, the Van Buren *Press* counselled giving Lincoln a

[302] Little Rock *Arkansas State Gazette*, Nov. 10, 1860.
[303] *Ibid*.
[304] *Ibid*. See also *ibid*., Nov. 17, 1860, which regretted that Sam Houston, a more available man, had not been nominated by the Union party in place of Bell.

trial. It did not see how he could execute abolition doctrines, even if he was inclined to do so. Finally, it would be well to ponder the problem of exchanging good government for uncertainty.[305]

Governor Henry M. Rector, in his inaugural address of November 15, took a different view of the grave crisis. He was not an alarmist, he said, nor was he blind to the desolation which would follow secession. The issue, formulated by the North, was stated by Governor Rector as "the Union without slavery, or slavery without the Union." The North had broken the compact and had violated the Constitution. "A most unprovoked and diabolical warfare, marked by ingratitude, malice and ignorance, is now being waged by the people of the non-slaveholding States, against the peace, dignity and independence of all those recognizing that institution." In the Governor's opinion, compromise and peace were "a bare possibility"; but if coercion were used against South Carolina, Arkansas should aid her.[306] Events were to prove the Governor more nearly right than the Bell and Douglas people.

TEXAS

The frontier slave state of Texas was involved in many difficulties as the election of 1860 approached, among which were border troubles, the activity of Cortina, the Indian problem, and the lawlessness of the population. Although there were some convinced and articulate Unionists in the state, the overwhelming majority were ready for radical action by which to defend what they considered to be Southern rights. The majority position was expressed in the resolutions adopted by the Democratic State Convention. This body endorsed the Cincinnati platform, repudiated Squatter Sovereignty, praised the Virginia and Kentucky Resolutions of 1798, and asserted state sovereignty and the right of secession. Congressional protection of slavery in the territories was approved, which was declared to be in harmony with Congressional non-interven-

[305] Van Buren *Press*, Nov. 9, 1860. Congressman Albert Rust believed that with the South "universally prosperous," that his section never had less cause for complaint than at present. Little Rock *Arkansas State Gazette*, Nov. 24, 1860.

[306] *Ibid.*, Nov. 24, 1860. For the official vote of the state, see *ibid.*, Dec. 1, 1860.

tion. The Texas Democrats also let it be known that if a Republican were elected, their state would be in readiness to cooperate with Southern states in convention to protect the rights of all, in or out of the then existing " Confederacy." Finally, it was affirmed that the United States government had been founded for the benefit of the white race, and that racial equality led to degradation.[307]   On the same occasion, the South Carolina-born Louis T. Wigfall, U. S. Senator from Texas, denied the existence of such a thing as a national " will " or the fact that a nation existed in America. In his opinion, the United States was but thirty-three confederated nations.[308]

Much intemperate language was uttered by Southern ultras during the campaign, and they seemed to carry all before them in Texas. At Charleston and Baltimore the Texas delegation acted with the seceders, and when Breckinridge was nominated, he was acclaimed as the only presidential candidate who was not an abolitionist at heart. He was one who had not " leaned so far North " as to be suspect. It was recognized, however, by one of his journalistic supporters that while he probably would carry the entire South, it was doubtful if he could be elected by the people. Said the same paper: " If we suffer defeat, let it be upon principle." True, the Union might be destroyed by the election of a "black" Republican, but "Democracy" would be saved.[309]   A prominent Texas Democratic Congressman, John H. Reagan, wrote a few days before election that, should Breckinridge fail to reach the House of Representatives, he would favor Bell or Douglas to defeat Lincoln. If the Republicans were elected, he favored resistance.[310]

Examples of Breckinridge arguments may be taken from campaign addresses of Senator Wigfall. On July 21, 1860, he said:

[307] Palestine *Trinity Advocate*, April 11, 1860.

[308] *Ibid.*, April 4, 1860. For sketch of Wigfall, see *D. A. B.*, XX, 187-188.

[309] Houston *Weekly Telegraph*, July 3, 1860. The Austin *State Gazette*, May 19, 1860, had predicted that if Baltimore and Richmond could unite, the Republicans might be defeated, but not otherwise. A correspondent wrote from Washington county, Texas, that Breckinridge men in Texas and other Southern states were disunionists. They divided the vote, and asserted that the bare fact of Lincoln's election would be sufficient to break up the Union. Geo. C. Reid to R. J. Breckinridge, Oct. 3, 1860, MS, Breckinridge Family Papers, Library of Congress.

[310] Reagan to George W. Paschal, Oct. 19, 1860, in Austin *State Gazette*, Nov. 3, 1860.

These Douglasites have the impudence to call us disunionists. Now, I am in favor of having this Union preserved if it can be retained in the possession of the Democratic party. If it should fall into the hands of a party that proclaims its intention, like John Brown, of freeing our slaves and murdering our wives and children, and despoiling us of our constitutional rights and privileges, a new question of self-preservation is presented. I love the Union . . . but . . . rather than submit to such tyranny would see it blown into as many fragments and particles as gunpowder could scatter a glass vase. If that be treason, make the most of it.[311]

At Tyler, Texas, September 3, 1860, Wigfall's theme was the sectional clash between manufacturing and agriculture, and an exposition of the compact theory of the Constitution, which he had long advocated. He declared that he could continue for hours his catalogue of Northern crimes against the South.[312]

The principle of Congressional protection of slavery in the territories was held to be far more than " a mere idle abstraction." The pro-Breckinridge Austin *State Gazette* claimed that in the past year five hundred slaves had been set free forcibly by the Kansas legislature and by mob law, and that owners had been murdered or driven out of that territory. It pointed hopefully elsewhere: " Our citizens have migrated from the South to New Mexico with their slaves, and rely upon the doctrines of the Constitution for their protection." [313]

Associated with the Breckinridge party on this issue was the large German population of Texas. The historian of the Texas Germans has written that they favored the territorial views of Calhoun and Jefferson Davis. The Germans were traditional Democrats, had opposed the Know-Nothing movement, and many were against slavery in principle. However, they believed that the states should solve the problem. At the same time, the Germans differed from many Breckinridge men in Texas by their opposition to secession.[314]

[311] Wheeling (Va.) *Union* quoted in New York *Tribune* (semi-weekly), July 21, 1860. This speech was delivered outside Texas.

[312] *Speech of Louis T. Wigfall, Sept. 3, 1860, Tyler, Texas* (Washington, 1860, 32 pp. pamphlet, Library of Congress).

[313] Austin *State Gazette*, May 26, 1860. But there were almost no slaves in New Mexico in 1860.

[314] R. L. Biesle, *The History of the German Settlements in Texas 1831-1861* (Austin, 1930), pp. 204-207. The New York *Tribune* (semi-weekly), Sept. 11, 1860, noted the antislavery attitude of the Texas Germans.

Probably one of the factors which swelled the Breckinridge support in Texas was the newspaper attempt in the summer of 1860 to create a terroristic psychosis there. The "Texas troubles" have been considered elsewhere, and may be briefly related to the campaign in Texas.[315] According to certain Texas newspapers, a vast and diabolical abolitionist plot existed to burn the towns and poison and murder the slaveholders of the state. Harrowing tales of abolitionist-inspired rapine, murder, and arson were printed in Texas papers, and these accounts were widely reprinted North and South. Although some Northern papers cited the Texas tales as authentic, and as a forerunner of more trouble for the South, moderate and Unionist papers in Texas and the South generally were skeptical. The Austin *Southern Intelligencer*, for example, quoted a correspondent from Fairfield, Texas, to the effect that vigilance would continue until after the election. This paper expressed indignation at the circulation of the terror stories, and denounced "lying, threatening, bullying, lynching, plotting, and treason," all of which were contrived in order that officeholders might retain their places.[316] But the Breckinridge press retorted that many Opposition papers also carried the stories.[317]

To Texas towards the close of the campaign came the adventurer and organizer of the Knights of the Golden Circle, "General" Bickley, in time to inject himself into the presidential election. He made several speeches in Texas in which the aggressive pro-slavery spokesman gave the impression of favoring Breckinridge. He was applauded vociferously by Breckinridge men, so a paper hostile to Breckinridge asserted.[318]

Although the Breckinridge Democrats constituted a large majority in Texas, their opponents were not backward in asserting the most uncompromising Unionism. The leader of the Unionist group in Texas was the recently chosen Governor, the redoubtable Sam Houston.[319] Defeated for the Governorship in

---

[315] See Chapter V, above.

[316] Quoted in Austin *State Gazette*, Sept. 15, 1860.

[317] Austin *State Gazette*, Sept. 15, 1860. Wigfall declared: "An enemy is in our midst, not with bayonet and broad sword, but with torch and poison. Is this a time for division?" *Speech of Louis T. Wigfall.*

[318] O. Crenshaw, "The Knights of the Golden Circle: The Career of George Bickley," *American Historical Review*, XLVII (Oct., 1941), 23-50.

[319] *D. A. B.*, IX, 263-267. Marquis James, *The Raven* (New York, 1929).

1857, and retired by his state from the United States Senate in 1859, he almost immediately returned to active leadership when he was chosen Governor in the same year by a large majority. On December 20, 1859, a mass meeting at Austin recommended a conservative Unionist for President, and specified Governor Houston as possessing requisite qualifications. A committee of correspondence was appointed to communicate with Houston's friends throughout the nation. This movement called itself the "National Democracy," and it opposed the reopening of the slave trade, secession, and all extremism. Houston's pet project, the establishment of a protectorate over Mexico was approved, and the doctrine of Popular Sovereignty was "unanimously declared . . . to be democratic sentiment." [320]

Sam Houston's inaugural address of 1859 reminded Texans that when their state became one of the United States, she did not join the North or the South, but the Union. In an age of excitement, Huston pleaded with his fellow citizens to discriminate between the acts of individuals and those of a whole people, "between the wild ravings of a fanatic and true sentiments of masses of a State." He argued strongly for diversity of opinion—at a time when his opponents were demanding unanimity—calling it a safeguard of republicanism, and vigorously objected to "making thought treason." The clamor for Southern rights accomplished only the strengthening of the enemies of the South, and all the din was music to their ears. [321]

When South Carolina invited Texas to participate in the proposed Southern conference, Houston sent a strong message to the legislature in which he not only rejected that proposition, but condemned the legality and expediency of secession. If a Southern Confederacy should be formed, he argued, South Carolina could not guarantee its permanence. Texas was a border state, as Virginia, Missouri, and Kentucky were border states. Let disunion come, and terrible consequences would follow, he continued, in language similar to that employed by border state Unionists in the campaign. Houston inquired if the border

[320] New Orleans *Daily Picayune*, Jan. 4, 1860. This paper regretted that the issue of the slave trade had been brought up, and contended that no substantial party in the South favored it. *Ibid.*, Jan. 5, 1860.

[321] Austin *State Gazette*, Dec. 31, 1859. Governor Houston's message was widely quoted outside Texas by those desiring to allay sectional strife.

states had demanded secession, well aware that they had not. After all, he pointed out, South Carolina was surrounded by a cordon of slave states and by the sea, and thus was protected. Houston, one of the fathers of Texas, cited the transfer of Texan sovereignty to the United States, and he denied that Texas possessed the reserved power to secede. He was, moreover, in accord with Webster's denial that the Constitution of the United States provided for its own destruction.[322]

Afterward, the Governor was asked how he stood on the " only issue "—" submission to Black Republican rule." His critics charged him with indifference to slavery, with unsound Constitutional views, and accused him of being an ally of Indians and Mexicans. Further, it was said that presidential aspirations had seized him, and that he was attempting " to divide and distract good and true Southern men." The hated New York *Tribune* was quoted to show Texans that Horace Greeley approved their Governor's course.[323]

On March 25, Houston set forth his views as a preliminary bid for the Presidency. The crisis of the country had destroyed the " grand idea " of political parties, as they formerly had existed. Views of finance and government such as were once held by Jackson and Clay, " both patriots," were obliterated by the " canker of sectionalism." He assailed men who had been laboring for a quarter century " under the guise of democracy to promote disunion." He predicted that such men would be present at the Charleston convention, and further, that their " subversive " ideas would prevail there. Houston recalled that " Old Hickory " had declined to allow his name to be presented to a party convention, but that he accepted " the spontaneous demand of the people." [324] Houston firmly set his face against sectionalism, as he had earlier. He had opposed the Kansas-Nebraska bill, and in 1860 was against a " narrow " political platform of any sort.[325]

Sam Houston proceeded to enumerate the qualifications of a presidential candidate, and his description of the ideal candidate exactly fitted the hero of San Jacinto. In the first place, he must

[322] Memphis *Morning Enquirer*, March 10, 1860.
[323] Austin *State Gazette*, Jan. 26, March 3, 1860.
[324] This allusion to Jackson's reticence regarding political parties seems forced.
[325] Augusta *Daily Chronicle and Sentinel*, April 20, 1860.

be a "bold, national man," who advocated an American protectorate over Mexico. If that rich country were not taken over legitimately, the "restless spirit" of the American people would seize it. None was more identified in the public mind during 1859-1860 with such a project than Governor Houston. A modern scholar has described Houston's threefold "Grand Plan," by which that intrepid leader would seize Mexico, settle the sectional controversy, and make himself President of the United States.[326] Houston concluded his bid by endorsing the proposed Pacific railroad, and more adequate border security. Like many another in a critical period, he desired to "do something to divert disaster." Entertaining such views, the Governor of Texas preferred to seek Union support, and he declined to permit his name to go before the Charleston convention.[327]

Of course, the logical nomination to seek for one of Houston's views was that of the Constituional Union party. In behalf of Houston, W. J. Pendleton of Austin wrote an influential figure in the Constitutional Union movement. He told Congressman Boteler of Virginia that the Baltimore convention should "recommend" a man whom national men of all parties could support, a man who had a hold on the "conservative masses." Houston was declared to be strong in the South and in the commercial states. His nomination on such a ticket would silence both the pro-slavery and antislavery agitation.[328]

A large assemblage gathered at San Jacinto battlefield on the twenty-fourth anniversary of General Houston's famous victory over Santa Anna, April 21, to nominate "Old Jacinto" for president. On this patriotic occasion, the Lone Star flag was hoisted, orators gave vent to nationalistic pride, and presidential electors pledged to Houston were chosen. But if this boom were intended to further his chances at the Baltimore Constitutional Union convention, his supporters were doomed to disappointment.[329] However, it was still possible for him to run

[326] Walter P. Webb, *The Texas Rangers* (New York, 1935), p. 197.

[327] Sam Houston to J. W. Harris, D. D. Atchison, *et al.*, March 25, 1860, in Augusta (Ga.) *Daily Chronicle and Sentinel*, April 20, 1860.

[328] W. J. Pendleton to Alexander R. Boteler, April 25, 1860, MS, A. R. Boteler Papers, Library of Duke University.

[329] Houston received 57 votes for President at this convention on the first ballot, and 68 on the second. He was runner up to Bell on both ballots, and

independently, and on May 17 he wrote the chairman of the San Jacinto mass meeting and accepted their nomination for President. In this communication, he expressed his confidence in the masses, deprecated party spirit, sectionalism, and slavery agitation. It was Houston's hope, he wrote, that the United States should never descend to the level of Mexico.[330]

There were varied reactions to Houston's presidential candidacy throughout the country. Before the San Jacinto meeting, the New York *Sun* and the New York *Express* proposed him as a coalition candidate of all elements opposed to the Republicans.[331] The Augusta *Chronicle and Sentinel,* a Georgia Opposition paper, praised Houston as a patriot, an old soldier, and a statesman. His eccentricities were acknowledged, but conservative voters were urged to work for his nomination and election. His identification with a grand filibustering scheme at Mexico's expense would commend him to those " restless, unquiet spirits which so abound in the States." For after all, concluded this journal, his plan was best for both Mexico and the United States.[332]

It was also apparent that Houston had made his share of enemies. The Columbus (Ga.) *Times,* a Southern ultra sheet, regretted that " a well-directed Mexican bullet did not ensure his fame by removing him while so much glory was his." [333] In his own capital, the hostile Austin *State Gazette* described him as " testy in temper, crafty in policy and shallow in information . . . ." [334] The New York *Times* displayed a vicious article which charged Houston with cowardice during the whole San Jacinto campaign and ascribed that victory to others. This Republican journal attributed his popularity in Texas to the influx of immigrants and to the new generation. In its opinion, he was not a hero, nor a skillful political leader or general.[335]

polled a heavy vote in the New York delegation. Murat Halstead, *Caucuses of 1860* (Columbus, 1860), pp. 114-115.

[330] New York *Herald,* May 30, 1860.

[331] Quoted in Augusta *Daily Chronicle and Sentinel,* April 19, 1860.

[332] *Ibid.,* April 19, 1860.

[333] Columbus *Daily Times,* Feb. 6, 1860.

[334] Austin *State Gazette,* April 7, 1860. His alleged vanity and ostentation were illustrated when he wore a leopard skin vest and a showy Mexican blanket on Pennsylvania Avenue in Washington. *Ibid.*

[335] New York *Times,* Aug. 15, 1860.

In spite of the unpromising reception and situation of the San Jacinto candidacy, Houston remained in the presidential race until the middle of August. As late as July 31, he professed to believe that the " politicians " would yet be routed. Said he : " My only hope is that all men who sincerely desire the preservation of the government will unite together in the present contest against sectionalism." The big issue remained Union versus disunion, and here he penned an eloquent tribute to the Union. The electors pledged to him were to be free to vote against sectionalism, which was an admission that his own chances were slim. Once more the veteran campaigner stated his opposition to abolitionism, sectionalism and the reopening of the African slave trade.[336]

Shortly afterward, the Houston *Telegraph* called upon Houston to withdraw from the presidential campaign on the ground that he could not carry a single state—a fact of which such a political realist as Houston was already aware. This was urged, moreover, to the end that his " vast popularity among a class of Northern voters " be transferred to Breckinridge. If Houston were to withdraw, and announce for Breckinridge, it was believed that the latter would receive several thousand sorely needed votes.[337] Yet the *Telegraph* demanded the impossible of Houston, as the tenor of his campaign was altogether opposed to the Breckinridge candidacy. It was asking him to do a political somersault.

At last, on August 18, in a letter to " My Friends in the United States," Sam Houston admitted that his cause was hopeless and withdrew from the contest, without, however, endorsing any candidate.[338] There could be no doubt where his sympathies lay. On September 22, a Union meeting was held in Austin at which Houston strongly rebuked secession plotters and endorsed the fusion Union ticket in Texas.[339] In the course

[336] New York *Herald*, Aug. 12, 1860. Houston's picture, biography, and platform were printed in *Wells' Illustrated National Campaign Hand-Book for 1860* (New York, 1860), pp. 177-187, 198-199.

[337] Houston *Weekly Telegraph*, Aug. 7, 1860.

[338] New York *Herald*, Sept. 2, 1860. See also Houston to George W. Crawford, Sept. 8, 1860, for Houston's evaluation of the presidential candidates. Amelia W. Williams and Eugene C. Barker (eds.), *The Writings of Sam Houston 1813-1863*, VIII, 135-136.

[339] Augusta (Ga.) *Daily Chronicle and Sentinel*, Oct. 14, 1860. A. M. Wil-

of his passionate Union argument, Houston described the paradox of the seceders: " They will vote for no candidate but the one of the bolting secessionists; all others, in their eyes, are worse than Lincoln, and yet if they thus elect Lincoln, they will plunge the country into civil war." [340]

Although Texas was that state where the anti-Breckinridge forces had the least chance of victory, fusion was effected there by the formation of an electoral ticket which included two Bell and two Douglas men. The fusion was pledged, however, to vote for that man in the electoral college who had the best chance of defeating Lincoln.[341] Indeed, Houston's unqualified Unionism was matched by others who supported fusion in Texas. Early in the year, the LaGrange *True Issue* printed a passionate Unionist editorial and welcomed the wise patriotism of such Northerners as Everett, Frelinghuysen, Pierce, Dickinson, and O'Conor. " The Presidential election of 1860," it said, " will determine this much-vexed question and solve the problem of Northern conservatism." [342]

This paper was favorably impressed by the Northern Union meetings, and spoke of the American Union as the " . . . central sun of Republican liberty and human freedom . . . ." It would be lamentable indeed if the American experiment should fail, and the world left to the " gloom of European despotism." If the Southern states should secede, they would be surrounded by a cordon of " enemy free states." European despots would maliciously rejoice at the bursting of the American " bubble." [343]

On the other hand, the Unionism of the *True Issue* was tempered by what it termed reckless disregard of Southern rights, by a prevalence at the North of " false philanthropy " and " love of the sons of Ham." Continuation of these trends would lead to the formation of a Southern Confederacy, which would defend " our principles and selves." Throughout the

liams, *Sam Houston and the War of Independence in Texas* (New York, 1893), pp. 341-342.

[340] Galveston *Civilian* in Baltimore *American*, Oct. 27, 1860.

[341] San Antonio *Ledger and Texan*, Nov. 3, 1860; Marshall *Harrison Flag*, Oct. 20, 1860.

[342] La Grange *True Issue*, Jan. 27, 1860.

[343] *Ibid.*

campaign, however, this paper stressed the desirability of maintaining the Union. It urged the nomination of a national Democrat at Charleston, who not only could win the South but enough of the North to elect him. Andrew Johnson of Tennessee, a self-made American, would "dignify and adorn" the Presidency.[344] On October 4, the *True Issue* carried an article which enumerated thirteen reasons why Douglas should be elected.[345]

Another paper, the *Harrison Flag,* strongly dissented from the notion that the seceders spoke for the South. It feared that if the South left the Union, a cotton-producing rival would rise as a competitor. The paper condemned the open avowal of disunion in Texas, and inquired, "Who is Lincoln but a *man?*"[346] Later the same paper contained a vigorous analysis of the "bonds of Union," of which the Mississippi river was one of the most important.[347] Congressman A. J. Hamilton of Texas was reported by the Galveston *News* as opposed to secession in any event, including the election of Lincoln, and as in favor of coercion.[348] On the eve of the election, I. A. Paschal said of the theory of secession as championed by Texas, South Carolina, and others: "I believe a greater heresy never existed and if carried into practice leads us inevitably to treason as unsuccessful revolution."[349] But the Republicans were detested by all political factions in Texas, and some Unionists began to wobble before election day. The outcome of the election showed that the state was overwhelmingly in favor of radical action.[350]

---

[344] *Ibid.,* Feb. 24, 1860.

[345] Victoria *Texan Advocate* in *ibid.,* Oct. 4, 1860.

[346] Marshall *Harrison Flag,* Sept. 15, 1860.

[347] *Ibid.,* Feb. 24, 1860.

[348] Quoted in Washington (D. C.) *Constitution,* Oct. 23, 1860.

[349] San Antonio *Ledger and Texan,* Nov. 3, 1860.

[350] For confident "Cotton is King" editorial, see "Results of Lincoln's Election," Dallas *Herald,* Nov. 14, 1860. For the LaGrange *True Issue's* vacillation, see issues of Oct. 4, 11, Nov. 15, 22, 1860. Texas was "represented" by a delegation at the Chicago Republican National Convention. New Orleans *Daily Picayune,* May 29, 1860.

SUMMARY FOR LOWER SOUTH

During the campaign many thoughtful people in the lower South, even those associated with the Breckinridge campaign, were weighing their future course. The extremist elements desired action instantly following Lincoln's election, as they had been unable to bring matters to a crisis before. The most ultra men, like Keitt, Miles, and the Rhetts, welcomed Lincoln's election, which would assure secession by South Carolina without waiting for others, but which action would " drag " along into a new government many other slave states. These leaders had long chafed at the unwillingness of the South to move, and they wished the break with the North to be complete. At the same time, there were other thoughtful men who, like Hamilton of South Carolina, while utterly exasperated with the North, privately expressed misgivings as to the desirability or durability of a Southern confederacy. These men were not outspoken in their doubts, and probably affected the trend towards secession but slightly; by their silence they increased the impression of unanimity in a state like South Carolina.

Elsewhere in the lower South, there were some who advocated extreme measures and the hoisting of intransigent dogmas, not in the hope of winning nominations or elections but eventually, somewhere short of complete destruction of the Union, to wring such concessions from the North—including Northern Democrats and " black " Republicans—as would create a reconstructed Union with specific guarantees which would still the slavery agitation and protect forever slave property. This approach may be observed in the call for a Southern conference early in 1860; in the hope of some seceders at Charleston that the Northern Democrats would bow to their demands and welcome them back at Baltimore; in the belief of some that after election a grand convention might be called which would at last grant the South her demands and thus end the sectional conflict. This idea persisted and may be seen in the debates over the Crittenden compromise and in the Virginia Peace Conference of 1861. As events unfolded, such Southerners were to be disappointed at each turn.

In the campaign, the Breckinridge party in the far South

sought to attain a monolithic one-party front with which to confront the North in any eventuality. In view of the long history of party cleavage in the South and the persistence of a deep-seated antagonism to the Democratic party, this was impossible in 1860. The Bell and Douglas parties were the objects of execration, and were characterized by the Breckinridge spokesmen as " submissionists," " vile cowards," " traitors," and " Union croakers "—the term " appeaser " had not yet come into political usage. The Bell and Douglas men retorted that such tactics were proscriptive and dictatorial and unbecoming to the American scene. How well the Breckinridge party succeeded in their task may be measured in the popular vote cast throughout the lower South, where a large dissenting vote was polled.

Other methods employed to secure the desired Southern unity included emphasis upon the alleged Negro-abolitionist uprisings and diabolical plots which were given wide publicity in the campaign. Talk of Negro equality, miscegenation, and even Negro domination under such " ultra abolitionists " as Lincoln and Hamlin, was calculated to horrify Southerners. All this would come about gradually, so that by the insidious use of the patronage, a creeping abolition would paralyze the South within the next several decades. Harrowing predictions were printed —and probably sincerely believed by some extremists—of the coming of a horde of Northern abolitionists, to seize Southern lands, to burn homes, and to imperil Southern womanhood. The Puritan was depicted as the leader in this wild assault of avarice. The Wide-Awakes of Northern cities were cited as preparing for just such attacks. Under Lincoln, even freedom of speech and of the press might be established in the South, and abolitionist presses set up. Moreover, continued reference in the papers to war, to the need for state preparation, and late in the campaign, to the activities of " Minute Men," transmitted sentiment of impending sectional collision.

In rebuttal, Bell and Douglas spokesmen in the far South, while generally admitting the validity of secession in theory, presented many arguments against the expediency of its application. They denounced a Southern conference as a " Hartford Convention." They pointed to the South's current prosperity, and denounced the " restless " Southern Democratic politicians, who would bring ruin in the form of secession and war. War, warned Bell men, would surely come, as peaceable secession was an impossibility. They contended further that the lower South should wait upon the border states and upper South, which had borne the brunt of frontal attacks and would likely afford the battlefield of civil war. The Bell managers in Mississippi, for example, ardently desired to poll a strong vote for their candidate in order to give the extremists pause, but they were not sanguine concerning their chances. They hoped that Northern speakers could come to Mississippi where the people could hear convincing pledges of Northern cooperation from their lips. Dissolution of the Union would not advance the pro-slavery interest, but indeed would put an end to it.

Douglas and Bell partisans dwelled upon the natural political alliance between the South and the West. It was pointed out by a Bell journal that Kentucky, Missouri, Tennessee, Louisiana, Arkansas, and Texas were more Western than Southern, and stressed the difficulties of finding a boundary of a proposed Southern confederacy. Time was needed to solve the knotty problems, but the West would unite the quarreling sections.

To counter the sensationalism of their opponents, the Bell and Douglas papers printed exposés of a fantastic, diabolical, secession plot, which were circulated throughout the lower South. A few Bell men defended the tariff, even in Mississippi, but on the whole comparatively little was heard in the campaign of the protective tariff and the exploitation of the South by the North. Occasionally, a Breckinridge man, such as Senator Wigfall, developed that theme. Now and then anti-British ideas cropped out, as when a Bell paper denounced secession as likely to link up the South with a monarchy, or when men like Governor Conway or Dr. Samuel A. Cartwright made the British responsible for dire abolitionist machinations in the South.

In recent years it has been fashionable for historians to interpret the coming of the Civil War in terms which largely discount the slavery issue and to minimize secession and war as issues in the campaign of 1860. While this interpretation may be accurate for certain areas of the free states, it is equally plain that in the lower South especially, and to some extent in the upper South, those questions were paramount, if one may judge from the overwhelming evidence of contemporaries. Nor indeed was the answer, as returned by the ballot box, completely clear as the following election results demonstrate:[351]

	BRECKINRIDGE	BELL	DOUGLAS
	%	%	%
Georgia	51,889 (48.77)	42,886 (40.34)	11,590 (10.89)
Florida	8,543 (59.54)	5,437 (37.90)	367 (2.56)
Alabama	48,831 (54.04)	27,875 (30.85)	13,651 (15.11)
Mississippi	40,797 (59.02)	25,040 (36.23)	3,283 (4.75)
Louisiana	22,681 (44.90)	20,204 (40.01)	7,625 (15.09)
Arkansas	28,732 (53.16)	20,094 (37.17)	5,227 (9.67)
Texas	47,548 (75.49)	15,438 (24.51)	Fusion with Bell

South Carolina Electors chosen by the legislature

[351] *Tribune Almanac and Political Register for 1865*, p. 68.

Chapter VIII

CONCLUSIONS

It is clear that by 1859-1860 there existed in the South a determined and exasperated group—with its center of gravity in South Carolina and manifestations in other slave states—which desired at all hazards to bring about unity of the fifteen slave states. Such a condition would enable the South to confront the dominant and ever-expanding North with demands looking to the Constitutional guarantee of Southern rights, or, if necessary, facilitate the formation of an independent Southern nation. It is also clear that, despite the exhortations and machinations of positive-action Southerners, diversity of Southern opinion continued up to and during the presidential election of 1860. Even such a startling event as the John Brown raid, in its repercussions, failed to close the ranks, and there were private expressions of despair at the "blindness" and "inertia" of the Southern people. Men debated, in the privacy of their personal correspondence, as to whether the Southern people were "ahead of" or "behind" their leaders.

Some positive actionists concluded that only by the occurrence of a sensational incident, indeed, an explosion, in 1859-1860, could the South be brought to act. To induce such a sensational incident was seriously discussed in private by influential South Carolinians, in the event that the national House of Representatives would elect to its speakership that "Helperite" and "black" Republican, John Sherman. This desperate expedient was dropped when Sherman failed of election, but other plans, not yet clearly understood, were under consideration at the same time.

Perhaps after the publication in 1921 of Chauncey S. Boucher's significant article, "*In Re* that Aggressive Slavocracy,"[1] students of the period tended to ignore the fact that, after all, aggressive, plotting cliques of secessionist "slavocrats" were at work. This is not to say that Boucher's central thesis is not still valid, because the South as a section remains exonerated

---

[1] *Mississippi Valley Historical Review*, VIII (June—Sept., 1921), 13-79.

of the indictment of having deliberately plotted the great events which produced the Civil War. The very persistent diversity of opinion in the South, for which there is ample proof, supports Boucher's thesis, and moreover, evidence is lacking which would link foremost Southern leaders such as Davis, Toombs, and Hunter, to these aggressive groups. Yet the activities of the Rhetts, Miles, Gist, Memminger, Isaac W. Hayne, Keitt, Yancey, and others were important, for in the end did not events unfold to the complete satisfaction of these aggressive leaders? Unfortunately, manuscript material relating to the inner plans of Southern leaders has not been available, and this is especially true of the correspondence of such men as Jefferson Davis, Breckinridge, Slidell, Yancey, and others.[2]

When earlier schemes failed to materialize, South Carolina turned to the project of a Southern conference by which she hoped to achieve the elusive slave-state solidarity. To promote this idea, the Palmetto state dispatched as Commissioner to Virginia, C. G. Memminger, who publicly and privately argued that the Old Dominion should assume the leadership in the Southern conference movement. Memminger was cordially received in Virginia, but that border state rejected his proposal, and also declined a similar invitation extended through Commissioners of Mississippi. Once again was Southern unity blocked, which elicited from certain prominent South Carolinians private denunciations of " submissionists " and compromisers. Several of these men privately asserted that separate state secession must be the last resort to gain their objectives, and that this step should be taken immediately subsequent to Republican triumph in the presidential contest. It may be concluded from this confidential correspondence that the purposes of the proposed Southern conference were twofold.

In the manner of the Hartford convention, the Southern conferees were to formulate Constitutional amendments which would guarantee Southern rights and serve as the basis of a continued but reconstructed Union. Acceptance by the North of these amendments was the price of Southern adherence to the

[2] For some reason, the papers of Southern " fire-eaters " dealing with the eve of secession are relatively scarce. The W. Porcher Miles Papers in the Southern Historical Collection, University of North Carolina, constitute a notable exception.

Union. At heart, however, the promoters of the conference entertained but scant hopes of success by such means; after the failure to obtain concessions from the North, the conference might then proceed to what was the real purpose of its organizers, secession of the slave states *en bloc*, and the formation of a new government. Many Southerners and some Northerners discerned the underlying motive of this proposed conference, and scorned it for that reason.

Simultaneously, in Alabama and in the United States Senate, a movement was launched to win Southern unity by means of platform demands upon the Democratic party. In the former, the " Alabama " platform, and in the latter, the Davis resolutions, were designed to accomplish this objective. By enunciating this unshakeable creed, the dogma of Congressional protection to slavery in the territories (its practicability and expediency were questioned by many Southerners), unity would be gained and Douglas destroyed. In this phase of the contest, Southern Democrats and Buchanan administration office-holders acted in close cooperation. But the Charleston convention rejected this territorial doctrine, adopted a platform satisfactory to Douglas, which led to the break-up of the historic Democratic party and the eventual appearance of two Democratic presidential tickets.

Careful examination of the correspondence of the leaders of the Breckinridge movement reveals that they entertained scarcely any sustained hope of electing their candidate to the Presidency either in the electoral college or in Congress. Despite the often-assumed superiority of Southern political management, there seems to have been no well defined plan in this regard. So deep was the party cleavage that frantic efforts at the last minute to effect fusion tickets to save essential free states from Lincoln were doomed to failure. Nor was the Buchanan " machine " of federal office-holders helpful in this process. Throughout various maneuvers, the irreconcilable component parts remained about as they had been, and the largest obstacle to harmony, from the Southern point of view, was the sway exercised by Douglas over the mass of Northern Democrats.

In the summer of 1860, coincident with the beginning of the presidential campaign in the South, the weapon of threatened and "discovered" abolitionist-inspired slave revolts, the *bête noir* of a slave society, was employed in an effort to herd all Southern voters into the Breckinridge camp. Harrowing tales of burnings and poisonings filled the Southern press, to which Southerners pointed as a prelude of things to come. Laurence Keitt believed that it portended an onslaught by Northern "barbarian hordes" which would utterly destroy Southern civilization. No doubt many, perhaps all, of these wild stories were of political inspiration, and this was recognized and denounced by moderate men. Emotionalism, it was hoped, would secure unity where all else had failed. There can be no doubt that some Southerners became apprehensive when they read these reports, and when the spectre of Negro equality was paraded in the press, it probably had the desired effect upon Southern readers. But, judged by the large vote polled by Bell and Douglas in the South, the use of emotionalism likewise failed to produce a unanimous South.

A central Breckinridge argument during the campaign in the South may be summed up approximately as follows: the dominant and increasingly powerful North witnessed a South torn by political divisions, and from such conditions concluded that the North might become bolder, because the South could make no resistance in behalf of Southern rights. (The calmer Republican journals, such as the New York *Times*, often quoted Southern moderate opinion to prove this, and Lincoln could be reassured as to the future by a letter from John Minor Botts of Virginia.) Therefore, the Breckinridge Democrats contended, let the South by unity and defiance assume a strong position by casting a unanimous vote for Breckinridge. This was the private advice conveyed to South Carolina from Joseph Lane of Oregon, candidate for Vice President on the Breckinridge ticket. Let the South stand firm, he wrote, and win an immense body of Northern support. This strategy would make an impression at last upon the obtuse Yankees, who would possibly in the end concede Southern rights. If, however, this failed, already a beginning would have been made for such future cooperation as would lead to the formation of a Southern Confederacy.

Avery Craven has described the diversities as well as the elements of coherence in that region which for convenience we call the South, and he has written of the forces which operated to produce the movement for Southern nationalism.[3] During the presidential campaign many Southerners privately and publicly weighed their future, balancing the merits and defects of the proposed confederacy against the disadvantages of the old government, with all its hallowed associations. Some of these, among them Carolinians, feared that centrifugal forces would soon render the new government impermanent, or that the old evils would reappear. By 1860 such characteristics of Southern nationalism appeared in demands for economic boycott, the establishment of direct trade with Europe, the development of Southern industry, the reopening of the African slave trade, the patronizing of Southern colleges and professional schools, and the concern with Southern literature and its nurture. Clement Eaton has demonstrated the effects of pressures upon Southern thought, especially as they touched the " peculiar institution." Above these were factors of climate, agriculture, and slavery which tended to make the South " southern." [4]

Even so, many remained unsure, and it was the election of 1860 which, by placing in power the dread "black " Republicans, at last brought unity—a unity which proved to be of short duration, but sufficient to enable the new government to begin its fateful career. Two eminent and popular historians have written: " No issue of secession and civil war had been submitted to the country in the election of 1860." [5] Quite to the contrary, so far as the South is concerned, the overwhelming evidence is that issues of secession and even civil war were frequently, almost constantly, discussed by party orators and newspapers. The decision came, precipitated by Lincoln's election, because some feared that to remain would invite abolition of slavery by 1880. The lesson of the census of 1860 was not lost upon the eager secessionists. Others foresaw that Lincoln's guile would utilize the pre-1861 divisions of the South, and by the skillful use of patronage of which Lincoln was to prove himself a master, build up a Republican party in the slave states.

[3] Avery Craven, *The Repressible Conflict 1830-1861* (University, La., 1939), pp. 1-31.
[4] The phrase is Professor Craven's.
[5] Charles A. and Mary R. Beard, *The Rise of American Civilization*, II, 56.

All this was rejected by the Southern moderates, the Bell and Douglas men. They contended that the best way to secure Southern rights was by continued cooperation with Northern allies, conservatives and Unionists who, through the years, had battled in their own bailiwicks for justice to the South. Again, the Southern moderates declared that slavery itself would receive better protection inside than outside the Union. As the late Professor Thomas has demonstrated, in general it was the large slaveholders who supported Bell and the Union, while inhabitants of non-slaveholding areas of the hills, the mountains, and the Piney woods, supported the aggressively proslavery candidate, Breckinridge, and advocated protective measures for slavery expansion into the territories.[6]

An occasional modern student has questioned the sincerity of the Unionism of the Southern Bell-Douglas men, and has pointed to their rapid conversion to secession after election as proof. It is true that the Unionism of some of these men was not what was meant by the same term in the North; such leaders as Watts of Alabama (Bell) and Hambleton of Georgia (Douglas) spoke defiantly while supporting Unionists. In this connection, it should be recognized that political parties have always contained men who differ even on fundamentals, and the Southern parties of 1860 constituted no exception. Nevertheless, probably a large majority of those who spoke and voted for these candidates did so because of their deep-seated Unionism, or because of their attachment to Whig principles. Indeed, the similarity of old Whig and Republican principles had suggested, at the outset of the campaign of 1860, that the two groups agree to merge, and nominate a Southern border-state old Whig of the type of Crittenden, Bates, or Botts. This movement failed for various reasons, chiefly because the Republicans did not need the Southerners and because of the slavery issue, but it is suggestive that it was seriously entertained. Many

[6] David Y. Thomas, "Southern Non-Slaveholders in the Election of 1860," *Political Science Quarterly*, XXVI (June, 1912), 222-237. Dr. Thomas' survey should be extended to include all the slave states. The largest slaveholder in the United States lived in Henry county, Virginia. Asked if he would vote for Douglas, if nominated at Charleston, he said he would do so cheerfully. The radicals in that region of Virginia never had owned Negroes, but they did not trust Douglas. Sam J. Mullins to S. A. Douglas, Horse Pasture, Henry Co., Va., Jan. 12, 1860, MS, Douglas Papers.

Bell-Douglas men favored Unionism long after election, even in the lower South.

The discussion during the campaign brought out the fact that, in the editorial words of the New York *Times,* there was a " far from solid South " in 1860.[7] It brought out that there existed mutual distrust and suspicion between the deep South and the upper-border slave regions, a condition underscored by the fact that the borderlands generally voted against the candidate of the lower South. The border feared that in the event of secession and civil war that region would bear the brunt of the fighting, and that their soil would be the scene of bloody invasion. On the other hand, extremists of the lower South raged at the " traitors " and " submissionists " who dominated the more northerly slave areas, and talked of violent action by which the upper South could be " dragged " out of the Union.

Analysis of the urban and rural election figures [8] has caused one recent scholar to observe that " urban support for the moderate candidates, both North and South, reveals the city as a potential deterrent to the Civil War." [9] This suggests, if it does not completely prove, that it was not Northern capitalist oppression which was so onerous to Southerners that they must disenthrall themselves from the domination of industry and commerce. To be sure there was some talk in the South of tariffs and Yankee exploitation, and it is also true that in some sections of the North, notably Pennsylvania, tariff and other economic proposals eclipsed other issues, including slavery. The Beards have quoted Reuben Davis of Mississippi to sustain their interpretation; it is also possible to quote Laurence Keitt of South Carolina, a better-known and more radical secessionist, to the effect that Southerners regarded Northern capital as friendly to the South and slavery. Keitt believed that the danger lay in the rural regions to the North, where fanatical antislavery preachers and agitators were most effective. Moreover, Dr. Foner's researches have demonstrated that in New York City business men and capitalists generally sympathized with the South until 1861.

[7] New York *Times,* Aug. 26, 1939 (editorial).

[8] Ollinger Crenshaw, " Aspects of the Presidential Election of 1860," Chapter X, MS, doctoral dissertation, the Johns Hopkins University, 1945.

[9] Bayrd Still, *Mississippi Valley Historical Review,* XXVIII (Sept., 1941), 291.

The student who has examined the mass of partisan misrepresentation which emanated from the principal actors in the drama of 1860, cannot but reflect upon its vicious effects upon the welfare of the nation. The more rabid in each section avidly sought out for quotation extremists' expression from the other section, where it would do the most damage—or partisan good. Southerners quoted the *Liberator*, the New York *Tribune*, and the Chicago *Democrat* as authentic spokesmen of the entire North, while the ululations of the Charleston *Mercury* or the Memphis *Avalanche* were reproduced to strengthen the stereotype of Southern society which was being presented to the Northern public. Calm voices were heard during the contest, but too often they were drowned in the furor. This gross misrepresentation bewildered when it did not mislead the voter of 1860.

Even in our time, when the issues of 1860 should be seen in clearer perspective, occasionally articles and books are written which are not a contribution to the better understanding of, because they are yet a part of, the slavery controversy. It should be emphasized that the election of 1860 was but a phase—although perhaps a precipitant—of the complex situation which led to war. Scholars such as Rhodes, Beard, Craven, and Randall have set forth theses or explanations of the coming of the war, and from their studies and those of others, we learn that behind all the surface furor lay the sectional moral and material interests, and that easy generalizations and oversimplifications must be viewed with skepticism.

BIBLIOGRAPHICAL NOTE

According to the editorial policy of the Johns Hopkins *Studies*, full bibliographical material is made available in the footnotes at the first citation of each reference, which may be found by consulting the Index. Inasmuch as this volume was written largely from manuscript and newspaper sources, some discussion of each of these categories may be in order.

I. MANUSCRIPT COLLECTIONS

The John Bell Papers, Library of Congress. These papers, consisting of letters to one of the candidates for President, although not so full for the period as the student could wish, are indispensable to an understanding of the Constitutional Union movement.

The Jeremiah S. Black Papers, Library of Congress. During the period Black, Attorney General of the United States, acted as political manager for the Buchanan administration. The objectives of the Southern Democratic faction which supported Breckinridge are reflected in letters to Black; likewise the difficulties of Northern administration men are revealed in this correspondence.

The Gist Blair Papers, Library of Congress. This large collection, composed of correspondence of the famous Blair family, throws light on conditions in the border slave states, especially in regard to the efforts of the Blairs to build up the struggling Republican party in those areas.

The Alexander R. Boteler Papers, Library of Duke University. Congressman Boteler, who represented the Harpers Ferry district of Virginia, was the national manager for the Bell campaign. There are a number of letters from various parts of the South, and one letter of July, 1860, from John Bell's pen, is of particular significance.

The Breckinridge Family Papers, Library of Congress. This large collection is of value for the views of Reverend Dr. Robert J. Breckinridge, and for Kentucky Unionist politics, 1859-1861. Unfortunately it is destitute of John C. Breckinridge material during these years.

The James Buchanan Papers, Library of Congress. This small collection has some correspondence from Southerners during the campaign, but on the whole is disappointing.

The James Buchanan Papers, Historical Society of Pennsylvania. This is the most important collection of Buchanan's papers, which must be consulted; but it is stronger on Pennsylvania politics than on

Southern. Such a supposed confidant of Buchanan's as John Slidell is unrepresented in this period.

The Anna Ella Carroll Papers, Maryland Historical Society. The intriguer and lobbyist, Anna Ella Carroll, knew politicians of all types and from all sections of the country, and there are letters from such men as Seward, Jefferson Davis, John C. Breckinridge, and Edward Everett. There is a good run of letters of John Minor Botts of Virginia, whose campaign for the Presidency Miss Carroll promoted, 1858-1860.

The John J. Crittenden Papers, Library of Congress. This collection supplements the Bell and Boteler papers in affording an insight into the Constitutional Union movement. Calendared.

The Caleb Cushing Papers, Library of Congress. There are a number of letters from Southern Democrats, including South Carolinians, in this large collection. Cushing was hand-in-glove with the Buchanan administration, and strongly supported Breckinridge.

The Stephen A. Douglas Papers, Library of the University of Chicago. This is the largest collection which I examined for the period 1859-1861. For the year 1860 there are approximately a dozen boxes containing much Southern material. Letters poured in upon Douglas from all the Southern states, usually from his supporters, offering advice and encouragement.

The James H. Hammond Papers, Library of Congress. Hammond, an important member of the United States Senate, was widely acquainted with politicians from his state and from the entire South. This correspondence includes letters from the ultras.

The Joseph Holt Papers, Library of Congress. Holt, a Kentucky Democrat, and Postmaster General in Buchanan's cabinet, received many letters from various parts of the South, descriptive of conditions there.

The Robert M. T. Hunter Papers, Alderman Library, University of Virginia. One of the leaders in Congress, Senator Hunter sought the Democratic presidential nomination in 1860. This correspondence is valuable for that phase, and for Virginia politics. His biographers have thus far not used this material.

The Andrew Johnson Papers, Library of Congress. This large collection is very satisfactory for the period, and throws light on Johnson's candidacy for President in 1860, on intra-party intrigue in Tennessee, and on the Charleston and Baltimore conventions. It is less valuable for the months following June, 1860.

The John P. Kennedy Papers, Peabody Institute Library, Baltimore.

This is an unusually large and rich collection, which remains relatively unexploited by scholars. Kennedy was a novelist, an old-line Whig, and a dignified civic leader. His wide contacts are represented in this correspondence, which should be compared with the Bell, Boteler, and Crittenden Papers. The collection consists of letters to and from Kennedy, and a Journal which records contemporary events.

The Christopher G. Memminger Papers, Southern Historical Collection, University of North Carolina. This collection is of especial importance in assessing the efforts of South Carolina to obtain the united cooperation of all the Southern states, 1859-1860.

The William Porcher Miles Papers, Southern Historical Collection, University of North Carolina. This is the most complete and fruitful collection of the papers of a Southern leader which I examined. Here may be read the inner plans of the ultra group of South Carolinians and their allies. Miles was the member of Congress from the Charleston district, and had close friends in South Carolina and in Virginia. This collection should be read in conjunction with the Hammond Papers and the Memminger Papers.

The John B. Minor Papers, Alderman Library, University of Virginia. Professor Minor, long a member of the Law faculty of the University of Virginia, corresponded with former students living in Virginia and other Southern states in regard to the crisis of 1860-1861.

The Pettigrew Family Papers, Southern Historical Collection, University of North Carolina. This family, the best-known member of which was James L. Petigru, exchanged ideas and information relative to the presidential election and secession. One group lived in Charleston and another in eastern North Carolina.

The Franklin Pierce Papers, Library of Congress. Former President Pierce had many warm admirers among Southerners in this era, and his papers contain letters from important Southerners. Calendared.

The Alexander H. Stephens Papers, Library of Congress. This is the largest and best collection of Stephens material. For the period it contains letters to Stephens and a few from him, and illuminates Stephens' well-concealed but real ambition to win the Democratic presidential nomination in 1860, and also the Douglas campaign in Georgia.

II. NEWSPAPERS

More than one hundred and twenty five newspapers were carefully examined for the limited period, 1859-1861. These included all the Southern newspapers which could be located, and also a number of

Northern papers were intensively studied. Newspapers were filled with political material in this epoch, and partisanship was extreme. It is of the first importance to understand the political complexion of a newspaper before evaluating its statements, editorial or otherwise. Below is a selected list of Southern papers supporting Bell, Breckinridge, Douglas, and Lincoln; and other selected newspapers outside the South. These files may be located by consulting *American Newspapers 1821-1836, A Union List of Files Available in the United States and Canada* (edited by Winifred Gregory, New York, 1937).

1. Bell

> Augusta (Ga.) *Chronicle and Sentinel*
> Baltimore *American*
> Fayetteville (N. C.) *Observer*
> Frankfort (Ky.) *Commonwealth*
> Knoxville *Whig*
> Little Rock *Arkansas State Gazette*
> Louisville *Daily Journal*
> Macon *Georgia Journal and Messenger*
> Nashville *Republican Banner*
> New Orleans *Bee*
> New Orleans *Daily Picayune*
> Richmond *Whig*
> Savannah *Daily Republican*
> Vicksburg *Daily Whig*

2. Breckinridge

> Athens (Ga.) *Southern Banner*
> *Daily Baltimore Republican*
> Charleston *Mercury*
> Columbus (Ga.) *Daily Times*
> Frankfort (Ky.) *Tri-Weekly Yeoman*
> Jackson *Daily Mississippian*
> Lexington *Kentucky Statesman*
> Little Rock *Arkansas True Democrat*
> Louisville *Daily Courier*
> Macon *Daily Telegraph*
> Memphis *Daily Avalanche*
> Montgomery *Daily Mail*
> Nashville *Union and American*
> New Orleans *Courier*
> New Orleans *Daily Delta*
> Norfolk *Southern Argus*

Raleigh *Semi-Weekly Standard*
Daily Richmond Enquirer
Richmond *Daily Examiner*

3. Douglas

Augusta *Daily Constitutionalist*
Huntsville (Ala.) *Southern Advocate*
Daily *Louisville Democrat*
Memphis *Daily Appeal*
Mobile *Daily Register*
Montgomery *Daily Confederation*
St. Louis *Daily Missouri Republican*

4. Lincoln

St. Louis *Daily Missouri Democrat*
Wheeling (Va.) *Intelligencer* (I did not consult original.)

5. Newspapers outside the slave states

New York *Herald* (anti-Lincoln)
New York *Times* (Lincoln)
New York *Tribune* (Lincoln)
Washington (D. C.) *Constitution* (Breckinridge)
Washington (D. C.) *National Intelligencer* (Bell)
Washington (D. C.) *States and Union* (Douglas)
Washington (D. C.) *Union Guard* (Bell)

INDEX